Families of Grace
through 1900

Remembering Radford

Volume I

by
Joanne Spiers Moche

HERITAGE BOOKS
2008

HERITAGE BOOKS

AN IMPRINT OF HERITAGE BOOKS, INC.

Books, CDs, and more—Worldwide

For our listing of thousands of titles see our website
at
www.HeritageBooks.com

Published 2008 by
HERITAGE BOOKS, INC.
Publishing Division
100 Railroad Ave. #104
Westminster, Maryland 21157

Front cover photo: Grace Episcopal Mission Chapel, Radford, Virginia, circa
1890s. Courtesy of Grace Episcopal Church, Radford.

Back cover photo: Bust of Dr. John Blair Radford, the city's namesake.
Courtesy of Hix Bondurant, Radford, Virginia.

International Standard Book Numbers
Paperbound: 978-0-7884-3744-1
Clothbound: 978-0-7884-7721-8

Dedication

For my mother, Josephine Alberta Hurley Spiers (1923-2007), who helped and encouraged me as I researched and wrote this volume. She was my best friend and my greatest fan,
and
For my maternal uncle, William Neal Hurley Jr. (1924-2003), author of many genealogy works, who graciously taught me his craft.

I miss you both!

Illustration 2: The Hurleys, In back, my grandparents William Neal Hurley and Josephine Davis Pratt Hurley. Sitting in front, left to right, my aunt Jacqueline Hurley Hinsley, my uncle William Neal Hurley Jr., and my mother Josephine Alberta Hurley Spiers.

Table of Contents

List of Illustrations

xii

"It is a useful employment for societies as well as individuals to look back through their past history and mark the dealings of a kind Providence towards them."

Bishop William Meade, *Old Churches, Ministers, and Families of Virginia: Recollections of the Protestant Episcopal Church of Virginia,* 1857.

Acknowledgements

This work would not have been possible if not for the original and current records keepers and residents of the New River Valley and the City of Radford. Any inaccuracies within this work are my own. In particular I would like to thank:

- Leslie Wolfinger and Heritage Books Inc. for support and quality production of this book.
- Eleanor "Tommy" Eakin Adams, for information regarding the Adams and Radford families.
- Bill Bondurant and Hix Bondurant of Bondurant Realty Corporation in Radford, for photographs, newspapers, and maps
- Sarah Carter, for information and photographs of the District, Palmer, and Jones families.
- Helen Dickens, for information and photos about the Delp Hotel.
- Explore Park in Roanoke County, Virginia, for provision of photographs of the Living History Totero Village. Explore Park is an outdoor educational program featuring early American life and operated at least through 2007.
- Betsy Naff Davis and the 1992 Grace Episcopal Church Centennial Committee, for information regarding Episcopal church history in Radford, Virginia. That committee included Betty Spillman, Mary Whitehead, Delma Bethea, Nona Smith, and Carroll Mason.
- Dr. Russell Davis, Radford physician, for use of his professional photographs of Grace Episcopal Church.
- Jane and Ken Farmer, for photographs of early Radford. Kenneth Farmer is the founder / owner of Farmer Realty & Auctions, Radford, VA, and a host of "Antique Roadshow" on PBS.
- Lewis Ingles Jefferies, for Ingles family information.
- Parishioners of Grace Episcopal Church, Radford, and of St. Thomas Episcopal Church, Christiansburg, Virginia, for information on church history and early parishioners.

- Robert Loeffelbein, my college journalism professor and lifelong friend, for advice and encouragement.
- John Lowman Sr., local researcher and historian, for information on area cemeteries.
- Rev. Claud Ward McCauley, Rector Emeritis of Grace Episcopal Church in Radford, for information on Episcopal symbols and ceremony.
- New River Valley Historical Society and Ann Bailey, Director, Wilderness Road Regional Museum in Newbern, Virginia, for information and photographs. The New River Valley Historical Society is committed to bringing together persons and organizations interested in the history of Radford City and the New River Valley region.
- Mary Ann Puglisi & Natural Bridge of Virginia, for provision of photos. Natural Bridge of Virginia, in cooperation with the Monacan Indian Nation, hosts a Living History Monacan Village reflective of native life 300 years ago.
- Radford Heritage Foundation of Radford, Virginia, and Peter Hans-Nagel, Director, Glencoe Museum in Radford, Virginia, for information and photographs. The Radford Heritage Foundation is a non-profit organization dedicated to preserving and promoting Radford's rich history.
- Sally Wharton van Solkema and Marvin Wharton, for information and photographs regarding the Wharton and Heth families.
- Betty Spillman, true friend, member of New River Historical Society and Pathways for Radford, for information, advice, and encouragement.
- Tom Starnes, Mayor of Radford, for illustrations.
- Betty Wright, for information and photographs regarding the Galway family.
- Frank Taylor, for photos and information on Adams Cave. Mr. Taylor is a science teacher at Radford High School, holds Masters Degrees in Education and in Zoology, and has received numerous awards including the Thomas Jefferson Medal for Outstanding Contributions to Natural Science Education, the Presidential Award for Excellence in Science Teaching, the Outstanding Teacher Award

from the National Association of Biology Teachers, and National Board Certification as a master teacher.

- Spero Moche Jr., my husband, for his patience and encouragement.

Illustration 3: Bust of Dr. John Blair Radford, the city's namesake. Courtesy of Hix Bondurant, Radford, Virginia.

Introduction

People of multiple cultures, ethnicity, and religions have been bringing strength, love, and their spiritual beliefs to this Virginia valley by the river, within which the City of Radford lies, since the 1700s. They've built homes, businesses, and churches where the community could gather to laugh together, cry together, and pray together. Their names and, to the extent possible, their stories are told here in celebration of the lives they lived, the lessons they taught, and the faith they shared.

This volume tells the stories of the many founding families of Radford, Virginia, and of the city's namesake. Chapters on the settlement and people of the community trace their growth through three community names (Lovely Mount, Central Depot, and Radford), and six geographical designations (Augusta County, Botetourt County, Fincastle County, Botetourt County again, Montgomery County, and Radford City bounded by Montgomery County and Pulaski County).

The Radford family attended the Episcopal chapel, as did many of their friends and business associates including the families of Heth, Wharton, Ingles, Preston, Washington, Kenderdine, and others. Because of the pivotal role of the church in the lives of the Radfords, that history is included in this volume as well. Each chapter on the early history of today's Radford City is followed by a chapter describing the growth of the Episcopal church and her parishioners. Their lives unfolded through three church names (St. James' Episcopal Mission Chapel, St. John's Episcopal Mission Chapel, and Grace Episcopal Mission Chapel) and two parish names (Montgomery Episcopal Parish and Radford Episcopal Parish). These chapters include narratives and genealogical data about those parishioners as available to the author at this time. Families are grouped into three divisions: clergy and their families, parishioners and their families, and servants living and/or working with those parishioners. A final chapter contains unpublished church records through 1899 printed verbatim. A list of Sources and Resources is followed by an Index.

Every attempt has been made to ensure the accuracy of information presented herein. Most states did not require birth and death records to be officially registered with the government until after 1900. Others did not register births and deaths until the 1920s. For those born during the 1700s and 1800s, family records such as family bibles, church records, cemetery records, and census data are the only source of vital statistics. My sources have included area Episcopal chapel and church records; records of births, marriages, and deaths from Augusta County, Botetourt County, Fincastle County, Montgomery County, Pulaski County, and Radford City; newspaper articles and obituary notices; information and photographs provided by families and friends; census data; and other research sources.

The Episcopalian community aforementioned does not comprise the totality of persons who developed our New River city. Many others of many faiths left their contributions of spirituality, promise, and success . . . BUT THAT'S A PROJECT FOR ANOTHER VOLUME!

A Note on the Family Research

The primary objective of this writing is to document local records and history of the City of Radford, Virginia and her people. This author has two goals. One is the hope that these writings assist the readers in understanding more about their community, their families, and their friends. The other is the hope that our body of knowledge on the history of the community and her people will grow as readers who have additional information including photographs will share them by contacting me at drjmoche@swva.net or by contacting me in writing care of Heritage Books Inc., 100 Railroad Ave. #104, Westminster, Maryland 21157.

CHAPTER ONE: THE CULTURES OF THE VIRGINIA FRONTIER THROUGH 1865

The risk and adventure of settling field and forest so different from their motherlands, shaped by political and economic events which offered both constraint and opportunity, set the context for a group of travelers to become a community. And so it was, through triumph and tragedy, old social customs mixed with new cultural venues and a community was formed. European ships full of courageous, hopeful individuals found their way across the Atlantic Ocean to the shores of the North American continent. The English embraced Virginia's shoreline in 1607. More would come, from many countries, to bond together and call themselves Americans.

During the mid-1700s, many adventuresome persons and colonial families made the trek to Virginia's western frontier from the northeastern colonies of Pennsylvania. Others made their way westward from the beaches across the Blue Ridge Mountains, to a lush southwestern valley through which glided the New River.

By 1900, Radford was an incorporated city whose residents past and present, active in the building of their community and their churches, included land speculators, railroad investors, laborers, businessmen, farmers, soldiers, state legislators, and descendants of some of the young nation's most famous players.

Their heritage lives on in the City of Radford, Virginia.

Many Nations, Many Cultures

The history of a land and its people determine the future of both. Their successes and failures may be viewed through the lens of their times and their cultures, and are the foundation on which today's City of Radford, Virginia, was built.

The western frontier of the Virginia Colony included the New River Valley and, between the settlement of Jamestown in 1607 and the early eighteenth century, extended west and northwest to the Mississippi River and into the Ohio River Valley. European colonists were not the first to love and appreciate this land. Southwestern Virginia provided sustenance and shelter for people of many nations for centuries. The tribal names of many of her earliest inhabitants are not now known. It is known that native villages were built, complex structures were erected, and sophisticated social orders emerged. These villages were later abandoned and nomadic peoples hunted and harvested the bounty of the New River Valley.

Numerous sites through the New River Valley bear witness to their presence. A palisaded village is known to have been built and occupied by a native culture around 1600 to 1635 at present-day Radford. Called the Trigg Site[1], excavations conducted in 1974 revealed that a native community of approximately one hundred and sixty three persons lived on the southeast bank of the New River, one hundred and fifty feet from the riverbank on the floodplain and western portion of an alluvial fan of Connelly's Run. Dome-shaped houses of bark and reed were arranged in circular rows around a central plaza of a palisaded village.

Artifacts found on the site provide a window into the lives of these early inhabitants. They cultivated corn, squash, beans, and other agricultural products, hunted animals in the surrounding hills and mountains, and enjoyed the river resources for food and for materials from which implements could be made. Their meals included elk, deer, turkey, groundhog, fox, skunk, bear, turtle, fish, and even mountain lion. Shells and animal bones were used to create weapons, awls, utensils, and even children's toys. Sand, shell, and limestone were ground and turned into pottery bowls and pots. It was doubtless a good life, surrounded by an abundance of food, unending beauty, and the fellowship of a small community.

Ancestors of the Monacan nation (a confederacy of several tribes) occupied the Piedmont and mountainous areas of Virginia and West Virginia by the early 1600s. Members of the Occaneechi, Saponi, Totero, Pisgah, and Cherokee nations occupied the Piedmont, Roanoke River, and New River valleys at least through the late 1600s.

---

[1] The Trigg Site was named for the family who owned the land in 1974, at which time it was sold to the City of Radford. Previous colonial owners were Francis Reilly, who sold it to James Rowland, who sold it to the Taylor and Addair families, who sold it to Dr. John Blair Radford, who sold it to the Trigg family.

By the 1670s, southern Virginia tribes were engaged in intense territorial conflict with northern members of the Six Nations of the Iroquois Confederacy (including the Seneca and the Shawnee). The Shawnees from northwest lands, the Cherokees of southwest lands, and the Senecas of the Iroquois Confederacy all laid claim to southwest Virginia as a hunting ground and, at times, a battle ground. The westward flowing waters of the New River and her tributaries provided an easy route for entry into Virginia's New River Valley.

Iroquois and Shawnee peoples from the Ohio Valley pushed the Totero, Saponi, Occaneechi, and, by 1672, the Cherokee people southward into today's state of North Carolina. So intensive was the fighting that, by the late 1600s, there were no longer permanent native settlements along the New River in present-day Virginia's southwestern slice. That land of promise became a neutral hunting ground for roving bands from several native nations.

Some of the early Piedmont Virginia tribes, including the Saponi, Occaneechi, and Tutelo, joined with Monacan ancestors in a confederacy of Siouan native peoples in Virginia. Monacans fought with settlers during the Revolutionary War and with Americans during the Civil War. Today's Monacan community at Bear Mountain in Amherst County is rooted in the purchase of four hundred and fifty-two acres of land which William Johns acquired as a settlement for his Native American relatives and descendants.

The Mattaponi-Pamunkey-Monacan Consortium was formed in 1981. The Monacan people banded together to obtain status as a state-registered corporation in Virginia in 1988. They were recognized by the Virginia General Assembly in 1989 as one of eight indigenous tribes of Virginia. The Monacan Nation is now headquartered at Bear Mountain in Amherst County and numbers almost one thousand members.

Others of the New River Valley's early Virginia inhabitants established themselves along the Virginia-North Carolina border and, subsequent to treaties with the Virginia government in 1677, 1680, and 1713, formed the Occaneechi Band of the Saponi Nation. This confederation of native peoples included the Saponi, the Occaneechi, the Eno, the Tutelo, the Cheraw, and a few other related bands. A large number of the Occaneechi fought with the

3

colonists against British foes during the Revolutionary War. The Saponi Nation is active today in programs to maintain their heritage and purchase North Carolina lands for the tribe.

Illustration 4: Circular dome housing typical of traditional Totero dwelling. Courtesy of Explore Park, Roanoke, Virginia.

Illustration 5: Living history Totero Village. Courtesy of the Explore Park, Roanoke, Virginia.

Illustration 6: Daily activity at Living History Monancan Village, Natural Bridge, Virginia. Courtesy of the Natural Bridge Living History Project.

Colonial Settlement in Southwest Virginia Through 1763

During an age of colonial expansion by European nations, England set its sights on the North American continent as a source of income through trade and food production. The new continent also provided an opportunity for expansion of the British realm for settlement by that overpopulated nation's unemployed and impoverished. King James issued charters to companies eager to establish colonies in England's name.

With the settlement of Jamestown in 1607, European colonists began to populate the eastern coast of Virginia. Exploration westward followed over the next several decades although it would be more than a century before western and southwestern Virginia became the site of permanent English settlements.

The majority of English settlers to the Virginia Colony were from England, Scotland, Ireland, and Wales. European immigrants flocked to the young colonies seeking an opportunity to own land, raise their families in a self-supportive manner, and pursue cultural and religious traditions. The Church of England saw an opportunity to convert native populations to the Anglican faith. Others came in pursuit of riches to be amassed through trade opportunities.

Besides the hope of discovering precious metals, explorers sought a mistaken opportunity to discover a trade route through Virginia's rivers and tributaries across to the North American continent's western shores. While exploration proved both notions incorrect, it was not a fruitless endeavor. The rivers and tributaries of the Virginia colony did not flow from the Atlantic Coast to the Pacific Coast, but the beauty and abundance of her mountains and river valleys was striking. European colonists were eager to call her home.

Younger sons of wealthy English families who did not stand to receive an inheritance as well as the impoverished of Great Britain saw the colonies across the waters as a fresh start. Englishmen convicted of certain offenses were also sentenced to a period of indenture until 1670, when the Virginia Assembly forbade the continued deportation of convicts to that locale. Others voluntarily contracted for a period of indenture in exchange for the cost of passage to the new world. An estimated seventy-five percent of white colonists in the 1600s were indentured servants.

The first African captives in the American colonies were brought to Jamestown in 1619 and sold as indentured servants. As that practice continued, Virginia admitted captured persons from the African continent only as servants held in a permanent status of servitude and American slavery came into being. Slavery was not unknown to the English colonization movement. The institution of slavery was practiced as early as the late 1400s. One hundred and five years before African servants were brought involuntarily to the Jamestown colony, and ninety-three years before the Jamestown colony itself was founded, in 1514 Pope Leo X of the Catholic Church formally protested the enslavement of individuals of any culture. Nonetheless, slavery became a part of life in the northern and southern American colonies by the late 1600s.

Although Southwest Virginia was largely unsettled until the mid-1700s, colonial explorations into those frontier lands began at least by the mid-1600s. John Lederer explored westward at least to the Piedmont and Shenandoah Valley by authority of a 1670 commission from the Governor of Virginia. General Abraham Wood, having engaged in western exploration towards the New River Valley around 1654, commissioned Robert Fallam[2] and Captain Thomas Batts in 1671 to proceed with westward explorations which took them to the Roanoke River Valley, the New River north of Radford, and across the Blue Ridge Mountains towards the New River Valley at least to present-day Floyd County.

The Virginia House of Burgesses encouraged settlement of the western frontier through a number of legislative moves. A 1701 plan made land available to individuals who would move to the western part of the state and build a fort as well as a community. That legislative incentive was not an overwhelming success. However, in 1730, large land grants were made available to individuals who would settle at least one family on the western lands of Virginia, the landowners not being required to live there. This settlement plan was successful in luring many families and land speculators to Virginia's frontier.

---

[2] Surname "Fallam", also known as "Fallowes".

7

By the mid-1700s, European colonists began settling the middle and western edge of the Virginia Colony. The first European settlers around Virginia's Bedford County, Campbell County, and the City of Lynchburg were Quakers and persons of the Presbyterian faith. Settlers of Swiss, German, English, and Scotch-Irish descent from Pennsylvania and eastern Virginia established their homes in western and southwestern Virginia. German Lutheran and Scotch-Irish Presbyterians formed their neighborhoods in southwestern Virginia during the mid-1700s.

The greatest period of Scotch-Irish movement from Pennsylvania to the Shenandoah Valley of Virginia occurred between the early 1730s and the mid-1740s. The Scotch-Irish in particular embraced Virginia's Shenandoah Valley, New River Valley, and lands of southwestern Virginia. They were assured by Virginia's government that they would enjoy religious freedom in their new settlements.

The Scotch-Irish were a people who had suffered religious persecution for their Presbyterian faith as well as agricultural losses, loss of land, and loss of position and power in their native Scotland and Northern Ireland. These determined souls were disinclined to be oppressed by any government forces again. Those Scotsmen who left the lowlands to settle in the Ulster area of Northern Ireland became a prominent force in the colonization of Virginia. They threw themselves into their communities and their new homelands as fierce protectors of land, life, and the liberty of their new country. Many realized economic success and political power.

Exploration continued in tandem with the migration of northern and coastal colonists toward Virginia's western mountains and rivers. Peter Salley, by permission of Virginia's governing body in 1742, explored Virginia's western waterways from the James River to the New River in northern Montgomery County. As Virginia's control and exploration western lands increased, counties were divided and new counties named. Augusta County as created by the Virginia House of Burgesses in 1745 extended from Virginia's present Augusta County west to the Mississippi River and included lands which would become Montgomery County, Pulaski County, and Radford City.

Land companies were granted large tracts of land for exploration, surveying, and settling. The Greenbrier and Ohio Companies were greatly involved in this process during the early years of growth in southwestern Virginia. The Woods River Land Company, organized by Colonel James Patton and associates in 1745, obtained land grants for acreage along the New River in the vast Augusta County.

Also by 1745, a pacifist and celibate religious sect had settled near the New River bottomland that would, in the Twentieth Century, become the site of a man-made lake called Claytor Lake. These Sabbatarians of Pennsylvania were called "Long Beards" and "Dunkards" by their fellow colonists. Their settlement was named Mahanaim, also known as Dunkard's Bottom. The Mahanaim area bore much importance to the New River Valley residents during the French and Indian War as residents took refuge against Shawnee assault at a fort built at Mahanaim and called Fort Frederick.

In 1746 the House of Burgesses extended governmental support of western Virginia settlement by authorizing the construction of roads from the South Fork and North Fork of Roanoke to New River and Dunkard's Bottom. James Connelly planned the roadway to the New River in 1749. The stream from the southern section of present Radford down to the northern point at which it enters New River is known as Connelly's Run.

Dr. Thomas Walker conducted explorations into southwest Virginia in 1748. In 1749 and 1750 the Loyal Land Company, formed by Colonel James Patton and Dr. Thomas Walker and associates, commenced exploration across the 800,000 acres along the New River granted to the Company by Virginia's Governor and governing Council. They were tasked with granting land titles to settlers across that region. The Governor and governing Council of Virginia also granted in 1749 approximately 500,000 acres to the Ohio Company.

Adam Harman settled the area on the Horseshoe Bend of the New River near the present-day Radford Arsenal during the mid-1700s. Ruth and Howard Heavin moved to the New River Valley and settled below the area that, in 1780, became known as Pepper's Ferry. The Ingles and Draper families created the Draper's Meadow community in 1748 near today's Town of Blacksburg.

9

Their experiences during the French and Indian War would have a major impact on the settlement of today's Radford City.

Disputes over territory and trade west of the Allegheny Mountains and into the eastern Ohio Valley brought an extensive and on-going conflict between the French and the English into western Virginia. The French and the English battled over ownership of colonial lands, control of trade with the native populations, and even religious differences between the primarily Catholic French and the primarily Protestant English. These battles would be fought across the colonial lands from the northern border at Canada down the east coast to Florida. The conflict from 1754 through 1763 was known to the colonists as The French and Indian War. Both the French and the English attempted to woo native nations into joining their fight for control, the French courting the Shawnee and others while the English primarily courted the Cherokee people.

Early settlers of Virginia's western frontier were caught in the middle of the conflict. They had the fortune and the misfortune to choose a new homeland which rested near the Appalachian Mountains and the westward Ohio Valley. Most were not of either French or English descent (in fact, most were Scotch-Irish), but they were inhabitants of English colonies near a much-disputed border which fell within Augusta County as established in 1738. The agreement between the French and the Shawnee people spelled disaster for the early New River Valley settlers. Shawnee raiding parties invaded the scattered homes and settlements, destroying and looting homes and murdering or kidnapping the colonial residents.

During July 1755 Shawnee warriors conducted a raid through Draper's Meadow. Col. James Patton, one of the original vestrymen for the Episcopal Church in Augusta County and one of Montgomery County's earliest settlers, was killed during the Draper's Meadow raid as was Caspar Barger, Eleanor Hardin Draper, and the infant son of John and Betty Robertson Draper. Mary Draper Ingles (daughter of Eleanor Hardin Draper and wife of William Ingles), her two sons Thomas and George Ingles, her sister-in-law Betty Robertson Draper, and neighbor Henry Lenard were taken captive. Mary Draper Ingles managed to escape and make her way home over hundreds of miles on foot through the forests and rivers from the Ohio Valley and Kentucky to the New River Valley[3]. The disbanding of the Dunkard's Bottom settlement around 1763 may be attributed to the dangers of the conflict fought throughout the New River Valley.

After the Shawnee raid of 1755, the surviving settlers from Draper's Meadow relocated. Some of them formed the first permanent New River Valley settlement which was known as the Ingles Ferry settlement. It was located close to the current City of Radford. The Ingles family owned land on both sides of the river, an ideal setup for the operation of the Ingles Ferry across the New River. Ingles Ferry was officially authorized by the Virginia legislature through charter in 1762.

The French and Indian War ended with the Treaty of Paris of 1763. England was recognized as the owner of the Virginia, West Virginia, and Ohio Valley lands. In order to ease lingering hostilities towards the English by Native Americans, particularly those of the Iroquois Confederacy, England's King George II signed the Proclamation of 1763 prohibiting English settlement west of the Appalachian mountains and requiring those already settled there to move East of that dividing line.

The path of settlers seeking land on Virginia's frontier and beyond continued and was aided by the construction of a national road. The western branch of the Great Wagon road from Philadelphia to the rugged lands of North Carolina, South Carolina, Kentucky and Georgia became known as the Wilderness Road. By 1775 it was the main route of migration ascending the Allegheny Mountains at Christiansburg and crossing the New River at Ingles Ferry, earning that section the name Ingles Ferry Road. Ingles Ferry Road was incorporated into the South Western Turnpike.[4]

---

[3] Mrs. Mary Draper Ingles' story of captivity and escape was the topic of "The Long Way Home" outdoor Radford from 1971 through 2001, of a 1981 book by Thom called Follow the River, and of a movie based upon the book and bearing the same title.

[4] Department of Historic Resources, 1998, Virginia Roadside Marker K 70, Ingles Ferry Road.

Illustration 7: Ingles Cabin, 1775. Courtesy of Glencoe Museum and the Radford Heritage Foundation.

Illustration 8: Ingles Ferry. Courtesy of Glencoe Museum / Radford Heritage foundation.

Freedoms and Hardships, 1764 – 1774

During the decade between the close of the French and Indian War and the beginning of the Revolutionary War, colonists in southwestern Virginia enjoyed significant freedoms as well as hardships. Much land was bought and sold, and settlers no longer so fearful of conflict with native populations began to settle along the southern reaches of Augusta County.

Daily life for early settlers revolved around challenges of materials procurement, difficult travel, and limited luxuries which their ancestors would one day take for granted. Travel was by foot, horse, or by wagons and carriages pulled by horses, mules, or oxen across dirt roads. The railway system would not revolutionize travel for another hundred years, and automobiles were the dream of a future generation. Electricity was yet to be discovered. Cloth, clothing, candles, and most necessities of the household were produced by member of the family living in the sparsely developed areas of the Virginia colony. Letter writing was the primary means for maintained contact with family and friends.

Physicians toiled with limited weapons against disease. They had access to medicinal plants and some medicines, primarily those such as mercury produced from minerals; the drug industry per se was not closed to fruition. Disease was often fatal, death in childhood was not unusual, young mothers often died in or shortly after childbirth, and the average life span was around fifty years. Anesthesia for use in surgery would not be introduced until the mid-1800s. Antibiotics would not save lives until the Twentieth Century.

To this life of freedom and hardships they came to face their challenges with optimism and anticipation. Large and small tracts of land were acquired and nurtured. Francis Riley, also spelled Reilly, received a large land patent in 1748 thought to be the first one granted to a settler in this area of the New River Valley. Others such as John Mills and James Addair were also granted large tracts of land near New River in the southwestern New River Valley during the mid-1700s. James Addair would build his landholdings to eight hundred and eighty acres on the north side of New River in an area called the Upper Horseshoe (some of which would later be known as the community of Fairlawn).

John Taylor and his wife, Elizabeth Campbell, left Ireland for the American colonies during the mid-1700s and eventually settled in the Upper Horseshoe area as well. In 1765 Taylor built an estate home and named it "Rockford", so named for a large rock which could be seen in the New River when the water was low enough for one to ford the river.

John Wylie owned four hundred acres in the eastern section of the New River Valley region by 1765. Samuel Pepper was a resident of the New River Valley by 1770, and the Ingles Ferry site contained a blacksmith shop and a general store by 1772. Colonel William Preston built his "Smithfield" estate on a section of his considerable land holdings.

As settlement and population increased, Augusta County was divided and subdivided several times. In 1770 Augusta County was divided into two counties, one maintaining the name Augusta and the other, encompassing lands west of the Blue Ridge Mountains, was named Botetourt. A farming village known as Big Lick for its location near the salt licks fell within the borders of Botetourt County. Botetourt was further divided in the counties of Botetourt and Fincastle in 1772.

Colonial Government and the Revolutionary War, 1774 – 1783

As conflict grew between the American colonists and her rulers across "the pond", life did not slow for Virginia's colonial government and her people. Still, political tensions between England and the colonies intensified, and a break with the Motherland was imminent. These tensions were felt by persons throughout the colonies, including those in young southwestern communities. A Revolution was in the wind and a citizenry awaited with concern, courage, hope and, undoubtedly, anxiety.

While little actual fighting occurred in the southwestern lands of Virginia, her community members were active in claiming a right to self-determination. In 1775, a committee of landholders from Fincastle County, Virginia, composed a document predating the Declaration of Independence that formally protested what they described as invasive and domineering policies of the British gov-

14

ernment in its relations with the American colonists. These Fincastle Resolutions were signed by early residents of the southwestern New River Valley including William Preston, William Ingles, and James McGavock.

British forces had arrived on the North American continent by 1775 to quell revolutionary measures in the colonies. The Second Continental Congress met that year to declare that the colonies must prepare to defend themselves and, by May 1776, authorized the colonies to establish local governments and local militias. The Continental Congress formally endorsed a Declaration of Independence on July 4, 1776.

Hard-fought battles were waged during 1776 to 1778, with military engagements continuing through 1783. Members of southwestern Virginia families fought with the rest of the colonials to gain freedom for the American colonies. Colonel William Preston, Captain James McGavock, and Major William Ingles fought in the colonial militia, to name but a few. Walter Preston, father-in-law of Francis Smith Preston's daughter Maria Thornton Carter Preston, performed his military service during the Revolutionary War at sites including Kings Mountain. General William Campbell, the father-in-law of William Preston's son Francis Smith Preston, was much-praised for his actions at the Battle of Kings Mountain in 1780. In 1810, Congressman Francis Smith Preston delivered a speech on the anniversary of Kings Mountain marking the importance of that battle: "every bosom glowed with the ardor of liberty. Wealth and splendor were things of no moment. The luxury they sought for was the enjoyment of freedom[5]".

France recognized America as an independent nation in 1777, and the Netherlands recognized the United States in 1782. It would not be until January 1784 that England and the colonial Continental Congress would formally end the American Revolutionary War and the Treaty of Paris would be signed.

The United States of America was a free nation. Virginia was one of the original thirteen states that comprised this union. A young government embodying the values of democracy, self-

---

[5] See Congressman Francis Smith Preston's speech "On the Anniversary of the Battle of Kings Mountain, Oct. 7, 1810, Abingdon, Va.", pages 8-16, of C. B. Slemp's 1940 compilation *Addresses of Famous Southwest Virginians.*

15

government by the people, freedom of ideas, and freedom of private religious practices emerged.

Independence for Church and State: Community Development, War and Peace Through 1861

Between 1777 and 1861, the southwestern Virginia families of the New River Valley experienced tremendous changes in their community development and in their nation. The County of Fincastle was dissolved in 1777, and the new County of Montgomery encompassed southwest Virginia including the future Radford city.

Land purchases and developments continued to increase. In 1780, John Taylor purchased four hundred acres in eastern Montgomery County on the south side of New River from the Wylies (John Wylie's land holdings bordering those of Francis Riley being passed on to sons Peter and Alexander Wylie. Also in 1780, Samuel Pepper established Pepper's Ferry.

Around 1789, Colonel John Ingles built an estate called "Ingleside", which still stands today and is owned by an Ingles descendant.

The growing national and local population had not been tracked prior to 1790. On March 1, 1790, Congress passed the Census Act. The federal census was to be taken every ten years and released as public information seventy-two years after the compilation date of individual census packets. The first official government census covered the years 1782 to 1785 and was presented by state. It was titled "Heads of Families at the First Census of the United States taken in the Year 1790". The Montgomery County, Virginia Census of 1790 described Montgomery County's population as consisting of 2,846 free white males of sixteen years and upward, 3,744 free white males under sixteen years, 5,804 free white females, 6 other free persons, and 826 slaves.

Personal property growth in the New River Valley marked the activities of the areas founders such as John Taylor, Abram Trigg, James Craig, William Lovely, Henry Banks, and John Heavin. John Taylor sold some of his one hundred and seventy acres, a tract called The Racepaths, to Abram Trigg in 1793. A portion of the Trigg property was sold to James Craig in 1794.

16

Illustration 9: Ingleside, the Ingles family home, built circa 1789. Courtesy of Glencoe Museum / Radford Heritage Foundation.

John Heavin[6] built a tavern called "Lovely Mount" in 1796. Heavin selected a site for his tavern which overlooked the Wilderness Road near the crossing of Connelly's Run. Construction on the Tavern occurred between 1796 and 1798. Slave quarters were built behind the two-story log tavern. Business enterprises and a settlement of homes were built nearby. The area around Lovely Mount Tavern became known as Lovely Mount.

Lovely Mount Tavern was located on land in what would become East Radford and which was once owned by William Lovely. The Tavern's name likely reflected the name of the original landowner (i.e. Lovely). Montgomery County, Virginia, land records of 1784 describe a tract of land owned by William Lovely as totaling 730 acres on Connelly's Branch and known as Lovely Mount. Records also reveal that Henry Banks owned seventy-three acres of land on Connolly's Branch in 1784 which was called Lovely Mount. Banks added to the size of that tract of land through the years and in 1795 sold seven hundred and seventy-three acres to Abram Trigg. Trigg later sold this tract, increased to nine hundred and fifty acres, to John Heavin. It was on this land that Heavin built his tavern. Heavin's son Howard Heavin purchased seven hundred and thirty-seven acres along the upper reaches of Connelly's Run from Abram and Susan Trigg in 1797. The Tavern property stayed in the Heavin family until its sale to William B. Baskerville around 1827.

By 1800, James Craig had extended his land holdings to the point that he owned most of the land in the Lovely Mount area around the Racepaths section as well as most of the land from Connelly's Run eastward to Plum Creek.

The late 1700s and early 1800s were a time of peacetime prosperity and spreading settlement of Montgomery County into the New River Valley. That peacetime prosperity was interrupted as Americans and British soldiers clashed along and below the Canadian border during the War of 1812. Several issues were involved, including the forced military duty of Americans for British forces (i.e. impressments of American sailors), European blockages that adversely affected western trade, and ownership and control of the American continents' Northwest Territories along the

---

[6] Surname "Heavin", sometimes spelled "Haven" and "Havens".

18

Canadian border. Southwestern Virginia's settlers did not turn their backs on this American cause. Military service was provided by New River Valley residents including Colonel Francis Smith Preston, who led a regiment of Montgomery County volunteers to fight to maintain their young country's independence and prosperity. General Edward Codrington Carrington, who married Francis Smith Preston's daughter Eliza Henry Preston, fought in the War of 1812 as well.

While the English succeeded at one point in making their way to the United States capitol in Washington and setting fire to the White House, the young Americans continued to fight and eventually pushed the English back beyond the Canadian border. The two-year War of 1812 concluded with a withdrawal by British forces north of the American-Canadian border. American soldiers were unable to drive the English out of Canada but held tight to their new homeland and ceded no territories. The Treaty of Ghent of 1814 officially ended the War of 1812. Montgomery County soldiers returned home to continue their community building, land development, and, once again, peacetime prosperity.

Optimistic economic times were briefly brought to a close again by an economic depression which lasted from 1819 through 1822. The Panic of 1819 plunged citizens throughout the country into loss of employment and for many loss of property due to foreclosure. Political tensions rose with soaring economic fears. Those tensions ran along geographic lines of Northern and Southern interests in conflict over the efficiency of national trade programs, the moral values revolving around the institution of slavery, disparate economic and political power, taxes, tariffs, and the national banking system. Those issues continued to challenge the stability of the nation even as the economy rebounded around 1823.

The Census of 1810 had reported nine hundred and five Montgomery County households, slaves being maintained at twenty-four percent of the households. By 1820, the county population had increased from 8,409 to 8,842. Ninety-three percent of the population was engaged in agriculture, with six percent engaged in manufacturing and one percent engaged in commerce. The total population grew by thirty-two percent between 1810 and 1830, although the number of separate households decreased from nine hundred and five in 1810 to eight hundred and forty-four in 1830.

Dr. John Ingles graduated from the University of Pennsylvania in 1826 and returned home to the New River Valley to serve his community as a much needed area doctor. He practiced medicine from his office at Ingleside until his death in 1849.

Scholar and teacher Edward Hammet brought their own skills to the area between 1800 and 1830. In 1831, he married Clementina Venable Craig (daughter of Montgomery County landowner James Craig). Clementina and Edward Hammet established their land holdings and home near the New River in the area that would become Central Depot, then East Radford.

Dr. John Blair Radford established a medical practice in the area around 1836 and, on May 31, 1836, wed Elizabeth Campbell Taylor. He and his wife received one hundred acres of land from her father, John McCanless Taylor, in 1838. That land lay on the south side of the New River and adjoined the lands of Edward Hammet. It was on that land, on a hill overlooking the New River, that the Radfords built their home and named it Arnheim[7]. In 1842, the Radfords received an additional six hundred and sixty-five acres of Taylor property on the east side of New River at the mouth of Connelly's Run "as an advancement", they being future heirs to John McCanless Taylor's estate.

Also in 1842, Dr. Radford tapped into perhaps the earliest significant event in the future city's development with the purchase of the Lovely Mount Tavern. Ownership of Lovely Mount Tavern and surrounding property had changed hands from John Heavin to William Baskerville in 1827. Baskerville operated a post office at the Tavern from 1836-1837. In 1837, the post office was relocated to Ingles Ferry and Baskerville sold Lovely Mount Tavern to James H. Cecil. Cecil sold the Tavern and surrounding land to Dr. John Blair Radford for $4,500 in 1841. The Tavern was still a centerpiece of social activity as well as a traveler's stopover before preceding to and across the New River via Ingles Ferry and, in 1842, the Ingles covered bridge. The Tavern served

---

[7] According to Radford descendant Minnie Adams Fitting, Dr. Radford considered naming the home "Bleak House" but rejected that name due to discontent with the author who made that name popular. Instead Radford chose to call his home Arnheim, a German word meaning "Home of the Eagle".

as an Inn, surrounded by a settlement which included home, a general store, a blacksmith shop, and a saloon.

The Radford deed[8] to the Lovely Mount property, certified by Montgomery County, Virginia, Justices of the Peace on April 8, 1841 and delivered to and endorsed by the Montgomery County Clerk's Office on February 19, 1842, reads: "a certain tract or parcel of land lying and being in the county of Montgomery on Conleys Branch, the water of New River, and bounded as follows: Beginning at a large white oak on the south side of the branch the beginning corner of said patent thenceforth 12 degrees west twenty-four poles croping[9] the branch to a white oak in a hillside north 66 west 119 croping same small branches to two white oak North 12 ½ West 106 poles to a red oak and white oak. North 23 degrees East 62 poles to two white oaks on a flat. North 54 degrees west 90 poles to a white oak by a sink hole . . . *[illegible]* . . . corner to a survey made by John Guills. North 28 degrees West 128 poles to four white oaks. North 87 degrees west 521 poles to a large white oak, and red oak near Conleys Branch corner to Robert Rawlands. South 75 West 155 poles to two white oaks and alpine. South 38 West 137 poles to three white oaks on a flat. South 30 West 102 poles to two white oaks. South 47 East 250 poles croping the waggon road to three pines blazed on two sides on the south side of Ingles Mountain, and North 62 degrees East 472 poles to the beginning. Together with all its appointinances."

Lovely Mount Tavern no longer stands. The precise location where it once stood is now unknown. It is known that the tavern stood one mile west of the Lovely Mount Church, also known as the Old Brick Church. John Blair Radford donated a tract of land for the erection of the church in 1835, and the church was a worship center for all area denominations by 1845. It was located on the south side of the road, owned by the Presbyterian congregation.

---

[8] See Montgomery County, Virginia Land Deeds, Book One, Pages 101-102, "Cecil to Radford".
[9] Note spelling of "cropping" in deed appears as "croping"; "wagon" is spelled "waggon", and "appointenances" appears as "appointinances".

Illustration 10: Above, Arnheim of old, the Radford home, built around 1836-1838. Courtesy of Glencoe Museum / Radford Heritage Foundation.

Illustration 11: Below, back of Arnheim today as seen from First / Main Street. Owned and under renovation by Radford Heritage Foundation. Photo by Joanne Spiers Moche.

Illustration 12: Lovely Mount Church, also known as the Old Brick Church, was built in 1845. The original church burned, but was rebuilt on the same site. Photo by Joanne Spiers Moche.

Southwestern Virginia county borders were redrawn, with a part of Botetourt County becoming designated as Roanoke County in 1838. Pulaski County was formed from parts of Montgomery County and Wythe County in 1839. The Valley Turnpike (Wilderness Road) was macadamized in 1850.

Part of the local expansion and economic promise was the anticipation of a railroad line through southwest Virginia. The first lines through the Town of Big Lick (present-day Roanoke) into the New River Valley were built in 1852.

As the Tennessee Virginia Railroad extended down through and past Lovely Mount around 1854, the north-eastern part of the settlement became known as Central Depot or simply Central. The 1854 name "Central Depot" reflected the area as a central (halfway) point on the railroad line from Lynchburg to Bristol. Dr. John Blair Radford was one of the stockholders and advocates of the creation of the railroad line in southwestern Virginia area.

Businesses grew, and the first public school in Central Depot was organized with classes being held in various buildings including one across the street from the site of an east end train station. The Virginia and Tennessee Railroad (which later became the Norfolk and Western Railroad) built an east end train station around 1857 despite an economic downturn nationally.

In southwestern Virginia and across the nation, there had been widespread investment in land and in railroad lines. That exciting period of economic investment and optimism ended in 1857. Overbuilt railroads began to fail. Land speculation programs failed as well. Farmers witnessed a drop in grain prices, and laborers throughout the country lost their jobs. A large shipment of gold from California to the East Coast of America was lost at sea. Confidence in the American economy plummeted both in the United States and abroad. The Panic of 1857 resulted in severe economic depression at least through 1859. Workers and investors did not fully regain their losses until after the Civil War.

24

The Civil War, 1861-1865

Slavery was the electric issue that brought the prior arguments over state's rights versus federal authority to a head. The first recorded written petition against slavery in the colonies was submitted by the Quaker community in Germantown, Pennsylvania, in 1688. The Continental Congress passed a resolution supporting the abolition of slavery in 1774. The trade of slaves (but not the ownership of slaves) was prohibited in 1778 in the New England states, the Middle states, Maryland, and Virginia. The system of slavery was abolished in all states north of Maryland except New York and New Jersey by 1790. A dual system developed in the nation comprised of "slave states" (those states in which slavery was legal) and "free states" (those states in which slavery was illegal).

The citizens of the slave states opposed any measures which limited state autonomy and slavery. The citizens of free states were opposed to any efforts to maintain the institution of slavery or to sever the national union, viewing federal sovereignty as the glue that held the young nation together. With the election of Abraham Lincoln to the office of United States President, southern states began to talk of seceding from the union of the states.

Seven southern states seceded from the Union between January and April 1861. A battle between federal forces and provisional Confederate forces at Fort Sumter, South Carolina lit the fuse of what was already a powder keg ready to explode. In April 1861, Virginia and four other states seceded from the union and formed the Confederate States of America. The capital was Richmond, Virginia and Jefferson Davis, named provisional President of the Confederacy in February 1861, became the President of the Confederate States of America. The Constitution of the Confederacy adopted in 1861 specifically prohibited the passage of any bills or laws that would deny one the right to own slaves. While only about twenty-five percent of southerners owned slaves, most if not all defended what they believed was their right to do so. The Constitution of the Confederacy also focused on state autonomy by specifying in the Preamble that each State would act in its own sovereign and independent character.

25

Young men from all states and of all faiths answered the call to battle. There were few if any families who did not have a father, a son, an uncle, or a cousin engaged in the War Between the States. Many of these soldiers would be wounded, captured, or killed. They fought minor skirmishes and major battles.

As northern forces made headway in their fight to maintain the states as one union, the federal Congress began to mandate the abolition of slavery. Southern slaves forced to fight against the Union were declared free men in 1861. In 1863, Congress declared that slaves supporting the Confederacy were free men as well. Fierce fighting waged on as President Lincoln issued an Emancipation Proclamation in 1863 declaring all southern slaves to be free. It would be two more years before the battles ended, the soldiers returned home, and the slaves became free men and women.

On May 9, 1864, the fighting came to southwest Virginia. Union forces under the command of Brigadier General George Crook[10] set out on a raid to destroy the Virginia and Tennessee Railroad tracks in southwestern Virginia which provided an important means of transport of Confederate supplies and troops. Outnumbered Confederate soldiers fought federal troops from the summit of Cloyd's Mountain into the fields of the Pulaski County, Virginia, farm of Joseph Cloyd. Brigadier General Albert Jenkins and, after his death, Colonel John McCausland led the southern forces as they attempted to repel the northern strike. The Confederates were forced to retreat back to Dublin Depot, which was Headquarters of their Army of Western Virginia and near the Confederate training grounds known as the Camp of Instruction, and on towards the Ingles Ferry crossing over the New River. After crossing New River by way of Ingles Bridge, they burned that covered bridge to slow the Union army's advance.

Union soldiers advanced to and briefly occupied the Town of Newbern before moving towards Dublin and the New River railroad bridge towards Lovely Mount on May 10, 1864. Union soldiers failed in an attempt to destroy the railroad bridge to Lovely Mount, burning only its wood cover and failing to completely destroy the tracks. They did succeed in temporarily disrupting vital

---

[10] Two Union soldiers who participated in the Battle of Cloyd's Mountain would go on to become United States Presidents. They were: Rutherford B. Hayes and William McKinley.

railway support for Confederate troop movement, transport of food, and other supplies including salt from Saltville necessary for the preservation of food stores. Those tracks were repaired and are still in use today. The Confederate Army retreated towards Christiansburg and north to Salem, following the Montgomery side of the river while the Union batteries attempted to assault them from the Pulaski side of the river on a hilltop which would become the location of St. Albans Boys Academy.

As the Battle of Cloyd's Mountain raged, Dr. John Blair Radford was a member of the Lovely Mount Home Guard and sometimes surgeon for troops on the battlefield. He was not at his home during the Battle of Cloyd's Mountain and subsequent skirmishes along the New River. That home, "Arnheim", did suffer mortar damage, although its inhabitants were unscathed. Ten percent of the Union troops and twenty-three percent of the Confederate troops lost their lives in that campaign.

During the shelling, eleven year old twins Amanda and Celia Taylor (who were slaves on the Arnheim estate) were so frightened that they fled from the house to Adams Cave and the ravine by Connelly's Run. There they hid until sure that danger had passed. The Radford family, unsure where they were and fearing the worst, met their return with relief according to the Taylor girls. They continued to live in the Central Depot / Radford City area, celebrating their eighty-fifth birthday when they recounted their experiences to a local reporter[11].

In 1865, the Confederacy collapsed. No American was untouched by the Civil War. The Radfords like so many others lost sons. On her application to join the United Daughters of the Confederacy, Mrs. Elizabeth Campbell Adams wrote of her brother John Taylor Radford: "Col. Radford was killed in a gallant charge on the 12th of November, 1864, at a little place called Cedarville, his last words being *Tell my mother I am dying, and I die fighting for my country and in the discharge of my duty, and my last thoughts are of her.*" Of her brother William Mosely Radford, who was killed on May 5, 1862 at Williamsburg, Virginia, she wrote "He was the joy and the sunbeam of our home". She wrote that her uncle Winston Radford was killed at Stone Bridge during the

---

[11] Unnamed newspaper, article reporting "Twins Celebrate 85th Birthday", Radford, March 21 (Special).

first Battle of Manassas "with his hand on the flag, in sight of the enemy and at the cannon's mouth". And of her future husband Richard Henry Adams Jr., who was imprisoned in a union facility in South Carolina "where 600 officers were put under retaliation and suffered the tortures of death many times over", she noted that he "was always a sufferer from his imprisonment. He was a true and noble soldier".

A new battle front was now to be conquered: there were lives to be rebuilt, an economy to be recovered, a new governmental union to be created, hatreds to heal, and a racially and regionally inclusive social system to be formed. Americans would need strength, courage and wisdom to overcome their national turmoil.

Illustration 13: Confederate soldier reunion, Wharton's Camp, at Central Depot. Collection of Jane and Ken Farmer.

Illustration 14: Bridge burned during Civil War, then repaired and rebuilt. Photo by Joanne Spiers Moche.

Illustration 15: Adams cave entrance, on hillside between Arnheim and Connelly's Run. Photo by Frank Taylor.

Illustration 16: Inside Adams Cave. Photo by Frank Taylor.

CHAPTER TWO: FAMILIES OF GRACE THROUGH 1865

The tragedies and triumphs of the early settlers of Virginia's New River Valley led them to desire a spiritual sanctuary. For Dr. John Blair Radford, the city's namesake, that spiritual sanctuary was the Episcopal Church. Other Anglican faiths met the needs of New River residents as well. The Episcopal faith will be discussed herein as it was the base of social, political, and religious activity for the Radford family.

The Church of England was the root of all Anglican faiths in the Virginia Colony. It's history as outlined below, therefore, sheds light on the history of all churches in the New River Valley. After the Revolutionary War, the Church of England was no longer the established church for Virginia. Her people supported various Anglican denominations including Baptist, Lutheran, Presbyterian, Methodist, and Episcopal.

Virginia's Episcopal church counted among her congregation politicians, councilmen, mayors, the murdered son of a Confederate officer, veterans of the War of 1812 and of the Civil War (one of whom was a member of the "Immortal 600" Confederate officers imprisoned in the line of fire outside Charleston, South Carolina), and the man for whom the City of Radford was named. They included descendants of escaped Shawnee captive Mary Draper Ingles, descendants of signers of the Fincastle Resolutions and of the Declaration of Independence, descendants of explorers George Rodgers Clark and William Preston, descendants of Virginia Governor James Hoge Tyler, and descendants of Presidents George Washington and Benjamin Harrison. Area street names, buildings, and landmarks pay homage to the contributions by Adams, Bullard, Clark, Cowan, Hammet, Heth, Howe, Ingles, Kenderdine, Preston, Washington, Wharton, and others.

Their heritage lives on in Grace Episcopal Church of Radford.

Colonial Settlement and the Church in Virginia

Church and state were closely bonded together in Europe and in the American colonies settled by those European interests. The English venture which began in Jamestown would expand to comprise the state of Virginia, incorporating England's system of civil and spiritual law under one governmental auspice[12]. The London Company followed to play a large role in Virginia's settlements, bringing with it a provision that each new settlement would become a Church of England parish with its own rector. By 1619, there were at least eleven parishes with representatives serving as Burgesses in Virginia's General Assembly.

King James was both the royal governing head of England and her colonies and the temporal head of the Church of England. He selected the church bishops, who were to remain in England, while rectors selected through the church and approved by the King were sent to the colonies to protect church interests and expand the teachings of the Church of England just as the governmental authorities were to expand the British Empire. King James attempted to strengthen his control over the colonies by disbanding the London Company in 1624 and taking control of Virginia as a Royal Colony. The King assumed the role of appointing both the colonial Governor and the Council. The Governor was then responsible for appointing rectors to specific parishes.

The Established Church of England was expanded to the Virginia colony as the Established Church of Virginia. Every minister who came to the Virginia colony was required to take an Oath of Conformity to the Church of England. Parishioners were required by Virginia statute to pay the minister's salary (tithes paid through set quantities of tobacco), provide their minister with a glebe farm and residence, and to attend the parish church. Traditional customs of daily services were not feasible given the distances between colonial residences in most areas of Virginia, so the tradition of

---

[12] The Church's colonial history is documented through several sources including Rev. William Meade's 1857 book <u>Old Churches, Ministers, and Families in Virginia</u>, G. M. Brydon's 1927 book <u>Mother Church and the Political Conditions Under Which it Grew</u> and Brydon's 1957 book <u>Religious Life of Virginia in the Seventeenth Century: The Faith of Our Fathers</u>. Meade and Brydon were historiographers of the Episcopal Diocese of Virginia.

one weekly service, held every Sunday, was created. Citizens were required by law to attend services at the parish church.

Colonial parish rectors were charged with transmitting the rules and rituals of the English mother church. Virginia parish boundaries were set by governmental statute and church wardens were appointed to maintain religious observance and other items which Rev. Edward L. Goodwin described as those related to charity and morals[13]. The colonial churches also served an important role in documenting the names of and the important events in the lives of the early colonists. Official governmental registration of vital statistics was not required in Virginia although the Church was authorized by statute to collect and maintain such data.

Given the absence of a Bishop on American soil, Virginia law required the appointment or election of laymen to conduct church business as well as to tend to issues of public welfare. These vestrymen had to be landowners and members of the Anglican faith. As a result of this requirement, many of the first vestrymen of the Episcopal Church in Virginia were Scotch-Irish Presbyterians.

The vestry functioned much like a local government in that this church body was charged with setting land assessments and tithes, investigating those accused of committing moral offenses, maintenance of the church property, and financial support of the local rector. The vestrymen were required to care for the sick, the elderly, the poor, the orphaned, and the children of the impoverished residing within their parish boundaries. Vestrymen paid private families or individuals to care for orphaned or needy citizens. Those unfortunates were often bound out as indentured servants to religious families who would provide for them until they reached adulthood (i.e. the age of eighteen).

Unlike the English settlers in the coastal and northern colonies, the German, Scotch-Irish, and English settlers to middle and western Virginia did not tend to build towns with houses closely situated. They were more likely to have a far-reaching community

---

[13] Rev. Edward L. Goodwin of the Episcopal faith recorded the history of the Church in Virginia through numerous writings including histories of various parishes written into the church registers where he served. As a Historiographer of the Episcopal Diocese of Virginia, he wrote an introduction with text edit and explanation for the 1907 printing of The History of Truro Parish in Virginia by Rev. Philip Slaughter.

of homes and farms that were somewhat isolated. Large land grants as payment or reward for military service also encouraged sparsely populated settlement. For the churches, this translated into a need for traveling preachers who could preach to more and smaller congregations.

As the number of parishes grew, provision of a rector to each church and chapel became problematic. With no central religious authority, i.e. Bishop, in the colonies, the vestry of a parish without a rector had to write a letter to a friend, relative, or business agent in England and ask that an English clergyman willing to come to the American colonies be located. The process could take a year or more.

For example, by 1655, there were approximately fifty Episcopal parishes in Virginia but only ten ministers. By 1700, barely half of the Episcopal congregations in Virginia had ministers. Those without an assigned rector were served by the occasional traveling minister and by vestry-appointed laymen. They functioned as church readers who would conduct prayer and read sermons to the parish flock.

Rectors were appointed to specific parishes by the central government of the Virginia Colony. Virginia vestries fought for the right to select their own rectors. That right was finally granted in 1703, as was the right to have laymen representatives in attendance at church councils and conventions by the early 1700s. Thus the cause of democratic representation was already being furthered on a local level well before the Revolutionary War was fought for total colonial independence.

There were few actual church buildings or chapels throughout the isolated Virginia settlements until the mid-1700s. The early Episcopalians were a people of faith. The Church was the congregation and not a building. Services were often held in the homes of the lay readers or vestry members, or at a local hotel lobby or parlor. The Church grew as exploration and settlement grew. Spiritual interest in and attendance at worship services jumped around 1734 during a period that became known as "The First Great Awakening". Spiritual interest and worship service attendance jumped.

The vast western section of present-day Virginia was organized as the County of Augusta in 1738. Draper's Meadow, a settlement founded in 1748, fell within the boundaries of Augusta

County. Augusta's first Episcopal vestry included Col. John Buchanan, Col. James Patton, John Madison, James Lockhart, John Smith, and John Archer. Only members of the Established Church of Virginia could hold such offices. The Church of Virginia continued to be a powerful force in the state through the late 1700s, until after the close of the Revolutionary War.

There were some Anglican denominations which dissented against the rigors of the Established Church. The Presbyterians and the Baptists complained of persecution; they did not feel that they enjoyed any favored or even equal status. They were the first to bring their forms of worship across the mountains into central and western Virginia. By the end of the eighteenth century, the Methodists would establish their own congregations as well.

Government, Worship, and the Revolutionary War, 1774 – 1783

Political tensions between England and the colonies did not leave the religious community untouched. A break with England and, to an equal extent, the Church of England was becoming increasingly unavoidable. The clergy of the Established Church of Virginia, an arm of the Church of England, were ordained in London and answerable to the bishops in England. They were also answerable to the governmental leaders and citizenry of their new homeland in Virginia. As talk of discontent and democratic government progressed to an imminent armed resistance in the colonies against England, one can but imagine the internal and external conflict of those early church rectors.

They, like their countrymen, faced separation from their original homelands and the conflicted emotions that created. They faced war with a country in which many of their family members still resided. They faced the inevitable loss of life and all horrors that war brings. The courageous clergy also faced a wrenching separation from their mother church in the country with which they would find themselves at war.

An additional public and private pain was projected through the eyes of their parishioners, some of whom were suspicious of a spiritual leader so closely tied to the English hierarchy. The vast majority of the clergy were loyal to the colonial cause while some were loyal to England, and many were painted with the same brush of "Tory sympathizer". It was not a time of bankrupt spirituality, but it was indeed a tenuous time for support of the church as an institution.

Through it all, the clergy would still fulfill their roles of spiritual counselors, religious instructors, and supporters for their parishioners as their communities went to war.

Independence for Church and State: Post-Revolutionary War Episcopal Church Development in Virginia Through 1861

The Montgomery Episcopal Parish, a part of the Montgomery County of 1777, was recognized by the Episcopal Diocese of Virginia in 1785. The seeds of that parish, and of Radford Parish, were already being sown.

The Book of Common Prayer for the new Protestant Episcopal Church was revised between 1785 and 1789, omitting prayers for the King and the Monarchy previously included in the Established Church (i.e. Church of England) prayers. Clergy found themselves in a position to take a new oath, one to the new Commonwealth. The Diocese of Virginia would become the first Anglican parish in the new United States of America.

The Commonwealth of Virginia secured an Episcopal bishop, consecrated and serving on American soil, in 1790. The first bishop of the Protestant Episcopal Church of Virginia was the Rt. Rev. James Madison, so assigned in 1790. While ordaining a large number of new clergymen to serve Virginia's parish, he was unable to significantly impact a decline in the number of Episcopal parishes and parishes witnessed across the new state following the Revolutionary War. At the time of his death in 1812, there were only forty Episcopal parishes in the state.

Rev. Richard Manning Moore became the second bishop of the Protestant Episcopal Church of Virginia in 1814. Moore had already received acclaim as an eloquent evangelist whose New York ministry attracted and held a growing congregation. As a bishop, the Rt. Rev. Moore expanded the popularity of the Episcopal faith throughout Virginia by increasing membership as well as financial support. It was also during his episcopate that both the Virginia Theological Seminary and the Diocesan Missionary Society were founded.

Bishop Moore died in 1841. William Meade succeeded him as the third bishop of the Protestant Episcopal Church of Virginia in 1814. Meade had been serving with the Rt. Rev. Moore as an assistant bishop since 1829. Both as assistant bishop and as bishop, he devoted much time to recording the history of Virginia's Episcopal parishes and her families. One of the most comprehensive early collections of Virginia history and family genealogy was that compiled by Virginia Episcopal Bishop William Meade, published in 1857 as a two-volume set titled <u>Old Churches, Ministers, and Families of Virginia</u>.

On July 19, 1858, Rev. Frederick Deane Goodwin and a group of men who would become members of the first vestry of Montgomery Parish met in Christiansburg at the home of Jeremiah Kyle. They designated Rev. Goodwin as rector, and the first vestry was elected. Only "married gentlemen" qualified for vestry service.

The Episcopal Church of Virginia continued to pursue plans to expand mission and worship opportunities into southwest Virginia. Those plans were delayed with the turmoil of the American Civil War during the years 1861 through 1865. As political and moral disagreements between northern states and southern states intensified, the Protestant Episcopal Church found itself in the untenable position of once again facing a separation within the church body much like that which parishioners and clergy faced during the Revolutionary War.

In 1861, near the end of Bishop William Meade's episcopate and of his life, America's greatest internal strife erupted into bloodshed. The American Civil War had begun. The southern branch of the Episcopal Church of the United States, also known as the Protestant Episcopal Church of America, severed the national church union and formed the Episcopal Church of the Confederacy. Many a southwestern Virginia church went without the services of a rector as some served as confederate army chaplains while travel for others was limited.

Before and during the Civil War, the Virginia Episcopal Rev. John Johns performed the duties of assistant bishop during Bishop Meade's episcopate. Upon Meade's death in 1862, John Johns was elected to become the fourth bishop of the Protestant Episcopal Church of Virginia. His 1862 consecration was the first consecration of an Episcopal bishop in Virginia. Bishop Johns was Virginia's church leader during one of the most historically difficult period for the young state's citizens and clergy.

Southern Episcopal chaplains turned from the face of war to the faces of grief-stricken congregations in the after-throws of military defeat, facing financial hardships and loss of loved ones (both southern and northern relations killed in battle as well as family schisms between northern and southern branches of many families). Many a young lady lost a fiancé or potential beau, the "marriage pool" as it were being quite diminished. Many a suitor found his own financial straits an impediment to the bride of his dreams. Wounded soldiers returned home with physical disabilities resulting in new lifestyle adaptations to conquer. Union and Confederate soldiers returned home to assume the roles of peacetime builders of their new societies, just as those who have experienced the cost of war have always become the greatest peacemakers.

The church organizations themselves were crippled financially. Funds of the Protestant Episcopal Church of the Confederacy were comprised of now-worthless Confederate dollars. Northern branches of the Episcopal Church offered support and reconciliation with their southern brethren, but southern Episcopalians were slow to reconcile either with the national church body or with the new governmental regime of the period which became known as Reconstruction.

Local rectors found themselves fulfilling the role of Christian peacemaker, encouraging their flocks to let go of wartime hostilities and accept the renewed United States of America and a renewed national Episcopal Church. Virginia's Episcopalians were the last of the southern churches to reunite with the Protestant Episcopal Church. They resisted inclusion of the Episcopal prayers for the President of the United States and for those in civil authority to the point that the national authorities issued orders forbidding omission of those prayers. Time passed and wounds healed, but Virginia's Episcopalians did not transition into a united nation with ease.

The Rt. Rev. John Johns led Virginia's Episcopal rectors in comforting their congregations during the upheaval of the Civil War. He also led his rectors in bringing their congregations back into the fold of the Protestant Episcopal Church of America when the War came to a close. The new annual conventions, renamed councils, were charged with the task of financial rebuilding as well as spiritual rebuilding within the national Episcopal faith. Bishop Johns was helped in conducting these huge tasks by a new assistant bishop in 1867 named Francis McNeece Whittle.

The Families of Grace through 1865

Information about the people who worshipped together and built an Episcopal parish together follows. This information has been culled from church records and, where possible, supplemented by local records including public records from the Virginia courthouses in Montgomery County and Radford City, articles from area newspapers, and information provided by family descendants.[14]

The Episcopal Bishops and Rectors through 1865

Moore, Richard Channing
1762-1841

Richard Channing Moore was born in New York on August 21, 1762. It was there that he was ordained as an Episcopal priest, and there that he served as an evangelical Episcopal priest until 1814. His inspired religious instruction and guidance increased the

---

[14] The author welcomes readers to share additional information, including photos and personal narratives, regarding early rectors and parishioners of the Episcopal faith in southwest Virginia and the area now known as Radford City. Dr. Joanne Spiers Moche can be contacted at drjmoche@swva.net.

Episcopal Church membership at a time when the Church still struggled to grow.

Moore was recruited to take charge of the ministry of the Monumental Church in Richmond, Virginia and accepted the call. He not only met with success in Richmond but became Bishop of the Episcopal Diocese of Virginia in 1814. It was Rt. Rev. Moore who attracted many to the priesthood including Nicholas Hamner Cobbs, the first Episcopal priest to conduct a service in Lovely Mount, Virginia in the Montgomery Episcopal Parish.

Moore served as Virginia's Episcopal Bishop for twenty-seven years, from 1814 until his death in 1841. He died during a visit at Lynchburg, Virginia, on November 11, 1841 at the age of seventy-nine.

Cobbs, Nicholas Hamner
1795-1861

Rev. Nicholas Hamner Cobbs is credited with conducting the first Episcopal Service to be held in Lovely Mount, Virginia. Lovely Mount was a part of the Montgomery Parish of the Episcopal Diocese of Virginia.

Nicholas Hamner Cobbs was born on his father's plantation "Rose Hill" near present-day Peaks of Otter, Virginia in 1795. He was baptized as an Episcopalian at Charlottesville, Virginia. The journey from "Rose Hill" to Charlottesville was no easy thing. His mother took him by horseback approximately sixty miles for the baptismal ceremony.

Cobbs first became a school teacher in Bedford County when he was seventeen. He was confirmed as an Episcopalian, received his first communion, and ordained as an Episcopal priest by the Rt. Rev. Richard Channing Moore in Staunton, Virginia, all on the same day.

Rev. Cobbs accepted a ministerial position in Bedford County. He also helped organize an Episcopal church in the Lynchburg, Virginia area and organized a small school called New London Academy, where he served as school principal for a time. Rev. Cobbs is credited with promoting and assisting with the organization of at least six additional churches in southwestern Virginia between 1815 and 1830.

During the early 1830s, he became well known as an advocate for the provision of religious instruction and worship services for American slaves. He also recognized that the church would continue to struggle in southwestern Virginia if parishioners were without prayer books, as so many were, and spearheaded efforts to distribute these important tools of worship throughout the southwestern Virginia parishes.

Rev. Cobbs was the rector of St. Stephen's Episcopal Church in Forest, Virginia, from 1824 through 1839. The family of John Blair Radford was one of his church families. Dr. Radford moved to the Lovely Mount area of Montgomery County and invited Rev. Cobb to perform the first Episcopal service held in that southwestern Virginia village. It was a baptismal service for Dr. Radford's first son John, held at the Radford family home "Arnheim" at some time between 1838 and 1841.

Rev. Cobbs went on to serve as chaplain at the University of Virginia in Charlottesville from 1839 through 1842. He then became rector of St. Paul's Episcopal Church in Cincinnati, Ohio and, in 1844, Bishop of Episcopal Diocese of Alabama. He died in Alabama in 1861.

Meade, William
1789-1862

William Meade was the third Bishop of the Protestant Episcopal Church of Virginia. The Rt. Rev. William Meade was the Protestant Episcopal Bishop of the Diocese of Virginia from 1841 until his death in 1862.

William Meade was born in 1789. He graduated from Princeton University, and was ordained as an Episcopal priest in 1811. He was a parish rector in Frederick County before becoming an Assistant Bishop of the Diocese of Virginia and, in 1841, became Virginia's Bishop. One of his major contributions as Bishop was the formation of "associations", which were the Episcopal equivalent of "revival meetings". Episcopal church membership had been low since the end of the Revolutionary War. Bishop Meade's as-

41

sociations did much to raise interest in the Episcopal Church and to raise church membership.

Meade's sermons and positions on colonial affairs were influential and widely published as pamphlets and as articles in Episcopal magazines. He was a prolific writer and an outspoken orator on community and religious affairs. He spoke of the rites of the Episcopal faith and the role of Episcopal rectors and parishioners. Meade, like Bishop Moore, advocated the simple and evangelical form of worship, i.e. the "low church", rather than the architecturally fancy and decorative churches of the "high church" style.

The Rt. Rev. Meade did not shy from controversy within the Church. When a Bishop H. U. Onderdonk was suspended by the Episcopal Church due to rumors that he suffered from alcoholism, he responded to arguments of unfair treatment in statements supporting the Church's position. His counterstatements were issued and published in 1854.

Meade took to heart the Gospel lessons of religious service to the poor and to those in bondage. Many Episcopalians were wealthy landowners, and the Rt. Rev. William Meade frequently expressed concern and disappointment that more freemen of limited wealth were not attracted to the Episcopal worship services. He encouraged those of the Episcopal faith to include and minister to the less financially endowed population as well as to the wealthy.

Well before Meade rose to the position of Bishop, he was concerned with the religious well-being of those persons in Virginia who were held in bondage. Impressed by the 1734 published sermons of Maryland Episcopal priest Thomas Bacon, Meade took up the case of religious instruction of slaves and servants when he was a Virginia preacher and in his later role as an Episcopal Bishop. Rev. Meade published Bacon's sermons and related materials in 1813 under the title of Sermons Addressed to Masters and Servants, and Published in the Year 1813, by the Rev. Thomas Bacon, Now Republished with Other Tracts and Dialogues on the Same Subject, and Recommended to All Masters and Mistresses to be Used in Their Families.

As a Bishop, he instructed his priests to meet the spiritual needs of the slave population in Virginia and bring them into the

42

Episcopal flock. His Pastoral Letter of the Right Rev. William Meade, Assistant Bishop of Virginia, to the Ministers, Members, and Friends, of the Protestant Episcopal Church in the Diocese of Virginia, on the Duty of Affording Religious Instruction to those in Bondage. Delivered in the Year 1834; Reprinted by the Convocation of Central Virginia in 1853 was published in 1853. He offered sermons "determined to be suitable" for slaves.

Meade recorded in two volumes, totaling almost six hundred pages, the history of early Episcopal parishes and genealogical information of early ministers and parishioners from at least twenty-five Virginia Episcopal parishes. He relied upon parish records, vestry records, official documents, family records, and tombstone inscriptions. His work was printed in 1857 and called Old Churches, Ministers, and Families of Virginia.

As the country entered into Civil War, the Rt. Rev. Meade was residing in and conducting his ministry from Richmond, Virginia. It was there that he died in March 1862.

Goodwin, Frederick Deane
Circa 1804-1881

The Rev. Frederick Deane Goodwin was an Episcopal missionary priest who served the Montgomery Parish from 1856 through 1862.

Rev. Goodwin was the rector of Trinity Episcopal Church in Staunton, Virginia, during the 1840s. In 1853, he visited the Montgomery Episcopal Parish and laid the groundwork for its organization. The Diocesan Missionary Society sent him to southwest Virginia again in December 1856 to pave the way for the extension of the Episcopal Church into that area. The following year, he accepted an invitation to become the rector of St. John's Episcopal Church in Wytheville, Virginia, where he provided spiritual guidance and support to that community and to Episcopal parishioners in neighboring communities including Central Depot of Montgomery County.

Rev. Goodwin traveled from Wytheville two Sundays a month to preach in Pulaski County, Tazewell County, Smyth County, and Montgomery County. The first vestry of Montgomery

Parish was elected in 1858 under his leadership. Rev. Goodwin resigned the Montgomery Parish in 1862, limiting his ministry to Wythe County where he resided. He attended the first Diocese Council to be held after the Civil War, traveling to Richmond in 1865 to help his Episcopal denomination regain its strength and unity.

Rev. F. D. Goodwin wrote extensively about his memories of Wytheville during the Civil War. Those writings, "The Goodwin Family Papers", are now housed at the Swen Library of William and Mary College in Williamsburg, Virginia.

When the 1880 United States Census was taken, Frederick Deane Goodwin and his family were living in Wythe County, Virginia. He was described as a seventy-year-old white retired minister; his middle initial was incorrectly recorded as "S". He had been born in Massachusetts, as had his parents. His wife was described as sixty-two year old Mary F. Goodwin. She was born in Virginia, as were her parents. Rev. and Mrs. Goodwin had three children, all born in Virginia. Also in the home was a single white twenty-two year old domestic servant named Sarah P. Rose. An area newspaper, the *South-West Virginia Enterprise*, reported on Sat., March 26, 1881 that Rev. F. D. Goodwin died that day at 12 noon. No other details were reported.

Mary F. and Frederick Deane Goodwin had children:
1. Robert A. Goodwin (circa 1850). This son of Rev. F. D. Goodwin was married and living in Salem, Virginia by 1880. The *South-West Virginia Enterprise* reported on Sat., August 28, 1880 that Mrs. Robert Goodwin of Salem, whose husband was the son of Rev. F. D. Goodwin of Wytheville, died the previous Thursday (i.e. August 26, 1880). The federal Census of 1880, Salem district, reported a Goodwin family as follows: white thirty year old Episcopal minister Robert A. Goodwin, his twenty year old wife Sallie C. Goodwin, and their one year old daughter Alice Goodwin. The household included eleven additional persons described as students, teachers, and at least two other ministers.
2. Sarah A. Goodwin (c. 1848). This daughter of Mary F. and F. D. Goodwin was thirty-two years old when the

United States census of 1880 was taken and was listed as a member of Rev. F. D. Goodwin's household.
3. Ella R. Goodwin (c. 1855). This daughter of Mary F. and F. D. Goodwin was twenty-five years old when the United States census of 1880 was taken and was listed as a member of Rev. F. D. Goodwin's household.
4. Edward L. Goodwin (c. 1856), of whom more. This son of Mary F. and F. D. Goodwin was twenty-four years old and studying for the ministry when the United States census of 1880 was taken, and was listed as a member of Rev. F. D. Goodwin's household.

The Episcopal Parishioners through 1865

Anderson, George
Circa 1800s

George Anderson served as a member of the Montgomery Parish vestry on July 19, 1858[15]. He was one of five gentlemen designated at an organizational meeting to serve on the first vestry. The meeting was held at the Christiansburg home of Jeremiah Kyle in Montgomery County, Virginia with the Rev. Frederick Deane Goodwin charged as rector.

Eskridge, Alexander P.
Circa 1800s

Alexander P. Eskridge served as a member of the Montgomery Parish vestry on July 19, 1858. He was one of five gentlemen designated at an organizational meeting to serve on the first vestry. The meeting was held at the Christiansburg home of Jeremiah Kyle in Montgomery County, Virginia, with the Rev. Frederick

[15] First Montgomery Parish vestry meeting, as written into church history records by Rev. J. E. Hammond (1800s).

45

Deane Goodwin charged as rector. He was again elected to the Montgomery County vestry in 1871.

Alexander P. Eskridge married Juliet G. Taylor. They lived in Fincastle, of Botetourt County, Virginia, and moved their family in 1848 to Montgomery County, Virginia. They had children:
1. Allen T. Eskridge (1844), son of Juliet G. and Alexander P. Eskridge. He was born in Fincastle, Virginia in 1844. He served as a Sergeant-Major, 25th Virginia Cavalry, of the Confederate Army during the Civil War. He married Ellen M. Edmundson, also known as Mary Ellen Edmundson, on April 27, 1870. The daughter of Mary and Henry A. Edmundson, she was born around 1843. Ellen and Allen Eskridge owned and worked a farm in Montgomery County, Virginia. When the 1880 United States Census data was recorded, thirty-six year old Allen "F." Eskridge was a white farmer residing in the Christiansburg District of Montgomery County with his thirty-seven year old wife "Mary E." Eskridge, three of their children, and servants: a single thirty-nine year old white cook named Mattie Leslie, thirteen year old Mary B. Leslie, and eight year old Thomas Leslie. Mary Ellen Edmundson and Allen T. Eskridge had children:
   a. Henry E. Eskridge (1871), son of Mary Ellen Edmundson and Allen T. Eskridge. He was born on April 27, 1871. He died young.
   b. Allen T. Eskridge Jr. (1873), son of Mary Ellen Edmundson and Allen T. Eskridge. He was born March 15, 1873. He was seven years old at the time of the 1880 United States Census; his middle initial was listed as "F".
   c. Alexander P. Eskridge (1874), son of Mary Ellen Edmundson and Allen T. Eskridge. He was born October 23, 1874. Called Alex, he was five years old at the time of the 1880 United States Census.
   d. S. Lewis Eskridge (1877), son of Mary Ellen Edmundson and Allen T. Eskridge. He was born February 22, 1877. He was listed as three year old "Lewis St. Eskridge" in the 1880 United States Census.

2. Charles Trigg Eskridge, son of Juliet G. and Alexander P. Eskridge, was born July 22, 1852, in Montgomery County, Virginia. He was described in the 1880 Census as a single white twenty-seven year old farmer in the Christiansburg District of Montgomery County. Five servants were listed as members of his household.

Kyle, Jeremiah
1791-1867

Jeremiah Kyle served as a member of the Montgomery Episcopal Parish vestry effective on July 19, 1858. He was one of five gentlemen designated at an organizational meeting to serve on the first vestry. The meeting was held at his Christiansburg home in Montgomery County, Virginia, with the Rev. Frederick Deane Goodwin charged as rector.

Jeremiah Kyle, the son of Margaret and William Kyle, was born in Tyrone, Ireland, in October 1791. The Kyle family immigrated to America and eventually settled in Botetourt County, Virginia. They were not listed in the Montgomery County 1810 census. William Kyle's household was described in the Montgomery County Census of 1820 as consisting of three white males, two white females, and three female slaves. Mr. Kyle was engaged in commerce. In 1830, the census described the household of William Kyle as consisting of thirty-four individuals: six white males, five white females, six male slaves, and seventeen white females.

Jeremiah Kyle married Elizabeth McKelvey. The daughter of Elizabeth and David McKelvey of Buckingham County, Virginia, Miss Elizabeth McKelvey was born around 1792. At some point Elizabeth and Jeremiah moved to Montgomery County, Virginia. Jeremiah Kyle died on December 5, 1867. His widow Elizabeth McKelvey Kyle died at age sixty-four on July 13, 1856. The Kyles were buried in the private Kyle family cemetery in Christiansburg, Virginia.

Preston, William Ballard
1805-1862

The Honorable William Ballard Preston served as a member of the Montgomery Episcopal Parish vestry on July 19, 1858. He was one of five gentlemen designated at an organizational meeting to serve on the first vestry. The meeting was held at the Christiansburg home of Jeremiah Kyle in Montgomery County, Virginia, with the Rev. Frederick Deane Goodwin charged as rector.

The son of Nancy Ann Taylor and Governor James Patton Preston, William Ballard Preston was born on November 29, 1805 at the family estate known as "Smithfield" in Montgomery County, Virginia. The Prestons trace their family roots back to Northern Ireland.

William Ballard Preston married Lucy Redd in 1839. During his lifetime, he served as Virginia's representative to the United States Congress from 1847-1849, as Secretary of the U. S. Navy under President Taylor from 1849-1850, a member of the United States Commission to France, delegate to the Virginia Conventions of 1850 and 1860, Senator of the Congress of the Confederate States, and a successful attorney. Preston died on November 16, 1862.

Lucy Redd and William Ballard Preston had children:

1. Walter Redd Preston (1841), son of Lucy Redd and William Ballard Preston. He was born on April 27, 1841 and died on August 1, 1872. He married Harriet Jane Milling Means (1846-1869).
2. Anne Taylor Preston (1843), daughter of Lucy Redd and William Ballard Preston. Called "Nannie", she was born in February 1843 and died during July 1868. She married Dr. Walter Coles. They had children: Lucy Coles., Walter Coles Jr., Coles son, twin of Walter Coles Jr., Anne Preston Coles., and James Patton Coles.
3. James Patton Preston (circa 1800s), son of Lucy Redd and William Ballard Preston.
4. Lucy Redd Preston (1848), daughter of Lucy Redd and William Ballard Preston. Lucy Redd Preston was named after her mother and was born on February 6, 1848. She married W. Beale. They had children: Ballard Preston

48

Beale, Anne Radford Beale, Preston Beale, and Lucy Beale.
5. Jane Grace Preston (1850). This daughter of Lucy Redd and William Ballard Preston was born on October 5, 1850. She married Aubin Lee Boulware. They had children: Ballard Preston Boulware (1882), Aubin Lee Boulware Jr. (1885), and Jane Preston Boulware (1891).
6. Preston infant, child of Lucy Redd and William Ballard Preston; died young.

A more detailed lineage of William Ballard Preston, including discussions of lineal relationships to other family members and other prominent area families, is as follows (John Preston > William Preston > James Patton Preston > William Ballard Preston):

1) <u>John Preston</u> 1st *GENERATION* (1687-1747). John Preston[16] was born in 1687 in Northern Ireland. He and his friend James Patton, both of Scotch-Irish descent, emigrated from Ireland to Virginia around 1738. Preston married Patton's sister, Elizabeth Patton. The daughter of Sarah Lynn and Henry Patton, she was born in Ireland on December 25, 1700 and died in Virginia on December 25, 1776. John Preston died in Virginia in 1747. Elizabeth Patton and John Preston had children:

   a) <u>William Preston</u> 2nd *GENERATION* (1729-1783). William Preston, son of Elizabeth Patton and John Preston, was born in Northern Ireland on December 5, 1729. He married Susanna Smith on January 17, 1761[17]. Susanna, the daughter of Eliza-

[16] Preston family lineage has been documented by the Daughters of the American Revolution, John Frederick Dorman (1982), Margaret Campbell Pilcher (1911), Robert Somerville Radford Yates (1986), Patricia Givens Johnson (1992), Philip C. Norfleet (2001), Minnie Adams Fitting (2002), as well as cemetery tombstones and public records as researched by this author.

[17] There are some discrepancies between information as submitted to the DAR by Preston descendant Elizabeth Cochran and other sources including the Yates book as consulted for the above narrative. The Lineage book of the National So-

beth Waddy and Francis Smith, was born on January 23, 1740. William Preston was active in the development of the Virginia counties of Augusta, Botetourt, Fincastle, and Montgomery. He was a surveyor, a member of the Virginia House of Burgesses, and a Lieutenant Colonel in the colonial militia. He also served during the Revolutionary War, and participated in the signing of a treaty with the Cherokee people in 1777. As conflict with the Shawnee people put the people of southwestern Virginia in danger, Colonel William Preston housed soldiers at his home and served as commander. The Preston estates were "Greenfield" in Botetourt County and, in 1773, "Smithfield" in Montgomery County; the name "Smithfield" being in honor of his wife's maiden surname. William Preston died in Montgomery County, Virginia, on June 28, 1783. His wife Susanna died at "Smithfield" on June 19, 1823. Susanna Smith and William Preston had children:

i) Elizabeth Preston 3rd GENERATION (1762).
Elizabeth Preston, daughter of Susanna Smith and Colonel William Preston, was born at "Greenfield" on May 31, 1762. She married William Strother Madison.

ii) John Preston 3rd GENERATION (1764-1827).
John Preston, son of Susanna Smith and Colonel William Preston, was born at "Greenfield" during May 1764 and died in 1827. General John Preston married Mary Susan Radford. She was born in 1781 and died in 1810. She was the daughter of Rebecca Winston and William Radford and the aunt of Dr. John Blair Radford for whom the City of

ciety of the Daughters of the American Revolution, Volume CXXVIII, 1916, page 64, as published in 1932 lists: the year of marriage of Susanna Smith and William Preston as 1760 instead of 1761; William Preston's year of death as 1781 instead of 1783; and Susanna Smith's year of birth as 1739 instead of 1740. However, William Preston's year of marriage is correctly reported as 1761 on pages 198-199 as by descendant Margaret Lynn Preston.

Radford was named [Rebecca Winston and William Radford were Dr. John Blair Radford's grandparents]. Mary Susan Radford and John Preston had children:

(1) William Radford Washington Preston 4th GENERATION (1799), son of Mary Susan Radford and John Preston.

(2) John Breckinridge Preston 4th GENERATION (circa 1800), son of Mary Susan Radford and John Preston.

(3) Elizabeth Madison Preston 4th GENERATION (circa 1803), daughter of Mary Susan Radford and John Preston.

(4) Susanna Smith Preston 4th GENERATION (circa 1805-1857), daughter of Mary Susan Radford and John Preston. She married her first cousin William Mosely Radford (1811-1873), a son of Elizabeth Mosely and William C. Radford and a brother of Dr. John Blair Radford for whom the City of Radford was named. Susanna Smith Preston and William Mosely Radford had children, including:

(a) Elizabeth Radford 5th GENERATION (1832), a daughter of Susanna Smith Preston and William Mosely Radford. She married her cousin William Alfred Preston (1808-1862), son of Margaret "Peggy" Brown Preston and John Preston. The sister of Elizabeth Radford's grandfather (General John Preston) was the mother of Elizabeth's husband William Alfred Preston (i.e. Margaret "Peggy" Brown Preston). With this marriage Mrs. Margaret "Peggy" Brown Preston became Elizabeth Radford's mother-in-law as well as her great-aunt. Elizabeth Radford and William Alfred Preston had children, including:

51

(i) Alfred G. Preston *6th GENERATION*
(1858-1933), son of Elizabeth Radford and William Alfred Preston. He married. He and his wife (name not known at present) had eleven children, including:
1. Lucy Alice Preston *7th GENERATION* (1889-1978), daughter of Alfred G. Preston.

iii) Francis Smith Preston *3rd GENERATION* (1765-1835). Francis Smith Preston, son of Susanna Smith and Colonel William Preston, was born at "Greenfield" in Botetourt County on August 2, 1765 and died at his son William Campbell Preston's home in Columbia, South Carolina on May 26, 1835. In 1793, he married Sarah "Sally" Buchanan Campbell. Born in 1778 and died in 1846, she was the daughter of Elizabeth Henry (born 1748; died 1825) and General William Campbell (born 1745; died 1782). Francis Smith Preston was an attorney who served as a member of the Virginia House of Delegates in 1788, 1789, and 1812-1814; a member of the Third and Fourth Congresses in 1793 through 1797; and as a member of the Virginia Senate from 1816 through 1820. Colonel Francis S. Preston commanded a regiment of Volunteers during the War of 1812. In 1832, he built a home in Abingdon, Virginia, where e lived with his family until his death in 1836 at the age of seventy-one. His wife died in 1846 at the age of sixty-eight. That home was sold by the family in 1858, operated as Mary Washington College until 1932, and reopened as the Mary Washington Inn in 1835. Sally Buchanan Campbell and Francis Smith Preston had children, at least four of whom did not survive childhood:
(1) William Campbell Preston *4th GENERATION* (1794-1860), the son of Sally Buchanan

Campbell and Francis Smith Preston. He became a Governor of South Carolina. He married Maria Eliza Coalter and, upon her death, Louisa Penelope Davis. Louisa Penelope Davis and William Campbell Preston had a child:

(a) Sarah Buchanan Campbell Preston *5th GENERATION*. She died young.

(2) Eliza Henry Preston *4th GENERATION* (1796-1877), the daughter of Sally Buchanan Campbell and Francis Smith Preston. She married General Edward Codrington Carrington, veteran of the War of 1812. They had six children.

(3) Francis Smith Preston Jr. *4th GENERATION* (1798-1801), the son of Sally Buchanan Campbell and Francis Smith Preston. He was born on June 21, 1798 and died at the age of three years and nine months on March 21, 1801.

(4) Susan Smith Preston *4th GENERATION* (1800-1847), also known as Susanna Smith Preston, the daughter of Sally Buchanan Campbell and Francis Smith Preston. She married her first cousin James McDowell III (1795-1851), son of Sarah Preston and James McDowell Jr. James McDowell III's mother (Mrs. Sarah Preston McDowell) was the sister of his wife's father (Francis Smith Preston). James McDowell III was a Governor of Virginia from 1843-1846. Susan Smith Preston and James McDowell III had nine children.

(5) Sarah Buchanan Preston *4th GENERATION* (1802-1879), the daughter of Sally Buchanan Campbell and Francis Smith Preston. She married her cousin John Buchanan Floyd, who was the son of Letitia Preston (Francis Smith Preston's sister) and John Floyd (who was a Governor of

Virginia from 1830 through 1834). John Buchanan Floyd was born on June 1, 1806 on the "Smithfield" estate in Blacksburg, Virginia. He was a Governor of Virginia from 1849-1852, served as Secretary of War under President James Buchanan, and served as a Brigadier General in the Confederate Army during the Civil War. Sarah Buchanan Preston and John Buchanan Floyd did not have children.

(6) Anne Sophonisba Preston *4th GENERATION* (1803-1844), the daughter of Sally Buchanan Campbell and Francis Smith Preston. She married Rev. Dr. Robert Jefferson Breckinridge (1800-1881). They had eleven children. After Anne's death, Robert J. Breckinridge married Virginia H. Hart (1809), daughter of Susanna Preston and Nathaniel Hart Jr. They had three children. Robert J. Breckinridge's third wife was Margaret Faulkner.

(7) Jane Robertson Preston *4th GENERATION* (1804-1804), daughter of Sally Buchanan Campbell and Francis Smith Preston. She was born during June 1804 and died at the age of two months during August 1804.

(8) Maria Thornton Carter Preston *4th GENERATION* (1805-1842), the daughter of Sally Buchanan Campbell and Francis Smith Preston. She married John Montgomery Preston (1788-1862), the son of Anne Montgomery and Walter Preston of Kentucky. Mrs. Maria Thornton Carter Preston Preston's father-in-law, Walter Preston (1752-1834), was born in Ireland, immigrated to the American colonies, served during the Revolutionary War including service at the Battle of King's Mountain, and lived in Virginia until his

54

death. John Montgomery Preston became a prosperous merchant in Abingdon, Virginia, a leader of industry in Southwest Virginia, and an advocate for state control of internal improvements including banking, characterizing internal improvements within states by the Federal Government to be "both unconstitutional and impolitic"[18]. Mrs. Maria Thornton Carter Preston Preston died in 1842. John Montgomery Preston died twenty years later, in 1862. Marie Thornton Carter Preston and John Montgomery Preston had at least one child:

(a) John Montgomery Preston Jr. *5th GENERATION* (1838), son of Maria Thornton Carter Preston and John M. Preston. In 1864, he married Mary Preston Cochran (born 1840). Mary Preston Cochran and John Montgomery Preston Jr. had children, including:

(i) Margaret Lynn Preston *6th GENERATION* (circa 1800s), daughter of Mary Preston Cochran and John Montgomery Preston. She married Rev. T. E. P. Woods. She was a member of the DAR (membership number 127611) based upon her lineage from Revolutionary War General William Campbell, Walter Preston, and Colonel William Preston.

(9) Charles Henry Campbell Preston *4th GENERATION* (1807-1832), son of Sally

[18] See John Montgomery Preston's speech "To the Voters of Russell, Scott, Lee and Washington, from the *Virginia Statesman*, a newspaper published in Abingdon, Virginia, October 8, 1836" on pages 97 through 100 of C. B. Slemp's 1940 compilation Addresses of Famous Southwest Virginians covering the years 1790 through 1939.

Buchanan Campbell and Francis Smith Preston, married Mary S. Beale of Virginia.

(10) John Smith Preston *4th GENERATION* (1809-1881), son of Sally Buchanan Campbell and Francis Smith Preston, married Caroline Martha Hampton. In 1864, he was promoted to Brigadier General in the Confederate Army.

(11) James Madison Preston *4th GENERATION* (1811-1812), son of Sally Buchanan Campbell and Francis Smith Preston. He was born on May 18, 1811 and died at the age of seven months on January 22, 1812.

(12) Thomas Lewis Preston *4th GENERATION* (1812-1903), son of Sally Buchanan Campbell and Francis Smith Preston, married first his cousin Elizabeth Breckinridge Watts and, second, Anna Maria Saunders.

(13) Robert Gamble Preston *4th GENERATION* (1815-1815), son of Sally Buchanan Campbell and Francis Smith Preston. He was born on October 9, 1815 and died at the age of two months on December 18, 1815.

(14) Margaret Buchanan Frances Preston *4th GENERATION* (1818), daughter of Sally Buchanan Campbell and Francis Smith Preston, married Wade Hampton III.

(15) Infant Preston *4th GENERATION* (circa 1800s). This child of Francis Smith Preston died in infancy according to Pilcher's 1982 work. Dorman reported in 1982 a last child of Francis Smith Preston as having been Isaac Trimble Preston, who first married Catherine Lawn Layton and, second, married Margaret Newman Hewes Layton.

iv) Sarah Preston *3rd GENERATION* (circa 1767). Sarah Preston, daughter of Susanna Smith and William Preston, was born at "Greenfield" around 1767 and died in 1841. She married Colonel James McDowell Jr. (1770-1835), the son of Elizabeth Cloyd and James McDowell. Sarah Preston and James McDowell Jr. had three children, including:

(1) James McDowell III *4th GENERATION* (1795-1851), son of Sarah Preston and James McDowell Jr. He married his first cousin Susan, also called Susanna, Smith Preston (1800-1847), the daughter of Sarah Buchanan Campbell and Francis Smith Preston. James McDowell III's mother (Mrs. Sarah Preston McDowell) was the sister of his wife's father (Francis Smith Preston). James McDowell III was a Governor of Virginia from 1843-1846.

v) Ann Preston *3rd GENERATION*. Ann Preston, who may have been a daughter of Susanna Smith and William Preston, was born at "Greenfield". Ann was also called Nancy. She died in 1782.

vi) William Preston Jr. *3rd GENERATION* (1770-1821). William Preston, son of Susanna Smith and William Preston, was born at "Greenfield". He married Caroline Hancock (1785-1847), a daughter of Margaret "Peggy" Strother (1763-1834) and Colonel George Hancock (1754-1820). The Preston, the Hancock, and the Kennerly families were related by marriage to the Radfords for whom the City of Radford was named. Mrs. Caroline Hancock Preston's paternal aunt Mary Hancock married Samuel Kennerly, whose sister Mary Kennerly married George Strother; their child was Margaret "Peggy" Strother who married Colonel George Hancock. They were the parents of William Preston Jr.'s wife Caroline Hancock. Their other daughter, Julia Hancock (born 1791), married General William Clark. Julia died at the age of sixty-two and was buried in the family tomb on the grounds of the Hancock estate "Fotheringay". Upon Julia's death, William Clark married Julia's cousin Harriet Kennerly (who was born in 1788), daughter of Mary Hancock and Samuel Kennerly. Harriet Kennerly was the widow of Dr. John Blair Radford's uncle John Radford (1785-1817).

vii) <u>Susanna Preston</u> *3rd GENERATION* (1772-1833). Susanna Preston, daughter of Susanna Smith and William Preston, was born at "Greenfield". She married Nathaniel Hart Jr. (1770-1844), son of Sarah Simpson and Nathaniel Hart. They had seven children, including:

(1) <u>Virginia H. Hart</u> *4th GENERATION* (1809), daughter of Sarah Simpson and Nathaniel Hart. She married Alfred Shelby (1804-1832) and, after his death, she married her cousin Robert Jefferson Breckinridge (1800-1881). He was the son of Mary Hopkins Cabell (1769-1858) and John Breckinridge (1760-1806). John Breckinridge (Mrs. Virginia H. Hart Breckinridge's father-in-law) was the son of Mrs. Letitia Preston Breckinridge (1729), the sister of William Preston (1729), who was the grandfather of Mrs. Virginia H. Hart Breckinridge. Virginia was the grand-niece of Mrs. Letitia Preston Breckinridge.

viii) <u>James Patton Preston</u> *3rd GENERATION* (1774-1843). James Patton Preston, son of Susanna Smith and Colonel William Preston, was born at the family home "Smithfield" in Montgomery County, Virginia, on June 21, 1774. He married Nancy Ann Taylor, who was born around 1783 [Her name is also written in sources as Ann Barraud Taylor, 1778-1861, the daughter of Sarah Curle Barraud and Robert Taylor]. James Patton Preston's public service included membership in the Virginia

State Senate in 1802, service as a Colonel in the 23rd Regiment during the War of 1812 during which he suffered a permanently disabling injury, service as Postmaster of Virginia's capital city Richmond, and duties as Virginia's 13th Governor in 1816 through 1819. As Governor who advocated for strengthening of the state militia which was receiving an inadequate amount of federal arms, enlargement of the public education system for the poor, and improvement of what he termed the "deplorable condition" of county jails[19]. James Patton Preston died at "Smithfield" on May 4, 1843. His wife Nancy Ann Taylor Preston died in Montgomery County, Virginia, during June of 1861 at approximately 81 years of age. Nancy Ann Taylor and James Patton Preston had children:

(1) William Ballard Preston 4th GENERATION (1805-1862), son of Nancy Ann Taylor and James Patton Preston. He was born on November 29, 1805 and died on November 16, 1862. He married Lucy Redd. Lucy Redd and William Ballard Preston had children: Walter Redd Preston, Mrs. Anne Taylor Preston Coles, James Patton Preston, Mrs. Lucy Redd Preston Beale, Mrs. Jane Grace Preston Boulware, and an infant son whose name is not now known.

(2) Robert Taylor Preston 4th GENERATION (1809-1880), son of Nancy Ann Taylor and James Patton Preston. He was born at "Smithfield" on May 26, 1809. He married Mary Hart (1808-1882). Col. Robert T. Preston was a confederate soldier during the Civil War, commanding of the 28th Virginia

---

[19] See Virginia Governor James Patton Preston's "Address to the General Assembly of Virginia, Council Chamber, December 7, 1818" on pages 41 through 49 of C. B. Slemp's 1940 compilation Addresses of Famous Southwest Virginians covering the years 1790 through 1939.

Regiment. Preston inherited the family estate called "Solitude", where he made farming his occupation and where he died on June 20, 1880.

(3) James Francis Preston *4th GENERATION* (1813-1862), son of Nancy Ann Taylor and James Patton Preston. James Francis Preston was born at "Smithfield" on November 8, 1813. He built his home "White Thorn" on a portion of the original "Smithfield" property. Preston married Sarah Ann Caperton. The daughter of Hugh Caperton, she was born in Virginia on June 29, 1826. Preston served as a Captain of the Virginia Volunteers of the United States Army during the Mexican War, and as a Colonel of the 4th Virginia Infantry of the Confederate Army during the Civil War. After the war, he was a private practice lawyer and a Montgomery County, Virginia, Commonwealth Attorney, as well as a member of the state legislature. Sarah Ann Caperton and James Francis Preston had children:

(a) Hugh Caperton Preston *2nd GENERATION* (1856), son of Sarah Ann Caperton and James Francis Preston, of whom more. He was born on September 5, 1856. He married Caroline Baldwin.

(b) William Ballard Preston *2nd GENERATION* (1858), son of Sarah Ann Caperton and James Francis Preston. He was born in Montgomery County on September 30, 1858. He became Commandant of Cadets and a Professor of English Literature at Virginia Agricultural and Mechanical College in Blacksburg in Montgomery County, Virginia.

(4) <u>Virginia Preston</u> *4th GENERATION*, daughter of Nancy Ann Taylor and James Patton Preston. She was born at "Smithfield" around 1819.

(5) <u>Susanna Edmonia Preston</u> *4th GENERATION*, daughter of Nancy Ann Taylor and James Patton Preston. Also called Susan, she was born at "Smithfield" around 1815.

(6) <u>Catherine Jane Preston</u> *4th GENERATION*, daughter of Nancy Ann Taylor and James Patton Preston. Known as Jane, she was born at "Smithfield" around 1817. She married George H. Gilmer.

ix) <u>Mary Preston</u> *3rd GENERATION*, daughter of Susanna Smith and William Preston, was born at "Smithfield" in 1772[20] and died in 1820. She married John Lewis in 1793. Mary Preston and John Lewis had children, including:

(1) <u>Margaret Lynn Lewis</u> *4th GENERATION*, daughter of Mary Preston and John Lewis, was born in 1808 and died in 1876. In 1826 she married John Cochran. He was born in 1793 and died in 1883. They had children, including:

(a) <u>James Cochran</u> *5th GENERATION*, son of Margaret Lynn Lewis and John Cochran, was born in 1830 and died in 1897. In 1856, he married Elizabeth Brooke. She was born in 1833 and died in 1891. They had children, including:

(i) <u>Elizabeth Cochran</u> *6th GENERATION*, daughter of Elizabeth Brooke and James Cochran. She was born in Augusta County, Virginia. She married Lionel S. Rawlinson. Mrs. Elizabeth Cochran

---

[20] Mary Preston's year of birth is written as 1776 in some sources. Her descendant Mrs. Elizabeth Cochran Rawlinson, DAR member #127205, reports her year of birth as 1772.

Rawlinson was a member of the DAR (membership number 127205) based upon her lineage from Revolutionary War Colonel William Preston[21].

x) <u>Letitia Preston</u> *3rd GENERATION* (1779), daughter of Susanna Smith and William Preston, was born at "Smithfield". She married John Floyd.

xi) <u>Thomas Lewis Preston</u> *3rd GENERATION* (1781), son of Susanna Smith and William Preston, was born at "Smithfield". He married Edmonia Madison Randolph.

xii) <u>Margaret Brown Preston</u> *3rd GENERATION* (1784), the daughter of Susanna Smith and William Preston. Also called Peggy, she was born at "Smithfield" on February 23, 1784 eight months after her father's June 1783 death. She married Colonel John Preston (1781-1864), the son of Margaret Rhea and Robert Preston. John Preston was a veteran of the War of 1812 and a colonel of the 105th Virginia Militia. Margaret Brown Preston and John Preston had children, including:

(1) <u>William Alfred Preston</u> *4th GENERATION* (1808-1862), the son of Margaret Brown Preston and John Preston. He married Elizabeth Radford. The daughter of Elizabeth Mosely and William C. Radford, she was born in 1832 and died in 1898. Through this marriage, Mrs. Elizabeth Radford Preston became both the great-niece and the daughter-in-law of Mrs. Margaret "Peggy" Brown Preston; the sister of Elizabeth Radford's grandfather (General John Preston) was the mother of Elizabeth's husband William Alfred Preston.

[21] *See* <u>The Lineage Book of the National Society of the Daughters of the American Revolution, Volume CXXVIII, 1916, Membership Numbers 127001 through 128000</u>, pages 64-65, as published in 1932.

Elizabeth Radford and William Alfred Preston had a child:

(a) Alfred G. Preston 5th GENERATION
(1858), the son of Elizabeth Radford
and William Alfred Preston.

(2) Jane Preston 4th GENERATION (circa
1800s), a daughter of Margaret Brown Preston and John Preston. In 1846 she married James Brown Craighead (1795-1860).

b) Mary Preston 2nd GENERATION (1740), daughter
of Elizabeth Patton and John Preston, was born in
Augusta County, Virginia in 1740. Either she or
her sister Ann may have married John Howard.

c) Letitia (also known as Lettice) Preston 2nd
GENERATION (1729-1797), daughter of Elizabeth
Patton and John Preston. She was born in 1729.
She married Colonel Robert Breckinridge (1720-
1772), who emigrated from Ireland to the American colonies around 1740. Letitia Preston and
Robert Breckinridge had six children, including:

i) John Breckinridge 3rd GENERATION (1760), son
of Letitia Preston and Robert Breckinridge. He
married Mary Hopkins Cabell (1769-1858).
They had nine children, including:

(1) Robert Jefferson Breckinridge 4th
GENERATION (1800). He married his
cousin Ann Sophonisba Preston (1803-
1844), daughter of Sarah Buchanan
Campbell and Francis Smith Preston. She
was his grandmother's grand-niece. Upon
Ann Sophonisba Preston's death, Robert
Jefferson Breckinridge married his cousin
Virginia H. Hart, the daughter of Susanna
Preston and Nathaniel Hart Jr. She was
also a grand-niece of his grandmother Mrs.
Letitia (Lettice) Preston Breckinridge.

d) Margaret Preston 2nd GENERATION (circa 1727),
daughter of Elizabeth Patton and John Preston,
was born around 1727. She married Rev. John
Brown.

e) <u>Ann Preston</u> *2nd GENERATION* (circa 1739), daughter of Elizabeth Patton and John Preston, was born around 1739. Either she or her sister Mary may have married John Howard.

f) <u>James Preston</u> *2nd GENERATION* (circa 1742), son of Elizabeth Patton and John Preston, was born around 1742. He died at a young age; additional information unknown at this time.

Illustration 17: Smithfield, the Preston plantation in Blacksburg, Virginia. Currently operated by Smithfield Association as museum entered through Virginia Tech campus. Photo by Joanne Spiers Moche.

Radford, John Blair
1813-1872

John Blair Radford, born on April 20th in the year 1813, was the son of Elizabeth Mosely and William Radford of Forest, Virginia, in Bedford County[22]. While his tombstone indicates that he was born at "Woodbourne", the family home in Forest, his descendant Minnie Adams Fitting[23] reported that he was actually born in Lynchburg. John Blair Radford had six brothers and sisters; most of the Radford family resided in Bedford County throughout their lives.

Dr. J. B. Radford began his medical practice in the New River Valley around 1836 and took a bride on May 31, 1836. He married Elizabeth Campbell Taylor. The daughter of Jane DeVigny Kent and Major John McCanless Taylor, Elizabeth was born on May 30, 1820 at the family home of "Rockford" in Montgomery County, Virginia (that location being a section of Montgomery County which is now Pulaski County, Virginia) near Pepper's Ferry. Elizabeth was sixteen and John Blair Radford was twenty-three when they were married on May 31, 1836 at "Rockford"[24].

The young couple received one hundred acres[25] of land from Major Taylor as recorded in Montgomery County, Virginia, Deed Book M Page 356 and dated April 25, 1838. It was described as "a certain tract or parcel of land containing one hundred acres (be the same more or less) lying and being in the county aforesaid *[Montgomery County]* adjoining the lands of Edward Hammet, and the said John M C Taylor being the same that the said Taylor purchased under a deed of trust assented by Anderson B. Matthews. Together with all and singular the appointenances to the said tract of land / premises to the said John B. Radford and Elizabeth his wife".

---

[22] John Blair Radford's date of birth as recorded on his tombstone was April 20, 1813. Other sources list the day of birth as the 26th of April.

[23] *See* Fitting, Minnie Adams (2002), The Radford Letters.

[24] The Taylor family home called "Rockford" no longer stands. The site and its cemeteries have been lost to time and business development.

[25] This property passed from Taylor to Radford is incorrectly described in some sources as totaling 1,000 acres.

The Radfords received approximately eight hundred and sixty-five additional acres of Taylor property in 1842, discussed by descendant Minnie Adams Fitting[26] as part of the division of his estate on the east side of New River at the mouth of Conley's Branch given prior to his death "as an advancement". Described in Montgomery County, Virginia, Deed Book N Page 139 and dated February 22, 1842, this second tract totaled seven hundred, sixty-five and a half acres. It was described as "a certain tract or parcel of land lying and being in the county of Montgomery on New River and Connellys [sic] Branch containing seven hundred and sixty-five and one half acres: Five hundred and ninety-five acres of which was granted to Francis Reily on the fifth day of April _____, one hundred and thirty-one acres was granted to George Rawland assignee of Jeremiah Barnett, on the ____ day of ____. Twenty-five acres granted to John McCanless Taylor on the first day of August 1809, and fourteen and one-half acres granted to the said Taylor on the first day of August 1809".

Radford continued to invest in real estate. Much of the original Radford family land is now the acreage on which much of central and western Radford City is now nestled.

Dr. Radford built a home for himself and his bride, finished by 1840 on land overlooking New River from the south. He named his home "Arnheim[27]". The building still stands today and the land surrounding it is now the site of Radford High School[28]. The old Radford Family Cemetery is located behind the Radford High School football stadium.

John Blair Radford was a man of many interests. In addition to the practice of medicine, he was engaged in farming and in land development. He owned land on both sides of the New River in the areas of both present-day Radford and present-day Pulaski County. By 1842 he was Montgomery County's Justice of the Peace in 1842.

---

[26] See Radford Family Letters by Minnie Adams Fitting (2002).

[27] Farrar and Hines, in their 1978 book on Virginia houses, incorrectly listed the owner of Arnheim as Dr. James Radford; the correct name being Dr. John Blair Radford. They also listed the home as being built in 1845.

[28] The Radford family sold "Arnheim" to the City of Radford in 1931. It was used as a classroom annex by Radford High School and is now held by the City and within the pervue of the Radford Heritage Foundation. Plans for renovation have been discussed but not realized.

He also had interests in the Allegheny Springs Turnpike and in the Yellow Springs resort. At one point, he was Director of the Lafayette and English (i.e. Ingles) Turnpike Company.

In 1842, Dr. Radford purchased the Lovely Mount Tavern. Lovely Mount Tavern, located along the Wilderness Road, served both as an Inn, the area post office, and a social center. It became the focal point of community activities including church services.

The Episcopal Church was very important to the Radford family. John Blair Radford's father, William Radford, helped to establish the St. Stephen's Episcopal Church in Forest, Virginia. It was there that Mrs. Elizabeth Campbell Taylor Radford was baptized as an adult on May 23, 1854. The confirmation was performed by the Rt. Rev. John Johns. Mrs. E. C. T. Radford's sponsors were her father-in-law William Radford and her husband John Blair Radford. Mrs. Elizabeth C. T. Radford and Dr. John Blair Radford were both confirmed at St. Stephen's that same day (i.e. May 23, 1854).

The Radfords were instrumental in the establishment of an Episcopal church in their home community. Their estate "Arnheim" was the site of the first Episcopal service known to have been performed in the area. The Rev. Nicholas Hamner Cobbs officiated. Elizabeth and John Blair Radford were among the catalysts behind the organization of Montgomery Parish and the St. James' Episcopal Mission congregation in Central Depot, Virginia. He was a member of the first Montgomery Episcopal Parish vestry. She held the first known Episcopal Sunday School class at the Radford home around the 1840s. Following the religious guidance of the Rt. Rev. William Meade, she included her servants, slaves, and their children in the religious lessons which she provided to her own children.

Dr. John Blair Radford served as a member of the Episcopal Parish vestry of Montgomery County, Virginia, on July 19, 1858. He was one of five men designated at an organizational meeting to serve on this first vestry. Dr. Radford continued to be actively involved in the area's Episcopal churches. He was a lay delegate from the Montgomery Parish to the Episcopal Diocesan Convention in 1860. He served on subsequent vestries and committees as the Montgomery Parish and then the Radford Parish grew. He was active in business and politics in the community which would later bear the name "Radford" in his honor.

Dr. Radford supported the Confederate efforts morally and financially during the Civil War. He did not accept a commission to serve as a soldier, but devoted most of his energy during that time as a member of the Home Guard. He offered his medical services to his community, and as needed to soldiers injured in battlefield settings including Manassas during 1861.

The Radford family suffered greatly, as did so many others in both the North and the South. The Radfords lost two sons in battle, and gained two son-in-laws from the Confederate ranks. Even the family home was not untouched. One day after the Battle of Cloyd's Mountain, "Arnheim" was struck by Union artillery shells aimed at Confederate troops on the southern side of New River. Mrs. Radford and son Lawrence Radford were home at the time but uninjured.

Dr. Radford was an active proponent of the extension of public transportation through the New River Valley. During the 1840s, he was the Director of the Lafayette and English[29] Turnpike Company.

Dr. Radford also promoted the creation of a railroad line through his community. After the Civil War, he and his son-in-law General Gabriel Colvin Wharton worked together to realize an extension of rail lines to the southwestern Virginia coal fields. The New River Railroad, Mining, and Manufacturing Company was incorporated on March 7, 1872, to meet that goal. Dr. Radford was its president. He died three months after New river Railroad, Mining, and Manufacturing had been incorporated.

John Blair Radford died on June 30, 1872, having suffered a stroke[30] at the age of fifty-nine. He was buried in the private Radford Family Cemetery.

At the time of the 1880 Census, Dr. Radford's widow Lizzie and son Lawrence were still living in the Central Depot area of Montgomery County and were still members of the St. James' Episcopal Mission congregation.

---

[29] "English" was often written for the surname "Ingles"; the Lafayette and English Turnpike was also called the Lafayette and Ingles Turnpike.
[30] Some sources list Dr. J. B. Radford's cause of death as a heart attack. Episcopal church records list cause of death as a stroke.

Mrs. Elizabeth "Lizzie" Campbell Taylor Radford died on December 17, 1886 of pneumonia. She was sixty-seven years old and residing in Central, Virginia, at the Radford family home. She was buried on December 19, 1886 at the private Radford Family Cemetery with the Rev. J. E. Hammond officiating.

The town of Central City was incorporated as the City of Radford on January 22, 1892, twenty years after Dr. Radford's death. His son James Lawrence Radford was instrumental in securing city status as a member of the Virginia House of Delegates.

The official reason that the city was named in honor of Dr. John Blair Radford was not recorded. A number of theories exist through local legend. The most popular theory is that the city's name commemorates the fact that much of the Radford city property was once owned by Dr. Radford. Another acknowledges his role in the land development as well as his active public service on councils and committees. Yet another theory alludes to Dr. Radford's personal characteristics including his caring medical services and his willingness to assist his neighbors financially through private loans.

Elizabeth Campbell Taylor and John Blair Radford had children:

1. John Taylor Radford, called Johnny, was born on June[31] 4, 1838, in the Overseer's Cottage while the Radford home, Arnheim, was being built. He never married. This oldest Radford son, called "Johnny", served during the Civil War as company captain of the Montgomery County, Virginia, Confederate company, called "The New River Grays". He was a colonel when he died near Charlottesville, Virginia, mortally wounded in the Battle of Cedarville on November 11, 1864. Johnny was twenty-six years old when he was killed.

2. William Mosely Radford, called "Willie", was born on August 12, 1840. Like his brother Johnny, he never had the opportunity to marry. Willie was first lieutenant with the Pulaski County, Virginia Confederate Company "The Pulaski Boys" of the 24th Virginia Volunteers regiment. When Union forces attempted to capitalize on their suc-

---

[31] Some sources list the birth month of John Taylor Radford as July. His tombstone lists his date of birth as June 4, 1838.

cesses at Yorktown by assaulting Fort Magruder near Williamsburg, Virginia, southern troops rallied to foil the foes' plans. The Confederate Army was victorious. However, William Mosely Radford was shot through the right breast and died instantly during this May 5, 1862 Battle of Williamsburg.

3. Anne Rebecca Radford, called "Nannie", was born on August 15, 1843 and died on April 15, 1890. She married Confederate Brigadier General Gabriel Colvin Wharton. He was born on July 23, 1824 and died on May 10, 1906. Nannie and Gabriel Colvin Wharton had a son named William Radford Wharton, of whom more.

4. Jane Kent Radford, also known as "Jennie", was born on May 15, 1845. She married Captain William Fox Moore. Moore served during the Civil War and was wounded at the Battle of Antietam. After the war, he worked with the Virginia and Tennessee Railroad near Central Depot as a civil engineer. Jane and William Moore were married at "Arnheim" on October 24, 1865, almost two years before her death. She bore a son, who died at or near the time of birth in 1866. She succeeded in achieving a second pregnancy, a male child who also died at or near the time of birth at the end of 1866 or the beginning of 1867[32]. Mrs. Jane Kent Radford Moore died on August 2, 1867. She was buried in the private Radford Family Cemetery[33]. Following Mrs. Jane Kent Radford Moore's death, William

---

[32] Information about the Radford family lineage can be found in works by Radford family descendants including <u>William Radford of Richmond</u> by Robert Somerville Radford Yates in 1986 and <u>The Radford Family Letters: A Radford Family History</u> by Minnie Fitting Adams in 2002. Details of early Radford family daily life and events were comprehensively covered by Adams based upon letters written by and to Radford relatives from at least 1799 through 1867. She donated the original letters to Radford Public Library, Radford, Virginia.

[33] Episcopal church records listed the death of a four-year old child named Mabel Moore, born circa 1887, as follows: Mabel Moore, age four years, died from diphtheria on March 6, 1891 in Radford, Virginia. She was buried at the "old Radford Cemetery (temporarily)", as recorded in Grace Episcopal Church records by Rev. Edward Lewis Goodwin. No marker for Mabel Moore has been found in the Radford Family Cemetery. Any relationship between this child, who was born around twenty years after the death of Mrs. Jane Kent Radford Moore, and Jane and William Fox Moore is not now known.

Fox Moore moved to Bedford County, Virginia. He later remarried.

5. Elizabeth Campbell Radford, called "Lizzie", was born at "Arnheim" in Montgomery County, Virginia on November 17, 1847 and died on February 22, 1930. She married Richard Henry Adams Jr. Capt. Adams was born on April 21, 1841 and died in Radford, Virginia, on October 8, 1896.

6. Mary McCanless Radford was born on April 28, 1851 and died on December 7, 1885. She married William T. Yancey Jr. He was born around 1847.

7. James Lawrence Radford, the youngest Radford child, of whom more. He was born on September 16, 1856.

Illustration 18: Dr. John Blair Radford, the city's namesake. Courtesy of Glencoe Museum / Radford Heritage Foundation.

A more detailed lineage of John Blair Radford[34], with discussions of lineal relationships is as follows (John Radford > John Radford Jr. > William Radford > William C. Radford Jr. > John Blair Radford):

1) <u>John Radford</u> 1st Generation (circa 1600s-1728) John Radford married Sarah (surname not known). Emigrated from England to American Colonies before 1677. He was a carpenter and a landowner in Maryland. He died in 1728. Sarah and John Radford had children, including:

    a) <u>John Radford Jr</u>. 2nd Generation (circa 1722), son of Sarah and John Radford, was born sometime between 1720 and 1725. He married Ruth Tannehill around 1758. He served in the militia during the Revolutionary War, then worked as a carpenter and lived in Frederick, Maryland, where he died in 1759. After his death Mrs. Ruth Tannehill Radford married Charles Prather. She died on October 7, 1807 in a section of Virginia which would become a part of the state of West Virginia. Ruth Tannehill and John Radford Jr. had children, including:

        i) <u>William Radford</u> 3rd Generation (1759-1803). This son of Ruth Tannehill and John Radford Jr. was born in Frederick County, Maryland in 1759 (the year of his father's death). He married Rebecca Winston on December 14, 1780 at the Winston family home called "Laurel Grove". Rebecca, the daughter of Mary Jordan and Geddes Winston, was born in 1761. Rebecca and William lived in Forest, Virginia. William died on April 3, 1803. Rebecca died on August 6, 1820. Rebecca Winston and William Radford had children:

---

[34] Radford family lineage has been documented by Robert Somerville Yates (1986), Randolph S. Hancock (1935), Minnie Fitting Adams (2002), Daughters of the American Revolution, and cemetery tombstone information, public records, and unpublished Radford family information researched by this author. See end book *Sources* for complete references.

(1) <u>Mary Susan Radford</u> 4th Generation (1781), daughter of Rebecca Winston and William Radford, was born in 1781 and died in 1810. Called Polly, she married General John Preston (1764-1827). General John Preston was the son of Susanna Smith and William Preston of Montgomery County, Virginia. Mary Susan Radford and John Preston had children:

    (a) <u>William Radford Washington Preston</u> 5th Generation (1799), son of Mary Susan Radford and John Preston.

    (b) <u>John Breckinridge Preston</u> 5th Generation (circa 1800), son of Mary Susan Radford and John Preston.

    (c) <u>Elizabeth Madison Preston</u> 5th Generation (circa 1803), daughter of Mary Susan Radford and John Preston.

    (d) <u>Susanna Smith Preston</u> 5th Generation (circa 1805), called Susan, was the daughter of Mary Susan Radford and John Preston. She married her first cousin, William Mosely Radford (1811-1873). He was the son of Elizabeth Mosely and William C. Radford (the father of Dr. John Blair Radford). Susanna Smith Preston and William Mosely Radford had children, including:

        (i) <u>Elizabeth Radford</u> 6th Generation (1832), a daughter of Susanna Smith Preston and William Mosely Radford, also known as "Lizzie". She married her cousin William Alfred Preston (1808-1862), son of Margaret "Peggy" Brown Preston and John Preston. After William Alfred Preston's death, Lizzie married John Durburrow Munford. They had at least one child:

73

1. Mildred Munford 7th Generation (c. 1800s), daughter of Mrs. Elizabeth Radford Preston Munford and Mr. John Durburrow Munford.

(2) Sarah Radford 4th Generation (1784), daughter of Rebecca Winston and William Radford, was born in 1784 and died in 1864. Called Sally, she married William Munford.

(3) John Radford 4th Generation (1785), son of Rebecca Winston and William Radford, was born in 1785 and died in 1817. He married Harriet Kennerly of Fincastle, Virginia. After John's death, Mrs. Harriet Kennerly Radford married widower William Clark (whose first wife Julia Hancock was a cousin to Harriet Kennerly). Harriet Kennerly was the daughter of Mary Hancock and Samuel Kennerly. Samuel Kennerly's niece, Margaret Strother, married Colonel George Hancock. Margaret Strother and George Hancock were the parents of Julia Hancock (first wife of William Clark) and Caroline Hancock (who married Major William Preston Jr.).

(4) William C. Radford 4th Generation (1787-1861). William C. Radford[35], son of Rebecca Winston and William Radford, was born on January 27, 1787 and died on January 5, 1861. He married Elizabeth Mosely. Born on November 13, 1785, she was the daughter of Ann Irvine and Revolutionary War General William Mosely and niece of Colonel George Hancock. The marriage ceremony was performed by Radford's uncle, the Rev. John D. Blair. Elizabeth and William lived in Forest, Vir-

[35] William C. Radford, also known as William Radford Jr.

74

ginia. He was an attorney who organized troops for the War of 1812 and helped to establish the St. Stephen's Episcopal Church in Forest in 1824. Elizabeth Mosely and William C. Radford had children:

(a) William Mosely Radford 5th Generation (1811-1873), son of Elizabeth Mosely and William C. Radford, was born on April 21, 1811 and died May 19, 1873. He married his first cousin, Susanna Smith Preston. She was the daughter of Mary Susan Radford (William C. Radford's sister) and General John Preston. Susannah Smith Preston and William Mosely Radford had children:

   (i) Mary Anne Radford 6th Generation (circa 1800s), called Minnie, was the daughter of Susannah Preston and William Mosely Radford. She married Peter Copland. They had five daughters.

   (ii) William Mosely Radford Jr. 6th Generation (circa 1800s), called Mose, was the son of Susanna Smith Preston and William Mosely Radford. He never married.

(b) Mary Lavinia Radford 5th Generation (1812), daughter of Elizabeth Mosely and William C. Radford, was born in 1812 and died in 1814 at the age of two.

(c) John Blair Radford 5th Generation (1813), son of Elizabeth Mosely and William C. Radford, was born in 1813 and died in 1872. He married Elizabeth Campbell Taylor, who was born in 1820 and 1876. She was the daughter of Jane DeVigny Kent and John McCanless Taylor, the granddaughter

75

of Elizabeth Campbell and John Taylor, and the grand-niece of Revolutionary War veteran General William Campbell. Elizabeth Campbell Taylor and John Blair Radford had children:

(i) <u>John Taylor Radford</u> 6th Generation (1838-1864), son of Elizabeth Campbell Taylor and John Blair Radford. He was born on June 1, 1838 and died at the age of twenty-six on November 11, 1864 as a Confederate soldier during the Civil War.

(ii) <u>William Mosely Radford</u> 6th Generation (1840-1862), son of Elizabeth Campbell Taylor and John Blair Radford. He was born on August 12, 1840 and died on May 5, 1862 as a twenty-two year old Confederate soldier during the Civil War.

(iii) <u>Anne Rebecca Radford</u> 6th Generation (1843-1890), daughter of Elizabeth Campbell Taylor and John Blair Radford. She was born on August 15, 1843 and died at the age of forty-seven on April 15, 1890. She married General Gabriel Colvin Wharton, who was born in 1824. The wedding was held at "Arnheim", conducted by Rev. Miller. Anne Rebecca Radford and Gabriel Colvin Wharton had a child:

1. <u>William Radford Wharton</u> 7th Generation (1864). He married Susan Hammet Heth, the daughter of Isabella Hammet and Stockton Heth and the granddaughter of Edward Hammet. Sue Heth and William Radford Wharton had children:

a. Stockton Heth Wharton 8th Generation (1892), son of Susan Hammet Heth and William Radford Wharton.

b. Anne Rebecca Radford Wharton 8th Generation (1894), daughter of Susan Hammet Heth and William Radford Wharton. She married Hugo Swaen von Poederoyen.

c. William Radford Wharton Jr. 8th Generation (1904-1990), son of Susan Hammet Heth and William Radford Wharton. He married Evelyn (maiden surname not now known). They had children:

   i. Sally Wharton 9th Generation (circa 1900s), daughter of Evelyn and William Radford Wharton Jr. She married Mr. van Solkema.

   ii. Sue Wharton 9th Generation (c. 1900s), daughter of Evelyn and William Radford Wharton Jr.

(iv) Jane Kent Radford 6th Generation (1845-1867), daughter of Elizabeth Campbell Taylor and John Blair Radford. She was born on May 15, 1845 and died at the age of twenty-two on August 2, 1867. She married Captain William Fox Moore.

(v) Elizabeth Campbell Radford 6th Generation (1847-1930), daughter of Elizabeth Campbell Taylor and John Blair Radford. She was born on November 17, 1847 and died on February 22, 1930 at the age of eighty-three. She married Richard Henry Adams Jr. They had children:

1. John Putnam Adams 7th Generation (1866), son of Lottie Putnam and Richard Henry Adams Jr.

2. Julia Putnam Adams 7th Generation (1868), son of Lottie Putnam and Richard Henry Adams Jr.

3. Radford Carter Adams 7th Generation (1872), son of Elizabeth Campbell Adams and Richard Henry Adams Jr. He married Mancye Doyle. They had children:

   a. Elizabeth Campbell Adams 8th Generation (1909), daughter of Mancye Doyle and Radford Carter Adams. She married Kenneth Frederick Small.

   b. Lucien Doyle Adams 8th Generation (1910), son of Mancye Doyle and Radford Carter Adams. He married Eleanor Elizabeth Eakin.

   c. Minnie Harris Adams 8th Generation (1912), daughter of Mancye Doyle and Radford Carter Adams. She married Robert Dancy Fitting.

   d. Radford Carter Adams Jr. 8th Generation (circa 1922), son of Mancye Doyle and Radford Carter Adams.

   e. Mancye Prince Adams 8th Generation (1925), daughter of Mancye Doyle and Radford Carter Adams.

(vi) <u>Mary McCanless Radford</u> 6th Generation (1851-1885), daughter of Elizabeth Campbell Taylor and John Blair Radford. She was born on April 28, 1851 and died at the age of thirty-four on December 7, 1885. She married William T. Yancey Jr.

(vii) <u>James Lawrence Radford</u> 6th Generation (1856-1901), son of Elizabeth Campbell Taylor and John Blair Radford. He was born on September 16, 1856 and died at the age of forty-five on October 20, 1901. This youngest member of the Radford family, nicknamed "Captain" by his parents and siblings, never married. He was a state representative, and was instrumental in getting the Town of Radford designated as the City of Radford in 1892.

(d) <u>Anne Rebecca Radford</u> 5th Generation (1816-1841), daughter of Elizabeth Mosely and William C. Radford, was born in 1816 and died in 1841. She married Charles Beale. Anne Rebecca Radford and Charles Beale had children:

(i) <u>William Radford Beale</u> 6th Generation (circa 1800s), son of Anne Rebecca Radford and Charles Beale, married Lucy Preston[36].

(ii) <u>John Robertson Beale</u> 6th Generation (circa 1800s), son of Anne Rebecca Radford and Charles Beale; never married.

---

[36] Lucy Preston, the wife of William Radford Beale, may have been Lucy Redd Preston. Lucy Redd Preston, the daughter of Lucy Redd and William Ballard Preston, was born in 1848.

(e) <u>Winston Radford</u> 5th Generation (1820-1861), son of Elizabeth Mosely and William C. Radford, was born in 1820 and died in 1861. He married Anne Marie Norvell. Their Bedford County, Virginia home was named "Ashwood". Captain Winston Radford was killed during the Battle of Manassas in 1861 during the American Civil War. His brother, Colonel Richard Carlton Walker Radford, was his commanding officer. Anne Marie Norvell and Winston Radford had children:

(i) <u>William N. Radford</u> 6th Generation (circa 1800s), son of Anne Marie Norvell and Winston Radford.

(ii) <u>Anne Radford</u> 6th Generation (circa 1800s), daughter of Anne Marie Norvell and Winston Radford.

(iii) <u>Emma Radford</u> 6th Generation (circa 1800s), daughter of Anne Marie Norvell and Winston Radford.

(iv) <u>Lucy H. Radford</u> 6th Generation (circa 1800s), daughter of Anne Marie Norvell and Winston Radford.

(v) <u>Winston Radford Jr.</u> 6th Generation (circa 1800s), son of Anne Marie Norvell and Winston Radford.

(vi) <u>Mina Radford</u> 6th Generation (circa 1800s), daughter of Anne Marie Norvell and Winston Radford.

(vii) <u>John B. Radford</u> 6th Generation (circa 1800s), son of Anne Marie Norvell and Winston Radford.

(viii) <u>Kate Radford</u> 6th Generation (circa 1800s), daughter of Anne Marie Norvell and Winston Radford.

(f) <u>Richard Carlton Walker Radford</u> 5th Generation (circa 1823-1886), son of Elizabeth Mosely and William C. Radford, was born around 1823 and died on November 2, 1886 at the age of sixty-four. Colonel R. C. W. Radford commanded a regiment of the Thirteenth Virginia Mounted Infantry, which was mustered by Colonel Jubal A. Early. Radford's command was the first mounted regiment organized in Virginia. Colonel Richard Carlton Walker Radford married Octavia DuVal, who was born in 1829 and died in 1877. After her death he married Frances Steptoe. Octavia DuVal and Richard Carlton Walker Radford had eleven children, only four of whom survived:

(i) DuVal Radford 6th Generation (circa 1800s), son of Octavia DuVal and Richard Carlton Walker Radford.

(ii) Octavius Carlton Radford 6th Generation (circa 1800s), son of Octavia DuVal and Richard Carlton Walker Radford.

(iii) Octavia Radford 6th Generation (circa 1800s), daughter of Octavia DuVal and Richard Carlton Walker Radford.

(iv) Loxley Radford 6th Generation (circa 1800s), son of Octavia DuVal and Richard Carlton Walker Radford.

(g) Munford Washington Radford 5th Generation (1825), son of Elizabeth Mosely and William C. Radford, was born in 1825 and died in 1887. He married Elizabeth Reed; they had five children. After Elizabeth's death, he married Laura Somerville; they had eleven children.

(5) Carlton Tannehill Radford 4th Generation (1792), son of Rebecca Winston and William Radford, was born in 1792 and died

in 1855. He married Virginia L. Martin, who was born around 1826.

(6) Marie Antoinette Radford 4th Generation (1793), daughter of Rebecca Winston and William Radford, was born in 1793 and died in 1873. She married Henry A. Edmundson (also spelled in some sources as Edmondson).

b) Henry Radford 2nd Generation (circa 1711), son of Sarah and John Radford, was born after 1710 and lived in Stafford County, Virginia.

c) Thomas Radford 2nd Generation (circa 1712), son of Sarah and John Radford, was born after 1710 and lived in Frederick, Maryland.

Mrs. Elizabeth Campbell Taylor Radford's ancestors, as well as the descendants of the Campbell and Taylor lines, were an impressive group of people as well. The Campbells and the Taylors lay claim to soldiers, politicians, and other citizens of esteem.

The Campbell clan is of Scotch-Irish descent. Research efforts[37] to trace this Campbell family, i.e. the ancestors of Mrs. Elizabeth Campbell Taylor Radford, have been unsuccessful in proving a lineal link to the Campbells of the Scottish Highlands where the Duke of Argyle and the village of Glencoe are located. Descent from American emigrant John Campbell is verified through several sources and outlined below. His heritage, i.e. ancestry, in Ireland and Scotland can not be verified by public or family records.

A detailed lineage of six generations of Elizabeth Campbell Taylor's maternal heritage (John Campbell > Patrick Campbell > Charles Campbell > Elizabeth Campbell > John McCanless Taylor > Elizabeth Campbell Taylor):

---

[37] Campbell family lineage has been documented by Margaret Campbell Pilcher (1911), John Frederick Dorman (1982), Robert Somerville Yates (1986), Gary Clark (2001), Phil Norfleet (2001), Minnie Fitting Adams (2002), the Daughters of the American Revolution, and public records as researched by this author. See end book *Sources* for complete references.

1) <u>John Campbell</u> 1st Generation (1674-1741). John Campbell was born in the Ulster area of Ireland on November 16, 1674. He may have been the son of Mary McCoy and Duncan Campbell. At some point he immigrated to the American colonies and eventually to Augusta County, Virginia where he died at his estate "Beverly Manor" around 1741. He married Grissell "Grace" Hay, daughter of Patrick Hay, around 1695. Grace was born around 1677 and died around 1770. Grace Hay and John Campbell were the great-grandparents of Virginia Governor David Campbell (1779-1859) and of his cousin Revolutionary War General William Campbell (1745-1781). The nine children of Grace Hay and John Campbell were as follows.

   a) <u>Patrick Campbell</u> 2nd Generation (circa 1696), son of Grissell "Grace" Hay and John Campbell, was born around 1696 and died during the mid-1700s. He married Delilah Thompson. Delilah Thompson and Patrick Campbell had four children as follows.

   i) <u>Martha Campbell</u> 3rd Generation (circa 1700s), daughter of Delilah Thompson and Patrick Campbell.

   ii) <u>Charles Campbell</u> 3rd Generation (circa 1720), son of Delilah Thompson and Patrick Campbell, was born around 1720. He served in the colonial militia and fought during the French and Indian War. He married Margaret Buchanan, the sister of Smyth County surveyor Colonel John Buchanan and the daughter of Jane Sayers and James Buchanan. Margaret was born in 1725. Margaret Buchanan and Captain Charles Campbell had six children as follows.

   (1) <u>William Campbell</u> 4th Generation (1745-1782), son of Margaret Buchanan and Charles Campbell, was born in 1745 and died at the age of thirty-six in 1782. He served his country during the Revolution-

83

ary War first as an army captain and then as colonel before achieving fame for his military action as a Brigadier General during the 1780 Battle of King's Mountain. In 1776 General William Campbell married Elizabeth Henry, who was born in 1748 and died in 1825. Elizabeth was the daughter of Sarah Winston Syme and Colonel John Henry and the sister of American statesman Colonel Patrick Henry[38]. Elizabeth Henry and General William Campbell had two children:

(a) Charles Henry Campbell 5th Generation (circa 1700s), son of Elizabeth Henry and General William Campbell. He died as a child.

(b) Sarah Buchanan Campbell 5th Generation (1778-1846), daughter of Elizabeth Henry and General William Campbell, was known as Sally. She was born on April 22, 1778 and died on July 23, 1846. After her father's death in 1825, Colonel Arthur Campbell was appointed as her guardian. Arthur Campbell was both a cousin and the husband of General William Campbell's sister Margaret, making him Sarah's uncle. Sarah Buchanan Campbell married General Francis Smith Preston in 1793. He was born on August 2, 1765 and died on May 26, 1835. He was a veteran of the War of 1812 and the son of Susanna Smith and Colonel William Preston. The Prestons built their home near Abingdon, Virginia in 1832. That home was sold by the family in 1858 and became the Mary Washington Col-

---

[38] Mrs. Elizabeth Henry Campbell's niece, a daughter of Patrick Henry, married a son of Alexander Campbell of Ireland.

lege for young women until it closed in 1932. The estate reopened as the Martha Washington Inn in 1935. Sarah Buchanan Campbell and General Francis Smith Preston had fifteen children[39]: William Campbell Preston (1794), Eliza Henry Preston (1796), Francis Smith Preston Jr. (1798), Susan (or Susanna) Smith Preston (1800), Sarah Buchanan Preston (1802), Anne Sophonisba Preston (1803), Jane Robertson Preston (1804), Maria Thornton Carter Preston (1805), Charles Henry Campbell Preston (1807), John Smith Preston (1809), James Madison Preston (1811), Thomas Lewis Preston, Robert Gamble Preston, Margaret Buchanan Frances Preston, and Isaac Trimble Preston.

(2) Elizabeth Campbell 4th Generation (circa 1700s), daughter of Margaret Buchanan and Captain Charles Campbell. She married John Taylor. Elizabeth Campbell and John Taylor seven children[40]: That 5th Generation included James Taylor (c. 1700s), Charles Taylor (c. 1700s), Allen Taylor (c. 1700s), John McCanless Taylor (1780), William Taylor, and Eliza Taylor. John McCanless Taylor and his wife Jane DeVigny Kent had children: those 6th Generation children were Elizabeth Campbell Taylor (1820) who married Dr. John Blair Radford (1813), . The 7th Generation offspring of Elizabeth Campbell Taylor and

[39] See PRESTON LINEAGE for additional information on these relatives of the Campbells.
[40] See TAYLOR LINEAGE for additional information on these relatives of the Campbells.

John Blair Radford[41] were: John Taylor Radford (1838), William Mosely Radford (1840), Anne Rebecca Radford (1843) who married General Gabriel Colvin Wharton (1824), Jane Kent Radford (1845) who married Captain William Fox Moore (c. 1800s), Elizabeth Campbell Radford (1847) who married Captain Richard Henry Adams Jr. (1841), Mary McCanless Radford (1851) who married William T. Yancey Jr. (c. 1847), and James Lawrence Radford (1856).

(3) Margaret Campbell 4th Generation (1716), daughter of Margaret Buchanan and Captain Charles Campbell, married Arthur Campbell. Arthur Campbell was the son of Mary Hamilton and David Campbell (referred to as "White David" Campbell, this father-in-law of Margaret Campbell was the brother of Margaret Campbell's grandfather Patrick Campbell, making him her great uncle). Margaret Campbell and Arthur Campbell were cousins. They had twelve children, as follows:

(4) Jane Campbell 4th Generation (circa 1700s), daughter of Margaret Buchanan and Captain Charles Campbell. She married Thomas Tate.

(5) John Campbell 4th Generation (circa 1700s), son of Margaret Buchanan and Captain Charles Campbell. He died young.

(6) Anne Campbell 4th Generation (circa 1700s), daughter of Margaret Buchanan and Captain Charles Campbell. She married Richard Poston.

iii) James Campbell 3rd Generation (circa 1700s), son of Delilah Thompson and Patrick Campbell.

---

[41] See RADFORD LINEAGE for additional information on these relatives of the Campbells.

iv) <u>William Campbell</u> 3rd Generation (circa 1700s), son of Delilah Thompson and Patrick Campbell.

v) <u>Patrick Campbell Jr.</u> 3rd Generation (circa 1700s), son of Delilah Thompson and Patrick Campbell. He married Anne Steele. They had four children, as follows:

   (1) <u>Robert Campbell</u> 4th Generation (circa 1700s), son of Anne Steele and Patrick Campbell Jr. He married.

   (2) <u>Jane Campbell</u> 4th Generation (circa 1700s), daughter of Anne Steele and Patrick Campbell Jr. She married Robert Love. They had children.

   (3) <u>Samuel Campbell</u> 4th Generation (circa 1700s), son of Anne Steele and Patrick Campbell Jr. He married.

   (4) <u>William Campbell</u> 4th Generation (circa 1700s), son of Anne Steele and Patrick Campbell Jr. He married Tabitha Russell, daughter of General William Russell. They had five children, as follows:

      (a) <u>Elizabeth Campbell</u> 5th Generation (circa 1700s), daughter of Tabitha Russell and William Campbell. She married Barton W. Stone. They had children.

      (b) <u>Tabitha Campbell</u> 5th Generation (circa 1700s), daughter of Tabitha Russell and William Campbell. She married Judge Alney McLean. They had children.

      (c) <u>Nancy Campbell</u> 5th Generation (circa 1700s), daughter of Tabitha Russell and William Campbell. She married Charles Wing. They had children.

      (d) <u>Mary Campbell</u> 5th Generation (circa 1700s), daughter of Tabitha Russell and William Campbell. She married Ephraim Brank. They had children.

(e) <u>Samuel Campbell</u> 5th Generation (circa 1700s), son of Tabitha Russell and William Campbell. He married a distant cousin named Cynthia Campbell, daughter of Major William Campbell of Tennessee.

b) <u>Robert Campbell</u> 2nd Generation (circa 1695), son of Grissell "Grace" Hay and John Campbell, was born around 1695. He died unmarried in Augusta County, Virginia around 1768.

c) <u>John Campbell Jr.</u> 2nd Generation (circa 1600s), son of Grissell "Grace" Hay and John Campbell. He returned to Europe and later died in England.

d) <u>William Campbell</u> 2nd Generation (circa 1600s), son of Grissell "Grace" Hay and John Campbell. He died unmarried.

e) <u>James Campbell</u> 2nd Generation (circa 1600s), son of Grissell "Grace" Hay and John Campbell. He died unmarried in Ireland.

f) <u>Catherine Campbell</u> 2nd Generation (circa 1600s), daughter of Grissell "Grace" Hay and John Campbell.

g) <u>Mary Campbell</u> 2nd Generation (circa 1700s), daughter of Grissell "Grace" Hay and John Campbell.

h) <u>David Campbell</u> 2nd Generation (1706-1790), the youngest son of Grissell "Grace" Hay and John Campbell, was born in Ireland on March 8, 1706 and died on October 19, 1790. He was known as "White David"[42]. He married Mary Hamilton of Scotland. She was born in 1716 and died in 1801. The thirteen children of Mary Hamilton and David Campbell were as follows:

---

[42] According to Pilcher (1911, page 130) this David Campbell, son of Grace Hay and John Campbell, was called "White David" based upon his fair complexion, blonde hair and blue eyes. The nickname was used to distinguish him from David Campbell, son of Mary Byers and William Campbell and grandson of Alexander Campbell, who was called "Black David" based upon his dark complexion, dark hair and dark eyes.

i) <u>Catherine Campbell</u> 3rd Generation (1736), daughter of Mary Hamilton and David ("White David") Campbell. She married Elijah McLannahan or McClannahan. They had children.

ii) <u>Mary Campbell</u> 3rd Generation (1737), daughter of Mary Hamilton and David ("White David") Campbell. Mary Campbell's husband was William Lockhart[43].

iii) <u>Martha Campbell</u> 3rd Generation (circa 1700s), daughter of Mary Hamilton and David ("White David") Campbell.

iv) <u>James Campbell</u> 3rd Generation (circa 1700s), son of Mary Hamilton and David ("White David") Campbell.

v) <u>William Campbell</u> 3rd Generation (circa 1700s), son of Mary Hamilton and David ("White David") Campbell.

vi) <u>David Campbell Jr.</u> 3rd Generation (circa 1700s), son of Mary Hamilton and David ("White David") Campbell.

vii) <u>Sarah Campbell</u> 3rd Generation (circa 1700s), daughter of Mary Hamilton and David ("White David") Campbell.

viii) <u>Robert Campbell</u> 3rd Generation (1755-1832), son of Mary Hamilton and David ("White David") Campbell. He was born in 1755 and died in 1832.

ix) <u>Margaret Campbell</u> 3rd Generation (circa 1700s), daughter of Mary Hamilton and David ("White David") Campbell.

x) <u>Arthur Campbell</u> 3rd Generation (1753-1811), son of Mary Hamilton and David ("White

---

[43] Pilcher reports the husband of Mary Campbell as William Lockhart. J. S. Gemmell Adams reported this Mary Campbell's husband as being Robert Cummings, and their daughter as Mary Cummings (born circa 1820), wife of Trigg (also born c. 1820). It is unlikely that this Mary Campbell was the mother of Mary Cummings in that Mary Campbell, the daughter of Mary Hamilton and David "White David" Campbell, would have been seventy or eighty years of age at the time that Mrs. Mary Cummings Trigg was born. Mrs. Mary Cummings Trigg was described by Adams as a granddaughter of David "White David" Campbell.

David") Campbell. Colonel Arthur Campbell married his cousin Margaret Campbell, the daughter of her husband's first cousin Captain Charles Campbell. She was born in 1753 and died in 1813. Margaret Campbell and Arthur Campbell had twelve children as follows:

(1) William Campbell 4th Generation (circa 1700s), son of Margaret Campbell and Arthur Campbell.

(2) Elizabeth Campbell 4th Generation (circa 1700s), daughter of Margaret Campbell and Arthur Campbell.

(3) John B. Campbell 4th Generation (circa 1700s), son of Margaret Campbell and Arthur Campbell.

(4) Arthur Campbell 4th Generation (circa 1700s), son of Margaret Campbell and Arthur Campbell.

(5) Margaret Campbell 4th Generation (circa 1700s), daughter of Margaret Campbell and Arthur Campbell.

(6) Mary Campbell 4th Generation (circa 1700s), daughter of Margaret Campbell and Arthur Campbell.

(7) James Campbell 4th Generation (circa 1700s), son of Margaret Campbell and Arthur Campbell.

(8) Charles Campbell 4th Generation (circa 1700s), son of Margaret Campbell and Arthur Campbell.

(9) David Campbell 4th Generation (circa 1700s), son of Margaret Campbell and Arthur Campbell.

(10) Martha Campbell 4th Generation (circa 1700s), daughter of Margaret Campbell and Arthur Campbell.

(11) Anne Campbell 4th Generation (circa 1700s), daughter of Margaret Campbell and Arthur Campbell.

(12)   Jane Campbell 4th Generation (circa 1700s), daughter of Margaret Campbell and Arthur Campbell.

xi) Patrick Campbell 3rd Generation, (circa 1700s), son of Mary Hamilton and David ("White David") Campbell.

xii) Ann Campbell 3rd Generation, (circa 1700s), daughter of Mary Hamilton and David ("White David") Campbell.

xiii)   John Campbell 3rd Generation, (1741-1825), son of Mary Hamilton and David ("White David") Campbell. He was born in 1741 and died in 1825. He served during the French and Indian War and during the Revolutionary War. He married Elizabeth McDonald. Born in 1753, she was the daughter of Mary Robinson and Edward McDonald. Elizabeth McDonald and John Campbell had eight children as follows.

(1) David Campbell 4th Generation (1779), son of Elizabeth McDonald and John Campbell. He was born in 1779 at "Royal Oak" in Washington County, Virginia and died in 1859 at his home "Montcalm" in Abingdon, Virginia. He was Governor of Virginia 1837-1840. He and his wife had no children, but did adopt a niece named Virginia Campbell who married Rev. William Shelton.

(2) Eliza Campbell 4th Generation (circa 1700s), daughter of Elizabeth McDonald and John Campbell. She was unmarried.

(3) Catherine Campbell 4th Generation (circa 1700s), daughter of Elizabeth McDonald and John Campbell. She was unmarried.

(4) John Campbell Jr. 4th Generation (circa 1700s), son of Elizabeth McDonald and John Campbell. He did not marry. Colonel John Campbell Jr. was the United States Secretary of the Treasury in 1837.

(5) <u>Arthur Campbell</u> 4th Generation (circa 1700s), son of Elizabeth McDonald and John Campbell. He was unmarried.

(6) <u>Edward Campbell</u> 4th Generation (circa 1700s), son of Elizabeth McDonald and John Campbell. He married Rhoda Trigg (c. 1700s). She was the great-aunt of Daniel "Dan" Trigg and aunt of Dr. Daniel Trigg. They had children, including:

    (a) <u>Joseph Trigg Campbell</u> 4th Generation (circa 1800s), son of Rhoda Trigg and Edward Campbell. He became an attorney in 1849, later attaining the position of Commonwealth Attorney in Abingdon, Virginia.

(7) <u>Mary Campbell</u> 4th GENERATION (circa 1700s), daughter of Elizabeth McDonald and John Campbell.

(8) <u>James Campbell</u> 4th Generation (circa 1700s), son of Elizabeth McDonald and John Campbell.

The Taylor clan is of Scotch-Irish descent. According to Pilcher's 1911 research, the Taylors were one of the families of the "Scotch-Irish" or "Ulster Scots" whose ancestors were among the Presbyterian lowland Scotsmen who migrated to Northern Ireland during the 1600s. Their descendants would later migrate to the American colonies and help settle the forested, undeveloped, and sparsely populated western frontier of Virginia. A detailed lineage of four generations of Elizabeth Campbell Taylor's paternal heritage (___ Taylor > John Taylor > John McCanless Taylor > Elizabeth Campbell Taylor) is as follows:

1) <u>Taylor</u> 1st Generation (late 1600s / early 1700s). Taylor (Christian name not now known) of Ireland was married to Mary McCanless. They had at least one child:

    a) <u>John Taylor</u> 2nd Generation (circa 1736), son of Mrs. Mary McCanless Taylor and her husband.

John Taylor was born in Ireland around 1736 and died in 1813. He married Elizabeth Campbell, the sister of General William Campbell. They left Ireland for the American colonies during the mid-1700s and eventually purchased large tracts of land on the north side of New River across from present Radford. Their estate was called "Rockford". Elizabeth Campbell and John Taylor had at least five children, as follows.

i) Charles Taylor 3rd Generation (1771-1843), son of Elizabeth Campbell and John Taylor. He married Mary Trigg.

ii) Allen Taylor 3rd Generation (circa 1700s), son of Elizabeth Campbell and John Taylor.

iii) James Taylor 3rd Generation (circa 1700s), son of Elizabeth Campbell and John Taylor. He married S. Smith.

iv) Margaret Taylor 3rd Generation (circa 1780), daughter of Elizabeth Campbell and John Taylor. She may have been the twin sister of John McCanless Taylor, which would place her year of birth at 1780.

v) William Taylor 3rd Generation (circa 1700s), son of Elizabeth Campbell and John Taylor. He married M. Saunders.

vi) Eliza Taylor 3rd Generation (circa 1700s), daughter of Elizabeth Campbell and John Taylor. She married a Mr. Crockett.

vii) Mary Taylor 3rd Generation (circa 1700s), daughter of Elizabeth Campbell and John Taylor. She married H. Smith.

viii) John McCanless Taylor 3rd Generation (1780–1856). John McCanless Taylor, son of Elizabeth Campbell and John Taylor, was born in 1780 and died at the age of seventy-seven years old on September 29, 1856. He married Jane DeVigny Kent[44]. Jane DeVigny Kent and

---

[44] Jane DeVigny Kent was a descendant of Jeanne DeVigny.

John McCanless Taylor had five children, as follows.

(1) Margaret Buchanan Taylor 4th Generation (circa 1814), daughter of Jane DeVigny Kent and Major John McCanless Taylor, was born in Montgomery County around 1814.

(2) James Lawrence Taylor 4th Generation (circa 1818), son of Jane DeVigny Kent and Major John McCanless Taylor, was born around 1818.

(3) Elizabeth Campbell Taylor 4th Generation (1820-1876), daughter of Jane DeVigny Kent and Major John McCanless Taylor, was born at Rockford on May 30, 1820. She married Dr. John Blair Radford on May 31, 1836. Elizabeth Campbell Taylor and John Blair Radford had seven children[45]. Those seven children (5th Generation in this Taylor lineage) were: John Taylor Radford (1838), William Mosely Radford (1840), Anne Rebecca Radford (1843), Jane Kent Radford (1845), Elizabeth Campbell Radford (1847), Mary McCanless Radford(1851), and James Lawrence Radford (1856).

(4) Mary Jane Smith Taylor 4th Generation (1826), daughter of Elizabeth Jane Kent and John McCanless Taylor, was born on September 4, 1826. She married James Edgar Eskridge on October 20, 1857. He was born on April 28, 1827. Mary Jane Smith Taylor and James Edgar Eskridge had two children:

(a) James W. Eskridge 5th Generation (1860), son of Mary Jane Smith Taylor and James Edgar Eskridge. He was

---

[45] See "RADFORD LINEAGE" for narratives on individuals with the Radford surname.

born on August 3, 1860 and died at the age of five months on January 2, 1861.

(b) Edgar Peyton Eskridge 5th Generation (1862), son of Mary Jane Smith Taylor and James Edgar Eskridge. He was born on June 7, 1862. He married Rosamond Gwenllian Terrell.

(5) Charles Joseph Taylor 4th Generation (1829), son of Jane Kent and John McCanless Taylor, was born in 1829. He died that same year before reaching his first birthday.

Servants, Slaves, and Freedmen

Servants (i.e. slaves, indentured servants, and paid servants) were part of the households of a number of the founding families of the Episcopal Church in the New River Valley. Their names can be found in estate ledgers and audits and in federal census data.

According to the 1850 Montgomery County, Virginia Census, there resided within the county 6,888 free persons (sixty-six of whom were black) and 1,471 slaves (which comprised 18.4% of the population). Ninety-five percent of the black population of Montgomery County was held in slavery. By 1860, that percentage had dropped one point, to 94% of Montgomery County's black residents being held in slavery.

Prior to the Civil War, many of these individuals received religious instruction in the Episcopal faith by these families and/or their Episcopal ministers. Those known to have resided with these families and/or resided in the Radford area (designated as Lovely Mount and as Central Depot) before or shortly after the Civil War are listed as follows[46].

---

[46] Information for the section "Servants, Slaves, and Freedmen" was culled from information shared by descendants, courthouse records, library resources, Minnie Adams Fittings 2002 book The Radford Letters, Richard W. Dickenson's 1978 and 1989 compilations of Slave and Freedmen Identities, research conducted by

American slaves were not always given surnames or their surnames were not recorded. This provides particular difficulty for African-Americans seeking to trace their family genealogy. Where surnames are unavailable, these individuals will be listed in the index and in the text under the estate family surname[47]. Index will also include the household surname and "Estate", again to aid those researchers who know the household surname but limited additional information.

Anderson, John
Circa 1843

John "Jack" Anderson and his wife Emily Saunders were slaves on the Smithfield estate of the family of Robert L. Preston before the Civil War. During the War, Jack was a Union soldier. He returned to Montgomery County, Virginia after the War, where he and his wife were employed by the Prestons. He was employed as a farm laborer. His wife Emily was a cook at Smithfield. His date of death is not now known. She died during October 1890. Upon their deaths, they were buried in the Preston family cemetery. Emily Saunders and John "Jack" Anderson had thirteen children, including:

1. James Preston Anderson (circa 1867). This son of Emily and Jack Anderson was thirteen years old at the time of the 1880 Census. He later served in the Spanish-American War. He died in Cincinnati, Ohio on June 26, 1936. James Preston Anderson married Laura Lee Saunders on October 21, 1889. The daughter of Rachel and James Saunders, she was born on February 6, 1870 in Blacksburg, Virginia. James Saunders was born around 1846. Rachel was born around 1847. They were married in Montgomery County in 1867. Mrs. Laura Lee Saunders Anderson died in Radford on August 5, 1977 at the age of one hundred and

---

Radford resident Sarah Elizabeth Carter, and Linda Killen's documentation of the black population in Radford and in New River, Pulaski County, Virginia.

[47] In the index, names of servants without given surnames will be written with a blank line where the surname should be, followed by the Christian name and the estate family name in brackets and italics.

96

seven. She was buried at the Westview Cemetery in Blacksburg; her mother had been buried there as well. Laura Lee Saunders and James Preston Anderson had children, including:

- a. Nettie Anderson (1891). This daughter of Laura Lee Saunders and James Preston Anderson was born during January of 1891.
- b. William Anderson (1892). This son of Laura Lee Saunders and James Preston Anderson was born during December 1892 and died May 16, 1916.
- c. Eugene Anderson (1895). This son of Laura Lee Saunders and James Preston Anderson was born on January 14, 1895 and died on August 5, 1929.

2. Frank Anderson (circa 1870). This son of Emily and Jack Anderson was ten years old at the time of the 1880 Census. He was "crippled" according to data obtained by Richard Dickenson in a 1977 interview with Nettie Anderson.

3. William Anderson (circa 1872). This son of Emily and Jack Anderson was eight years old at the time of the 1880 Census.

4. Nashville Anderson (circa 1877). This son of Emily and Jack Anderson was three years old at the time of the 1880 Census.

5. Auburn Anderson (1879). This son of Emily and Jack Anderson was nine months old at the time of the 1880 Census. He was born during August of 1979.

Austin, Marie
Circa 1800s

Marie Austin was a slave of and, after the Civil War, a servant of Gabriel Calvin Wharton and his family. She may have first been a slave of John Blair Radford, whose daughter married General Wharton. The Whartons gave Marie a section of land to live on for her life, with an option for her or her descendants to buy that land located at what was known as Butcher's Crossing. Marie Austin may have had two sons, Robert Austin and George Austin.

97

It is not known at this time if Marie had other children. No Austins appeared on the Montgomery County Freedman's Bureau Censuses. Descendants of Marie Austin were still living in the Radford City and New River areas in the twentieth century, according to local author Linda Killen.

There were three black Austin families with members by the names of Robert or George residing in the New River / Dublin section of Pulaski County at the time of the 1880 Census: the households of fifty-seven year old George Austin (born circa 1823), of twenty-two year old George Austin (born circa 1858), and of forty-five year old Robert Austin (born circa 1835). These may have been descendants of Marie Austin.

Blueford, Mattison
Circa 1842

At least three members of the Bufort family were slaves of John Blair Radford prior to the Civil War. The original spelling of the surname was "Bufort", changed to Blufort or Bluefort by 1867; later Blueford. Former slaves were Mattison Blueford, his wife Ann Blueford, their daughter Matilda Blueford, and their son Radford Blueford. Two younger children, Jennie Blueford and Stanford Blueford, were born near or shortly after the Civil War and were therefore born as free persons.

The Bluefords were living in Central Depot in 1867 as reported in Freedmen's Bureau records. Mattison Blueford was employed for wages by John B. Radford, as was his wife Ann. The Blueford household of 1867 was described as follows: twenty-five year old farmer Mattison Blueford (born circa 1842), his twenty-two year old wife Ann Blueford (born circa 1845) who was employed as a servant, seven year old Matilda Blueford (born circa 1860), five year old Radford Blueford (born circa 1862), three year old Jennie Blueford (born circa 1864), and two year old Stanford or Steinford Blueford (born circa 1865).

Boles, Patzy
Circa 1849

Mrs. Patzy Boles was a slave before the Civil War. In 1867, she was an eighteen year old widow living in Central Depot and working as a servant for wages in the household of John Blair Radford.

Bowls, Nathan
Circa 1861

Nathan Bowls was nine years old at the time of the 1870 Census and residing in the household of Gabriel Colvin Wharton with his seven year old sister Susan Bowls (spelled "Bowles" in 1870). In 1800, he was described as a black nineteen year old servant in the Wharton household. Susan Bowls was not included as a member of that household.

Brown, Robert
Circa 1846

Robert Brown was a free man before the Civil War. In 1867, he was an unmarried twenty-one year old employed for wages by General Gabriel C. Wharton. Brown lived 1 ½ miles southwest of Central Depot.

Burton, William
Circa 1836

Mrs. Rachel (also spelled Rachael) Anderson Burton and Mr. Solin Burton were slaves on the estate of Alexander P. Eskridge prior to the Civil War. Their relationship is unknown at this time. Solin Burton's name did not appear in Freedmen's Bureau records in 1867. Rachel Anderson Burton's name did appear in those records. The surname Burton was written as "Briton" in census records prior to 1867.

Rachel Anderson was born between 1829 and 1835. Census records by the Freedman's Bureau listed her age as thirty-six in 1865 and as thirty-two in 1867. When she married thirty year old William Burton, she was thirty-seven. He was formerly a slave on the estate of Edward Christian of Bath County, Virginia. An additional member of the Burton household was John Burton, born around 1865.

Campbell, David
Circa 1850

David Campbell, the oldest member of the five-person Campbell family, was employed for wages by John Blair Radford in 1867. The Campbells resided in Central Depot.

All of the Campbells were slaves prior to the Civil War. At least one member of the Campbell family, Hiram Campbell, was a slave of John Blair Radford. Before 1867, his name was written as "Herman Campbell". Freedman's Bureau records describe him as thirteen year old Herman Campbell in 1865 and fourteen year old Hiram Campbell in 1867. He was the only Campbell listed as having been a slave on the Radford estate.

Members of the 1867 Campbell family were as follows: seventeen year old servant David Campbell (born circa 1850), fourteen year old Hiram Campbell (born circa 1853), eleven year old Sylvester Campbell (born circa 1856), eight year old Granville Campbell (born circa 1859), and five year old Lawrence Campbell (born circa 1862).

Clark, Harriet
Circa 1849

Harriet Clark, born around 1849, was listed as a twenty-two year old cook at the Wharton household in the 1870 federal census. It is not now known if she was a slave or a free person prior to the Civil War.

Dill, Fanny
Circa 1847

Four members of the Dill family were living in Central Depot in 1867. Two of them, Fanny Dill and Gracie Dill, were employed as servants for wages by Edward Hammett (misspelled in Freedman's Bureau records as "Hammitt").

The 1867 Dill household was described as: twenty year old widow Fanny Dill (born circa 1847), eighteen year old Gracie Dill (born circa 1849), fourteen year old James Dill (born circa 1853) who had an "injured hand", and six year old Obediah Dill (born circa 1861).

District, William
Circa 1800s

Seven members of the District (also spelled "Destrict") family were slaves of John McCanless Taylor and then of Dr. John Blair Radford and his wife Mrs. Elizabeth Campbell Taylor Radford (daughter of John McCanless Taylor) prior to the Civil War. The surname was spelled "District" in census records prior to 1867 and both "District" and "Destrict" after 1866. The District family members were William District, Nancy Palmer (surname previously written as "Parmer") District, John District, Edmond District, James District, Pocahantus *[sic]* District, and Lila District (whose name was written in census records as "Tucrla *[sic]* District" prior to 1867).

William District married Nancy Palmer. They were both slaves of the Radford estate. The District lineage as now known follows.

1) <u>William District</u> 1st Generation (circa 1786). William District married Nancy Palmer. Records of the Montgomery County, Virginia Courthouse report that Nancy "Parmer" married "William D. Street" on July 10, 1841. She was born in Montgomery County, and was a member of the estate of John Blair Radford. Nancy was born between 1800 and 1835; her ages were reported as

forty-one at the time of her 1841 marriage, thirty in 1865 as per Freedman's Bureau records, and thirty-four in 1867 as per Freedman's Bureau records. William District (incorrectly listed as "William D. Street") is listed as a fifty-five year old in 1841, which would place his year of birth at around 1786 and his age at the time of the Civil War at around seventy-nine years. William was born in Wythe County although his last owner was John Blair Radford of Montgomery County. Nancy and William District had children:

   a) Millie District 2nd Generation (circa 1844), daughter of Nancy Palmer and William District. She was described as twenty-two years of age in 1866 Montgomery County, Virginia courthouse records.

   b) John District 2nd Generation (circa 1847), son of Nancy Palmer and William District. He was described as twenty-five years of age in 1865 Freedman's Bureau records, nineteen years of age in 1866 Montgomery County courthouse records, and twenty-one years of age in 1867 Freedman's Bureau records. A John District household in the 1880 Census for the Alleghany District of Montgomery County is described as follows: a black thirty-three year old laborer named John District, his twenty-five year old wife Emma District, their two year old daughter Laura District, and John's single eighteen year old brother James District, who was employed as a laborer.

   c) William District 2nd Generation (circa 1850), son of Nancy Palmer and William District. He was described as eighteen years of age in 1865 Freedman's Bureau records, sixteen years of age in 1866 Montgomery County courthouse records, and seventeen years of age in 1867 Freedman's Bureau records. The 1880 United States Census describes the household of a William District in the Auburn section of Montgomery County as follows: twenty-eight year old black farmer named William District, his twenty-five year old wife Ellen District, and a black thirty-five year old teacher named Henry Jones. This may have been the household of William District (Jr.), the son of Nancy Palmer and William District.

d) Pocahantus District 2nd Generation (circa 1855), daughter of Nancy Palmer and William District. She was described as ten years of age in 1865 Freedman's Bureau records, twelve years of age in 1866 Montgomery County courthouse records, and eleven years of age in 1867 Freedman's Bureau records.

e) Lila District 2nd Generation (circa 1858), daughter of Nancy Palmer and William District. She was described as seven year old "Tucrla District" in 1865 Freedman's Bureau records, nine year old "Lydia A. District" in 1866 Montgomery County courthouse records, and as nine year old "Lila District" in 1867 Freedman's Bureau records.

f) Buford District 2nd Generation (circa 1860), son of Nancy Palmer and William District. He was listed as the six year old son of Nancy and William in 1866 Montgomery County courthouse records, but was not listed as a member of the District household in the 1865 and 1867 Freedman's Bureau records.

g) James District 2nd Generation (circa 1862), son of Nancy Palmer and William District. He was described as seven years of age in 1865 Freedman's Bureau records, four years of age in 1866 Montgomery County courthouse records, and five years of age in 1867 Freedman's Bureau records. A James District was described in the 1880 Census as living in the Alleghany district of Montgomery County with his brother John District. James was then single, eighteen, and a laborer.

h) Julia District 2nd Generation (circa 1864), daughter of Nancy Palmer and William District. She was described as the one year old daughter of Nancy and William in 1866 Montgomery County courthouse records, but was not listed as a member of the District family in 1865 and 1867 Freedman's

103

Bureau records. She was also described in the 1880 Census as a sixteen year old mulatto woman.

i) <u>Edward District</u> 2nd Generation (circa 1859), son of Nancy Palmer and William District. His name is written in various sources as "Edmond", "Edmund", and "Edward". He was called "Edmond" District and described as ten years of age in 1865 Freedman's Bureau records, fourteen years of age in 1866 Montgomery County courthouse records, and thirteen years of age in 1867 Freedman's Bureau records, and as twenty-one year old "Edward District" on the 1880 Census. Combined these four sources of information place his year of birth between 1852 and 1859. Edward District married Polina (also spelled Paulina) Fields in 1876. She was the daughter of Hannah and John Fields. In the 1880 United States Census, Edward District was described as a twenty-one year old black laborer and a member of the household of Angelina and McClannahan Ingles in the Auburn section of Montgomery County, Virginia. A Native American named Polina (spelled "Palina" in the Census) was described as a mulatto twenty-one year old servant and the wife of Edward District. Polina and Edward District had children:

i) <u>Anna District</u> 3rd Generation (circa 1875), daughter of Polina Fields and a caucasian father whose name is not recorded. When the 1880 United States Census was taken, she was described as a five-year old mulatto living with her parents in Auburn, Virginia. She married William Lewis, son of Margaret and Beverly Lewis, in 1894. Her second husband was Charles Bell, who she married in 1920. Anna had children, including:

(1) <u>Julia A. Lewis</u> 4th Generation (circa 1800s), daughter of Anna District and William Lewis. She married Henry C. Jones. Born in 1887, Henry was the son of Ella Jane

104

Beverly and Charles B. Jones. His paternal grandparents were Amelia and Abraham Jones; Abraham Jones was a slave of the Sallust and Zolls estates. Abraham died in 1881. At the time of the 1880 Census, the family of Abraham Jones was living in Central Depot and described as follows: black eighty year old married farmer "Abram" Jones, his sixty-five year old wife "Melia" Jones, their single thirty-four year old son and minister Henry Jones, a thirty-five year old widow named Victoria Mares, and her three year old daughter Manda Mares; a black thirty-eight year old servant by the name of Victoria "Mars" was also listed in the 1880 Census as a member of the Wharton household. Another son, William Jones (born between 1832 and 1835), and his wife Eliza Rose (born between 1843 and 1855) was included in the 1870 Census but not in the 1880 Census. The family of their other son, Charles Jones, was listed both with Abraham Jones in Central Depot and as a separate household in the Auburn district of Montgomery County, with differing ages at time of census, as follows: black married farmer aged forty or forty-two named Charles Jones, his twenty-three or thirty year old wife Ella Jones, their fifteen year old daughter Mahulda Jones, their twelve or thirteen year old daughter Mary Jones, their nine or ten year old daughter Betsy (called Bettie) Jones, and their two year old son William Jones. Their son Henry Jones would not be born for another seven years. Julia Lewis and Henry Jones had children, including:

(a) <u>Sybil Arnette Elizabeth Jones</u> 5th Generation (1929), daughter of Julia Lewis and Henry Jones. She was born in

1929. She first married Randolph Brown; they had no children. Second, she married Earnest Lee Carter. Born in 1932, he was the son of Fannie Rozetta Price and James Edward Carter. Fannie Rozetta Price's parents were Alice Johnson and Thomas Marrs Price. Her father Thomas Marrs Price of Blacksburg died around 1893 or 1894. He was one of a party of men tearing down the old bridge over Connelly's Branch to make room for a new iron bridge when several sections of the old bridge collapsed. The men fell seventy-five feet. Price among others died from injuries. Sybil Arnett Elizabeth Jones and Earnest Lee Carter (grandson of Thomas Price) had children:

(i) <u>Sarah Elizabeth Carter</u> 6th Generation (1951), daughter of Sybil Arnette Elizabeth Jones and Earnest Lee Carter. She was born in Radford, Virginia in 1951. She married Larry D. Reed, who was also born in Radford. Sarah resumed using her maiden surname following her divorce from Reed. Sarah Elizabeth Carter and Larry D. Reed had two children:

1. <u>Rozetta Christine Reed</u> 7th Generation (circa 1900s), daughter of Sarah Elizabeth Carter and Larry D. Reed.

2. <u>Collins Broadus Chatham Reed</u> 7th Generation (circa 1900s), son of Sarah Elizabeth Carter and Larry D. Reed. He was called Chad.

ii) <u>Mary District</u> 3rd Generation (circa 1879), daughter of Polina Fields and Edward District.

She was described in the 1880 United States Census as a one-year old mulatto child living with her parents.

iii) Emma District 3rd Generation (circa 1880), daughter of Polina Fields and Edward District. She married Edman Franklin in 1900.

iv) Carrie District 3rd Generation (circa 1889), daughter of Polina Fields and Edward District. She married first Martin Benjamin around 1907. She married second to a gentleman by the name of Ross. Her third husband, whom she married in 1918, was George Valentine.

v) Harvey District 3rd Generation (circa 1890), son of Polina Fields and Edward District. He married Lena Dean around 1912.

vi) Dessie District 3rd Generation (circa 1891), daughter of Polina Fields and Edward District. She married Early Haley.

vii) Minnie District 3rd Generation (circa 1894), daughter of Polina Fields and Edward District. She married A. P. Armstrong in 1924.

viii) Maud District 3rd Generation (circa 1894), daughter of Polina Fields and Edward District. Minnie and Maud may have been twins. Maud married Ennis Taylor around 1914.

ix) Sherman District 3rd Generation (circa 1897), son of Polina Fields and Edward District.

x) Willie District 3rd Generation (circa 1899), son of Polina Fields and Edward District. He married Lydia Cox around 1921. They divorced in 1928.

Illustration 19: Mrs. Polina Fields District, wife of Edward District. Courtesy of descendant Sarah Elizabeth Carter of Radford, Virginia.

Illustration 20: Mrs. Anna District Lewis [Bell], daughter of Mrs. Polina Fields District. Courtesy of Sarah Elizabeth Carter.

Illustration 21: Mrs. Ella Jane Beverly Jones, wife of Charles B. Jones and mother of Henry Jones. Courtesy of Sarah Elizabeth Carter.

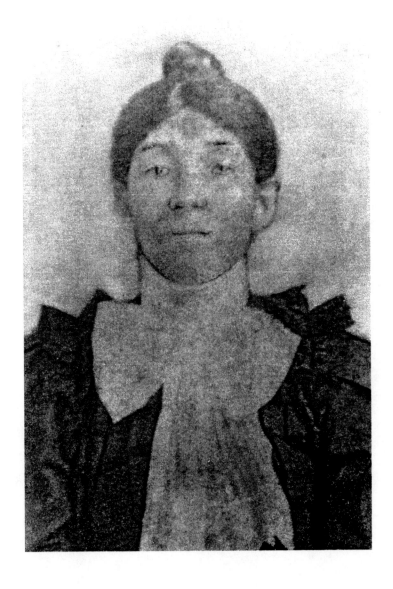

Illustration 22: Sarah Elizabeth Carter of Radford, Virginia, descendant of District, Jones, Lewis, and Palmer families.

Dill, Charles
Circa 1800s

Charles Dill was a slave of George W. Anderson prior to the Civil War. Two other slaves had the surname Dill as well. They were Adeline Dill (surname Dill was adopted sometime between 1865 and 1867) and Mary Dill.

Eskridge Estate

The 1860 United States Census for Montgomery County described Alexander P. Eskridge of Blacksburg as being a fifty-four year old white farmer and a slaveholder of twenty-six individuals. The value of his personal property was listed as $20,000. The cash value of his farm in agriculture was listed as $61,400.

Names of slaves and servants are listed elsewhere in this section by their surnames.

Fields, Mary
Circa 1853

Mary Fields was a slave on the estate of Alexander P. Eskridge before the Civil War. She was listed by the Freedmen's Bureau as a twelve-year old in 1865, and again as a fourteen year old in 1867.

Fraction, John
Circa 1801

John Fraction was a slave on the estate of Robert Taylor Preston before the Civil War. His last name was spelled "Fracton" in 1865 and "Fraction" in 1867. His name appeared on the estate inventory of James Patton Preston in 1843 as a forty year old slave, placing his year of birth at around 1804. He was recorded by the Freedman's Bureau in 1865 as being sixty-five years old, and in 1867 as being sixty-seven, placing his year of birth around 1800.

Montgomery County marriage records place his age at sixty years when he married fifty-seven year old Fanny Johnson (born circa 1802) on December 24, 1859. Her slave owner prior to the Civil War was William Ballard Preston.

Kent Estate

The 1860 United States Census for Montgomery County described James Randal Kent of both Blacksburg and Central Depot as being a sixty-seven year old white farmer and a slaveholder of one hundred and twenty-three individuals. The value of his personal property was listed as $195,750,000. The cash value of his farm in agriculture was listed as $125,840. James Randal Kent was born on October 23, 1792. He married Mary Cloyd on March 31, 1818. J. R. Kent's date of death was May 29, 1867.

Names of slaves and servants are listed elsewhere in this section by their surnames.

McDaniel, Hampton
Circa 1834

The McDaniel family members were listed as servants of the Wharton family in the 1870 federal census. They may have been Radford slaves, slaves from another area, or freedmen prior to the Civil War. Members of the McDaniel family were Hampton McDaniel (born circa 1833 or 1835), described as a thirty-five year old blacksmith in 1870 and as a forty-seven year old farmer in 1880; his wife Ann or Anna McDaniel (born circa 1839 or 1846), described as the twenty-four year old wife of Hampton McDaniel in 1870 and as his forty-one year old wife in 1880; and two children:

1. Marie or Mariah McDaniel (circa 1864), daughter of Ann and Hampton McDaniel, described as age seven in 1870 and as age fifteen in 1880.
2. Amelia McDaniel (circa 1866), daughter of Ann and Hampton McDaniel, described as age four in 1870 and as age thirteen in 1880. She was also called Melia.

3. Henry McDaniel (circa 1871), son of Ann and Hampton McDaniel. He was nine years old at the time of the 1880 census.

Mitchell, Maria
Circa 1814

The Mitchell family members were listed as African-American servants of the Wharton family in the 1870 federal census. They may have been Radford slaves, slaves from another area, or freedmen prior to the Civil War.

Members of the Mitchell family were as follows:
1. Maria Mitchell (circa 1814), age fifty-six in 1870.
2. Peggy Mitchell (circa 1852), described as an eighteen year old house servant in 1870.
3. Daniel Mitchell (circa 1800s), described as a milker.
4. Alla Mitchell (circa 1800s).

Mitchell, Archer
Circa 1800s

Archer Mitchell and his wife Maria Dobbins were living in Central Depot by 1885. They were married on December 20, 1885 by Episcopal Rev. J. E. Hammond. Maria was then twenty-one years of age. Archer Mitchell's age was not recorded, nor were the birth dates of the young couple or the names of their parents. The couple was described in church records as "Negro".

Archer Mitchell, according to local sources, was the son of L. and Abe Mitchell. Maria and Archer purchased land and lived in the racially integrated community of New River Depot, Virginia. Although married in the Episcopal faith, they may later have joined the Baptist Church.

Maria Dobbins and Archer Mitchell had children[48]: James Mitchell (1889), Thomas Mitchell (1891), Johnny Mitchell (1894), Oni Mitchell (1895), Shiller Mitchell (1895), Alice Mae Mitchell

[48] As recorded by author Linda Killen.

(1899), William Mitchell (1906), Fred Mitchell (1902), and Aurelia Mitchell (circa 1900s) who married Robert Whitsett.

Palmer, Allen
Circa 1800s

The Palmers were members of the John McCanless Taylor and John Blair Radford estates. Some of the Palmers were part of the household of Mrs. Elizabeth Campbell Taylor Radford in 1856. "Palmer" was also spelled "Parmer" in some records. Palmer family members from the estate of John Blair Radford were: Allen Palmer, Adam Palmer, Nancy Palmer (Mrs. Nancy Palmer District, having married William District), Mrs. Mary Middleton Palmer (wife of Allen Palmer), Harriett Palmer (whose 1866 Freedman surname was Stewart as per her marriage to Anderson Stewart), Margaret Palmer (who married Beverly Lewis), Albert Palmer, and Samuel Palmer.

Palmer descendants are buried in the Mountain View Cemetery in Radford, Virginia. Samuel Palmer was a Trustee of "the colored cemetery"[49], known today as Mountain View Cemetery, during the early 1800s. His plots were located near the lower and middle areas at the left (eastern) sections of the cemetery.

Samuel Palmer was a trustee of the Zion Baptist Church in 1896 when Julia and H. C. Mitchell deeded to church trustees a tract of land "beginning at a stake corner to Milton Turner's lot" on the macadamized road, "said lot to be used for the erection of a church for use of the colored Baptists" (*see* Montgomery County, Virginia, Deed Book 44, page 84). The Zion Baptist Church trustees were Samuel Palmer, Whit Tate, Charles Jones, Milton Turner, Lewis Powell, and A. J. Anderson. Isabella Hammet Heth and her husband Stockton Heth had previously, in 1887, deeded a parcel of land to "Trustees of the Col Babtist *[sic]* Church". That parcel was described as being bounded on the west by the road leading into the main road from Central, and bounded on the south and east by land owned by Isabella and Stockton Heth (*see* Montgomery County, Virginia, Deed Book W, page 19).

[49] Montgomery County Deed Book 76, page 49.

Samuel Palmer was also one of the persons instrumental in the establishment of Radford's Mountain View Cemetery. In 1908, Fannie S. and W. J. Hall sold about an acre and a half of land to G. H. Pettis and Samuel Palmer for use as a family cemetery plot. That land was described as "beginning at a stake on the south side of the said road [i.e. *Montgomery County, Virginia, macadamized road near Radford, now known as Rock Road in Radford)*, and standing N 16 degrees E 22 feet from the northeast corner of the Church, and being a corner to the Church lot, and running with the south side of the macadamized road (*see* Montgomery County, Virginia, Deed Book 69, page 407). That tract of approximately one acre was deeded in 1919 by P. M. and G. H. Pettis and Ella and Samuel Palmer to trustees "to hold as a cemetery for colored people" (*see* Radford City Deed Book 70, page 544). Those trustees were D. P. Morton, William Edwards, Charles Lee, Ranley Morton, Samuel Akers, Flem Sanders, Alec Johnson, James Perry, and P. W. Caesar.

That cemetery land was also increased in 1912 when Mrs. Elizabeth Campbell Radford Adams, William Radford Wharton, and his wife Mrs. Sue Hammet Heth Wharton sold approximately one acre of land to Samuel Palmer and Carolina Bell as a cemetery plot. That parcel of land was described in Montgomery County, Virginia, Deed Book 65, page 560, as "beginning at southeast corner of the cemetery lot; thence with same S 65 ¾ W 127 feet; thence S 33 E 170 feet; thence N 65 ¾ E 127 feet; thence N 33 W 170 feet to beginning", and in Radford City Deed Book 69, page 406, as "beginning at the southeast corner of Samuel Palmer's cemetry [*sic*] lot; thence S 35 degrees E 85 feet; thence S 65 ¾ degrees W 260 feet to the east side of the 20 foot right of way reserve; thence with same N 33 W 255 feet to the cemetry [*sic*] lot; thence with same N 65 ¾ E 133 feet to corner of Samuel Palmer's cemetry [*sic*] lot and with same N 65 ¾ E 127 feet to the beginning".

Preston Estate

Slaveholder James Patton Preston was born in 1774 and died on Nov. 16, 1843. He was the son of Susanna Smith and William

Preston. The 1843 appraisal of his estate listed a "total appraisement of 91 negroes" valued at a total of $26,650; individual values are not transcribed herein. In 1860, Robert Taylor Preston of Smithfield in Blacksburg, Montgomery County was described as a white fifty-one year old farmer and holder of thirty-three slaves. Robert Taylor Preston was born on May 26, 1809. His personal property was valued at $37,500. The cash value of his farm in agricultural production was $44,000.

The names of individuals listed on Patton's 1843 appraisal of Preston's Smithfield estate follow[50].

1. Philip (circa 1788), age 56.
2. Nancy (circa 1818), age 26.
3. Jacob (circa 1829), age 15.
4. Esau (circa 1829), age 15.
5. Cynthia (circa 1832), age 12.
6. Sam (circa 1788), age 56.
7. Mouser or Monser (circa 1788), age 56.
8. Nelly (circa 1773), age 70.
9. Louisa (circa 1816), age 28.
10. Sarena (circa 1818), age 26.
11. Ugenia (circa 1842), age 18 months.
12. Andy (circa 1819), age 25. ["Diseased"].
13. Peter (circa 1824), age 20.
14. Isaac (circa 1826), age 18.
15. James (circa 1829), age 15. ["Same", *i.e. Diseased*].
16. Carolina (circa 1833), age 11.
17. Sally (circa 1836), age 8.
18. Martha (circa 1838), age 6.
19. Oceola or Occola (circa 1839), age 5.
20. Joseph (circa 1842), age 2.
21. Mary Jane (circa 1843), 7 months.
22. William Mc (circa 1802), age 42.
23. Cato Mc (circa 1802), age 42.
24. Marsha (circa 1818), age 26.
25. Harrison (circa 1841), age 3.
26. Taylor (circa 1822), age 22.
27. Monticello or Montiroille (circa 1823), age 21.

[50] See James P. Preston estate list, Montgomery County, Virginia Courthouse, Montgomery County Will Book 7, page 130.

28. Eliza (circa 1825), age 19.
29. Charlotte (circa 1843), age 1.
30. Emily (circa 1827), age 17.
31. Ballard (circa 1829), age 15.
32. Grace (circa 1831), age 13.
33. Daniel (circa 1832), age 12.
34. Nancy (circa 1834), age 10.
35. John (circa 1835), age 9.
36. Florence (circa 1835), age 9.
37. Walter or Walterson (circa 1838), age 6.
38. Orval (circa 1842), age 2.
39. Robert (circa 1843), age 1.
40. Joshua (circa 1827), age 17.
41. John Fraction (circa 1804), age 40.
42. Easther (circa 1803), age 41.
43. Mary (circa 1822), age 22.
44. Daniel Jones (circa 1843), age 1 month.
45. Georgia or George (circa 1824), age 20.
46. Chloe (circa 1827), age 17.
47. Juda (circa 1828), age 16.
48. Verguson or Virginia (circa 1830), age 14.
49. Ellen (circa 1834), age 10.
50. Oscar (circa 1835), age 9.
51. Rebecca (circa 1837), age 7.
52. Tom Jr. (circa 1830), age 14.
53. Wilson (circa 1842), age 2.
54. Peggy (circa 1802), age 42.
55. Flora (circa 1827), age 17.
56. Margaret (circa 1843), age 1.
57. Robert (circa 1828), age 16.
58. Amy (circa 1830), age 14.
59. Edmonia (circa 1832), age 12.
60. Edward (circa 1834), age 10.
61. Charles (circa 1836), age 8.
62. David (circa 1838), age 6.
63. Rebecca Peggy (circa 1840), age 4.
64. Clary or Clay Amanda (circa 1844), age 2.
65. Caty Saunders (circa 1843), age 1.
66. Hiram (circa 1825), age 19.

67. Preston (circa 1831), age 13.
68. Saunders (circa 1829), age 15.
69. Francis (circa 1838), age 6.
70. Clay (circa 1793), age 61.
71. Rherra or Rhena (circa 1829), age 15. [Idiotic]
72. Betsy (circa 1819), age 25.
73. Beverly (circa 1837), age 7.
74. Row (circa 1839), age 5.
75. Biddy (circa 1841), age 3.
76. Orange (circa 1843), age 1.
77. Isaac Son ? (circa 1838), age 6.
78. Mary Ann (circa 1807), age 37.
79. Edmund (circa 1811), age 33.
80. Eliza (circa 1829), age 15.
81. Peyton (circa 1832), age 12.
82. Mariah (circa 1835), age 9.
83. Easther Daut. of M (circa 1834), age 10.
84. Susan (circa 1842), age 2. [Diseased]
85. Moses (circa 1817), age 27.
86. Lively (circa 1822), age 22.
87. Sarah Jane (circa 1840), age 4.
88. Lucinda or Lucenda (circa 1825), age 19.
89. Charles [Dan.] (circa 1807), age 37.
90. Willis (circa 1815), age 29.
91. Anthony (circa 1821), age 23.
92. Diana (circa 1822), age 22.

While the appraisement states that there are 91 slaves, 92 names are listed. Financial values were listed beside each individual's name except the name of nine year old "John" (#35 above). Excluding this name, the total number of persons becomes 91.

Radford Estate

In 1856, Mrs. Elizabeth Campbell Taylor Radford inherited thirteen slaves from her father John McCanless Taylor. James Lawrence Taylor, son of Mrs. Elizabeth Campbell Taylor Radford and Dr. John Blair Radford and grandson of John McCanless Taylor inherited slaves from the Taylor estate as well. John Blair Radford was described in the 1860 United States Census as a white forty-seven year old farmer and physician residing in Lovely Mount (i.e. Central Depot). He was a slaveholder of seventy persons. John Blair Radford was born on April 26, 1813 and died on June 30, 1872. He married Elizabeth Campbell Taylor on May 31, 1836.

The names of individuals listed in John McCanless Taylor's 1856 bequest to his daughter and grandson are listed below. Names of others are listed elsewhere in this section by surname. The following persons were transferred in 1856 from the estate of John McCanless Taylor to the estate of James Lawrence Radford:

1. Amy.
2. Ann.
3. Ann $2^{nd.}$
4. Edmund 2nd.
5. Hiram.
6. Easter.
7. Easter Jr. He was a member of the John McCanless Taylor estate, although his name was not listed in Taylor's 1856 will. It is not known if he was still alive in 1856, a free person, or if he was with another family of slaveholders.
8. Edwinna. She was a member of the John McCanless Taylor estate, although her name was not listed in Taylor's 1856 will. It is not known if she was still alive in 1856, a free woman, or if she was with another family of slaveholders.
9. Jim.
10. Joe.
11. Joe Jr.
12. Margaret.
13. Martha.
14. Peter.
15. Stephen.
16. Wesley.

The following persons were transferred in 1856 from the estate of John McCanless Taylor to the estate of Mrs. Elizabeth Campbell Taylor Radford:

1. Allen.

2. Billie.
3. Delia.
4. Edmund.
5. Edward.
6. John.
7. Joshua.
8. Lucy.
9. Millie.
10. Nancy.
11. Pocahontas.
12. Susan.
13. Willie.

Reed, Isaac
Circa 1841

Isaac Reed was a slave on the estate of John Blair Radford prior to the Civil War. Freedman's Bureau records describe him as twenty-five years of age in 1865 and again as twenty-five in 1867.

Sales, Henry
Circa 1853

Four children of the Sales family were slaves on the estate of Alexander P. Eskridge prior to the Civil War. Those individuals were documented by the Freedmen's Bureau in 1865 and in 1867. The 1867 information describes them as: fourteen year old Henry Sales (born circa 1853), eleven year old Betsey Sales who changed her Christian name from Betsey to Bettie by 1867 (born circa 1856), eight year old Joseph Gragen Sales who changed his surname from Gragen in 1865 to Sales in 1867 (born circa 1859), and six year old P. Betzey Sales (born circa 1861). Bettie Sales and Joseph Sales were described as mulatto, a term which meant a lighter skinned individual who may have either had one caucasian parent or parents whose origins were racially mixed.

Sanders, Robert
Circa 1830

Robert Sanders was recorded by the Freedman's Bureau as being thirty-four in 1865 and thirty-nine in 1867, placing his year of birth between 1828 and 1831. He had previously been a slave on the estate of Robert T. Preston.

Stewart, Anderson
Circa 1800s

Anderson Stewart was a slave of John Blair Radford. He married Harriet Palmer, who was born around 1849. They had children:

1. John Stewart (circa 1871), son of Harriet Palmer and Anderson Stewart.
2. Albert Stewart (circa 1800s), son of Harriet Palmer and Anderson Stewart.
3. Sam Stewart (circa 1800s), son of Harriet and Anderson Stewart.
4. Jacob or James Stewart (circa 1800s), son of Harriet and Anderson Stewart.

Taylor Estate

Slaveholder John McCanless Taylor was born in 1780 and died in 1856. He bequeathed his slaves to his heirs (daughter Mrs. Elizabeth Campbell Taylor Radford and grandson James Lawrence Radford). The names of individuals listed in the Will of John McCanless Taylor are listed within this section under the heading "Radford Estate" and be individuals last names when available.

Turner, Milton
Circa 1800s

Milton Turner was a slave at "Arnheim" when he was a child. He became a preacher and was active in his church in the Radford area before and after the Civil War.

Rev. Milton Turner was one of several ministers who took charge of the worship at the Methodist Episcopal Church during times when that congregation was without a permanent rector in the late 1800s.

Turner was a Trustee of the Methodist Episcopal Church in 1841 when Matilda and James Smith deeded a tract of land to George Godbey, Richard Buckingham, Henry Bishop, David Hale, and Milton Turner, who "shall build or cause to be erected and built a Methodist Episcopal Church" (*see* Montgomery County Deed Book 37, page 357). That Church became part of the Christiansburg Circuit of the Mount Olive Methodist Episcopal Circuit, organized around 1867. A church building was erected around 1884. That building burnt down in 1890, and the Mount Olive Methodist Church building was erected below a tract of land that would become known as the Mountain View Cemetery.

Rev. Milton Turner was also listed as a trustee of the Zion Baptist Church when land was acquired in 1896 for the erection of that building of worship (*see* Montgomery County, Virginia, Deed Book 44, page 84).

Wade, John
Circa 1812

The Freedman's Bureau recorded six members of the Wade family as having previously been slaves on the estate of John Blair Radford. Those persons were: John Wade, Mrs. Lucy Bouser Wade, Wyatt Wade (whose surname was listed as "Wade" in 1865 and "Washington" in 1867), Henrietta Wade, Judy Wade (whose Christian name was listed as "Judy" in 1865 and "Julia" in 1867), and Hamilton Wade. John Wade was described as fifty-five years old on Montgomery County, Virginia marriage records from 1848, as fifty years old on 1865 Freedman's Bureau records, and as fifty-eight years old on 1867 Freedman's Bureau records. This places his year of birth between 1809 and 1815. His wife Lucy Bouser was described as thirty-one years old on Montgomery County courthouse records when she married John Wade on February 28, 1848, as fifty years of age on 1865 Freedman's Bureau records, and as twenty-nine years of age on 1867 Freedman's Bureau records. That places her year of birth between 1815 and 1838.

The Wade lineage as now known follows.

1. John Wade 1st Generation (circa 1812) was the husband of Lucy Bouser Wade (circa 1820). They lived on the Radford estate prior to the Civil War. Lucy Bouser and John Wade had children.

  a. Anderson Wade 2nd Generation (c. 1851), son of Lucy and John Wade. He was described as fifteen years of age on 1866 Montgomery County courthouse records, placing his year of birth at about 1851. He married Anna Morris. She was born around 1851. He married second to Lizzie Smith in 1894. Lizzie married again in 1928, to Peter Slaughter. Anna Morris and Anderson Wade had children:

    i. Lucy Wade 3rd Generation (circa 1873), daughter of Anna Morris and Anderson Wade. She married Grant Sanders in 1891.

    ii. Clara Wade 3rd Generation (circa 1874), daughter of Anna Morris and Anderson Wade. She married Sidney H. Alexander in 1892.

    iii. J. Ella Wade 3rd Generation (circa 1877), daughter of Anna Morris and Anderson Wade.

    iv. Annie Phoebe Wade 3rd Generation (circa 1885), daughter of Anna Morris and Anderson Wade. She married Sam Jones around 1905.

    v. Lucretia Wade 3rd Generation (circa 1891), daughter of Anna Morris and

Anderson Wade. She married William Calfee (or Clafee) in 1910.

b. Washington Wade *2nd Generation* (circa 1853), son of Lucy and John Wade. He was described as fourteen year old Wyatt Wade in 1865 Freedman's Bureau records, as the eleven year old son of Lucy and John Wade named Washington Wade in 1866 Montgomery County records, and as thirteen year old Washington Wade in 1867 Freedman's Bureau records. That places his year of birth between 1851 and 1855.

c. Henrietta Wade *2nd Generation* (circa 1855), daughter of Lucy and John Wade. She was described as twelve years of age in 1865 Freedman's Bureau records, as the nine year old daughter of Lucy and John Wade in 1866 Montgomery County courthouse records, and as eleven years of age in 1867 Freedman's Bureau records. This places her year of birth between 1853 and 1857.

d. Julia Wade *2nd Generation* (circa 1857), daughter of Lucy and John Wade. She was described as ten year old Julia Wade in the 1865 Freedman's Bureau records, as the six year old daughter of Lucy and John Wade named Julia Wade in 1866 Montgomery County courthouse records, and as nine year old Julia Wade in 1867 Freedman's Bureau records. This places her year of birth between 1855 and 1860. She may also have been called Judy.

e. Hamilton Wade *2nd Generation* (circa 1859), son of Lucy and John Wade. He was described as eight years of age on 1865 Freedman's Bureau records, as the five year old son of Lucy and John Wade in 1866 Montgomery County courthouse records, and as seven years of age on 1867 Freedman's Bureau records. This places his year of birth between 1857 and 1861.

f. Mary Wade *2nd Generation* (circa 1863), daughter of Lucy and John Wade. She was described as the three year old daughter of Lucy and John Wade in 1866 Montgomery County courthouse records. She was not listed with the Wade family on either the 1865 nor the 1867 Freedman's Bureau records.

g. John Wade *2nd Generation* (circa 1866), son of Lucy and John Wade. He was described as the five month old son of Lucy and John Wade in 1866 Montgomery County courthouse records. His twin brother was William Wade. They were not listed with the Wade family on either the 1865 nor the 1867 Freedman's Bureau records.

h. William Wade *2nd Generation* (circa 1866), son of Lucy and John Wade. He was described as the five month old son of Lucy and John Wade in 1866 Montgomery County courthouse records. His twin brother was John Wade. They were not listed with the Wade family on either the 1865 nor the 1867 Freedman's Bureau records.

CHAPTER THREE: THE POST-CIVIL WAR YEARS, 1866 - 1887

The years following the Civil War were a time of rebuilding not only for the nation and the states, but for the communities in southwestern Virginia. The State of Virginia was slow to nurse her war wounds; Virginia officially re-entered the United States of America in 1870. The post-war years were called "Reconstruction".

National Reorganization

Governmental, scientific, economic, and social advances occurred despite national financial crises between 1873 and 1879. The Panic of 1873 resulted from inflation, an abundance of land and railroad investments, and the closure of banks and businesses when investors could not make their payments. The country pulled out of the depression in 1879 and the economy grew quickly and broadly.

Social changes were vast as a free society adapted to a newly integrated social fabric. Roles changed in racial relationships and in gender relationships. Women began their long fight for suffrage (they won the right to vote in the state of Utah in 1870; it would take some time and dedication for gender bias in voting to be eliminated nationally). The era of prohibition of alcoholic beverages began with a ban on the sale and consumption of alcohol in Kansas in 1881. A Prohibition Movement spread across the country. As social changes were evolving, the scientific community reveled in new inventions. For example, the first telephone was invented in 1876, and Thomas Edison patented the phonograph in 1878.

As part of the nation and a young community, Lovely Mount and Central Depot in Montgomery County, Virginia continued to grow.

Local Reorganization: the Montgomery County Board of Supervisors

Around the area that would become Radford City, local governmental affairs were handled by the Montgomery County Board of Supervisors. The county was divided into four townships, each of which had its own Township Board: Alleghany Township, Auburn Township, Christiansburg Township, and Blacksburg Township. Additional administrative divisions were established as the Alleghany Springs Precinct, Big Spring Precinct, Crumpecker's Precinct, Guerrants Precinct, Auburn Precinct, Central Depot Precinct, Christiansburg Precinct, Blacksburg Precinct, and Price's Fork Precinct. The Central Depot Precinct and the Auburn Precinct fell within the boundaries of the Auburn Township. Within the Board meeting minutes, references were made both to the Central Depot Precinct and to the community of Lovely Mount.

The Supervisors addressed those ordinary and extraordinary issues which keep a county functioning as a vital entity that protects and pleasures its citizens. They set toll rates, assigned levies, approved jail repairs, insured county buildings and properties, drafted regulations regarding wildlife and domestic animals, managed the county Poor House, supported public schools, and acted on state legislation.

In 1871, a tithe amount of fifty cents per person and five cents per "$3.144.188" (or a total $1572.09, 5% of a total $31,441.88) for land and personal property was levied. The $2691.29 revenue gained from these levies was divided among the townships as follows: 32% to the Blacksburg Township, 25% to the Auburn Township, 22% to the Alleghany Township, and 22% to the Christiansburg Township.

Also in 1871, the Board of Supervisors set new rates to be charged at the Christiansburg Toll Gate. Toll charges for travelers were set by method of travel and, when herding livestock, by number of animals. Those rates for travelers were set at 3 cents for a horse, mule, or gelding, 5 cents for a one-horse wagon or cart, 15 cents for a two-horse wagon or cart, 20 cents for a four-horse wagon or cart, 10 cents for a two-wheel pleasure carriage, and 20 cents for a four-horse pleasure carriage. Those herding livestock were required to pay 5 cents for twenty head of hogs or sheep and

10 cents for twenty head of cattle. The need for an additional toll road was acted upon: "It is ordered that a toll gate be erected at or near Lovely Mount, the same rate of tolls as above charged".

Township Boards were given the responsibility of procuring the services of toll gatherers and controlling the receipt of tolls for the road section running through their respective townships. By 1872, the Board of Supervisors decided to sell the Christiansburg Toll House at auction, and to turn over the responsibility for repairing and maintaining "the McAdamized [sic] Road" to the townships.

Governmental expenses were documented in the Board minutes. In the Central Depot Precinct, John Elliott was paid $5.00 for his services during the election of a judge and B. F. Ammen received $2.00 for his services during the Central Depot Precinct clerk election in 1872. Much Central Depot electoral business was conducted in 1874 and reflected as follows: $1.00 to Levi Bibb for the rental of a room for election purposes; $8.00 to J. H. Carper, $2.00 to William L. French, $2.00 to Frank N. Stone, and $2.00 to William E. Stone for services during clerk elections; and, for services during judge elections, $5.00 to John Elliott, $4.00 to John R. Stone, and $5.00 to J. K. Shanklin.

In 1873, the Montgomery County Board of Supervisors ordered a levy of 2309 tithes at 50 cents each and "20 per cent $3.073.000", to collect $1,154.50 in tithes and $6,146.00 in property taxes (20% of $30,730.00). Board minutes read "the treasurer is directed to collect .50¢ from every titheable person and .20¢ on every $100.00 worth of real and personal property".

Montgomery County Supervisors continued to act on behalf of their community and attend to the business of government as new towns formed and local leaders emerged.

Local Reorganization: the Communities of Lovely Mount and Central City

In the Lovely Mount, Central Depot, and Auburn settlements, the community worked together to rebuild their lives, their churches and businesses, their community. Ingles Ferry was re-established. Old businesses re-emerged, hotels were built, and new businesses were started. A thickly populated residential area grew north of the railroad tracks. Experience community leaders stepped up, and new leaders migrated to the area.

An ironic twist to the Civil War fighting which occurred near Pulaski's Cloyd Mountain and across to the New River area north of Lovely Mount was that it brought later economic benefit to that southwestern Virginia region. Such was the case when a Union soldier by the name of Watson returned to his home in Philadelphia, Pennsylvania, and extolled the beauty and mineral resources of the New River Valley. He returned to the area with his Quaker employer, R. D. Wood, around 1867. R. D. Wood & Sons was established to develop those natural resources and, by 1868, a furnace operated by the Radford Iron Company in Max Creek of Pulaski County was producing pig iron.

Another new community leader was General Gabriel Colvin Wharton. General Wharton, a civil engineer turned war hero turned farmer and developer, married Dr. John Blair Radford's daughter Anne Rebecca Radford in 1863. After the Civil War, he returned to southwest Virginia. His father-in-law deeded land in the Auburn district of Montgomery County to him, and he built a home for himself and his wife in 1870. That home was named "Glencoe".

Business ideas continued to ripen in the communities despite the financial panic which deterred progress during the years 1873 through 1879. For example, General Wharton proceeded to engage himself as a farmer, land developer, and railroad investor. He worked to develop a railroad line, business, and community in New River, across the river from the Wharton home. By 1876, the New River community included a hotel, businesses, and a depot.

Wharton founded the New River Railroad, Mining, and Manufacturing Company. He also built a school building in the west ward (i.e. Auburn District, Montgomery County) of future-Radford City, the first public one-room schoolhouse having been established in 1876 and burned to the ground in 1881.

In 1881, the Virginia and Tennessee Railroad and other railroad companies consolidated to form Norfolk and Western Railroad. The first Vice President was Frederick J. Kimball, who moved to the Central Depot area and established his residence in the Auburn District of Montgomery County one block south of the Kenderdine home.

According to Chataigne's Virginia Gazetteer and Business director of 1880-1881,there were two hotels in Central Depot. The Bibb Hotel, located north of the railroad tracks, was owned and operated by Levi Bibb. The Hoffman House was owned and operated by James Hoffman. It was located on Virginia Avenue south of the railroad tracks. The Bibb Hotel burned down in 1884, on the same day and at about the same time as workers were injured and killed when a bridge being built over Connelly's Run collapsed. The Virginia House hotel, built around 1874 and located on the corner of today's Norwood Street opposite of the area known as Heth Grove, was not listed in the 1880-1881 directory.

There were three general merchants in the area in 1880. In Lovely Mount, Levi Bibb had his business. G. E. Roberts and Ambrose Robinson were merchants in Central Depot. J. Turner operated both a saw mill and a mill for grinding corn and flour. The only doctor listed in the directory was doctor John W. Farmer.

Thirteen principal farmers were listed for Central Depot: James Lawrence Radford with 1260 acres, John Ingles with 1175 acres, J. H. Simpkins with 730 acres, Gabriel Colvin Wharton with 580 acres, Russell Carper with 517 acres, Stockton Heth with 430 acres, Elijah Wall with 418 acres, Joseph K. Shanklin with 300 acres, Michael Gibson with 279 acres, Hezekiah Whitt with 218 acres, J. H. Harman with 215 acres, and Thomas Gibson with 205 acres.

General Wharton was the founder of the New River Railroad, Mining, and Manufacturing Company. By 1883, the company was carrying coal and iron ore from Central Depot to Bluefield. He was also the owner of the *New River Bulletin*, with C. W. Scott as Editor. By 1886, a second newspaper was established by R. H. Payne and called the *Central Courier*.

Also in 1883, John Godolphine Osborne came to Central Depot from Eggleston, Virginia, having moved there from Philadelphia, Pennsylvania. He was later named as Superintendent of the Radford division of the Norfolk and Western Railway.

Col. Warner Justice Kenderdine moved to Central Depot around 1884 and also established his home in the Auburn district. He became the Superintendent of the Radford Land and Improvement Company, which was officially incorporated by the Virginia General Assembly in 1887.

The first public school building was built on land donated by Mrs. Isabella Hammet Heth in 1884. Construction on the building was completed in 1886, on Third and Downey Streets.

Land development in southwestern Virginia boomed for local and for northern investors. One group of investors who would play a huge roll in the development of the town and of the Episcopal church became known locally as "the Philadelphia Group".

The General Assembly of Virginia approved an act to incorporate the Radford Land and Improvement Company on May 10, 1887, allowing the company to establish principal offices in either Montgomery County or Pulaski County with the power to purchase, hold, and convey dwellings, lands and interests in lands in those two counties. The incorporators were Joseph I. Doran of Philadelphia, Pennsylvania, William A. Dick, Evans R. Dick, William W. Justice, Sabin W. Colton Jr., George T. Mills, Henry Fairfax, Charles A. Mellon, Alexander H. Stevens, Fairman Rogers, and J. Hampton Hoge. By 1891, Joseph I. Doran was the President of the Radford Land and Improvement Company, Charles H. Mellon was the Secretary and Treasurer, Warner Justice Kenderdine was the Superintendent, William Smith was the Engineer, and E. Bennett was the Assistant Engineer.

Some of these same investors of the Radford Land and Improvement Company incorporated the Clinch Valley Coal and Iron Company that same year. The Clinch Valley incorporators included Philadelphia attorney Joseph I. Doran, William A. Dick, and William C. Bullitt[51]. Joseph I. Doran, William A. Dick, Evans R. Dick, George T. Mills, Henry Fairfax, and William C. Bullitt were also among the incorporators of the Clinch Valley Railroad Company.

On May 6, 1887, the New River Steamboat Company was incorporated "for the purpose of constructing a steamboat or steamboats, and plying the same on New river in the State". The incorporators included A. L. Ingles, Joseph H. Chumbley, William Ingles, and W. B. Hodges. A. L. Ingles was President of the New

---

[51] Two of Joseph I. Doran's associates in his Philadelphia law firm were Logan M. Bullitt and John C. Bullitt. Relationship if any between these gentlemen and investor William C. Bullitt is unknown at this time.

River Steamboat Company, and Joseph H. Chumbley was the Secretary and Treasurer. Also in May 1887, the community of Central Depot became the incorporated town of Central City.

On May 23, 1887, the General Assembly of Virginia approved an act to incorporate Central City. That act in part read "Be it enacted by the general assembly of Virginia, That the town of Central, in the county of Montgomery, shall be and the same is hereby declared to be a town corporate, under the name and style of Central City, and by that name shall have and exercise the powers hereinafter granted". The General Assembly went on to describe the new corporate town: "The following is hereby declared to be the boundary of the town of Central City: On west by Connelly's Branch, north by New river, south and east by three-fourths of a mile from the brick depot in said town." The town government was to be comprised of a mayor and seven councilmen to be elected annually each May. The first mayor was named in the Act to A. J. Lucas. Named town councilmen were Walter Roberts, Levi Bibb, James Hoffman, Stockton Heth, R. Pyle, E. T. Gill, and F. Collins. John A. Wilson was appointed as Clerk, J. C. Porterfield was appointed as Sergeant, and Ambrose Robinson was appointed to be the town treasurer.

Illustration 23: The Community of New River; map 1880s by Radford Land and Improvement Company.

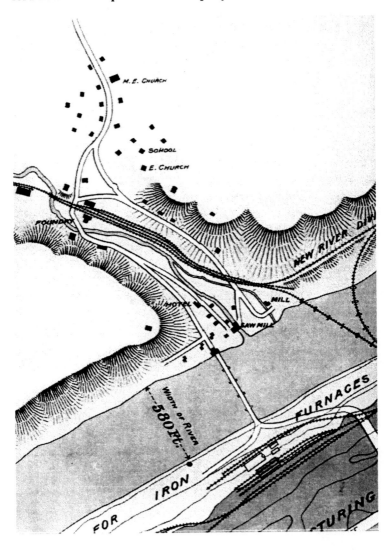

Illustration 24: Glencoe, the Wharton residence, built around 1870. Located on Unruh Drive. Courtesy of Glencoe Museum / Radford Heritage Foundation.

Illustration 25: The three bridges of Radford. Collection of Jane and Ken Farmer.

Illustration 26: The Kenderdine home, on the corner of Second and Fairfax (now Harvey) streets. Photo by Joanne Spiers Moche.

Illustration 27: Warner Justice Kenderdine. Courtesy of Epsie Wilson and Grace Episcopal Church, Radford, Virginia.

CHAPTER FOUR: THE FAMILIES OF GRACE, 1866 - 1887

The Growth of Grace and the Episcopal Faith

It was against this historical backdrop that the Episcopal Diocesan Missionary Society began to look again at expanding the church within and beyond the Montgomery County Parish.

The Episcopal Church entered a phase of heightened mission work and religious instruction following the Civil War. Parishes were encouraged to initiate Sunday school programs where none existed. The southern Episcopal leadership also encouraged the formation of Episcopal parochial schools to educate the newly freed slaves. Episcopal laypersons devoted themselves to mission work during the late 1860s. Men's and women's benevolent societies flourished.

Occasional Episcopal worship services were conducted by a variety of itinerant clergymen visiting Central Depot between 1866 and 1872. The St. James' Episcopal congregation was formed in Central in 1866 (although their mission chapel would not be built until eleven years later, in 1877).

Also in 1866, Episcopal Rev. Edward H. Ingle met with the St. James' congregation, as well as the congregations of Christ Episcopal in Blacksburg and the Episcopal congregation from Christiansburg, Virginia. All three congregations pledged to support a shared rector. Rev. Lyman B. Wharton served them briefly, as did his father, Rev. John Austin Wharton.

Clementina Hammet, mother of Episcopal parishioner Isabella Hammet Heth donated land for the erection of church building to be used by the Presbyterian congregation as well as other congregations lacking a permanent site. The building became known as "the Lovely Mount Church" and "The Old Brick Church". The Rt. Rev. Francis McNeece Whittle, Bishop of the Episcopal Diocese of Virginia, occasionally preached there as did the Episcopal Rev. H. Melville Jackson.

Under the leadership of Rev. Edward H. Ingle in 1871, Montgomery Parish was reorganized with a vestry comprised of members elected from all sections of the large parish. The 1871 vestry of the Montgomery Parish was composed of Richard Henry Adams Jr., Alexander P. Eskridge, J. H. Kipps, John Blair Radford, and William F. Tallant. Dr. John Blair Radford attended the Episcopal Diocese Council meeting during 1872, but was unable to secure a Diocesan commitment for the services of a clergyman at that time. It would take additional parish growth before Rev. H. Melville Jackson would take charge of the Montgomery Parish for the years 1873 through 1875.

Episcopal sermons of the time changed from moral instruction based upon biblical teaching to sermons based on the bible as an instrument both of religious and historical instruction. Many rejected the notion of worldly goods as items of import, and "high church" (elaborate) forms of worship were rejected by many congregations.

The congregation of St. James' Episcopal, which had been established in Central Depot in 1866, developed a mission church in New River Depot, Virginia, with much support and advocacy from parishioner Mrs. Anne Rebecca Radford Wharton, wife of General Gabriel Colvin Wharton. The mission congregation was named St. John's in 1876, but often referred to as "Mrs. Wharton's Church".

In 1877, the St. James' Episcopal Mission Chapel was built in the East Ward of Central on property donated by Capt. Stockton Heth and his wife Isabella Hammet. It was the first Episcopal church building in Central, Virginia; a silver "ewer", or pitcher, said to be from the St. James' Episcopal Mission Chapel is still displayed and used in Grace Episcopal Church today. Many area Episcopalians were committed to support of St. James'. One parishioner, Mary Robinson, worked particularly hard to see its creation. In fact, the Chapel was sometimes referred to as "Mrs. Mary Robinson's Church" because of her devotion to seeing the building completed. The first structure, built of brick, was destroyed in a storm. The Chapel was rebuilt of timber on the same site.

The Chapel was served by a number of visiting clergymen through the late 1800s. Rev. Nelson Dame served the Montgomery Parish, including the St. James' Chapel and St. John's, from 1877 through 1880.

The church was undergoing some interesting and important conflicts during the time of Rev. Mr. Nelson Dame. Following the Civil War, the national Episcopal Church body was increasing its emphasis on the use of established ritual and what might be called elaborate dressing within the churches. Parishioners were adopting the practice of providing flowers for the altar, vestments for the church choirs, and various church altar hangings for each liturgical season. The carrying of processional crosses and activities of young crucifers were introduced and were quite popular. Many of the church's bishops were committed to less elaborate forms of worship with an emphasis on evangelical preaching, particularly in remote southern areas.

The Rt. Rev. F. M. Whittle became the fifth bishop of Virginia in 1876. During his time as assistant bishop and then bishop, he led a revival both of church membership and church building. He was opposed the "high church" rituals and church adornments. Whittle was the bishop of the Episcopal Diocese of Virginia when the Diocese was split into two separate dioceses, the Episcopal Diocese of West Virginia and the Episcopal Diocese of Virginia, in 1877. Whittle chose to maintain his post as bishop of the Episcopal Diocese of Virginia.

Bishop Francis McNeece Whittle went so far as to forbid the use of altar flowers and liturgical hangings in the churches of the Episcopal Diocese of Virginia in 1879. He was unable to stem the tide of change, and many southwestern Virginia churches adopted the popular decoration of the church and use of ritual within their forms of worship. Grace Episcopal Mission Chapel and, later, Grace Episcopal Church, would adopt much of these styles in years to come.

Just as each ritual symbolized a tenet of the faith, the church decorations were full of symbol and meaning. The altar, i.e. the holy table, as well as the lectern or pulpit were symbols of God's presence at the Episcopal worship service. The flowers on the altar were placed their as symbols of the parishioner's joy in the resurrection. The candles represented Jesus Christ's light, also called the Light of the World. Altar hangings and clergy vestments were adorned in colors representing events and virtues critical to the faith.

139

White and gold stood for purity and victory of faith. Violet, crimson, and purple were the colors of preparation. Purple and blue also represented royalty and repentance. The color red represented martyrdom. Green, the most common color in nature, proclaimed growth.

Twentieth century Episcopal Rev. Claud McCauley shared the following to explain the symbolic colors and corresponding Episcopal seasons:

Advent (Purple) tells us Christ is near.
Christmas (White) tells us Christ is here.
In Epiphany (Green) we trace
All the glory of His Grace
That we may keep a faithful Lent.
Holy Week (Purple) and Easter, then,
Tell who died and rose again.
Oh that happy Easter Day!
"Christ is risen indeed" we say. (White)
Yes, and Christ ascended, too, (White)
To prepare a place for you;
So we give Him special praise
After those great forty days.
Then he seats the Holy Spirit
On the day of Pentecost, (Red)
With us soon to abide;
Well may we keep Whitsentide.
Last of all we humbly sing,
Glory to our God and King,
Glory to the One in Thee
On the Feast of Trinity. (Green)
St. John's Day is White.
The other Saints are Red
In that they were martyred.

Rev. Dame departed from the Montgomery Episcopal Parish, which was briefly without a rector. During 1882 and 1883, the Rev. William M. Walton accepted the call to serve. He departed in 1884, and was replaced by the Rev. James E. Hammond in 1885. Rev. Hammond served through 1887. The Parish was without an assigned rector during the year 1888.

140

Illustration 28: St. James' Episcopal Mission Chapel, built around 1877. Courtesy of Grace Episcopal Church, Radford.

THE FAMILIES OF GRACE
1866 THROUGH 1887

Information about the people who worshipped together and built a parish together is contained herein. This information has been culled from church records and, where possible, supplemented by local records including public records from the Virginia courthouses in Montgomery County and Radford City, articles from area newspapers, and information provided by family descendants.[52]

---

[52] The author welcomes readers to share additional information, including photos and personal narratives, regarding early rectors and parishioners of the Episcopal faith in southwest Virginia and the area now known as Radford City. Dr. Joanne Spiers Moche can be contacted at drjmoche@swva.net.

The Episcopal Bishops and Rectors
1866 through 1887

Wharton, John Austin
1803-1888

John Austin Wharton of Liberty, Virginia held occasional services at Central Depot, Virginia during the year 1866 and during the year 1871. The son of Sarah ("Sally") Lillburne Logwood and John Wharton, he was born in Bedford County, Virginia on March 22, 1803. He married Isabella ("Irene") Brown. She was born around 1810. They made Bedford, Virginia, their home and raised eight children.

John A. Wharton had been a Presbyterian until, inspired by Episcopal priest Nicholas Hamner Cobbs, he joined the Episcopal faith in 1831. Wharton was lawyer and a banker in Liberty, Virginia. He accepted the call to become a priest in 1847 and was ordained as a Deacon that year by Bishop William Meade.

Perhaps a highlight of his career was when his son, Lyman Brown Wharton, chose the priesthood as well and was ordained in 1856. Almost ten years later, after the close of the Civil War, he and his son preached together and supported a great revival in interest in the Episcopal faith. He followed his son in serving the Montgomery Parish, including Central Depot, in 1866 and in 1871.

The 1880 United States Census listed the Wharton family as being comprised of Head of Household John A. Wharton, described as a white seventy-five year old lawyer, his sixty-year old wife Irene, daughters Mary and Alice, sons John and Charles, and Charles' wife Estelle. They resided together in Bedford County, Virginia.

Rev. John Wharton served his religious community in Bedford County for forty-one years as a subdeacon, then deacon, and then rector. He died on June 20, 1888.

Isabella Brown and John Austin Wharton had children:

1. Lyman Brown Wharton (circa 1831), of whom more. He was born around 1831 in Bedford County, Virginia and followed in his father's footsteps by becoming an Episcopal priest.
2. Sarah Virginia Wharton (circa 1835).
3. Frances Isabella Wharton (circa 1838).
4. Mary Jane Wharton (circa 1844). She was thirty-five and living with her parents in Bedford County when the United States Census of 1880 was taken.
5. John Edmund Wharton (circa 1845). He was thirty-five years old and living with his parents in Bedford County when the United States Census of 1880 was taken.
6. Charlotte Eliza Wharton (circa 1847).
7. Alice Wharton (circa 1850). She was twenty-nine years old and living with her parents in Bedford County when the United States Census of 1880 was taken.
8. Charles William Wharton (circa 1852). When the United States Census of 1880 was taken, he was a twenty-seven year old bank cashier living with his parents and his twenty-four year old wife Estelle. Estelle was born around 1856; her maiden surname is not now known.

Wharton, Lyman Brown
Circa 1831

The Rev. Lyman Brown Wharton served as Episcopal clergy for Montgomery Parish, which encompassed Blacksburg, Christiansburg, and Central Depot during the year 1866. Holding Services at "The Inn" in Central Depot and other nearby locations, he was the first clergyman assigned to this section of Virginia by the Episcopal Diocese.

Rev. Wharton graduated from the Virginia Seminary in 1856. When the Civil War battles began, he served as an army chaplain. At the War's end, young Lyman returned to Bedford County where his father was a great Episcopal clergyman and revivalist. Rev. Lyman B. Wharton and his father Rev. John A. Wharton formed a father-son team of great inspiration, conducting daily morning services and other religious worship throughout the county of Bedford. The following year, in 1866, he brought his spiritual inspiration to parishes throughout southwest Virginia including that of Montgomery.

Lyman Brown Wharton, son of Isabella Brown and John Austin Wharton, was born in Bedford County, Virginia, around 1831. At the time of the United States Census of 1880, he was living in Williamsburg, Virginia. Lyman B. Wharton was described as a forty-nine year old Professor of Languages. His wife was thirty-six year old Martha P. Wharton (maiden surname unknown at this time).

Ingle, Edward H.
Circa 1840

The Rev. Edward H. Ingle served as Episcopal clergy for Montgomery Parish, which encompassed Blacksburg, Christiansburg, and Central City (i.e. Central Depot) during the year 1866 and the year 1871.

When the Episcopal Seminary in Staunton, Virginia, was closed at the outbreak of the Civil War, a number of professors continued to teach their young seminarians in private homes. One of those would-be preachers was Edward H. Ingle. He graduated seminary in 1864 and was assigned as rector of the two-year-old Emmanuel Episcopal Church in Bristol. In 1865, this young preacher had the unusual honor of participating in the first Episcopal Diocese conference held after the end of the Civil War.

The following year, in 1866, Rev. Ingle became the Deacon of St. Thomas' Episcopal Church in Abingdon, Virginia. That same year traveled to the Montgomery County area and held a church service in the dining room of the hotel at Central Depot. Based upon parishioner interest and pledged support, the Diocesan agreed to provide the Montgomery County area with a clergyman. Ingle visited Christiansburg again in 1871 to help the fellowship there organize a vestry.

Ingle did not slow down after his 1866 and 1871 visits to southwest Virginia. He went on to serve as rector for both St. John's Episcopal Church in Roanoke and for St. Paul's Episcopal Church in Salem, Virginia. He served them diligently for ten years, when he decided to accept a position at an Episcopal Church in the state of Georgia.

The Ingle family was living in Athens, Georgia, when the United States Census of 1880 was taken. They were living in the home of a sixty-one year old married school teacher, Alen M. Scudder, and his fifty-eight year old wife Susan A. Scudder (maiden surname not now known). Edward H. Ingle was described as a forty year old white married Episcopal rector. He was born in Washington D.C., as were his parents. His wife was thirty-five year old Emma Ingle (maiden surname not now known). She was born in Virginia, as were her parents.

Jackson, H. Melville
Circa 1850

The Rev. H. Melville Jackson served as Episcopal clergy for Montgomery Parish, which encompassed Blacksburg, Christiansburg, and Central Depot, from 1873 through 1875. He moved to Greenville, South Carolina during the autumn of 1875.

By 1880, Rev. Jackson and his wife were living in Richmond, Virginia. Rev. H. Melville Jackson was born in Virginia, as were his parents. He was described in the 1880 United States Census as a thirty-year-old preacher residing with his nineteen-year-old wife Violet L. Pace in the home of her parents. Her parents were thirty-nine year old Bettie W. Pace and forty-three year old James B. Pace. Violet was born in Virginia, as were her parents. Her father was a tobacconist.

Norwood, John J.
Circa 1800s

Montgomery Parish had no rector during the years 1876 and 1877. The Episcopal Diocese of Virginia provided the parish with the services of missionary priests to hold occasional services. One of those missionary priests was the Rev. John J. Norwood.

Lloyd, John J.
Circa 1800s

Rev. John J. Lloyd was one of the missionary priests sent by the Episcopal Diocese of Virginia to the Montgomery parish during the years 1876 and 1877 when the parish was without a rector. Rev. John J. Lloyd began a family tradition of service to the Episcopal community. His grandson, Rev. R. B. Lloyd, served Grace Episcopal Church in Radford in 1904.

Dame, Nelson P.
Circa 1853

Rev. Mr. Nelson P. Dame served as Episcopal clergy for Montgomery Parish from 1877 through 1880.

It was during 1877 that the first Episcopal church building was built in Central, Virginia. When that brick structure was destroyed by storm, a wooden chapel was built in its place.

When the 1880 United States Census was taken prior to the Dame family's move to Maryland, Rev. Dame was a twenty-seven year old minister living in Blacksburg, Virginia. With him were his twenty-four year old wife, Mary N. Dame, and his eleven month old daughter, Margaret P. Dame. They were born in Virginia, as were their parents. The Dame family lived in the home of a forty-nine year old butcher named D. Sidney Painter and his thirty-eight year old wife, V. Jane Painter. The Painters and their parents were also born in Virginia. According to church records, Rev. Dame and his family moved to West River, Maryland during September 1880.

Mary N. and Nelson P. Dame had a child:

1. Margaret P. Dame (circa 1879). She was reported as being eleven months old at the time of the 1880 United States Census.

Walton, William M.
Circa 1800s

The Rev. William M. Walton served as Episcopal clergy for Montgomery Parish from 1882 through 1883. His primary station was Christ Episcopal Church in Blacksburg, Virginia. Around the beginning of 1884, he moved to Michigan.

Whittle, Francis McNeece
1823-1892

The Rt. Rev. Francis McNeece Whittle confirmed four St. James' Episcopal Mission Chapel parishioners in Central Depot in 1866, and another nine new communicants there in 1888 and 1889.

Francis McNeece Whittle was born in Virginia in Chesterfield County on July 7, 1819 or 1823[53]. His parents were Mary Ann Davies and Fortescue Whittle from Ireland; Fortescue Whittle immigrated to America from Ireland before beginning a family. Other children of Mary Ann Davies and Fortescue Whittle were William Whittle, Fortescue Whittle Jr., James M. Whittle, Conway D. Whittle, John S. Whittle, Lewis Neal Whittle, Stephen D. Whittle, and Powhatan Whittle.

The Rt. Rev. Francis McNeece Whittle was elected to be the Assistant Bishop of the Episcopal Diocese of Virginia in 1867. His early efforts involved helping his priests and parishioners recover from human and financial losses suffered during the Civil War, help them adjust to a new post-War society, maintain current parishes, and, to a small degree, encourage the growth of new parishes. Growth in parishes did occur once the southern society was back on its feet. During that time, a movement was about in the Episcopal community supporting more ritualistic decorations in the church. The Rt. Rev. Whittle was adamantly opposed to this movement, going so far as to prohibit the use of altar flowers and

---

[53] Both years of birth have appeared in written records; the correct year of birth is at this point undetermined by this author.

altar cloths in the Virginia Episcopal Churches in 1879. He was, however, unable to stem the tide of the ritualistic movement.

Mary Ann Davis and Francis McNeece Whittle were living in Richmond, Virginia, at the time of the 1880 United States Census. Head of Household was described as a white fifty-six year old preacher named F. M. Whittle, living with his fifty-four year old wife Emily, their two children, and two servants: a black twenty-five year old servant named Lucy Perkins and a black sixty year old servant named Sarah Robinson. The children of Emily Fairfax and Francis McNeece Whittle, both born in Virginia, were:

1. Frank Whittle (circa 1856). At the time of the 1880 Census, he was a twenty-four year old store clerk in Richmond, Virginia.
2. Emily Whittle (circa 1862). She was eighteen when the 1880 Census was taken.

Hammond, James E.
Circa 1839

Between May 1885 and October 1887, the Episcopal Rev. James E. Hammond served the Montgomery Parish. At St. James' Episcopal Mission Chapel in Central Depot, he officiated at sixteen baptisms for five families. He performed four marriage ceremonies. He also conducted four funerals during 1885 and 1886, two of which were for infants. Rev. J. E. Hammond attested to four confirmations performed by the Rt. Rev. Francis McNeece Whittle.

The Episcopal Parishioners 1866 through 1887

Adams, Richard Henry Jr.
1841-1896

Richard Henry Adams Jr., son of Ann Carter Harrison and Richard Henry Adams, was born at the Adams family home, "Altwood", in Marengo County, Alabama on April 21, 1841. He was known as Dick by some and as Rich by others; Montgomery County, Virginia residents knew him as "Captain" (apparently an honorary title adopted by the First Lieutenant).

Capt. Richard Henry Adams Jr. served in the Confederate Army during the Civil War, first as a Private in the Alabama Infantry and later as a First Lieutenant of Company D, Alabama Infantry Regiment, 51st Alabama Partisan Rangers of the Confederate States of America. Adams was wounded at the Battle of Seven Pines. He was captured near Nashville, Tennessee and held as a prisoner of the Union Army from 1863 through 1865. He became one of a group of captured Confederate officers dubbed "The Immortal Six Hundred" held in a federal prisoner-of-war camp near Charleston, South Carolina as human shields in harm's way of fire from Confederate batteries. Adams wrote in his journal that the Morris Island prison was "in sight of Charleston, the smoke, and under the range of Rebel guns". He did not gain his release until the close of the Civil War.

It was during the War that, prior to his capture, he met Miss Charlotte "Lottie" Putnam of Nashville, Tennessee. After his capture, R. H. Adams and Lottie Putnam corresponded and a romance was forged. It was Lottie, during the waning days of the Civil War, who encouraged him to gain his freedom by taking the required Oath of Allegiance to the government and President of the United States. Adams spent an additional three months of captivity trying to gain his freedom while avoiding the swearing of the Oath of Allegiance. He became one of the last 115 of the 600 prisoners to take the Oath and return to his southern home.

Captain Richard Henry Adams Jr. and Miss Charlotte "Lottie" Putnam were married at the Putnam home, "Wayside", in Nashville, Tennessee on August 23, 1865. Lottie, born around 1844, was the fourth and youngest child of Cornelia V. Sevier and Albigence Waldo Putnam and the great-granddaughter of Revolutionary War hero General Israel Putnam. The newly-weds made their home at "Altwood" and were confirmed in an Alabama Episcopal church in 1866. Their first child, John Putnam Adams, was born at "Altwood" in Marengo County on December 10, 1866.

Their second child, Julia "Lottie" Putnam Adams, was born almost two years later on August 29, 1868. Twenty-five year old Mrs. Charlotte "Lottie" Putnam Adams died on September 8, 1868

149

ten days after giving birth to her daughter, likely from complications related to childbirth. She was buried in Nashville, Tennessee, where her parents still resided. Her young daughter died eight days later on September 16, 1868 at the age of eighteen days.

In 1870, Captain Adams moved with his parents and young son to Montgomery County, Virginia. Richard Adams Sr. established a home which he named "Espanola". Montgomery County was also the home to Adams cousins: the Radford family. Dr. John Blair Radford's grandmother, Mrs. Rebecca Winston Radford, was sister to Capt. Richard Henry Adams Jr.'s grandmother, Mrs. Margaret Winston Adams.

In 1871, Captain Richard Henry Adams Jr. wed a second time, to Miss Elizabeth Campbell Radford. Born at "Arnheim" on November 17, 1847 in Montgomery County, Virginia, she was the daughter of Elizabeth Campbell Taylor and John Blair Radford. Elizabeth Campbell Radford and Richard Henry Adams Jr. had a son, Radford Carter Adams, in September 15, 1872.

The family of R. H. Adams Jr. made their home in Montgomery County, Virginia. He was an active public servant and Episcopal parishioner. He was a notary public by 1873; his name and signature appear on numerous land deeds as notary for Montgomery County during the 1870s.

He also served as a member of the Montgomery Episcopal Parish vestry in 1871 and in 1874; he was vestry secretary in 1874. Richard Henry Adams Jr. was elected to be an alternate delegate from the Montgomery parish to the 1874 Episcopal Diocesan Council of Virginia.

The United States Census of 1880 shows the family residing in the town of Dublin in Pulaski County, Virginia. Richard Henry Adams Jr. was a married thirty-nine year old white farmer living with his thirty-two year old Lizzie C. Adams, his thirteen-year-old son John P. Adams, his seven-year-old son Radford C. Adams, and two servants.

Episcopal records list the Adams's 1885 residence in the West Ward of Central Depot on Second Street. This was likely a reference to "Arnheim", where they are known to have lived. They moved to Alabama in 1886 according to church records.

They returned to the Central Depot community, then known as the Town of Radford, Virginia, in 1889 and renewed their active involvement in the affairs of St. James' Episcopal Mission Chapel. Captain R. H. Adams Jr. served on the Montgomery Episcopal Parish vestry in 1890 and 1891. He was a member of the church committee planning the construction of a new Episcopal chapel building "west of Connelly's Branch". That chapel was built in 1892 and named Grace Episcopal Mission Chapel.

Adams was a member of the vestry committee which prepared and presented a petition to the Episcopal Diocese of Southwestern Virginia requesting the division of the Montgomery Episcopal Parish into two parishes. A new parish, the Radford Episcopal Parish, was created with the remainder of the old Montgomery parish retaining the name of Montgomery Episcopal Parish. The congregation of the Radford parish was officially formed on June 1, 1891. Captain Adams was a member of the Radford parish vestry during 1891 and 1892.

Captain Adams was also a Radford postmaster and a civil engineer. In his capacity as civil engineer, he drew one of the most detailed maps available of the West Ward of Radford as it stood around 1891 or 1892. His detailed drawing included original street names, locations of current and proposed businesses, homesteads of a few of the wealthier landowners, the location of two churches, and the proposed location of the new Episcopal chapel.

Richard Henry Adams Jr. died from heart disease at the age of fifty-five on October 8, 1896. He was buried in the Radford Family Cemetery following an Episcopal funeral service conducted by the Rev. Frederick Goodwin Ribble. His tombstone reads "Richard H. Adams, Lieut., 51 ALA Partisan Rangers, CSA, October 8, 1896".

Mrs. Elizabeth Campbell Radford Adams died forty-three years after her husband's death. She was eighty-three and still living at "Arnheim" in Radford. She died on February 22, 1930. Cause of death, according to church records, was "pneumonia" and "old age". She was buried in the Radford Family Cemetery. Her tombstone reads "Elizabeth Campbell Adams, Nov. 17, 1847. Feb. 22, 1930. Wife of Capt. Richard H. Adams, dau. of Dr. John B. Radford, a member of the family for whom the City of Radford was named". Her estate administrator and sole heir was her fifty-eight year old son Radford Carter Adams.

Richard Henry Adams Jr. had children:

1. John Putnam ("Put") Adams (1866), the son of Charlotte "Lottie" Putnam and Richard Henry Adams Jr. He was born at the Altwood estate in Marengo County, Alabama on December 10, 1866. He married Elizabeth Kent Cowan on October 26, 1898. The daughter of Margaret Gordon Kent and John T. Cowan and the granddaughter of Mary Cloyd and James R. Kent, she was born in Montgomery County, Virginia on September 29, 1870. She inherited tracts of the Montgomery County "Kentland" farm at Whitethorne[54] (also known as Buchanan's Bottom) through the Kent-Cowan Line. Elizabeth Kent Cowan and John Putnam Adams had children: Richard Putnam Adams, Julia Putnam Adams, and Elizabeth Kent Adams.

    a. Richard Putnam Adams (circa 1899), son of Elizabeth Kent Cowan and John Putnam Adams. He inherited tracts of "Kentland" from his aunt Miss Mary Cloyd Cowan and from his mother Mrs. Elizabeth Kent Cowan Adams. He was living at Whitethorne, Virginia at the time of his mother's death[55]. He married. The children of Richard Putnam Adams were:

        i. Thomas Kent "T. K." Adams (circa 1900s), son of Richard Putnam Adams.

---

[54] Kentland was located at the Whitethorne community in Montgomery County, Virginia, bounded by McCoy Road to the north, the New River and old Virginia Railway lines to the south, Robert Price's 1910 tract of land to the east, and encompassed part of Tom's Creek to the southeast. Kentland at Whitethorne should not be confused with the "White Thorn" house built on a tract of the original "Smithfield" estate built by James Francis Preston. Preston's "White Thorn" was bounded by Price's Fork Road on the north, Merrimac Road on the south, and included a section of Strouble's (also spelled Strubble's) Creek. That "White Thorn" home came into the possession of Isabella and Stockton Heth by 1891, and was owned by Jeanette Cowan Heth in 1931. Surrounding property belonged to Linkous, Kipps, E. Dobbins, and Henry Heth.

[55] Information on the descendants of Richard Putnam Adams and their lands can be found in Montgomery County records including: Land Deed Book 93, page 150 and page 271, Year 1931, Richard P. Adams et als. vs. J. R. K. Cowan et als; Land Deed Book, Year 1962, Richard P. Adams et al. to Thomas K. Adams; and Land Deed Book 254, page 3, Year 1964, Wills Renunciation, Julia Roop Adams vs. Richard P. Adams, Estate; also Radford City Will Book 2, page 108, List of Heirs of Elizabeth C. Adams and Will Book 2, page 33, List of Heirs of John Putnam.

He inherited the "Kentland" property from his father; T. K. Adams, sold that acreage to Virginia Tech around 1985.

    b. Julia Adams (circa 1906), daughter of Elizabeth Kent Cowan and John Putnam Adams. She married a Henson and was living in Bristol, Virginia by 1936.

    c. Elizabeth Kent Adams (circa 1909), daughter of Elizabeth Kent Cowan and John Putnam Adams. She was living in Radford, Virginia at least by 1936.

2. Julia "Lottie" Putnam Adams (1868), the daughter of Charlotte "Lottie" Putnam and Richard Henry Adams Jr. She was born on August 29, 1868 and died at the age of eighteen days on September 16, 1868.

3. Radford Carter Adams (1872), of whom more. The son of Elizabeth Campbell Radford and Richard Henry Adams Jr., he was born at the Arnheim estate in Montgomery County, Virginia on September 15, 1872. He married Mancye Doyle. The children of Mancye Doyle and Radford Carter Adams were: Elizabeth Campbell Adams, Lucien Doyle Adams, Minnie Harris Adams, Radford Carter Adams Jr., and Mancye Prince Adams.

A detailed lineage of Richard Henry Adams Jr.'s maternal heritage[56] follows (Benjamin Harrison Jr. > Benjamin Harrison III > Benjamin Harrison IV > Benjamin Harrison V > Carter Bassett Harrison >Benjamin Carter Harrison > Ann Carter Harrison > Richard Henry Adams Jr.):

a) <u>Benjamin Harrison Jr.</u> 1st Generation (circa 1645-1712), son of Mary and Benjamin Harrison. Benjamin Harrison Sr., who was born in 1600 and died in Jamestown, Virginia in 1643, emigrated from England to the American colonies prior to

---

[56] The Adams / Harrison family lineage has been documented by Robert Somerville Yates (1986), Minnie Fitting Adams (2002), Daughters of the American Revolution, and this researcher via public records and unpublished Adams family information. See end book *Sources* for complete information.

1643. He married Mary (maiden surname not now known), who was born around 1624 and died around 1687. Their son Benjamin Harrison Jr. was born in Virginia around 1645 and died in Virginia in 1712. He married Hannah Churchill, who was born in 1651 and died in Virginia around 1698. Hannah Churchill and Benjamin Harrison Jr. had children: those members of the *2nd Generation* were Nathaniel Harrison (1677), Hannah Harrison (1678), Sarah Harrison (circa 1679), Henry Harrison (circa 1679), Anne Harrison (1680), Elizabeth Harrison (1685), and Benjamin Harrison III (1673). Son of Hannah Churchill and Benjamin Harrison Benjamin Harrison III was born in Virginia in 1673. He married Elizabeth Burwell, who was born in 1675 and died in 1734. The Honorable Benjamin Harrison III died in 1710. Elizabeth Burwell and Benjamin Harrison III had children:

i) Elizabeth Harrison 3rd Generation (circa 1693), daughter of Elizabeth Burwell and Benjamin Harrison III.

ii) Elizabeth Harrison 3rd Generation (circa 1700s). There may have been a second daughter, also named Elizabeth Harrison, born around 1705.

iii) Benjamin Harrison IV 3rd Generation (circa 1695-circa 1744), son of Elizabeth Burwell and the Honorable Benjamin Harrison III. He was born in Charles City County, Virginia around 1695. He married Ann Carter, the daughter of Judith Armistead and Colonel Robert Carter (c. 1663). Ann was born around 1696 in Lancaster, Virginia; her date of death is not now known. Benjamin Harrison and his family lived in Charles City County, Virginia. In 1726, he built the "Berkeley Plantation" on the James River in present-day Charles City. He was a member of the House of Burgesses and a High Sheriff. He died around 1744. Ann

Carter and Benjamin Harrison IV had children:

(1) Ann Harrison 4th Generation (circa 1723-circa 1735), daughter of Ann Carter and Benjamin Harrison IV. She married William Randolph.

(2) Elizabeth Harrison 4th Generation (circa 1725), daughter of Ann Carter and Benjamin Harrison IV. She married The Honorable Peyton Randolph (born circa 1721), who served as President of the First continental Congress of 1774 and the Second Continental Congress of 1775.

(3) Robert Harrison 4th Generation (circa 1730-circa 1770), son of Ann Carter and Benjamin Harrison IV.

(4) Charles Harrison 4th Generation (circa 1731), son of Ann Carter and Benjamin Harrison IV. He served as a Brigadier General during the Revolutionary War.

(5) Carter Henry Harrison 4th Generation (1732-1796), son of Ann Carter and Benjamin Harrison IV. He was born in Charles City County, Virginia on August 22, 1732. He served as a Captain during the French and Indian War and as a Brigadier General during the Revolutionary War. General Carter Henry Harrison was also a member of the Committee of Safety of Clifton, Cumberland County, in 1775 and a member of Virginia House of Delegates in 1784. He married Susanna Randolph on November 9, 1760 in Gloucester County, Virginia. General Harrison died in Kentucky in 1796. Susanna Randolph and Carter Henry Harrison had children, including:

(a) Peyton Randolph Harrison 5th Generation (circa 1700s), son of Susanna Randolph and Carter Henry Harrison.

He married Elizabeth Barclay. They had children, including:

(i) Robert Peyton Harrison 6th Generation (circa 1800s), son of Elizabeth Barclay and Peyton Randolph Harrison. In 1829, he married Elmira C. Wilcox. They had children, including:

1. John M. Holmes Harrison 7th Generation (1830-1914), son of Elmira C. Wilcox and Robert Peyton Harrison. In 1853, he married Margaret Wilson. They had children, including:

   a. Henry Holmes Harrison 8th Generation (1866), son of Margaret Wilson and John M. Holmes Harrison. In 1888, he married Ellen Douglas Mitchell. They had children, including:

      i. Helen Harrison 9th Generation (circa 1800s), daughter of Ellen Douglas Mitchell and Henry Holmes Harrison. She became a member of the Daughters of the American Revolution (DAR membership #127164) based upon her lineage to General Carter Henry Harrison.

(6) Henry Harrison 4th Generation (circa 1700s), son of Ann Carter and Benjamin Harrison IV. Captain Henry Harrison married Elizabeth Avery.

(7) Lucy Harrison 4th Generation (circa 1700s), daughter of Ann Carter and Benjamin Harrison IV.

156

(8) Maria Harrison 4th Generation (circa 1700s), daughter of Ann Carter and Benjamin Harrison IV.

(9) Nathaniel Harrison 4th Generation (1742-1782), son of Ann Carter and Benjamin Harrison IV. He served as a member of the Virginia Senate in 1780 and as a High Sheriff from 1779 through 1780. He married Mary Ruffin and, after her death, Anne Gilliam.

(a) Benjamin Harrison V 4th Generation (1726-1791), son of Ann Carter and Benjamin Harrison IV. He married Elizabeth Bassett (1730-1792). They lived on Berkeley Plantation. He was a member of the Virginia House of Burgesses 1749-1775, the Continental Congress 1774-1777, a signer of the Declaration of Independence, a member of the Virginia House of Delegates 1778-1781, and the Governor of Virginia from 1781 through 1784. Elizabeth Bassett and Benjamin Harrison V had children: Judith Harrison (circa 1742), Tabitha Harrison (circa 1749), Elizabeth Harrison (circa 1751), Anna Harrison (circa 1753), Lucy Harrison (circa 1754), Benjamin Harrison VI (circa 1755), Nathaniel Harrison (circa 1756), Sarah Harrison (circa 1765), Eleanor Harrison (circa 1788), William Henry Harrison (circa 1773), and Carter Bassett Harrison (circa 1756). William Henry Harrison was born on "Berkeley Plantation" in Charles City County, Virginia on February 9, 1773. He married Anna Tuthill Symmes (1775-1864). Nicknamed "Tippecanoe" based upon his successful military campaign at the Battle of Tippecanoe

157

during the Indian Wars, he became the Ninth President of the United States in 1841. He died one month later of pneumonia on April 4, 1841. Anna Tuthill Symmes and President William Henry Harrison had children. William Henry Harrison's brother, Carter Bassett Harrison, was another son of Elizabeth Bassett and Benjamin Harrison V. He was born in 1756 and died in 1804. Carter Bassett Harrison married first Jane Byrd and, after he death, Mary Allen. During his lifetime, he served as a member of Congress from Virginia. He died on April 18, 1808 in Prince George County, Virginia. Carter Bassett Harrison had children:

(i) William Allen Harrison 6th Generation (1778), son of Carter Bassett Harrison.

(ii) Benjamin Carter Harrison 6th Generation (circa 1780), son of Carter Bassett Harrison. He was born in Virginia around 1780. He married Elizabeth Collier. They had children:

    1. Mary Howell Harrison 7th Generation (circa 1800s), daughter of Elizabeth Collier and Benjamin Carter Harrison.

    2. Ann Carter Harrison 7th Generation (circa 1810), daughter of Elizabeth Collier and Benjamin Carter Harrison, was born in Marengo County, Alabama around 1810. She married her cousin Richard Henry Adams, who was also born in Marengo County around 1810. They had children, including:

a. <u>Richard Henry Adams Jr.</u> 8th Generation (1841-1896). The son of Ann Carter Harrison and Richard Henry Adams, he was born in Marengo county, Alabama on April 21, 1841. He married first Lottie Putnam. He married second to Elizabeth Campbell Radford. The children of Richard Henry Adams Jr. were:
   i. <u>John Putnam Adams</u> 9th Generation (1866). The son of Lottie Putnam and Richard Henry Adams Jr. He married Elizabeth Kent Cowan.
   ii. <u>Radford Carter Adams</u> 9th Generation (1872), son of Elizabeth Campbell Radford and Richard Henry Adams Jr. He married Mancy Doyle.

Richard Henry Adams Jr.'s paternal heritage was equally impressive and included cousins of the Radford family for whom the City of Radford was named.

A detailed lineage of Richard Henry Adams Jr.'s[57] paternal heritage follows (Richard Adams > Ebenezer Adams > Richard Adams > John Adams > Richard Henry Adams > Richard Henry Adams Jr.):

---

[57] Adams family lineage has been documented by Robert Somerville Yates (1986), Minnie Fitting Adams (2002), and this researcher via public records and unpublished Adams family information. See end book *Sources* for complete information.

1) <u>Richard Adams</u> 1st Generation (circa 1670). Richard Adams was born in England. He married Ann (maiden surname not now known). They had children, including:

   a) <u>Ebenezer Adams</u> 2nd Generation (circa 1685-circa 1735), son of Ann and Richard Adams. Born in England, he is believed to be the first member of the Adams family to immigrate to the American colonies. He married; his wife's name is not now known. Mr. and Mrs. Ebenezer Adams had children, including:

   i) <u>Richard Adams</u> 3rd Generation (1726-1800), son of Ebenezer Adams. Richard Adams was a Revolutionary War veteran, serving as a Colonel. He was a member of the House of Burgesses in 1772, the Committee of Safety from 1774-1775, the Continental Congress, the Virginia House of Delegates from 1775-1778, and the Virginia Senate. He was also the father-in-law of Virginia Governor George William Smith. Richard Adams married Elizabeth Griffin in 1755. She was born in 1738 and died in 1800. He also died in Richmond, Virginia in 1800. Elizabeth Griffin and Richard Adams had children, including:

   (1) <u>Samuel Griffin Adams</u> 4th Generation (1776-1821), son of Elizabeth Griffin and Richard Adams. In 1799, he married Catherine Innes. Her date of birth is not now known; she died in 1839. They had children, including:

   (a) <u>George William Adams</u> 5th Generation (1815-1853), son of Catherine Innes and Samuel Griffin Adams. In 1850, he married Jane R. Robertson. She was born in 1827 and died in 1912. They had children, including:

   (i) <u>Catherine Innes Adams</u> 6th Generation (circa 1800s), daughter of Jane R. Robertson and George William

160

Adams. She was born in Lavaca County, Texas. She married Wilson B. Dobbins. She was a member of the Daughters of the American Revolution (DAR membership #127797) based upon her lineage from her great-grandfather Colonel Richard Adams (1726-1800).

(2) <u>John Adams</u> 4th Generation (circa 1700s), son of Elizabeth Griffin and Richard Adams. He was the Mayor of Richmond, Virginia from 1819 through 1825. He married Margaret Winston. They had children, including:

(a) <u>Richard Henry Adams</u> 5th Generation (circa 1810), son of Margaret Winston and John Adams. He married Ann Carter Harrison. They had children, including:

(i) <u>Richard Henry Adams Jr.</u> 6th Generation (1841-1896). The son of Ann Carter Harrison and Richard Henry Adams, he was born in Marengo county, Alabama on April 21, 1841. He married Charlotte "Lottie" Putnam (c. 1844). They had a son and a daughter. Following Lottie's death, he married Elizabeth Campbell Radford. The daughter of Elizabeth Campbell Taylor and John Blair Radford, she was born on November 17, 1847 in Montgomery County, Virginia. They had a son. Capt. Adams died in Radford, Virginia, on October 8, 1896. The children of Richard Henry Adams Jr. were:

1. <u>John Putnam Adams</u> 7th Generation (1866). The son of Charlotte "Lottie" Putnam and Richard Henry Adams Jr., he was

161

born on December 10, 1866. He married Elizabeth Kent Cowan, who was born on September 29, 1870. Elizabeth Kent Cowan and John Putnam Adams had children:

a. Richard Putnam Adams 8th Generation (circa 1899), son of Elizabeth Kent Cowan and John Putnam Adams. He was born around 1899. He married. The children of Richard Putnam Adams were:

  i. Thomas Kent "T. K." Adams 9th Generation (circa 1900s), son of Richard Putnam Adams.

b. Julia Adams 8th Generation (circa 1906), daughter of Elizabeth Kent Cowan and John Putnam Adams. She married a Henson.

c. Elizabeth Kent Adams 8th Generation (circa 1909), daughter of Elizabeth Kent Cowan and John Putnam Adams.

2. Julia "Lottie" Putnam Adams 7th Generation (1868), the daughter of Charlotte "Lottie" Putnam and Richard Henry Adams Jr. She was born on August 29, 1868 and died at the age of eighteen days on September 16, 1868.

3. Radford Carter Adams 7th Generation (1872), of whom more. Mancye Doyle and Radford Carter Adams had children:

162

a. <u>Elizabeth Campbell Adams</u> 8th Generation (1909), daughter of Mancye Doyle and Radford Carter Adams. She married Kenneth Frederick Small. They had children:
   i. <u>Elizabeth Campbell Small</u> 9th Generation (1933), daughter of Elizabeth Campbell Adams and Kenneth Frederick Small. She married first to Gordon D. Price, and second to William Barham. Elizabeth Campbell Small and Gordon D. Price had children: Stephen O'Hara Price, David Price, and Susan Elizabeth Price.
   ii. <u>Kenneth Hollingshead Small</u> 9th Generation (1937), son of Elizabeth Campbell Adams and Kenneth Frederick Small.
b. <u>Lucien Doyle Adams</u> 8th Generation (1910), son of Mancye Doyle and Radford Carter Adams. He married Eleanor Elizabeth Eakin. They had children: John Gordon Adams, Ann Carter Adams, and Sally Taylor Adams.
c. <u>Minnie Harris Adams</u> 8th Generation (1912), daughter of Mancye Doyle and Radford Carter Adams, also known as "Mickey". She authored the book *Radford Family Letters*

163

about the early history of the Radford family. She married Robert Dancy Fitting. The children of Minnie "Mickey" Harris Adams and Robert Dancy Fitting were Robert Eric Fitting and Richard Kent Fitting.

d. Radford Carter Adams Jr. 8th Generation (circa 1922), son of Mancye Doyle and Radford Carter Adams. He married Jamie Elizabeth Bagwell.

e. Mancye Prince Adams 8th Generation (1925), daughter of Mancye Doyle and Radford Carter Adams.

Allen, Alice
Circa 1800s

Alice Allen was a Montgomery County, Virginia Episcopal parishioner during the year 1885, and continued to attend the church at least until 1895. She was born during the 1800s, was baptized as a Methodist, and became a St. James' Episcopal Mission Chapel communicate in Central Depot during the year 1885. She was confirmed at St. James' on May 18, 1895, with the Rt. Rev. Alfred M. Randolph officiating as attested to by the Rev. A. A. Pruden. Miss Alice Allen's name was recorded in the church register. It was never removed, nor was additional information about this parishioner entered into the Episcopal records in Montgomery County.

Bennett, Frank M.
Circa 1858

The Bennett family lived in Central Depot, Virginia and attended St. James' Episcopal Mission Chapel from approximately 1881 through 1892. Dr. Frank M. Bennett (a physician), his wife Judith W. (her maiden name may have been Watkins), and their two children were members of St. James' until they moved to South Carolina around 1892.

The United States Census of 1880 lists a twenty-two year old Frank M. Bennett as a medical student residing with his mother, Mary C. Bennett, in Richmond, Henrico County, Virginia. Also in the home were his sisters Helen A. Bennett and Anna A. Bennett, both teachers, both having been born in Virginia. Their parents were born in Massachusetts. Frank was born in North Carolina. It is likely that this Frank M. Bennett is the same Dr. Frank M. Bennett who, with his wife and children, later attended St. James' Episcopal Mission Chapel and resided in Central Depot, (i.e. Radford City), Virginia.

Judith and Frank M. Bennett had children:

1. Carrington Watkins Bennett (circa 1800s), daughter of Judith and Frank M. Bennett. She was baptized as an infant at St. James's Episcopal Mission Chapel in Radford, Virginia on September 27, 1891. Rev. Edward Lewis Goodwin performed the baptismal ceremony. Capt. Ambrose Robinson and Miss R. C. Watkins were her sponsors (godparents).
2. Frank M. Bennett Jr. (circa 1800s), son of Judith and Frank M. Bennett. His name was on the Episcopal parishioner rolls by 1891.

Bibb, James D.
Circa 1800s

James D. Bibb[58] and his wife Zestera A. (maiden surname not now known) Bibb moved to the Radford area in 1882. Previously members of St. John's Episcopal Church in Roanoke, Virginia, they became communicants of Grace Episcopal Mission Chapel and worshipped there at least from 1882 through 1895. They resided in the West Ward of Radford on First Street by 1892.

James Bibb was a member of the Grace Episcopal Mission Chapel vestry in 1895. Zestera Bibb was a member of the Rector's Aid Society of Grace Parish Episcopal Chapel from 1893 through 1895. One of her activities included membership on the Refreshments Committee for Socials held as Society fundraisers. The last meeting she attended was held on August 2, 1895.

Zestera A. and James D. Bibb had children:

1. John Edward Bibb (1873), son of Zestera A. and James D. Bibb. According to church baptismal records, the son of Z. A. and J. D. Bibb was born November 11, 1873 in Albemarle County, Virginia. He was baptized as an adult at Grace Episcopal Mission Chapel, Radford, Virginia, on July 7, 1895 at the age of twenty-two. His baptismal sponsors were Mr. and Mrs. Warner Justice Kenderdine. The Rev. A. A. Pruden officiated.

2. Edna Kinsolving Bibb (circa 1800s), daughter of Zestera A. and James D. Bibb. She was baptized as an adult at Grace Episcopal Mission Chapel on May 8, 1893. Her baptismal sponsor was "Mrs. W. S. Bibb (by proxy)". Rev. Edward Lewis Goodwin officiated. Miss Edna K. Bibb was confirmed at Grace Episcopal Mission Chapel four days later, on May 12, 1893, by the Rt. Rev. Alfred M. Randolph as attested to by Rev. E. L. Goodwin.

---

[58] A note on name abbreviations is necessary at this point. Church records of the late 1880s frequently contain the abbreviation "Jas." for the name "James" and "Jno." for the name "John". The 1882 church roster of communicates lists "Jno. D." Bibb, husband of Zestera, indicating that his first or Christian name was John. However, Mr. J. D. Bibb, husband of Zestera, is written as "Jas. D." on the church parishioner rolls of 1885, indicating that his Christian name was "James". His son's name is written as James D. Bibb Jr.

3. James D. Bibb Jr. (circa 1800s), son of Zestera A. and James D. Bibb.

Bibb, Lewis
Circa 1800s

Lewis Bibb and his wife, Louisa Carolina Lock, lived in Central, Virginia, and were Episcopal Parishioners at least from 1885 through 1888.

Notations in the church register indicate that Lewis was a member of the church congregation until his death, and that Louisa was a parishioner until her name was "removed" when she moved to Norfolk, Virginia, in 1888. An additional notation reports that Louisa Bibb's name was changed to "Mrs. Deal". In 1893, she was again a St. James' Episcopal Mission Chapel parishioner and residing with her parents Wilhemina Juliana and "Fredrick" Lock[59]. "Mrs. Louise C. Deal" was listed in the church register as a communicant in 1893, being an "old communicant who returned to the area". She was still living with her parents on Third Street in the East Ward of Radford in 1885.

Louisa Lock, daughter of Wilhemina Juliana (maiden surname not now known) and Frederick Lock, was married first to Lewis Bibb. They were living in Central, Virginia and attending St. James' Episcopal Mission Chapel at least from 1885 through 1888; the town of Central was renamed "Radford" while they were still in residence. Lewis Bibb may have died sometime between 1888 and 1893; 1888 being the year Louisa moved to Norfolk and 1893 being the year she returned to Radford. At some point prior to or during the year 1893, she married a Mr. Deal (Christian name not recorded in church records).

Mrs. Louisa Carolina Lock Bibb Deal was a member of the Radford Chapter of the Virginia Daughters of the Confederacy and the United Daughters of the Confederacy. She was also a member of the Woman's Guild of Grace Chapel in 1902. She served as Vice President of the Guild. Among her many activities was the

[59] Surname "Lock", also spelled in church records as "Locke". The correct spelling is "Lock".

hosting of a refreshment table at the 1903 Christmas bazaar with "Mrs. Wright" and "Mrs. Fink".

Collins, William Francis
1848-1897

William Francis Collins, his wife Mary Jane Gregory, and their children lived in the East Ward of Radford on Norwood Street by 1885. A notation in the St. James' Episcopal Mission Chapel register records that the Collins family members were communicants until 1891, when their names were dropped from church rolls as "not communing". W. F. Collins was a member of the church vestry and was vestry secretary in 1885, and occasional vestry meetings were held at his office in 1886. In 1891, when the Collins name was dropped from church rolls, the family was living on Third Avenue in Radford. Apparently they resumed "communing", as W. F. Collins was a church trustee in 1893 and family members were parishioners through 1898.

He accepted an important role when the new Radford Parish was recognized in 1891 as an independent parish separate from the Montgomery Episcopal Parish. William Francis Collins was one of the four original trustees of the Episcopal chapels of Radford. He served as trustee at least from 1892 through 1898 along with Warner Justice Kenderdine, Aaron Jeffrey, and Charles W. Sanders.

William F. Collins was a railroad depot agent from North Carolina when the 1880 United States Census was taken. He, his wife, and their three daughters were residing in Central Depot and reported as follows: white thirty-two year old head of household W. F. Collins, his twenty-seven year old wife Mary J. Collins, his seven year old daughter "Elisabeth" (spelled "Elizabeth" in church records) Collins, his five year old daughter Lettie Collins, and his two year old daughter Ruth Collins. Also in the household was a seventeen year old housekeeper named Sallie E. Spangler.

William Francis Collins died at the age of forty-nine on November 8, 1897 in Radford, Virginia from "apoplexy[60]". He was buried the following day, on November 9, 1897 in the "Radford Cemetery" (a reference to Central Cemetery, one of two public cemeteries in Radford). The Rev. F. G. Ribble officiated. His Central Cemetery marker reads: "W. F. Collins. He was a good man. June 22, 1848. Nov. 8, 1897." An insignia on his marker identifies him as a member of the Woodmen of the World.

Mrs. Mary Jane Gregory Collins died two months shy of her ninetieth birthday on March 21, 1944. Rev. Wilfred E. Roach recorded her death as occurring on March 20, 1944 from "old age". She was living in Appomattox, Virginia at the time of her death, and was buried in Radford. Her Central Cemetery marker reads "Mary J. Gregory Collins, May 29, 1854. Mar. 21, 1944".

Mary Jane Gregory and William Francis Collins had children:
1. Mary Elizabeth Collins (circa 1873). She married Joseph R. Kemp on December 23, 1890. She was eighteen and he was twenty-four. Joseph, born around 1866, was the son of T. E. and B. C. Kemp of Radford. The Rev. Edward Lewis Goodwin officiated, with the St. James' Episcopal Mission congregation in attendance. Their daughter, born in 1891, died one hour after her birth.
2. Lettie Kate Collins (1875). Her Christian name is spelled both as "Lottie" and as "Lettie" in church records, and as "Lettie" in census records and on her tombstone. She was christened at St. James' Episcopal Mission Chapel on October 4, 1890, a little more than two months before her sister Mary Elizabeth Collins's wedding. The Rt. Rev. A. M. Randolph officiated, as attested to by Rev. Edward Lewis Goodwin. Lettie Kate Collins married John S. Mackenzie. She died at the young age of twenty-eight. Her husband lived to be eighty-two. They were both buried in Central Cemetery in Radford. Her marker reads "Lettie K. Collins, wife of J. S. Mackenzie. Jan. 27, 1875. April 17, 1903".

---

[60] The terms "apoplexy", "paralysis", and "softening of the brain" appear in early church records as cause of death. These terms refer to what is now known as "stroke", i.e. cerebral or brain hemorrhage resulting in loss of motor control, loss of consciousness, and/or death resulting from complications related to the stroke.

His marker reads "John S. Mackenzie. May 14, 1869. October 29, 1951".

3. Ruth Collins (1878). According to a grave marker in Central Cemetery, Radford, Virginia, Mrs. Ruth Collins Spelman was born on August 16, 1878 and died on April 10, 1962. She is buried in the Collins family plot.

4. William Francis Collins Jr. (circa 1882).

5. L. Collins (1892). According to Pulaski County, Virginia birth records, a white female named L. Collins, daughter of M. J. and W. F. Collins, was born on October 9, 1892.

Croft, D. N.
Circa 1800s

D. N. Croft and his wife were not listed as communicants of St. James' Episcopal Mission Chapel, although they did choose the church for the final services of their infant child. The infant child of Mr. and Mrs. D. N. Croft died on October 30, 1886, age not noted in church records and cause of death listed as "unknown". The family lived in Central Depot, Virginia. Rev. J. E. Hammond officiated at the funeral service held the following day. The child was buried in the "Gibson's Cemetery". The tombstone is either absent from Gibson's Cemetery in Radford or illegible today.

Croy, Erastus W.
Circa 1800s

Erastus W. Croy of Pulaski County, Virginia, married Adeline Weddle of Montgomery County, Virginia, at St. James' Episcopal Mission Chapel. They were married in Central on April 18, 1885 with the Rev. J. E. Hammond officiating and family and friends in attendance.

The 1880 Census listed one "Erastus Croy" as a resident of Pulaski, Virginia. However, his wife's name was reported as being "Martha A.", and there were no other individuals by the name of

Erastus Croy in that Census. It is not known at this time if the initial "A" stood for "Adeline".

Eskridge, James Edgar
1827 - 1892

James Edgar Eskridge was a parishioner of St. John's Episcopal Mission congregation by 1871. He was also a member of the 1871 Montgomery Parish Vestry. By 1891, he and his wife were attending Grace Episcopal Mission Chapel in Radford; a notation by their names reading "old communicants of St. John's Church, New River Depot, VA".

James Edgar Eskridge married Mary Jane Smith Taylor. Mary Jane was a daughter of Jane DeVigny Kent and John McCanless Taylor. She was thirty-one when they wed, three days after the settlement of her late father's estate, on October 20, 1857.

James Edgar Eskridge was born on April 28, 1827. Mary Jane Smith Taylor was born on September 4, 1826. Their names were listed as Episcopal parishioners in 1891, as heads of household and residing in the Pepper's Ferry area with their son Edgar Peyton Eskridge, his wife Mrs. Rosamond Gwenllian Terrell Eskridge, their children, and a Margaret Peyton Eskridge. Mr. and Mrs. James E. Eskridge and their daughter-in-law, Rosamond, were "entered as old communicants of St. John's Church, New River".

The 1880 Census reports this family as residing in the Blacksburg District of Montgomery County. A fifty-three year old white male named J. E. Eskridge as Head of Household. He was, at the time, a state senator. His wife, Mary J. Eskridge, was recorded as being fifty-two. While census data would indicate that her birth year was 1828, family, burial, and church records list her year of birth as 1826, making her one year older than her husband rather than one year younger.

The last member of the household was Edgar P. Eskridge, a seventeen year old student. Edgar P. Eskridge was also reported as being an eighteen year old student residing with the family of Gabriel Colvin Wharton as a student boarder. It would appear, then, that young Edgar Peyton Eskridge was reported in the census

171

twice, both at the residence of his parents, Mary Jane and James Edgar Eskridge, and at the Wharton residence where he was pursuing his studies when the census was taken.

James Edgar Eskridge of Montgomery County, Virginia, passed away at the age of sixty-five on October 25, 1892, of Bright's Disease (a form of kidney disease, now known as nephritis or glomerulonephritis, originally named for English physician Dr. Richard Bright). He was buried on October 27, 1892, place of burial noted as "private cemetery", with the Rev. James McGuill officiating as noted in church records by clergyman Edward L. Goodwin. Grave markers for J. A. Edgar Eskridge and his wife Mary J. S. T. Eskridge may be found, not in a private cemetery, but in Radford's Central Cemetery. Those markers read "J. A. Edgar Eskridge, Apr. 28, 1827, Oct. 25, 1892" and "Mary J. S. T. Eskridge, Sept. 4, 1826, Jan. 12, 1903". A Masonic emblem adorns Edgar's grave marker. Mary Jane Smith Taylor and James Edgar had children:

1. James W. Eskridge (1860), died in childhood. He was born on Aug. 3, 1860 and died on Jan. 2, 1861.
2. Edgar Peyton Eskridge (1862), of whom more follows.

Farmer, John W.
1843

Dr. John W. Farmer and his family were parishioners of St. James' Episcopal Mission Chapel and Grace Episcopal Mission Chapel at least from 1885 through 1898. The lived in the East Ward of the Radford on Norwood Street. He was a dentist.

John W. Farmer, son of Martha W. Melton and William Farmer, was born in Pulaski County, Virginia on December 21, 1843. He graduated from the University of Maryland in 1863. He served in the 63rd Virginia Infantry of the Confederate Army during the Civil War and was wounded in the Battle of Murfreesboro, Tennessee. After the War, John W. Farmer attended the Baltimore College of Dental Surgery and graduated in 1875.

He married Flora E. Welch on December 23, 1872. Flora, the daughter of Mary Snydor and Isaac A. Welch of Montgomery County, Virginia was born on May 22, 1849.

At the time of the 1880 United States Census, John W. Farmer was a thirty-four year old white physician living in Central Depot with thirty-one year old wife Flora E. Farmer, their children and a black twenty year old servant named Sallie Taylor.

The Farmers lived in Radford. Dr. Farmer had a dental office on the corner of Norwood & Third Streets in East Radford at least by 1892. Flora E. Welch and John W. Farmer had children:

1. William Welch Farmer (1874), son of Flora E. Welch and John W. Farmer. Called Willie, he was born on May 2, 1874. He was five years old at the time of the 1880 Census. He was baptized "in the Church". At age fifteen, he was confirmed by the Rt. Rev. Alfred M. Randolph as attested to by Rev. Edward L. Goodwin. The confirmation took place on October 4, 1890. William W. Farmer died on April 13, 1898 at the age of twenty-three. Cause of death was not noted in church records maintained by clergyman Floyd L. Kurtz. Farmer was buried on April 15, 1898 in "Radford Cemetery". A grave marker in Radford City's Central Cemetery reads "William Welch Farmer, D. D. S., son of Dr. J. W. & F. E. Farmer, May 2, 1874, Apr. 13, 1898".

2. Ernest Farmer (1876), son of Flora E. Welch and John W. Farmer. His name was spelled "Earnest" in the 1880 Census and "Ernest" in church records. He was born on July 19, 1876. He was three years old at the time of the United States Census of 1880.

3. Mary Milton Farmer (1878), daughter of Flora E. Welch and John W. Farmer. She was two years old at the time of the 1880 Census and living in East Radford with her parents. She was born on April 17, 1878. She was baptized "in the Church". Mary Milton Farmer was confirmed at St. James' Episcopal Mission Chapel on May 12, 1893 by the Rev. Rev. A. M. Randolph as attested to by Rev. Edward L. Goodwin. On December 8, 1897, she married Walter Ingles of East Radford, Virginia as per the Radford City Marriage Register and the Grace Episcopal Mission Chapel Register. Walter was the son of Ellen and Elijah M. Ingles of Pulaski County, Virginia. The marriage ceremony was held at the Farmer family residence. Rev.

173

F. G. Ribble officiated, with Captain Ambrose and Mary Milton Farmer's father and brothers in attendance.

4. Raymond L. Farmer (1880), son of Flora E. Welch and John W. Farmer. He was born on January 3, 1880. He was five months old at the time of the 1880 United States Census.

5. Susan E. (or C.) Farmer (1882), son of Flora E. Welch and John W. Farmer. She was born on March 1, 1882.

Hammet, Isabella
1842-1916

Isabella Hammet[61], the daughter of Clementina Venable Craig and Col. Edward Hammet, married Capt. Stockton Heth and attended Grace Episcopal Mission Chapel and Grace Episcopal Church.

Belle's father Edward Hammet is believed to have immigrated to America from Ireland. On April 16, 1831, he married Clementina Venable Craig. She was born on February 21, 1809 and died on September 25, 1879. Clementina was the daughter of James Craig. The Craig Estate, portions of which are still owned by Craig and Hammet descendants, figured prominently in the early development of the City of Radford.

Stockton Heth's in-laws, i.e. Isabella's parents, lived in the Radford, Virginia. Edward Hammet was Captain of the 5th Regiment of Cavalry in the militia in 1836, and was later promoted to the position of Colonel. Colonel Edward Hammet was heir to the Lammermoor estate of his brother Dr. William Henry Hammet of Mississippi, as well as being a large landowner in the Montgomery County, Virginia. Another Hammet estate was called Aldomar. The Montgomery County home of the Hammet's was located in the area that would become known as East Radford. Edward Hammet was known as a scholar and taught school for a period of time. Upon Edward Hammet's death, his son-in-law and a Governor of Virginia named James Hoge Tyler was executor for his es-

---

[61] Hammet, also spelled as "Hammett".

tate. Isabella Craig and Edward Hammet had children, including the following:

1. Isabella Hammet (1842), daughter of Clementina V. Craig and Edward Hammet. Called "Belle", she was born on June 29, 1842 in Montgomery County, Virginia. Belle married Capt. Stockton Heth in Central Depot on October 17, 1867. They had children. Mrs. Belle Heth died on February 24, 1916, and was buried in the Heth Family Private Cemetery in Radford.

2. James Preston Hammet (circa 1800s), son of Clementina V. Craig and Edward Hammet. He was a physician in Montgomery County, Virginia.

3. John Radford Hammet (circa 1841), son of Clementina V. Craig and Edward Hammet. John was twenty-nine years of age when the 1870 Census was taken.

4. Robert Hammet (circa 1800s), may have been a son of Clementina V. Craig and Edward Hammet.

5. Susan Montgomery Hammet (1845). She married James Hoge Tyler of Central City, who would become a Governor of Virginia. Susan Montgomery Hammet and James Hoge Tyler had children: Edward Hammet Tyler (1869), James Hoge Tyler Jr. (1871), Stockton Heth Tyler (circa 1875) who married Nellie Serpell, Belle Norwood Tyler (1876) who married Frank P. McConnell, Sue Hampton Tyler (1877) who married Robert Ware Jopling, Henry Clement Tyler (1878), and Lily Tyler (circa 1800s) who married Henry H. Wilson.

Heth, Stockton
1840 - 1927

Captain Stockton Heth and his wife, Isabella Hammet, lived in the East Ward of Central Depot[62] on Norwood Street and were communicants of St. James' Episcopal Mission Chapel at least by 1885. Isabella, called Belle and in honor of whom Radford City's

[62] Central Depot, Virginia, became known as the Town of Radford in 1887 and was incorporated as the City of Radford in 1892.

Belle Heth Elementary School and Radford University's Heth Hall would later be named, was born on June 29, 1842 and died on February 24, 1916. She was the daughter of Col. Edward Hammet and his wife, Clementina Venable Craig. Stockton Heth was the son of Margaret Pickett and John[63] Heth. Stockton's mother Margaret was the daughter of George E. Pickett.

Capt. Stockton Heth moved to the Central Depot area from Chesterfield County, Virginia, during the mid- 1800s. He married Isabella Hammet at the Hammet family home on October 17, 1867. The service was performed by the rector of St. John's Episcopal Church of Wytheville, Virginia, who also provided spiritual support to the Episcopal community in Central Depot.. According to information on their marriage license, Stockton Heth was born in Richmond, Virginia, and residing in Culpepper County in 1867. His occupation was farming.

Stockton was a Confederate Captain in the Thirteenth Virginia Infantry of the E Company during the Civil War. He served under his cousin, Brigadier General Henry (also called "Harry") Heth. Gen. Henry Heth commended his personal staff, one of whom was then-Lieutenant Stockton Heth, for their service in his 1863 official report to Major General J. E. B. Stuart regarding the Battle of Chancellorsville. Capt. Stockton Heth also fought in the Battle of Gettysburg under the command of Brigadier General Henry Heth.

The family of Belle and Stockton Heth lived in several Virginia locations. Their oldest daughter, Sue, was educated at Edge Hill School in Albemarle County, although she spent most of her childhood in Central Depot (i.e. Radford) and is believed to have been born at the Heth home in Radford. The Heth family owned the land around and on which Radford University would later be built. At the time, the Heth land was referred to as "Heth Grove". The Heth home, built around 1866-1867, was called "Norwood" in honor of his wife's grandmother Isabella Norwood. It was referred to simply as "Heth House" by college folks during the twentieth century.

---

[63] The name of Stockton Heth's father is written in sources both as "John" and as "Jacob". Stockton's marriage license states his parents' names as Margaret and John Heth (see Montgomery County, VA, marriage records).

The members of the Heth family were very active in the Episcopal parish. They were also active in their community. Several Radford City streets were named for the family and the family property, including "Norwood Street", "Hammet Street", "Stockton Street", and "Grove Avenue".

Capt. Stockton Heth was an active member of the Episcopal Parish in Montgomery County and, later, in Radford City. He was a vestryman and general treasurer for the Montgomery Parish in 1874. By 1885, he was serving on the Montgomery Parish vestry representing St. James' Episcopal Mission Chapel in Central Depot. James Lawrence Radford and John Andrew Wilson of the St. James' Episcopal Mission Chapel property committee worked with Stockton Heth and the Radford Land Company in 1889 to locate a lot for the building of a new Grace Episcopal Mission rectory. Stockton Heth, Ambrose Robinson, and John A. Wilson were trustees of St. James' Episcopal Mission Chapel in 1890 when James Lawrence Radford deeded the original property for the planned Grace Episcopal Mission Chapel.

Heth was again a member of the vestry in 1890 and 1891. He was an alternate lay delegate to Diocesan Council in 1891. When the new Radford Parish was created in 1891, he was a member of the first vestry and served at least through 1892. He was also the first Clerk of Court for the City of Radford in 1892. Captain Stockton Heth may have been a President of the Exchange Bank of Radford at some point.

Mrs. Isabella Heth at some point purchased "White Thorn", the house built on Gov. James Patton Preston's "Smithfield" estate by Preston's son and daughter-in-law, James Francis Preston and Sarah Caperton Preston. Isabella and Stockton Heth assumed ownership of White Thorn in 1891. That is likely where Capt. Stockton Heth was living when he died in 1927.

Belle, her mother, her husband, and her children were buried in the Hammet Family Cemetery (also known as the Heth Family Cemetery). That cemetery is located today located on Stockton Street in Radford, is owned by Heth descendants, and is marked on the Radford City map as a Confederate Cemetery. Belle's mother's burial marker reads "Clementina V. Hammet, wife of Edward Hammet, born Feb. 21, 1809, Died Sept. 25, 1879". Belle's marker reads "Isabella H., wife of Capt. Stockton Heth,

177

June 29, 1842, Feb. 24, 1916, daughter of Col. Edward & Clementina Craig Hammet", along with the tender words "Many daughters have done virtuously, but thou excellest all".

Church records, as written by Rev. James A. Figg, report that Capt. Stockton Heth was living in Blacksburg, Virginia when he died from "old age" at the age of eighty-eight. Captain Heth died on March 26, 1927 and was buried on March 28, 1927 at the "Hammet Family Cemetery on New River, East Radford, VA". His marker reads "Stockton Heth, Capt. Company E, 13 Va Inf CSA". Isabella Hammet and Stockton Heth had children:

1. Susan Hammet Heth (1868) was born on August 23, 1868. She was baptized in the Episcopal church, and was confirmed on November 11, 1884 by the Rt. Rev. A. M. Randolph "when Parish was without a Rector", as entered into the St. James' Episcopal Mission Chapel records by Rev. Edward L. Goodwin. She became a communicant in 1889. Susan, called Sue, married William Radford Wharton at Capt. Heth's home "Norwood" in Radford on October 1, 1890. Sue died on May 17, 1958 and was buried in the Radford Family Cemetery. They had children: Heth Wharton, Ann Wharton, and William Radford Wharton.

2. Virginia C. Heth (1872). She was born in 1872, baptized in the Episcopal church, and confirmed on September 15, 1886 at age fourteen. The Rt. Rev. Francis M. Whittle officiated, as attested to by the Rev. J. E. Hammond. Her name was listed on the roster of communicants in 1887 at least through 1906. She was a member of the Radford Chapter, Virginia Daughters of the Confederacy, of the United Daughters of the Confederacy in 1906. She died in 1946. Virginia was buried in the Heth Family Cemetery in Radford.

3. Sallie Pickett Heth (1874), whose first name was sometimes spelled "Sally" and who was called "Pickett", was born in 1874. She was a communicant of St. James' Episcopal Mission Chapel in 1894, and then a communicant of Grace Episcopal Mission Chapel at least through 1906. She was baptized in the Episcopal church. She was also confirmed at St. James' on May 23, 1894, by the Rt. Rev. Alfred M. Randolph "when Parish was without a Rector",

as entered by the Rev. A. A. Pruden. She was a member of the Radford Chapter, Virginia Daughters of the Confederacy, of the United Daughters of the Confederacy. Pickett died in 1951 and was buried in the Heth Family Cemetery.

4. Stockton[64] Heth Jr. (1879). He was born in 1879. Called "Stock" by family and friends, he was listed as an Episcopal Parishioner throughout his life. His murder by a one-time friend resulted in a local scandal and trial which prompted the judge to order the removal of women from the courtroom during certain testimony related to the relationships between Stockton Heth Jr., the alleged murderer Professor Charles E. Vawter of Virginia Polytechnic and State University in Blacksburg, and Professor Vawter's wife Rachel. Evidence in the trial indicated that Heth had been having an affair with Mrs. Rachel Vawter, had previously discovered them in bed together in the Vawter house, and, on March 13, 1917, mortally shot Heth in the Vawter home after observing Mrs. Vawter leaving Heth's room during the early morning hours. Vawter first defended himself based upon what was known as "the unwritten law", a principle that a man had an unwritten right to seek redress for grievances against family or self by any means. When evidence at trial indicated that Professor Vawter not only knew of the affair but had given tacit permission for its continuation, he defended himself under a claim of temporary insanity based upon his pervasive and well-known battle with alcoholism. The jury returned a verdict of not guilty, determining that Professor Vawter had been insane when he shot Heth[65]. Stockton Heth Jr. died on March 14, 1917, and was buried in the Heth Family Cemetery.

5. Clement Craig Heth (1883). According to church baptismal records, he was born on November 11, 1883 and bap-

[64] Grace church records report that this man's full name was "Stockton Tyler Heth". However, his name appears as "Stockton Heth Jr." in all other sources. The name "Tyler" does not appear as a part of his or his father's name in any other sources to date.

[65] A thorough discussion of the murder of Stockton Heth Jr. was written by Jeffrey Newman and published in the 2001 issue of the Journal of the New River Historical Society.

tized on May 23, 1894 at his parents' home when he was eleven. The baptismal ceremony was conducted by the Rt. Rev. A. M. Randolph, as entered by Rev. A. A. Pruden. His sponsors were his sister Mrs. Susan H. Heth Wharton, his father Capt. Stockton Heth, Mrs. A. H. Heth, and Mrs. Richard Henry Adams Jr. He was listed as an Episcopal parishioner throughout his life or at least through 1906. His friends and family called him "Clem". Clement Craig Heth married Jeanette Cowan, daughter of

A brief paternal lineage of Stockton Heth is as follows (Henry Heth > Henry Heth Jr. > John Heth > Stockton Heth):

1) Henry Heth 1st Generation (circa 1700s). He married Agnes Mackey. They had children:
   a) Henry Heth Jr. 2nd Generation (circa 1700s), son of Agnes Mackey and Henry Heth. He was known as Captain Heth. He married Nancy Hare. They had at least one child:
   i) John Heth 3rd Generation (1798-1842), son of Nancy Hare and Henry Heth Jr. He was born in 1798 and died in 1842. He married Margaret Pickett. They had eleven children, including:
   (1) Stockton Heth 4th Generation (1840-1927), son of Margaret Pickett and John Heth. He was born in 1840 in Richmond, Virginia. He married Isabella Hammet on October 10, 1867 in Central Depot, Virginia. Isabella was born in Montgomery County, Virginia on June 29, 1842. Stockton Heth died on March 26, 1927. Isabella Heth predeceased him, having died on February 24, 1916. Isabella Hammet and Stockton Heth had children:
   (a) Susan Hammet Heth 5th Generation (1868), daughter of Isabella Hammet and Stockton Heth. She married William Radford Wharton. They had chil-

dren: Heth Wharton, Ann Wharton, and William Radford Wharton Jr.

(b) Virginia C. Heth 5th Generation (1872), daughter of Isabella Hammet and Stockton Heth.

(c) Sallie, also spelled Sally, Pickett Heth 5th Generation (1874), daughter of Isabella Hammet and Stockton Heth.

(d) Stockton Heth Jr. 5th Generation (1879), son of Isabella Hammet and Stockton Heth.

(e) Clement Craig Heth 5th Generation (1883), son of Isabella Hammet and Stockton Heth. He married Jeanette Cowan. He died in 1930 from injuries sustained due to a fall from his horse "Annie Montgomery". They had at least one child: Henry Heth (1925), was born on December 10, 1925 and died on October 4, 2001.

b) John Heth 2nd Generation (circa 1700s), son of Agnes Mackey and Henry Heth.

c) William Heth 2nd Generation (circa 1700s), son of Agnes Mackey and Henry Heth.

Hite, Deborah V.
1867 - 1950

Deborah V. Hite, a St. James' Episcopal Mission Chapel parishioner from Montgomery County, Virginia, married Malachi McGhee on October 10, 1886. Rev. J. E. Hammond performed the Episcopal wedding ceremony in Central, Virginia, before friends and family of the bride and groom. Her grave marker in Radford's Central Cemetery reads: "Deborah V. McGhee, July 4 1867, Apr. 9 1950".

Illustration 29: the Heth Family Home. During early 1900s, became part of the Heth Reservations lands which comprised the Radford Normal School for Women. Courtesy of Radford Heritage Foundation.

Jones, J. E.
Circa 1800s

J. E. Jones, his wife Jennie W. (maiden surname not now known), and their daughters lived in Central, Virginia, and were St. James' Episcopal Mission Chapel parishioners at least by 1885. They moved to Ronald, Virginia, around 1886.

Jennie W. and J. E. Jones had children:

1. Susan Stevenson Jones (1878), daughter of Jennie W. and J. E. Jones. According to church baptismal records, she was born October 12, 1878 and baptized at St. James' Episcopal Mission Chapel in Central, Virginia, when she was seven. Rev. J. E. Hammond officiated at the September 6, 1885 ceremony. Her sponsors were Capt. Richard H. Adams Jr., his wife Lizzie C. Adams, and Bessie N. Jordan.

182

2. Mary Elizabeth Jones (1880), daughter of Jennie W. and J.
E. Jones. According to church baptismal records, she was
born November 30, 1880 and was baptized with her sister
Susan on September 6, 1885. Mary Elizabeth was five.
Rev. J. E. Hammond conducted the baptismal rites at St.
James' Episcopal Mission Chapel in Central, Virginia.
Like her sister Susan, Mary Elizabeth's sponsors were
Capt. Richard H. Adams Jr., Lizzie C. Adams, and Bessie
N. Jordan. According to a notation in church parishioner
records, Mary Elizabeth Jones married a Mr. Hoffman.
She may have moved away from the area around 1896. A
cross which now adorns the roof of Grace Episcopal
Church in Radford City was donated by "Miss Molly
Jones", likely a nickname for Mrs. Mary Jones Hoffman.

Jordan, Bessie N.
Circa 1800s

Bessie N. Jordan was a communicant of St. James' Episcopal
Mission Chapel of Central Depot (i.e. Radford), Virginia at least
from 1885 through 1889. She transferred to St. Thomas Episcopal
Church in Christiansburg, Virginia in 1889.

Kenderdine, Warner Justice
1848 - 1932

Warner Justice Kenderdine, his wife Mary Lytle, and his two
daughters were members of the Episcopal congregation in Montgomery County and then Radford City from 1884 until their
deaths.

Warner Justice Kenderdine, named for his father's business
partner Warner Justice, was born August 30, 1848 and died De-
cember 26, 1932. He was the son of Sarah C. Wright and Joseph
Rakeshaw Kenderdine. Warner Justice Kenderdine married Mary
Lytle. The daughter of Hannah and John Lytle, she was born on
March 17, 1850 and died on October 8, 1931.

Mary Lytle and Warner Justice Kenderdine were married in a Quaker ceremony in Philadelphia, Pennsylvania during the year of 1874. Their wedding regalia reflected the Victorian society standards of the time. She wore an ivory silk bridal gown. He wore a gentleman's broadcloth morning coat. They were both baptized at the Church of the Resurrection in Philadelphia.

The Kenderdines moved to Central Depot, Virginia in 1884 and set up residence in a section of the Auburn District of Montgomery County which would become the West Ward of Radford City. They built a home on a large corner lot located at Walker and Second Streets, facing north with a view of the New River.

Col. Kenderdine[66], as he was known, assumed the position of Superintendent of the Radford Land and Improvement Company. He also assumed an important role in the development of his young community through real estate, religion, and government.

Mary Lytle and Warner Justice Kenderdine, along with their two daughters, were active and lifelong members of the Episcopal faith in their new home town. They were first parishioners of St. James' Episcopal Mission Chapel located near the business section of Central Depot. They then attended Grace Episcopal Mission Chapel located in the west ward of the Central Depot community. The chapels were a part of the Montgomery Episcopal Parish until 1891, when a separate independent Radford Episcopal Parish was created.

Col. Kenderdine was a member of the 1891 Episcopal parish building committee charged with the building of a new church "west of Connally's [sic] Branch" according to church vestry records. Through the Radford Land and Improvement Company, he deeded the original church property to Episcopal church trustees for the erection of the new building which would be called Grace Episcopal Mission Chapel.

Warner Justice Kenderdine was a member of the first Radford Parish vestry and served as vestryman, Junior Warden, and Senior Warden at least during 1891 and 1892. He was a church trustee from 1892 through 1898. He joined with Mrs. E. S. Jones to purchase the first church organ which was used in Randolph Hall by

---

[66] Although Warner Justice Kenderdine was known as "Colonel Kenderdine", no record of military service has been found. "Colonel" may have been an honorary title bestowed upon him.

184

both the Episcopalian and the Methodist congregations. When the Grace Episcopal Mission Chapel was built in the west ward, Col. Kenderdine bought Mrs. Jones' share of the organ and donated that organ to the chapel.

Mrs. Mary Lytle Kenderdine was very active in all of the Episcopal ladies' societies. She was a member of the Rector's Aid Society of Grace Parish Episcopal Chapel from 1893 through 1895, joined the renamed Ladies Chapel Fund society in 1896 and was again active in the reorganized Rector's Aid Society in 1900. She hosted meetings in her home, welcoming the ladies to meet in her parlor and in her library. Mrs. Kenderdine served on church society committees and held the offices of Treasurer, Vice-President, and President. Her activities for the Woman's Guild of Grace Chapel in 1902 and 1903 included serving as Vice-President in 1902, helping to prepare a reception for the students of St. Albans Boys Academy, and hosting a "Fancy Table" with Mrs. Clark for the 1903 church Christmas bazaar.

Col. Kenderdine was interested in his local government as well. He was a member of the first Radford City Council when the city was incorporated in 1892.

The Kenderdines of Radford did not lose contact with their Pennsylvania associates and relatives. During the 1890s, Warner Justice Kenderdine placed his home and other possessions as surety on a bond for the purchase of the Kenderdine &Paul Mill in Babylon, Horsham County, Pennsylvania. Those possessions included five shares of capital stock in the Radford Trust Company, an account of $500 due to him by the Dwelling Improvement Company of Philadelphia, current and future amounts due to him by the Radford Land & Improvement Company for his services, all furniture in his house on Second and Fairfax Streets in Radford, one organ at Grace Episcopal Mission Chapel in Radford, one bay horse with two carriages and harness, one roller top desk, and one Remington typewriter.

The Kenderdine family had long been mill-wrights and saw-yers. The purchasers of the Kenderdine & Paul Mill were Isaac W. Kenderdine, the brother of Warner Justice Kenderdine, and their father Joseph R. Kenderdine. Warner Justice Kenderdine received a Deed of Release[67] for the surety he had placed on the bond for that mill on March 23, 1896. He also received a Deed of Release for a home on the intersection of Fairfax and Fourth Streets fronting Fairfax based upon a final payment to the National Mutual Building and Loan Association of New York in 1897.

According to church records entered by Rev. James A. Figg and Rev. J. M. Dick, Warner Justice Kenderdine died in Radford from "old age" on December 28, 1932. He was eighty-four. He was buried in Radford on December 29, 1932. Mary Lytle Kenderdine died in Radford at the age of eighty-one from "pneumonia following paralysis". She died on October 8, 1931 and was buried in West View Cemetery on October 10, 1931. Their daughters donated a set of three stained glass Chancel Windows for the Grace Episcopal Church in memory of their parents. The chancel windows read "Warner Justice Kenderdine, 8/30/1848, Sr. Warden and Vestryman", "Ye Shall Overcome   St. John", and "Mary Lytle Kenderdine, 5/17/1850 - 10/8/1931". Mary Lytle and Warner Justice Kenderdine had children:

1. Anna Lytle Kenderdine (1876). The oldest of the two Kenderdine daughters, of whom more.
2. Bess also known as "Bessie" and "Kenderdine (1880), Miss Bess", of whom more. She married Fred Sayles Bullard.

The Kenderdine family[68] came to the American colony from Wales during the early 1700s. Thomas Kenderdine, the first American immigrant, was a member of the Quaker faith; the majority of the Welsh Kenderdines were members of the Church of England. A detailed lineage of Warner Justice Kenderdine's paternal heritage follows (Thomas Kenderdine > Joseph Kenderdine > John Kenderdine > Joseph Kenderdine > Joseph Rakestraw Kenderdine > Warner Justice Kenderdine):

---

[67] See Radford City Deed Book 1, page 240.
[68] The Kenderdine family lineage information has been culled from sources including Radford City public records, Grace Episcopal Church register and meeting minutes, and information compiled by Thaddeus Stevens Kenderdine in 1901.

1) <u>Thomas Kenderdine</u> 1st Generation (circa 1650-1713). He was born in North Wales around 1650 and immigrated to the American colonies. He married Margaret Robert, daughter of Mr. and Mrs. John Robert of North Wales. Thomas Kenderdine died in Philadelphia County, Pennsylvania in 1713. Margaret Robert and Thomas Kenderdine had children:

   a) <u>Richard Kenderdine</u> 2nd Generation (c. 1680-1733), son of Margaret Robert and Thomas Kenderdine. He was born in Wales around 1680. He married Sarah Evans. Richard owned Shay Mill in Pennsylvania, which passed to Richard's younger brothers Thomas and Joseph. Sarah Evans and Richard Kenderdine had children:

      i) <u>Thomas Kenderdine</u> 3rd Generation (circa 1700s), son of Sarah Evans and Richard Kenderdine.

      ii) <u>Sarah Kenderdine</u> 3rd Generation (circa 1700s), daughter of Sarah Evans and Richard Kenderdine. She married Enoch Morgan. They had children, including:

        (1) <u>Hannah Morgan</u> 4th Generation (circa 1700s), daughter of Sarah Kenderdine and Enoch Morgan. Hannah Morgan married John Kenderdine, who was the nephew of her grandfather Richard Kenderdine (i.e. John Kenderdine was the son of Joseph Kenderdine, Richard Kenderdine's brother).

      iii) <u>Ellinor Kenderdine</u> 3rd Generation (circa 1700s), daughter of Sarah Evans and Richard Kenderdine.

      iv) <u>Mary Kenderdine</u> 3rd Generation (circa 1700s), daughter of Sarah Evans and Richard Kenderdine.

      v) <u>Elizabeth Kenderdine</u> 3rd Generation (circa 1700s), daughter of Sarah Evans and Richard Kenderdine.

   b) <u>Jenkins Kenderdine</u> 2nd Generation (c. 1600s), son of Margaret Robert and Thomas Kenderdine.

c) <u>Thomas Kenderdine Jr.</u> 2nd Generation (c. 1692-1779), son of Margaret Robert and Thomas Kenderdine. Thomas and his brother Joseph became owners of Shay Mill; upon the death of Thomas, brother Joseph Kenderdine became sole owner of Shay Mill. Thomas and his wife (name not now known) had children during the 1700s, as follows: Benjamin Kenderdine, Jacob Kenderdine, Joseph Kenderdine who married Rachel Kenderdine, Margaret Kenderdine, Jane Kenderdine, Mary Kenderdine, and Hannah Kenderdine.

d) <u>John Kenderdine</u> 2nd Generation (c. 1694), son of Margaret Robert and Thomas Kenderdine.

e) <u>Margaret Kenderdine</u> 2nd Generation (c. 1700-1714), daughter of Margaret Robert and Thomas Kenderdine.

f) <u>Mary Kenderdine</u> 2nd Generation (c. 1700s), daughter of Margaret Robert and Thomas Kenderdine.

g) <u>Joseph Kenderdine</u> 2nd Generation (1703-1778), son of Margaret Robert and Thomas Kenderdine. He was born on December 14, 1703 in Wales and died in America on February 23, 1778. On July 28, 1738 he married Mary Jarrett, the daughter of Mr. and Mrs. John Jarrett. Joseph Kenderdine and his brother Thomas inherited Shay Mill from their eldest brother, Richard Kenderdine. Joseph became the sole owner upon Thomas' death. Upon Joseph's death, the mill became the property of his six daughters. The daughters transferred ownership to their cousin and brother-in-law, Joseph Kenderdine (son of Thomas Kenderdine Jr.), in 1785. Mary Jarrett and Joseph Kenderdine (son of Margaret Robert and Thomas Kenderdine) had children:

    i) <u>Jane Kenderdine</u> 3rd Generation (circa 1700s), daughter of Mary Jarrett and Joseph Kenderdine.

ii) <u>Mary Kenderdine</u> 3rd Generation (1739), daughter of Mary Jarrett and Joseph Kenderdine. She married Benjamin Tompkins.

iii) <u>John Kenderdine</u> 3rd Generation (1740-1790), son of Mary Jarrett and Joseph Kenderdine. He was born in Philadelphia, Pennsylvania in 1740 and died on January 2, 1790. John Kenderdine married his cousin, Hannah Morgan, in 1778. She was the daughter of Sarah Kenderdine and Enoch Morgan and the granddaughter of John Kenderdine's uncle Richard Kenderdine. Hannah Morgan and John Kenderdine lived at Shay Mill. They had children:

(1) <u>Joseph Kenderdine</u> 4th Generation (1778), son of Hannah Morgan and John Kenderdine. He was born on November 26, 1778 and died on September 13, 1822. He married Hannah Rakestraw, daughter of Sarah Milner and Joseph Rakestraw, in 1799. Hannah Rakestraw and Joseph Kenderdine had children:

(a) <u>John Kenderdine</u> 5th Generation (1800), son of Hannah Rakestraw and Joseph Kenderdine.

(b) <u>Justinian Kenderdine</u> 5th Generation (1801), daughter of Hannah Rakestraw and Joseph Kenderdine.

(c) <u>Hannah Kenderdine</u> 5th Generation (1803), daughter of Hannah Rakestraw and Joseph Kenderdine.

(d) <u>Sarah Kenderdine</u> 5th Generation (1806), daughter of Hannah Rakestraw and Joseph Kenderdine.

(e) <u>Elizabeth Kenderdine</u> 5th Generation (1808-1813), daughter of Hannah Rakestraw and Joseph Kenderdine.

(f) <u>Mary Kenderdine</u> 5th Generation (1811), daughter of Hannah Rakestraw and Joseph Kenderdine.

(g) Joseph Rakestraw Kenderdine 5th Generation (1813-1903), son of Hannah Rakestraw and Joseph Kenderdine. He was born in Horsham, Pennsylvania on April 26, 1813. He died in Germantown, Pennsylvania on December 14, 1903. Joseph married Sarah C. Wright, the daughter of Elizabeth Child and Isaac Wright, on November 18, 1841. Sarah and Joseph R. Kenderdine made their home in Philadelphia where he worked as a carpenter, builder, and contractor. He and his business partner Warner Justice owned a hardware store in Philadelphia called "Kenderdine & Justice". Joseph later operated a second hardware store which he called "Joseph R. Kenderdine & Sons". Joseph and his son Isaac, with financial assistance from son Warner Justice Kenderdine, became partners in "Kenderdine & Paul Mill". Sarah C. Wright and Joseph Rakestraw Kenderdine had children:

(i) Albert Kenderdine 6th Generation (1843), son of Sarah C. Wright and Joseph Rakestraw Kenderdine. He was born on April 22, 1843 and died on April 20, 1845.

(ii) Isaac Wright Kenderdine 6th Generation (1845), son of Sarah C. Wright and Joseph Rakeshaw Kenderdine. He was born on February 13, 1845. As a young adult, he became partners with his father in ownership of the Kenderdine and Paul Mill.

(iii) Warner Justice Kenderdine 6th Generation (1848-1932), son of Sarah C. Wright and Joseph Rakeshaw

190

Kenderdine. He was born on August 30, 1848 in Pennsylvania. He was named for his father's business partner Warner Justice. Warner Justice Kenderdine married Mary Lytle, daughter of Hannah and John Lytle. Mary was born on March 17, 1850. She died in Radford, Virginia on October 8, 1931. Warner died in Radford a year later, on December 26, 1932. Mary Lytle and Warner Justice Kenderdine had children:

1. Anna Lytle Kenderdine 7th Generation (1876-1955), daughter of Mary Lytle and Warner Justice Kenderdine. She was born on May 25, 1876 and died unmarried on December 18, 1955. She and her sister Bess lived in the Kenderdine family home in Radford, Virginia.

2. Bess Kenderdine 7th Generation (1880), daughter of Mary Lytle and Warner Justice Kenderdine. She was born on September 27, 1880 and died on March 10, 1968 in Radford, Virginia. She married Fred Sayles Bullard. He died young during the national flu epidemic of 1918. The couple had no children.

(iv) Frank Kenderdine 6th Generation (1850), son of Sarah C. Wright and Joseph Rakeshaw Kenderdine. He was born in Philadelphia, Pennsylvania on October 9, 1850 and died in Wilmington, Delaware on December 7, 1936.

(v) Elizabeth Wright Kenderdine 6th Generation (1852), daughter of Sarah C. Wright and Joseph Rakeshaw Kenderdine. She was born on September 17, 1852 and died unmarried on April 28, 1891.

(vi) Laura Kenderdine 6th Generation (1855), daughter of Sarah C. Wright and Joseph Rakeshaw Kenderdine. She was born on May 17, 1855.

(h) Elizabeth Kenderdine 5th Generation (1816), daughter of Hannah Rakestraw and Joseph Kenderdine. She was born three years after the death of her sister, also named Elizabeth. This Elizabeth Kenderdine who was born in 1816 married Thomas T. Childs. They had children: Charles Starr Kenderdine (1818) and Rebecca Kenderdine (1821). They had children: Issacher Kenderdine (1780) and John Kenderdine (1782).

iv) Margaret Kenderdine 3rd Generation (1742), daughter of Mary Jarrett and Joseph Kenderdine. She married John Hickman.

v) Hannah Kenderdine 3rd Generation (1745), daughter of Mary Jarrett and Joseph Kenderdine. She was born in Pennsylvania in 1745. She married James Paul, who bought Shay Mill from Joseph Kenderdine (husband of Hannah's sister Rachel).

vi) Rachel Kenderdine 3rd Generation (1747), daughter of Mary Jarrett and Joseph Kenderdine. She married her cousin Joseph Kenderdine. Joseph was the owner of Shay Mill in 1785. In 1795 he sold it to James Paul, husband of Rachel's sister Hannah.

vii) Sarah Kenderdine 3rd Generation (1750), daughter of Mary Jarrett and Joseph Kenderdine. She married John Lloyd.

Kessler, William E.
Circa 1867

William E. Kessler was the son of Virginia C. and William S. Kessler of Radford, Virginia. At the time of the 1880 population census, the family was living in Central Depot. The surname was incorrectly spelled "Keslir", and Head of Household was listed as "William J. Keslir" instead of William S. Kessler. The family was described as follows: thirty-five year old white railroad engineer William J. Keslir, his thirty-three year old wife Virginia C. Keslir, their thirteen year old son William E. Keslir, and their ten year old daughter Maggie J. Keslir.

The Kessler family attended Grace Episcopal Mission Chapel in Radford, Virginia. On December 30, 1890, William E. Kessler married Virginia F. McCarty. The daughter of John and Mary McCarty of Radford, she was baptized at Christ Church in Blacksburg and was listed as a Grace Episcopal Mission Chapel communicant by 1887. The wedding of Virginia F. McCarty and William E. Kessler was held at the home of the bride's parents in Radford, with family members witnessing the ceremony performed by the Rev. Edward Lewis Goodwin.

A notation in the church register states that Mrs. Virginia Kessler transferred to Christ Church in Roanoke September 1892. It is unclear whether this notation referred to Mrs. Virginia C. Kessler (mother of William E. Kessler) or to Mrs. Virginia McCarty Kessler (wife of William E. Kessler). Virginia F. McCarty and William E. Kessler had at least one child: Thelma Estelle Kessler. She died at the age of eight months on June 20, 1892 in Roanoke, Virginia, according to Grace Episcopal Mission Chapel records. Cause of death was not noted. She was buried on June 22, 1892 in "Radford Cemetery". Rev. E. L. Goodwin performed the burial service.

Kipps, J. H.
Circa 1842

J. H. Kipps was a member of the Montgomery Episcopal Parish vestry in 1871.

By 1880 he was living in Christiansburg, Virginia, with his wife, five children, a niece, and nine servants. The census of 1880 described the family as follows: married white thirty-eight year old hotel keeper J. H. Kipps, his twenty-eight year old wife Bettie L. Kipps, four daughters, one son, and an eight year old niece named Florence Mason. All family members were born in Virginia, as were their parents and grandparents. Also in the Kipps establishment were nine servants: a white thirty-year old barkeeper named Henry Bohn (circa 1850), a single mulatto twelve year old chamber maid named Nannie Briggs (circa 1868), a white twenty year old store clerk named J. G. Charlton (circa 1860), a white twenty-four year old house keeper named Sallie Dunn (circa 1856), a white eighteen year old seamstress named Catherine Gray (circa 1862), a white twenty-five year old store clerk named H. R. Kipps (circa 1855), a white twenty-two year old hotel clerk named J. E. Mitchell (circa 1858), a black twenty-five year old dining room servant named Teory Parnel (circa 1855), and a mulatto thirty-three year old dining room servant named Edward Woods (circa 1847).

In the 1900s, a Montgomery County, Virginia, public school was named Kipps Elementary School in honor of J. H. Kipps. The children of Bettie L. and J. H. Kipps were:

1. Lou L. Kipps (circa 1873). She was seven years old at the time of the 1880 United States Census.
2. Lennie D. Kipps (circa 1874). She was six years old at the time of the 1880 United States Census.
3. Fayetta Kipps (circa 1875). She was five year old at the time of the 1880 United States Census.
4. Fannie K. Kipps (circa 1873). She was three years old at the time of the 1880 United States Census.
5. Lewis D. Kipps (circa 1880). He was one month old at the time of the 1880 United States Census.

Kohlhousen, Theodore F.
Circa 1800s

Captain Theodore F. Kohlhousen was baptized as a Lutheran but confirmed as an Episcopalian at St. James' Episcopal Mission

Chapel on April 5, 1882. Rev. Edward Lewis Goodwin attested to the confirmation performed by the Rt. Rev. Alfred Magill Randolph.

Captain Kohlhousen and his wife, Julia V., were parishioners of St. James' Episcopal Mission Chapel at least by 1889 and living on Commerce Street in the East Ward of Radford. Julia, who was baptized at Grace Episcopal Church in Berryville, Virginia, became a communicant of St. James' in 1890. Her husband became a communicant of St. James' in 1891. He was also an alternate lay delegate to the Episcopal Diocesan Convention at some point. The Kohlhousens were still attending the Episcopal Church in Radford as late as 1905.

According to church records as entered by Rev. James A. Figg, seventy-three year old Julia V. Kohlhousen, female from East Radford, died on August 12, 1930 from "indigestion". She was buried on August 15, 1930 at Mt. Huberon Cemetery in Winchester, Virginia.

Julia V. and Theodore F. Kohlhousen had children:

1. Frederick K. Kohlhousen (circa 1872), called Fred. He was born around 1872 and was baptized "in the church" according to church records. He was a communicant of St. James' Episcopal Mission Chapel in 1889 and confirmed on October 30, 1889 by the Rt. Rev. F. M. Whittle, attested to by Rev. Edward Lewis Goodwin. Fred died in San Antonio, Texas, at the age of nineteen years from "fever" on November 28, 1891. His remains were brought back to his hometown, where he was buried eight days after his death in "the Radford Cemetery". Rev. Edward Lewis Goodwin recorded the burial date as December 5, 1891.

2. Grace Kohlhousen (circa 1800s). She was baptized "in the church" and confirmed with her father at St. James' Episcopal Mission Chapel on April 5, 1892. Rev. Edward Lewis Goodwin attested to the confirmation performed by the Rt. Rev. Alfred Magill Randolph.

Lock, Frederick
1822-1898

Frederick Lock[69] and his wife Wilhemina Juliana M. (maiden surname not now known) were communicants of Grace Episcopal Mission Chapel at least by 1885. The lived in the East Ward of Radford on Third Street. Also living in the Lock household in 1885 was their daughter, Mrs. Louisa Lock Deal (previously known as Mrs. Louisa Lock Bibb).

The 1880 United States Census lists the Lock family, living in Central Depot of Montgomery County, Virginia, as follows: Frederick Lock was a white fifty-eight year old blacksmith living with his forty-seven year old wife "Wilmina", their twenty-eight year old daughter Louisa Lock, and a boarder. The boarder was white twenty-four year old farmer Thomas Cunningham. Wilhemina and Frederick Lock were born in Germany. Their daughter Louisa was born in Virginia.

A note in church records indicates that Frederick Lock's name was dropped from the roll of communicants in 1891 because he was "not communing". His name was added back to the list of communicants in 1895 as an "old communicant restored". He died on January 18, 1898 at the age of seventy-five years and nine months. He was buried in Radford's Central Cemetery. His will was filed and entered in Radford City on November 20, 1899 (Radford City Will Book One, Page 30, April 30, 1898) under "Fredrick Lock" of Central City. His trustees were William F. Collins and J. H. Dudley. He left $1 to each of his three daughters and the balance of his estate to his wife. The children of Wilhemina Juliana M. and Frederick Lock were as follows:

1. Louisa Carolina Lock (circa 1852), daughter of Wilhemina Juliana M. and Frederic Lock. She married Lewis Bibb and later, as a widow, married a Mr. Deal. In 1885 she was living with the "Locke" family (i.e. her parents Mr. Frederick "Locke" and his wife "Wilhelima J. Locke") on Third Street in the East Ward of Radford, ac-

[69] Frederick Lock's name is also spelled in church records as "Fredrick Lock" and as "Frederick Locke". It is spelled on his grave marker in Central Cemetery as "Frederick Lock". His wife's name is spelled both as "Wilhemina" and as "Wilhelima".

cording to church records, and attending St. James' Episcopal Mission Chapel at least from 1885 through 1888. The community of Central was renamed the Town of Radford while she was in residence. Lewis Bibb may have died sometime between 1888 and 1893; Louisa moved to Norfolk, Virginia around 1888 and returned to Radford City around 1893. Sometime after Lewis Bibb's death, his widow Louisa married a "Mr. Deal" (Christian / first name not now known). Mrs. Louisa Lock Bibb Deal was a St. James' Episcopal Mission Chapel communicant in 1893, being an "old communicant who returned to the area" according to church records. Mrs. Louisa Deal was a member of the Radford Chapter of the Virginia Daughters of the Confederacy. "Mrs. Deal" was a member of the Woman's Guild of Grace Chapel in 1902. She served as Vice President. Among her many activities was the hosting of a refreshment table at the 1903 Christmas bazaar with "Mrs. Wright" and "Mrs. Fink" (i.e. Mrs. Irene Robinson Fink).

2. Mary Elizabeth Lock (circa 1800s). She married a Mr. Franklin (Christian / first name not now known).

3. Mary Catherine Lock (1855). She was born on February 22, 1855 and died on April 29, 1933. She married John Andrew Wilson, who was born on February 12, 1849 and died on April 14, 1910. They were both buried at Central Cemetery. Mary Catherine Lock and John Andrew Wilson had four children.

Newman, Samuel D.
1851

Samuel D. Newman and his wife Sarah J. were listed as communicants of St. James' Episcopal Mission Chapel from 1886 through 1897. Samuel was born in 1851 and was living in the East Ward of Radford at Lawrence Hill by 1885. He was baptized as a Baptist but confirmed in the Episcopal faith when he was thirty-five. The Rt. Rev. Francis McNeece Whittle performed the rite of confirmation in Radford on September 15, 1886 as attested to by

Rev. J. E. Hammond. Sarah J. and Samuel D. Newman had children:

1. Elias G. Newman (circa 1800s), son of Sarah J. and Samuel D. Newman.
2. Eliga R. Newman (circa 1800s), son of Sarah J. and Samuel D. Newman.
3. Sallie Yingling Newman (1884), daughter of Sarah J. and Samuel D. Newman. Sallie was born on December 12, 1884. She was baptized at St. James' Episcopal Mission Chapel in Central, Virginia when she was one and a half years old. Rev. J. E. Hammond performed the rite of baptism on May 2, 1886. Mrs. Wilhemina M. Lock was the infant's sponsor. Sallie may have married Ika Einstien and moved to Cleveland, Ohio.

Pickering, J. H.
Circa 1800s

J. H. Pickering and his wife, Lillian A., lived in Central, Virginia (also known as the town of Radford) and were parishioners of St. James' Episcopal Mission Chapel at least by July 10, 1887 through 1888. They had transferred to the southwestern Virginia Episcopal parish from Grace Episcopal Church in Petersburg, Virginia. Their names were removed from the list of parishioners in 1888.

Pile, David Landon
1849-1907

Annie Roper and David Landon Pile chose the Episcopal church in Radford for the marriage of their daughter Gertrude.

The Pile family was living in Central Depot at the time of the 1880 United States Census. They were described as follows: white twenty-eight year old railroad engineer D. L. Pile (incorrectly listed as "D. H." Pile) living with his twenty-two year old wife Annie Pile, his seven year old son William Pile, his five year old daughter Gertrude Pile, his three year old daughter Minnie Pile, and his one year old son Henry Pile.

David Landon Pile was born in Tennessee on September 6, 1849. He died on August 14, 1907. His wife Annie Roper was born on September 12, 1857 and died on January 21, 1925. They were both buried in Central Cemetery in Radford.

Annie Roper and David Landon Pile had children:

1. William David Pile (1873), son of Annie Roper and David Landon Pile. He was born on June 7, 1873, died on August 22, 1894, and was buried in Central Cemetery.
2. Gertrude Landon Pile (1874), daughter of Annie Roper and David Landon Pile. She was born on December 24, 1874. She was born on December 24, 1874 and died on July 13, 1934. She applied and was accepted for membership in the Radford Chapter of the Virginia Daughters of the Confederacy on September 29, 1915 based upon her grandfather William Edward Black's service as a Confederate soldier. Black served with the Washington Mountains Riflemen and was later a member of the Company D, First Virginia Calvary of the Confederate Army under Commander William E. Jones. Gertrude Landon Pile married John Custis Peter, who was born on December 4, 1867 and died on January 14, 1952. They had a child, Eleanor Custis Peter, who was born in Radford, Virginia on Tuesday, July 7, 1896 and died on Thursday, November 23, 1905.
3. Minnie Pile (circa 1877), daughter of Annie Roper and David Landon Pile.
4. Henry Pile (1878), son of Annie Roper and David Landon Pile. He was born on December 15, 1878, died in a railroad accident on October 14, 1906, and was buried in Central Cemetery.
5. L. E. Pile (circa 1800s), child of Annie Roper and David Landon Pile.

Radford, James Lawrence
1856-1901

James Lawrence Radford, the youngest son of Elizabeth Campbell Taylor and John Blair Radford, was born at the family home "Arnheim" on September 16, 1856, thirteen days before the death of his maternal grandfather John McCanless Taylor. He was called Lawrence and nicknamed "Captain" by his family.

When Rev. Edward H. Ingle was rector to the St. James' Episcopal Mission congregation of Central Depot, Virginia. James Lawrence Radford served on the 1871 vestry. He again served as a member of the Episcopal Montgomery Parish vestry in 1885 and of the Radford Parish vestry during the years 1892 through 1895. James Lawrence Radford served as Junior Warden and played a key role on committees related to the growth of the Parish. He and John A. Wilson comprised the 1889 committee that worked with Captain Stockton Heth and the Radford Land and Development Company to find a lot on which to build the Grace Episcopal Mission rectory. That followed with membership on the 1890 and 1891 committee to work with the Radford Land and Improvement Company to secure land for the building of a new church building (i.e. Grace Episcopal Mission Chapel) "west of Connally's Branch". He served on the first vestry of the newly formed Radford Parish during the years 1891 and 1892.

J. L. Radford received his education at Virginia Polytechnic Institute in Blacksburg, Virginia. He spent his adult years actively serving both his community and his church. He was a member of Virginia's House of Delegates representing Montgomery County from 1889 through 1892. The Honorable James L. Radford worked on behalf of his community to obtain a charter for the Town of Radford to become a city. Central Depot had been renamed Radford after the delegate's father John Blair Radford around 1887. Dr. Radford passed away in 1872 but his family lived to see him honored as the town's namesake. In 1892, twenty years after Dr. Radford's death, his son was successful in his duties as a delegate to the Commonwealth and the City of Radford was incorporated.

J. L. Radford never married, and died after an extended illness on November 12, 1901 at the age of forty-five. He was living at the Taylor family home "Rockford" at the time of his death. The living heirs of James Lawrence Radford settled a Quit-Claim Deed[70] for the estate in 1940 regarding an 1890 property sale conducted by J. L. Radford. His heirs released to Mary F. Carter a piece of property which she purchased from J. L. Radford in the J. L. Radford Addition to the City on September 29, 1890 with the explanation that the original deed was either lost, destroyed, or never placed in either Montgomery County or Radford City courthouse records. Those thirteen living heirs were: Mrs. Mancye Doyle Adams (widow of J. L. Radford's nephew Radford Carter Adams), Lucien Doyle Adams (son of J. L. Radford's nephew R. C. Adams), Eleanor Elizabeth Adams (wife of Lucien Doyle Adams), Radford Carter Adams Jr. (son of J. L. Radford's nephew R. C. Adams), Mrs. Elizabeth Campbell Adams Small (daughter of J. L. Radford's nephew R. C. Adams), Kenneth F. Small (her husband), Mrs. Susan Hammet Heth Wharton (widow of J. L. Radford's nephew William Radford Wharton), William Radford Wharton Jr. (son of J. L. Radford's nephew W. R. Wharton), Dorothea Vaughan Wharton, (relationship unclear at this point), Katherine K. Wharton (relationship unclear at this point), Anne Rebecca Radford Wharton von Poederoyen (daughter of J. L. Radford's nephew W. R. Wharton), and Hugo Swaen von Poederoyen (her husband).

Robinson, Ambrose
1835-1931

Ambrose Robinson and his wife, Mary M., were living in the East Ward of Radford on Railroad Avenue. They were communicants of St. James' Episcopal Mission Chapel and then transferred to Grace Episcopal Mission Chapel at least by April 1, 1885.

Capt. Ambrose Robinson was a member of the Montgomery Parish vestry representing St. James' Episcopal Mission Chapel of Central Depot in 1874, serving as treasurer, and at least during the years 1885, 1887, and 1890 through 1891. Vestry meetings were frequently held at "Robinson's Store" and "Robinson Hall" during

[70] See Radford City Deed Book 39, page 253.

201

the years 1887 and 1889. He chaired the 1889 building committee charged with the task of obtaining a signed contract with the Radford Land Company for lots on which to erect the proposed Grace Episcopal Mission Chapel and rectory. He continued that committee membership to build a new church "west of Connally's Branch" in 1891 and served on the 1891 committee to petition the Episcopal Diocese of Virginia to divide Montgomery Parish and form from it a new Radford Parish. Capt. Robinson was Senior Warden of the new Radford Parish vestry during the years 1891 and 1892.

He was the City Treasurer of the new Radford City in 1892. At least during the 1890s he was proprietor of Robinson Store where, according to his advertisements in the 1896 *Radford Advance* newspaper, he was a "dealer in clothing, gents' furnishings, ladies' and gentlemen's shoes, dry goods and notions" and provided "gentlemen's suits made to order".[71]

The Robinson family is recorded in the 1880 United States Census as living in Central Depot, Montgomery County, Virginia, although the last name is misspelled as "Robison" and two of the children's first names are misspelled (not an unusual situation in early census data). Members of the household, with census spellings maintained, were as follows: Head of Household was a white forty-six year old merchant named Ambrose Robison, his thirty-six year old wife named Mary M. Robison, his nine year old son named Foredic Robison, his eight year old son named Preston M. Robison, his seven year old son named Albert D. Robison, his six year old son Charles A. Robison, and his four year old daughter, Ireen Robison. At the time, there were also three servants and one boarder in the residence as well. Ambrose's country of birth was reported as having been Canada. His father was born in England and his mother was born in France. His wife, her parents, and their children were all born in America in the state of Virginia.

Ambrose Robinson was born on March 6, 1835. He died on January 24, 1931 of "old age" at "age 95", according to church records. He was buried at Central Cemetery in East Radford on January 25, 1931. His family purchased a pew for the church; a

---

[71] See Robinson ad in the *Radford Advance*, Vol. 5, No. 36, Radford, Virginia, Friday, July 10, 1896.

small brass plaque on the pew reads "In memory of Ambrose Robinson 1835-1931".

Mrs. Mary M. Robinson was born on October 26, 1840. She died on September 10, 1891 from heart failure. She was buried at the "Radford Cemetery", i.e. Central Cemetery, on September 11, 1891 with clergyman E. L. Goodwin officiating. Mary M. and Ambrose Robinson had children:

1. Fordyce William Robinson (c. 1870). Note that his first name was incorrectly spelled in the 1880 Census as "Foredic".
2. Preston Madison Robinson (c. 1871).
3. Albert Duvall Robinson (1872). He was baptized in the Church and confirmed at Grace Episcopal Mission Chapel on October 10, 1889. The confirmation rite was performed by the Rt. Rev. F. M. Whittle, attested to by Rev. Edward Lewis Goodwin. Church records list his name as "Albert Duvall Robinson"; a marker in Radford's Central Cemetery reads "Alva D. Robinson, Nov. 27, 1872, Sept. 9, 1941".
4. Charles Ambrose Robinson (c. 1874).
5. Irene Robinson (1876); note that her first name was incorrectly spelled as "Ireen" in the 1880 Census. She was born on March 8, 1876. Irene was baptized in the church and was confirmed at Grace Episcopal Mission Chapel on October 30, 1889. The confirmation rite was performed by the Rt. Rev. F. M. Whittle, attested to by Rev. Edward Lewis Goodwin. Eight years later, on May 26[72], 1897, she married Edward Jacob Fink at St. James' Episcopal Mission Chapel. The wedding service was performed by the Rev. F. G. Ribble. Mrs. Irene Robinson Fink died on May 24, 1952. She was buried in Central Cemetery in Radford.

---

[72] The Robinson-Fink marriage records in the Radford City Courthouse list the marriage date as May 25, 1897.

Sampson, Samuel T.
Circa 1800s

Samuel T. Sampson and his wife, Ida R., were parishioners of St. James' Episcopal Mission Chapel in Central Depot, Virginia, at least between 1885 and 1892. Samuel T. Sampson was also involved in community activities; S. T. Sampson was Secretary of the Virginia May Lodge No. 88 of A. F. & A. M. in 1892. At some point, Mr. and Mrs. Sampson moved to Roanoke, Virginia according to church records. Ida R. and Samuel T. Sampson had children:

1. Ernest Vivian Sampson (1882). This child of Ida R. and Samuel T. Sampson was born on September 22, 1882. Ernest Vivian was baptized at St. James' Episcopal Mission Chapel on September 6, 1885 by Rev. J. E. Hammond. Baptismal sponsors were William Francis Collins and his wife Mary Jane Gregory Collins. Church records indicate that Ernest Vivian may have never been confirmed at an Episcopal Church and may have become active in another church.
2. Edwin Haney Sampson (1884). He was born on September 9, 1884. He was baptized at St. James' Episcopal Mission Chapel by Rev. J. E. Hammond on September 6, 1885 and, like his sibling Ernest Vivian Sampson, his sponsors were Mary J. and William F. Collins.

Tallant, William F.
Circa 1845

William F. Tallant, son of Henry Tallant from Ireland and/or London, England was born in section of Virginia that later became part of West Virginia. William F. Tallant set up residence in Christiansburg in Montgomery County, Virginia, by 1870. He was an important figure in the establishment of the Episcopal Church in southwestern Virginia, serving as a member of the first Montgomery Parish Vestry in 1871.

He was a citizen from Wheeling, West Virginia, when he married Elizabeth M. Montague of Montgomery County, Virginia. At the time of the 1880 United States Census, he was described as a thirty-five year old white Montgomery County tinner and farmer named W. F. Tallant[73]. Living with him were his wife, a daughter, and servants: a black sixty-three year old laborer named Alford Johnson (born around 1817), his wife Grace Johnson who was then a mulatto thirty-eight year old cook (born around 1842), their three month old son William Johnston, and a single black fifty-five year old farmhand named Marshall Talioferro (born around 1825). His wife was described as a thirty-two year old woman named Lizzie. She was born in Virginia, as were her parents. Their daughter, born in Virginia, was described as six year old A. K. Tallant. Elizabeth M. Montague and William F. Tallant had at least one child: A. K. Tallant (c. 1874). She was six years old and living with her parents in Montgomery County, Virginia, at the time of the 1880 United States Census.

Tyler, John Jr.
Circa 1800s

John Tyler Jr. came to St. James' Episcopal Mission Chapel from Monumental Church in Richmond. He became an Episcopal communicant on April 26, 1887. Tyler's name was removed from the roster of communicants in 1888.

Further information and identification of this parishioner is not now known, John Tyler being a common name among the Virginia Tyler families. There was a John Tyler Jr., son of President John Tyler, who was born in 1819 and died in 1896. No records have been found to indicate whether or not he ever lived in the Radford area.

More likely this John Tyler is a member of the family referred to as "Tylers of Richmond City" in Lyon Gardiner Tyler's extensive writings of 1896[74]. Rev. John Tyler, born in 1742, was ordained in the Church of England and, in 1769, became rector of Christ Episcopal Church in Norwich, Connecticut. His grandson,

---

[73] The surname "Tallant" was misspelled as "Fallant" in the 1880 United States Census.
[74] Lyon Gardiner Tyler, son of President John Tyler, wrote three volumes on *The Letters and Times of The Tylers*, one published in 1884, one published in 1885, and one published in 1896.

John H. Tyler, settled in Richmond, Virginia, before the Civil War. John H. Tyler had three sons by the names of John Tyler, James Tyler, and Henry Tyler, all of whom were residing in Richmond in 1896. This John Tyler who briefly transferred in 1887 to St. James' Episcopal Mission Chapel in Central Depot / Radford from Monumental Church in Richmond was likely the son of John H. Tyler.

According to family historian Lyon Gardiner Tyler, the families of President John Tyler (i.e. "Tylers of York, James City, and Charles City Counties), of John H. Tyler (i.e. "Tylers of Richmond City"), and of Radford resident and Virginia Governor James Hoge Tyler (i.e. "Tylers of Essex and Caroline Counties") shared a common ancestry. The direct lines of these familial lineages were not drawn in L. G. Tyler's writings.

Given the importance of the Tyler family in Virginia, both in the Presbyterian and Episcopal faiths as well as on the state and national political stage, the lineage of United States President John Tyler is of interest and import herein. The John Tyler lineage is as follows: [John Tyler > John Tyler Jr. > Gov. John Tyler III > Pres. John Tyler (IV) > Lyon Gardiner Tyler > John Tyler].

1) John Tyler 1st Generation (circa 1684-circa 1728). He was a grandson of Ann and Henry Tyler (born circa 1604), and one of six children of Elizabeth Chiles and Henry Tyler Jr. Henry Tyler Jr. was a church warden and vestryman at Bruton Parish. John Tyler married Elizabeth (maiden surname unclear[75]). They had seven children: John Tyler (who died in 1714), John Tyler Jr. (born around 1715), Joanna Tyler, Elizabeth Low Tyler, Mary Tyler, Edith Tyler, and Anne Tyler.

    a. John Tyler Jr. 2nd Generation (circa 1715-1773). This son of Elizabeth and John Tyler was born during the early 1700s and

---

[75] Lyon Gardiner Tyler, in *The Letters and Times of the Tylers*, surmises that the wife of John Tyler Jr. was Elizabeth Low, noting that one of their daughters was named Elizabeth Low Tyler after her mother. Other sources list this wife of John Tyler Jr. as Elizabeth Jarrett.

prior to 1727. He married Anne Contesse, who was born around 1718. She was the daughter of Mary Morris and Dr. Louis Contesse. Anne Contesse and John Tyler Jr. had seven children: Mary Tyler, Elizabeth Tyler, Rachel Tyler, Anne Tyler, Louis Tyler, John Tyler, and Joanna Tyler. Additional information on their son John Tyler III follows.

    i. John Tyler III 3rd Generation (1747-1813), son of Anne Contesse and John Tyler III. John Tyler III was born on February 28, 1747. He attended the College of William and Mary in Williamsburg, Virginia. He married Mary Marot Armistead, daughter of Anne Shields and Robert Booth Armistead. They had eight children. Tyler served in the colonial army during the Revolutionary War. Interested in the politics of his country and of his state, John Tyler III served as a Governor of Virginia from December 1808 until around January 1811. He then served as a United States District Court Judge until his death on January 6, 1813. One of his children, also named John Tyler, would follow in his footsteps as a Governor of Virginia and go on to become the President of the United States. The eight children of Mary Marot Armistead and John Tyler were Anne Tyler, Elizabeth Tyler, Martha Jefferson Tyler, Maria Henry Tyler, Watt Henry Tyler, John Tyler, William Tyler, and Christiana Tyler. Their son John would follow in his father's footsteps as a Governor of

Virginia and then go on to become the President of the United States. His biography and descendants are as follows:

1. <u>John Tyler IV</u> 4th Generation (1790-1862), son of Mary Marot Armistead and John Tyler III. John Tyler IV was born on the Greenway Plantation in Charles City County, Virginia, on March 29, 1790. He was a member of the Episcopal church. Tyler graduated from the College of William and Mary (his father's alma mater) in 1807, and later became a lawyer at a Richmond law firm. He also participated in a long political career. He served in the Virginia House of Delegates and was a state legislator from 1811-1816, was an army captain during the War of 1812, and served in the United States House of Representatives from 1816-1821. Like his father before him, he served as a Governor of Virginia. Gov. John Tyler IV's term ran from 1825-1827. He served as a Senator from Virginia from 1827-1836. In 1813, John Tyler IV married Letitia Christian (born 1790); they had eight children before her death in 1842. In 1840, he ran on the Whig ticket with William Henry Harrison for President

and John Tyler IV for Vice President. Their slogans were "Log Cabin and Hard Cider" and "Tippecanoe and Tyler Too". They won the election. President Harrison caught pneumonia during his presidential address and died shortly thereafter, with John Tyler succeeding him as President. Thus John Tyler IV became the tenth President of the United States, serving from 1841 through 1845. Tyler kept President Harrison's cabinet, and did not have a Vice President. He was called the "Accidental President" and "His Accidency" based upon the manner in which he became President. When his wife Mrs. Letitia Christian Tyler died in 1842, Pres. John Tyler IV's acting First Lady was his daughter-in-law Priscilla Cooper Tyler (wife of the President's son Robert Tyler). Two years after the death of his first wife Letitia, President John Tyler IV married Julia Gardiner (born 1820) in 1844; they had seven children. After his one term as U. S. President, the Tylers returned to Richmond, Virginia. He was a member of the Richmond Convention proceeding the Civil War, where he advocated for reconciliation between the North and South. When those efforts were unsuccessful, he became a proponent of Southern secession. President John Tyler died seventeen years later, on January 18, 1862, and was buried at Richmond's Hollywood Cemetery. The widow Mrs. Julia Gardiner Tyler lived another twenty-seven years, dying in 1889. The children of John Tyler IV were as follows.

   a. Mary Tyler 5th Generation (1815-1848), daughter of Letitia Christian and President John Tyler IV.

   b. Robert Tyler 5th Generation (1816-1877), son of Letitia Christian and President John Tyler IV. He married Elizabeth Priscilla Cooper (called Priscilla), who functioned as the First Lady of the United States during her father-in-law's Presidency.

   c. John Tyler Jr. 5th Generation (1819-1896), son of Letitia Christian and President John Tyler IV. Although he was the fifth "John Tyler", he was known as "John Tyler Jr." He may have married Martha Rochelle.

d. Letitia Tyler 5th Generation (1821-1907), daughter of Letitia Christian and President John Tyler IV.

e. Elizabeth Tyler 5th Generation (1823-1850), daughter of Letitia Christian and President John Tyler IV.

f. Anne Contesse Tyler 5th Generation (1825), daughter of Letitia Christian and President John Tyler IV.

g. Alice Tyler 5th Generation (1827-1854), daughter of Letitia Christian and President John Tyler IV.

h. Tazewell Tyler 5th Generation (1830-1874), son of Letitia Christian and President John Tyler IV. He may have married Nannie Bridges.

i. David Gardiner Tyler 5th Generation (1846-1927), son of Julia Gardiner and President John Tyler IV. He was also known as D. Gardiner Tyler. His maternal grandfather

was David Gardiner.
D. Gardiner Tyler
served in the Virginia
state legislature as a
Democrat, was a
United States Repre-
sentative from 1893
through 1897, and a
Virginia state judge.
Upon his death in
1927, he was buried
in Richmond's Holly-
wood cemetery.

j. John Alexander Tyler
5th Generation (1849-
1871), son of Julia
Gardiner and Presi-
dent John Tyler IV.
Called Alex, he may
have married Sarah
Griswold Gardiner.

k. Julia Gardiner Tyler
5th Generation (1849-
1871), daughter of
Julia Gardiner and
President John Tyler
IV.

l. Lachlan Tyler 5th
Generation (1851-
1902), son of Julia
Gardiner and Presi-
dent John Tyler IV.

m. Lyon Gardiner Tyler
5th Generation (1853-
1935), son of Julia
Gardiner and Presi-
dent John Tyler IV.
He became President
of the College of Wil-
liam and Mary in Wil-

liamsburg, Virginia. He also wrote and published three volumes of Tyler family history, The Letters and Times of the Tylers. He married Annie Baker Tucker. They had three children: Julia Gardiner Tyler (1881), Elizabeth gilmer Tyler (1885), and John Tyler (1887).

n. Robert Fitzwalter Tyler 5th Generation (1856-1927), son of Julia Gardiner and President John Tyler IV. He was called Fitz.

o. Pearl Tyler 5th Generation (1860-1947), daughter of Julia Gardiner and President John Tyler IV.

Wallace, W. W.
Circa 1800s

W. W. Wallace and his wife Emily were Grace Episcopal Mission Chapel communicants in 1885. They lived in the East Ward on Radford on Railroad Avenue. Mrs. Emily Wallace (maiden surname not now known) may have died in 1889. Emily and W. W. Wallace had at least one child: Eugenia Sue Wallace was born during the 1800s was listed as an Episcopal communicant at least in 1885.

Wharton, Gabriel Colvin
1824-1906

General Gabriel Colvin Wharton settled in the present-day Radford area after the Civil War. In 1863 he married Anne Rebecca Radford, a member of the family for whom the City of Radford would be named.

Gabriel Colvin Wharton was born in Culpeper County, Virginia, on July 23, 1824. His parents were Eliza Hansbrough Colvin and John Redd Wharton. He graduated from Virginia Military Institute with a degree in civil engineering in 1847. Like so many of his peers, his military career took a different track than that anticipated prior to the country's Civil War. Gabriel Colvin Wharton joined the Army of the Confederate States of America and distinguished himself as a Brigadier General. His "Wharton's Brigade" distinguished themselves in battle and protected supply lines in western Virginia.

General Wharton married Anne Rebecca Radford, called "Nannie". Nannie was born on August 15, 1843. Her parents were Elizabeth Campbell Taylor and John Blair Radford. Anne Rebecca Radford was twenty years old when she married thirty-nine year old Gabriel Colvin Wharton. The wedding ceremony was held at the Radford family home, Arnheim, on May 14, 1863.

After the War, the Whartons settled in Central Depot (i.e. present-day Radford). The General built a home in the western section of the settlement during the 1870s. He named his home "Glencoe".

Wharton had interests in land development and in the establishment of railroad lines through southwestern Virginia. He owned land on both sides of the river in the areas that today are a part of Radford City and Pulaski County, Virginia. As the Virginia-Tennessee expanded to and through Central Depot, Wharton sold some of his land across the river for the railroad to build a depot and bridge. He then developed much of that surrounding land across the river that would become known as New River Depot. The New River Depot became locally known as "General Wharton's Town" because of his involvement in its development, just as his wife's involvement in the establishment of an Episcopal chapel named St. John's Episcopal Mission Chapel in New River Depot earned it the nickname of "Mrs. Wharton's Church".

General Wharton founded the New River Railroad, Mining, and Manufacturing Company which in 1883 carried coal and iron ore from Central Depot to Bluefield, Virginia. An industrious and loyal Virginian, General Wharton served in the Virginia Legislature. Among other things he supported the Morrill Land Grant Act which established the Virginia Polytechnic Institute in Montgomery County.

The 1870 United States Census described Wharton as a white forty-six year old civil engineer living with his twenty-six year old wife Ann (i.e. Mrs. Anne "Nannie" Rebecca Radford Wharton) and his six-year old son William. The 1880 Census described him as a fifty-two year old farmer who was the Head of Household in the Auburn District of Montgomery County. His wife was thirty-six year old Nannie R. Wharton and his son was fifteen-year old William R. Wharton. Also living in the home as a boarder was a twenty-two year old teacher named A. B. Meade and two student boarders: sixteen year old William L. Priven and eighteen year old Edgar P. Eskridge. This student was Edgar Peyton Eskridge, son of Mary Jane Smith Taylor and James Edgar Eskridge, who was reported in the same 1880 Census as living with the Eskridge family and was described as a student. Mr. Meade was providing instruction to William Priven, Edgar Eskridge, and William Wharton in the Wharton family home.

The Wharton family reported another boarder, twenty-two year old civil engineer named John B. Radford, who was a civil engineer. It is probable that this young man was the son of John Blair Radford's brother Captain Winston Radford who married Anne Marie Norvell; Captain Winston Radford was killed during the Battle of Manassas in 1861. Their son John B. Radford would have been Mrs. Nannie Radford Wharton's cousin.

Mrs. Anne Rebecca Radford Wharton died at the young age of forty-seven from pneumonia on April 15, 1890. She was buried on April 17, 1890 at the "Old Radford Cemetery" (i.e. Radford Family Cemetery), with the Rev. Edward Lewis Goodwin officiating.

In 1891, General Wharton was still living in Radford's West Ward on Wadsworth Street (i.e. living at Glencoe). His son William R. Wharton and family were living there as well. The Whartons were listed in Episcopal church records as communicants in March 1891, General Wharton being described as an "old communicant of St. John's church, New River Depot". Gabriel C. Wharton was a member of the Montgomery Episcopal Parish vestry and a member of the committee to petition the Episcopal Diocese for a division of the parish. When new boundary lines were drawn and the parishes of Montgomery and Radford were formed, his son William R. Wharton was elected to be a member of the Radford Episcopal Parish vestry. William declined, and General Wharton agreed on June 8, 1891 to serve on the vestry "in his stead".

Wharton was active in his community throughout his life. His name was listed in an 1892 copy of the *Radford Advance* newspaper as the contact person for his civic group as follows: "Glen OE Lodge, U.D., G. C. Wharton, W.M..".

General Wharton died on May 10, 1906 at the age of eighty-two. He was buried in the Radford Family Cemetery. Markers in the Radford Family Cemetery read "Anne Rebecca Wharton, Born Aug. 15, 1843, Died Apr. 15, 1890" and "Genl. G. C. Wharton, C.S.A., Aged 82 years. Erected by Wharton Camp C. V., sister and niece, September 29, 1918". A memorial gift to the new Grace Episcopal Parish House fund was made by Mr. and Mrs. William Radford Wharton in memory of Mrs. and General Gabriel Colvin Wharton.

During the late 1900s, Glencoe was turned into the Radford City's museum and was named "Glencoe Museum". For those who like to ponder ghost stories, it is said that the General, who was very particular in life about his home and its construction, could be heard walking the stairs and hallways during the 1997 and 1998 renovations of Glencoe. Anne Rebecca Radford and Gabriel Colvin Wharton had one child: William Radford Wharton (1864), of whom more.

The paternal lineage of Gabriel Colvin Wharton was as follows (George Wharton > George Wharton Jr. > George Wharton III > Samuel Wharton > John Redd Wharton > Gabriel Colvin Wharton).

216

1) <u>George Wharton</u> 1ˢᵗ Generation (1617-1681). George Wharton and his wife had children, including:

a) <u>George Wharton Jr.</u> 2ⁿᵈ Generation (circa 1600s). George Wharton Jr. and his wife Lee had children:

i) <u>George Wharton III</u> 3ʳᵈ Generation (circa 1600s), son of Lee and George Wharton. He was born around the late 1600s and died around 1770. He married Elizabeth Alsop of South Carolina. Elizabeth Alsop and George Wharton III had children:

(1) <u>John Wharton</u> 4ᵗʰ Generation (circa 1700s), son of Elizabeth Alsop and George Wharton III.

(2) <u>Joseph Wharton</u> 4ᵗʰ Generation (1734), son of Elizabeth Alsop and George Wharton III. He was born in 1734 and died at the age of forty in 1774.

(3) <u>William Wharton</u> 4ᵗʰ Generation (1736), son of Elizabeth Alsop and George Wharton III. He was born in 1736. He and his wife (name not now known) had at least one child:

(a) <u>Gabriella Wharton</u> 5ᵗʰ Generation (circa 1700s), daughter of Mr. and Mrs. William Wharton.

(4) <u>George Wharton IV</u> 4ᵗʰ Generation (1737), son of Elizabeth Alsop and George Wharton III. He was born in 1737 and died at the age of fifty-three in 1790.

(5) <u>Zachary Wharton</u> 4ᵗʰ Generation (1738), son of Elizabeth Alsop and George Wharton III. He was born in 1738 and died at the age of forty-two in 1780.

(6) <u>Samuel Wharton</u> 4ᵗʰ Generation (1761-1841), son of Elizabeth Alsop and George Wharton III. He was born on July 27, 1761 and died on December 11, 1841 at the age of eighty. He married Letitia Hutchinson (also spelled Hutcheson). She was born in Spotsylvania County, Virginia in 1762 and

died in Culpepper County, Virginia in 1864. They had children:

(a) Sarah Wharton 5th Generation (1794), daughter of Letitia Hutchinson and Samuel Wharton.

(b) John Redd Wharton 5th Generation (1796), son of Letitia Hutchinson and Samuel Wharton. He was born on January 1, 1796 in Louisa County, Virginia and died in Culpeper County on August 1, 1868. He married Eliza Hansbrough Colvin in Culpeper County on June 6, 1823. She was born on January 7, 1803 and died on June 16, 1873. Eliza Hansbrough Colvin and John Redd Wharton had children:

(i) Gabriel Colvin Wharton 6th Generation (1824), son of Eliza Hansbrough Colvin and John Redd Wharton. He was born on July 23, 1824 and died on May 10, 1906. He married Anne Rebecca Radford. She was born on August 15, 1843 and died on April 15, 1890. Anne Rebecca Radford and Gabriel Colvin Wharton had one child:

1. William Radford Wharton 7th Generation (1864), son of Anne Rebecca Radford and Gabriel Colvin Wharton. He was born on June 11, 1864 and died on May 16, 1918. He married Susan Hammet Heth, daughter of Isabella Hammet and Stockton Heth. She was born on August 23, 1868 and died on May 17, 1958. Susan Hammet and William Radford Wharton had children:

a. Stockton Heth Wharton 8th Generation (1892), son of Susan Hammet and William Radford Wharton.

b. Anne Rebecca Radford Wharton 8th Generation (1894), daughter of Susan Hammet and William Radford Wharton.

c. William Radford Wharton Jr. 8th Generation (1904), son of Susan Hammet and William Radford Wharton. He was born on March 3, 1904 and died on May 27, 1990. He married Evelyn (maiden surname not now known). They had children: Sue Wharton and Sally Wharton (who married Frith van Solkema).

(ii) Letitia E. Wharton 6th Generation (1825), daughter of Eliza Hansbrough Colvin and John Redd Wharton.

(iii) Mary Amelia Wharton 6th Generation (1831), daughter of Eliza Hansbrough Colvin and John Redd Wharton.

(iv) Eliza J. Wharton 6th Generation (1834), daughter of Eliza Hansbrough Colvin and John Redd Wharton.

(v) Sallie B. Wharton 6th Generation (1835), daughter of Eliza Hansbrough Colvin and John Redd Wharton.

(vi) Emma Frances Wharton 6th Generation (1838), daughter of Eliza Hansbrough Colvin and John Redd Wharton.

(vii)   Nannie B. Wharton 6th Generation (1840), daughter of Eliza Hansbrough Colvin and John Redd
Wharton.

(viii)   Mattie Wharton 6th Generation
(circa 1800s), daughter of Eliza
Hansbrough Colvin and John Redd
Wharton.

(ix) John James Wharton 6th Generation (1845), son of Eliza Hansbrough Colvin and John Redd
Wharton.

(c) William Wharton 5th Generation (1800),
son of Letitia Hutchinson and Samuel
Wharton.

(d) Malcolm Hart Wharton 5th Generation
(1805), son of Letitia Hutchinson and
Samuel Wharton.

(e) Samuel Wharton Jr. 5th Generation
(1808), son of Letitia Hutchinson and
Samuel Wharton.

(f) Permelia Wharton 5th Generation (circa
1800s), daughter of Letitia Hutchinson
and Samuel Wharton.

(g) Susan Wharton 5th Generation (circa
1800s), daughter of Letitia Hutchinson
and Samuel Wharton.

(h) Lavinia Wharton 5th Generation (circa
1800s), daughter of Letitia Hutchinson
and Samuel Wharton.

(i) Joseph Powell Wharton 5th Generation
(circa 1800s), son of Letitia Hutchinson
and Samuel Wharton.

(j) Amelia Wharton 5th Generation (circa
1800s), daughter of Letitia Hutchinson
and Samuel Wharton.

(k) Betsy Wharton 5th Generation (circa
1800s), daughter of Letitia Hutchinson
and Samuel Wharton.

(l) <u>Huldah Wharton</u> 5th Generation (circa 1800s), daughter of Letitia Hutchinson and Samuel Wharton.

ii) <u>Thomas Wharton</u> 3rd Generation (circa 1600s), son of Lee and George Wharton.

iii) <u>Jesse Wharton</u> 3rd Generation (circa 1600s), son of Lee and George Wharton.

iv) <u>John Wharton</u> 3rd Generation (circa1600s), son of Lee and George Wharton.

v) <u>Samuel Wharton</u> 3rd Generation (circa 1600s), son of Lee and George Wharton. May also have been known as Joseph Wharton.

Illustration 30: General Gabriel Colvin Wharton. Courtesy of Glencoe Museum / Radford Heritage Foundation.

Illustration 31: Mrs. Anne Rebecca Radford Wharton. Both photos Courtesy of Mrs. Sally Wharton van Solkema.

Illustration 32: General Gabriel Colvin Wharton.

CHAPTER FIVE: THE END OF A CENTURY, 1888-1900

Settlement and Organization

"Be it enacted by the General Assembly of Virginia, That the territory contained within the limited prescribed and herein designated as follows, viz:

Beginning at a point where Plum creek empties into New river, thence in a southerly direction to the intersection of Auburn and Euclid[76] avenues on the lands of the South Radford Land and Improvement[77], thence passing west of the house of M. Gibson, due south to the south side of the old National turnpike, and with the south side of the same to a point opposite the western boundary line of the Radford West End Land Company's property, thence with said boundary line to New River, and with New River to the beginning, be deemed and taken as the City of Radford, and the inhabitants of the City of Radford, for all purposes for which towns and cities are incorporated in this Commonwealth, shall continue to be one body, politic in fact and in name, under the style and denomination of the City of Radford, and as such shall have, exercise and enjoy all

[76] Note: boundary avenue intersections described in Virginia Acts of Assembly as "intersection of Auburn avenue and Commerce avenue" and in Radford City Charter as "intersection of Auburn and Euclid avenues".

[77] See Acts of Assembly, Virginia, Session of 1891-1892, pages 131-155 "An Act to incorporate the city of Radford" , approved, January 22, 1892, and pages 926-934 "An Act to amend the charter of the city of Radford", approved January 22, 1892" approved on March 2, 1892.

the rights, powers and privileges, and be subject to all the duties and obligations now incumbent and pertaining to said city as a municipal corporation. It having been ascertained that there now exists over five thousand population within the said limits."

Charter and General Ordinances of the City of Radford. Compiled by Ordinance Committee, By Order of Council. 1892; ordinances effective April 1, 1892.

The nineteenth century drew to a close with a new city incorporated, new businesses chartered, new and consolidated railroad companies, new residents altering the landscape of the population, and, along the way, economic dips and peaks. Town trolleys became a popular means of public transportation. The first automobile changed the face of travel in 1893and the first subway further enhanced the public's mobility in 1898.

Locally, the railroad's convenience effected both travel and commerce. Trains were used both for travel and for mail transport. Lovely Mount Tavern was abandoned, and the stagecoach no longer stopped in the Lovely Mount or Central Depot area. The Post Office was moved to Central City in 1888.

The railroad expanded its operations beyond Central City, building another depot and station around 1889 or 1890 in the west end of the settlement (i.e. eastern section of the Montgomery County Auburn District). That station was known as the Randolph Street Station. A bridge across the New River was built to the east of the station by the Radford Land and Improvement Company. That bridge became known as the Iron Bridge, the Wagon Bridge, and the Toll Bridge. The bridge officially opened on September 7, 1891.

By 1890, the La Belle Inn was open in the East End near Heth Grove and the current location of Radford University and, by 1891, the Radford Inn graced the hill directly to the east of the

Randolph Street Station. South of and behind the station was the Bee Hive Department Store.

Between 1890 and 1891, the Radford Trust Company built headquarters for their new enterprise on the corner of First and Fairfax (i.e. Harvey) Streets, fronting First Street. The 25,000 square foot bank building sported chestnut floors, chestnut stairway railings, decorative limestone columns with "Radford Trust" engraved in the corner column at First and Fairfax, two bay windows with fancy metalwork around the exterior, prominent arched windows, and a second floor porch. A plaque by the walk-in vault in the first floor Radford Trust offices still sports the "Radford Trust" name today. W. H. Galway was Cashier for the Radford Trust Company, and associates included Philadelphia attorneys Logan M. Bullitt and Joseph I. Doran.

The East End sported the La Belle Inn, and the Hotel Shere was built across from the east ward train depot during the 1890s. The Radford Inn near the west end train depot was lost in a fire. The Radford Trust building housed not only the bank offices but the West End Hotel. Hotel porters escorted guests up the hill from the depot, a livery stable was located down the road, and across the street from the West End Hotel, on Arlington, were the trolley barns. Trolley tracks extended from the west end Foundry to the east end train depot. The family of William Marshall Delp lived at the West End Hotel. Mr. Delp worked at the Hotel Shere before purchasing the West End Hotel in 1904 and operating it as the Delp Hotel; William Marshall Delp would later become a Mayor of Radford.

The Town of Central Depot and adjacent section of Auburn in Montgomery County became the incorporated City of Radford in January 1892, having reached a population of 5,000 residents.

The Town's namesake, Dr. John Blair Radford, had passed away in 1872. His son, the Honorable James Lawrence Radford, was in 1891 a Montgomery County representative to the Virginia House of Delegates. J. L. Radford contributed his efforts to obtaining a charter for the town to become a city. Members of the Radford Charter Committee were James Lawrence Radford, J. W. Marshall, Hugh Caperton Preston, William Radford Wharton, Samuel Harris Hoge, and Robert Jackson Noell. Attorney G. E. Cassel took the charter for the city to Richmond where, with Delegate J. L. Radford's assistance in obtaining a speedy enactment, the charter was approved on January 22, 1892.

George A. Sullivan, as acting mayor of the new city, appointed four residents to act as city officials. Capt. Ambrose Robinson became City Treasurer and Capt. Stockton Heth was appointed to be the Clerk of Court. In addition, J. M. Fisher was appointed as City Sergeant and J. W. Hopkins became Commissioner of Revenue.

Hugh Caperton Preston was elected by the people in 1892 to serve a two-year term as Mayor which would expire on June 30, 1894. Also elected by the people were S. H. Hoge to serve as Commonwealth's Attorney until June 30, 1894, J. M. Fisher to serve as City Sergeant until June 30, 1894, and A. T. Caldwell to serve as Constable through June 30, 1894.

Arthur Roberts replaced Stockton Heth as Clerk of Court. Roberts was elected by the people to serve a term of six years expiring on June 3, 1898. The Honorable G. E. Cassel served as Judge. Cassel was elected by the Legislature to serve a six year term expiring on February 5, 1898.

J. W. Hopkins was elected by the people to serve a two year term as Commissioner of the Revenue. Ambrose Robinson was elected by the people to serve a three-year term as City Treasurer.

The Virginia Acts of Assembly in January 1892 and March 1892 appointed the first city council to serve until May 1892 elections could be held as follows. The six East Ward appointed councilmen were named as G. T. Kearsley, H. P. Briggs, E. F. Gill, J. P. Kelly, G. W. Tyler, and D. V. Sturdevan. Members from the East Ward on the first elected council were George T. Kearsley, Henrick Parsons Briggs, Emmett F. Gill, as before, and new councilmen Robert Jackson Noell (spelled Noel in the 1892 city charter), W. W. McElrath, and Walter R. Roberts.

The six West Ward appointed councilmen were J. H. Washington, C. A. Biencampen *[sic]*, W. I. *(corrected to W. J.)* Kenderdine, H. H. Powers, W. R. Whorton *[sic]*, and J. D. Moffett. The elected West Ward members were John Henry Washington, Charles A. Bienkampen, Warner Justice Kenderdine, Harry Hazard Powers, and William Radford Wharton, as before, and new councilman Lewis Harvey. John Henry Washington was elected to be President of the new City Council of Radford.

The Council then acted to appoint city officials. Two-year terms expiring on June 30, 1894 were to be served by R. L. Jordan as both Clerk of the Council and as City Auditor, and S. H. Hoge as City Attorney (who was also elected by the people to serve as Commonwealth's Attorney). Dr. L. B. Moore was appointed as the City Physician and Physician to the Alms House. The Board of School Trustees was comprised of J. D. Peters (who had been appointed Justice of the Peace of the East Ward prior to city elections), E. S. Jones, and S. H. W. Lucas.

The Superintendent of Public Schools had not been appointed when the City Charter was published. Also pending appointments were the offices of City Engineer, Superintendent of the Market, Chief Engineer of the Fire Department, Health Committee, Keeper of the city Cemetery, Board of Overseers of the Poor, and Superintendent of the Alms House.

Law enforcement persons appointed through the Virginia Assembly were R. T. Smith as city constable, J. D. Peters as Justice of the Peace for the East Ward, and W. W. Boswell as Justice of the Peace for the West Ward. Upon elections, J. M. Fisher became Chief of Police, W. W. Boswell became the Justice of the Peace for the East Ward (having been listed as a West Ward justice by the Virginia Assembly) and I. B. Adams became Justice of the Peace for the West Ward. Members of the Council's Police Committee were Charles A. Bienkampen, R. J. Noel, and W. R. Wharton.

The Fire Committee members were H. H. Powers, George T. Kearsley (incorrectly listed as C. T. Kearsley in the city charter), and Lewis Harvey. Council committees were as follows: Kenderdine, Beinkampen, Wharton and Harvey on West Ward Standing Committee; Noel, Gill, Roberts and Briggs on East Ward Standing committee; Noel, Beinkampen, and Wharton of Committee On Accounts; Beinkampen, Noel, and Wharton of Committee On Police; Powers, Kearsley and Harvey of Committee On Fire; Kearsley, Kenderdine, and Harvey of Committee On Streets; Roberts, Kearsley, and Beinkampen of Committee On Sewerage; Kenderdine, Briggs and Kearsley of Committee On Public Property; Gill, Noel and Kenderdine of Committee On Finance; Wharton, Roberts, and Powers of Committee On Ordinance; Harvey, McElrath, and Powers of Committee On Light; McElrath, Roberts and Powers of Committee On Sanitary; Briggs, Kenderdine and McElrath of Committee On Water; and Washington, Gill and McElrath of Committee On Parks and Cemetery.

The City Council met every first and second Monday in each month, as announced in the 1892 *Radford Advance* newspaper along with the names of all office holders and council members. Also in 1892, a corporation or hustings *[sic]* court[78] was established in Radford with jurisdiction over probate, records, deeds, wills, contracts, and other cases at law or chancery. The clerk of the Radford School Board was authorized to conduct a census of all persons ages five through twenty-one residing in the new Radford school district.

The Radford Water and Light Company was incorporated on February 16, 1892 to furnish and supply water, light, power and heat in Montgomery County, Radford City, and adjacent towns, cities, or counties. The first Board of Directors included J. L. Radford, , W. W. Justice, Joseph I. Doran, Charles H. Mellon, F. J. Kimball, A. A. Phlegar, and J. H. Dingee. The incorporation of the Radford Water-Power Company was approved by the Virginia General Assembly on February 13, 1901. The act of incorporation described company goals to engage in a manufacturing business in Pulaski County, Montgomery County, and Radford City and operate mines, stone quarries, and street railways to enhance the provision of electricity and water to public and individual dwellings. The principal office of the corporation was in Radford City.

On March 1, 1892, "An Act to incorporate the Radford street railway company" was approved by the Virginia General Assembly. The Radford Street Railway Company was authorized to construct and operate a street railway on any streets or highways in Radford City, Montgomery County and Pulaski County, "for public conveyance of passengers by any power other than locomotive" and to collect tolls and fares. The incorporators were James L. Radford, W. W. Justice, Joseph I. Doran, Charles H. Mellon, William Ingles, J. Hoge Tyler, W. R. Wharton, and W. H. Barclay.

New railroad enterprises were also in the works. The Southwest Virginia Central Railroad Company was incorporated on

[78] Called Hastings Court in area records and Hustings court in Acts of Assembly, Virginia, Session 1891-1892.

February 2, 1892 by H. D. Ribble, Charles Kanode, N. R. Stanger, Robert Kirkwood, Ambrose Robinson, J. L. Radford, R. H. Adams, James W. Marshall, A. L. Boulware, Decatur Axtell, and William H. Palmer. The Radford and Little River Railroad Company formed in 1889 and 1890 applied for and received a two year extension from the 1890 incorporation for commencing construction on their railroad lines (until March 1892), and completion of their main line within five years of the 1890 incorporation date (until 1895).

In 1892, the Radford Pipe works, known as "The Foundry", began production. J. K. Dimmock established the Foundry. His home on the corner of Fairfax and Eighth Streets was designed by architect Frank Miles Day. The house still stands, purchased by Betty and Lewis Harvey in 1906, and is known locally as "the Harvey House". Fairfax Street was renamed Harvey Street.

On a hill across the New River from Radford's West End Depot, a scholar named George Miles established the St. Albans Boys Academy. The exclusive preparatory school met the educational needs of residential and local students. It became known for its superior athletics program. The school also inspired new business, such as the tailor business of Mr. Garking. He specialized in making and maintaining the boys' uniforms.

During the early 1890s, John G. Osborne built a three-story home on the corner of Second and Randolph Streets. Osborne was a real estate developer, and insurance salesman, and Radford Superintendent for the railroad.

William Ingles, known as "Captain Billy", designed and built a large mansion on the south side of the New River in 1892. Named La Riviere, his home included ten large rooms, numerous smaller rooms or cubicles, and a grand winding staircase of cherry. He spared no expense, including solid cherry woodwork, silver doorknobs, and elaborate furnishings. The evening before he and his wife were to take up residence, a devastating fire destroyed the interior and its furnishings including china and silver already in the house. Despite the loss, Ingles presented his original plans to a contractor and had his La Riviere rebuilt. It was finished in 1893 and, while lacking the elaborate cherry woodwork, it included William Ingles' plans such as window shutters that slid into the wall when opened, a Dutch front door that opened separately top

229

and bottom like a stable door, a curved radiator tucked into the stairwell, a parlor push button bell for summoning servants, a large wraparound porch, and a side tower earning it the local nickname of "Ingles Castle".

All was not business, however. The residents of the young city made time for leisure activities. On February 4, 1892, the General Assembly approved the incorporation of the Montgomery Club of Radford. The Montgomery Club was organized "for the promotion of social intercourse and for the purpose of maintaining a library and reading room". Its incorporators and first officers were John G. Osborne, Robert Kirkwood, R. H. Adams, William Ingles, James N. Norfleet, A. P. Page, M. C. Jamison Jr., D. H. Barger, and W. H. Galway.

The Radford Wheelmen club was approved for incorporation one month later, on March 4, 1982, "for the purpose of the mutual enjoyment of its members in the pursuit of cycling as a pastime; the promotion by force of example of the use of the bicycle or similar machines, as practical and enjoyable aids to locomotion, the advancement of cycling interests generally, including the awakening of greater interest in better roads and the promotion of good fellowship and comfort among its members". The incorporators and first officers were Warner J. Kenderdine, Melmmoth M. Osborne, William W. Darnell, Richard H. Lytle, George W. McGregor, Arthur Roberts, Joseph R. Kemp, Charles M. Caldwell, and Theodore Labrum.

During the early and mid-1800s, the local guard company was called the Radford Rifles. Local residents raised money to support the guard, including one production of Gilbert and Sullivan's comic opera "H. M. S. Pinafore" in which citizens comprised the cast of characters. Held at Randolph Hall in the early 1890s, cast members included H. H. Powers as Sir Joseph Porter, H. C. Preston as Captain Corcoran, Prof. E. Z. Moyer as Dick Deadeye, and A. Owen as the Boatswain.

W. L. Wardle, author, described Radford's advantages in 1892 as a central point both between major cities and the main line of the Norfolk and Western Railroad. He suggested that Radford City would fall in the middle of an "X" intersection drawn on a map given a northwest to southeast line drawn from Chicago, Illinois to Wilmington, North Carolina and a northeastern to southwestern line drawn from New York, New York to New Orleans, Louisiana. He further described Radford's location on the main railroad line from Norfolk, Virginia to Bristol, Tennessee as being in the center of a mineral "storehouse" of coal and iron ore.

By 1892 Radford had three miles of macadamized streets, a water works plant and fifteen miles of water pipes, a public library established through the Doran Library Association, two public schools (Belle Heth Academy named in honor of Mrs. Isabella Hammet Heth and the Radford school, i.e. Wadsworth Academy), and an institution of higher learning called the Radford Female Seminary. A boys' preparatory school called the St. Albans Academy would be established across the river from Radford during the 1890s. Four church buildings had been erected in Radford, with an additional two under construction.

Banking businesses were housed in the Radford Trust Company building and in the three-story Radford Bank Building, according to Wardle. The Ashmead block of buildings housed stores and apartments. The Randolph Building provided store spaces as well as a stage and anterooms. The Sill block housed railroad offices and a telegraph office. The Radford Pipe Foundry Company in the West Ward employed four hundred workers.

A financial "Panic of 1893" foreshadowed a stall in the young city's economic boon. The American currency was based upon a set value at which currency could be exchanged for gold. During and leading up to 1893, so many people exchanged their currency for gold that the federal reserve reached its allowable limit on gold reserves withdrawal. Silver prices fell. In addition, major railroads including the Philadelphia and Reading Railroad, the Northern Pacific Railway, the Union Pacific Railway, and the Atchison Topeka & Santa Fe Railroad failed. The nation did not begin to rally until 1896.

A bridge over Connelly's Run was finally completed, joining the east and west wards of Radford. As Radford citizens sought to continue the building of their city, those efforts were not without tragedy. In 1894, the bridge being built over Connelly's Run to collapsed. Six workmen were killed and two were injured. That same day, the Bibb Hotel was destroyed by fire. Citizens, firemen and rescue personnel split their services between the two disasters.

231

Citizens were resilient. New hotels and the anticipated bridge were built. Local newspapers kept the community informed about local and national issues. Newspapers of the 1890s included the *Radford Advance, the New Democrat,* and the *Radford Enterprise.* The Democrat Job Office produced its daily and weekly paper and offered printing services for businesses and authors. Merchants and professionals plied their trade and advertised in these local papers.

A. I. Harless and Vaughan had a law office in the Briggs Building. George E. Cassell and William Radford Wharton had their own separate law offices as well. Dr. John W. Farmer was a local physician and Dr. F. J. Welch was a dentist. Lewis Washington Clark advertised as both an optician and a jeweler. Drug stores included Radford Drug Company and G. W. Lyle & Brother Druggists and Pharmacists in East and West Radford. T. F. Kohlhousen's Novelties, Jewelry, and silverware. Wygal Drug Company on Norwood Street.

A number of merchants served the Radford community. East and West Ward stores included P. Simon's Clothing and Dry Goods Store, G. W. Tyler's Dry Goods and Grocery Store, C. F. Thomas' grocery store, S. M. Carter's grocery in East Radford, and J. W. Tinsley's Dry Goods and Notion on Norwood Street in East Radford. W. R. Roberts Co. sold general merchandise in East Radford. E. S. Jones and Bro. sold general merchandise as well. Clothing needs were met both by Ambrose Robinson in East Radford and by W. H. Bonnage & Sons. J. E. Lewton sold Willer Sliding Blinds and screen doors. T. F. Kohlhousen sold Novelties, Jewelry, and Silverware.

As new residents came to the area seeking land and housing, realtors, insurance agents, architects, and engineers were there to meet their needs. Those businessmen included architect and builder J. F. Tilly Jr., civil and mining engineer R. H. Kello, contractor and builder J. E. Parrish, and contractor and builder J. T. Stump. H. H. Powers & Co. located their realty and insurance company in Room 6 of the Trust Building in West Radford. Kearsley & Crockett also worked as general insurance agents. Land was available from companies such as the Radford Development Company with J. Hoge Tyler as President.

A variety of other businesses located in Radford. J. W. Lester operated the Daisy Saloon on Norwood Street, opposite Radford Drug Company. St. Greenspon advertised as a dealer in wine and whiskey. The business districts included New River Furniture Company in the Tyler Building in East Radford, Radford Furniture Company, Radford Steam Laundry, and G. C. Walker's Ice Cream Parlor located at "Arringdale's old stand". The city attracted three photographers: Hugh Mangum, W. A. Johnston with his New Photograph Gallery over J. W. Tinsley's store on Norwood Street in East Radford, and W. W. Darnell with his studio on Norwood Street. Jenkin's News Depot advertised business in both the East and West Wards.

The Radford Trust Company continued to operate a bank, as did the Exchange Bank of Radford and the Virginia Mutual Building and Loan Association. The board of the Virginia Mutual Building and Loan Association were James Hoge Tyler as President, G. E. Cassell as Attorney, S. W. Burton as Secretary and Treasurer, and R. J. Noell as Manager of the Loan Department.

James Hoge Tyler became Governor of Virginia in 1898. His home in Radford, called Halwyk and built around 1892, still stands as a historic landmark.

Radford City rallied after local tragedies and the national financial crash. It continued its corporate growth, but never realized the prosperity town fathers had anticipated when they projected that their community would become either "the Philadelphia of the South" or "the Pittsburgh of the South".

The Nineteenth Century ended with a new military conflict off the American shores. Cuba's citizens became engaged in a fight for self-rule, having been governed by Spain. Given a significant number of Americans living in the island country, the United States government sent a naval vessel to Cuba to protect its citizens there. The U.S.S. Maine exploded and sank in the Havana Harbor on February 2, 1898. This pulled American forces into the conflict. Americans joined Cubans in their successful fight for independence. A number of those American soldiers, including William Radford Wharton, Elliott Howe, Eugene Mundy, and Frank Cannaday, hailed from Central Depot, Virginia. The Spanish-American War ended in victory for the Americans and for the Cubans.

The city of Radford crossed into the Twentieth Century with more history to make and more residents to welcome.

Illustration 33: Map of downtown Radford, East Ward, by Radford Land and Improvement Company map of Central Depot business district, late 1800s. Courtesy of Hix Bondurant.

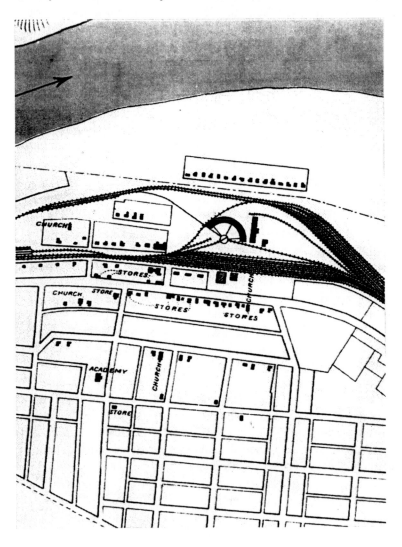

Illustration 34: RLIC map, late 1800s, showing location of west end train depot. Courtesy of Hix Bondurant.

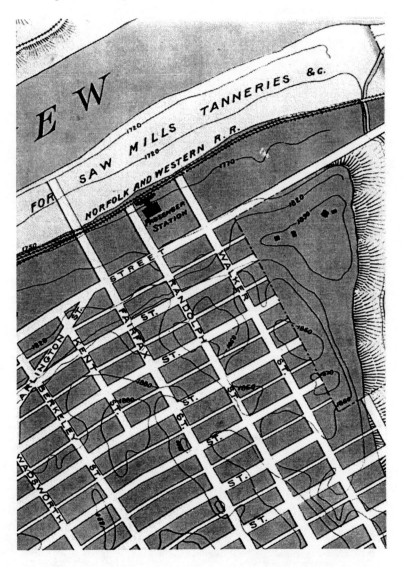

Illustration 35: The Radford Inn and the West End Train Depot (Randolph Street Station). Photo by W. W. Darnell. Collection of Jane and Ken Farmer.

Illustration 36: Radford City Courthouse, 1892.

Illustration 37: Radford Trust Building and West End Hotel. Courtesy of Helen Dickens.

Illustration 38: Bridge over Connelly's Run. Collection of Jane and Ken Farmer.

Illustration 39: The trolley ran from east end Radford to the foundry in the West End. Photo courtesy of Helen Dickens.

Illustration 40: Charter committee for the incorporation of Radford as a city. Members of the charter committee were J. L. Radford, J. W. Marshall, H. C. Preston, W. R. Wharton, S. H. Hoge, and R. J. Noell. Photo courtesy of Hix Bondurant.

Illustration 41: The 1892 first City Council of Radford, Virginia: G. T. Kearsley, R. J. Noell, H. P. Briggs, J. H. Washington (Pres.), C. A. Bienkampen, W. J. Kenderdine, H. H. Powers, W. R. Wharton, E. F. Gill, W. W. McElrath, W. R. Roberts, and L. Harvey.

Illustration 42: Captain John G. Osborne. Collection of Jane and Ken Farmer.

Illustration 43: The Osborne home. Photo by Joanne Spiers Moche.

Illustration 44: La Riviere, the Ingles home.

Illustration 45: Halwyk, the Tyler home.

Illustration 46: Bicycling became a popular sport nationally. W. W. Darnell was a member of the Radford Wheelmen. Collection of Jane and Ken Farmer.

Illustration 47: Warner Kenderdine and friends enjoy bicycling below the St. Albans Boys School. Courtesy of the Wilderness Road Regional Museum, Newbern.

Illustration 48: St. Albans Boys Academy, circa 1892. Courtesy of Glencoe Museum / Radford Heritage Foundation.

CHAPTER SIX: FAMILIES OF GRACE, 1888-1900

The Growth of Grace

The late 1800s was a time of change for those of the Episcopal faith in Radford. In 1890 the Grace Rectory was built in Radford's West Ward on Fourth Street near Fairfax Street. Stockton Heth, Ambrose Robinson, and John A. Wilson were trustees of St. James' Episcopal Mission Chapel when James Lawrence Radford deeded the original property for the planned West Ward chapel. Rev. Edward L. Goodwin served both St. James' and the new Grace Episcopal mission chapels.

St. James' Episcopal Mission Chapel in the East Ward became self-supporting in 1891, and the Radford Parish was designated by the Episcopal Diocese as a separate parish from Montgomery Parish in 1891. A new vestry was elected to conduct business for the new parish. Members of the first Radford Episcopal Parish vestry were Richard Henry Adams Jr., Dr. R. Bruce James, Dr. Aaron Jeffrey, George T. Kearsley, Warner Justice Kenderdine, Harry Hazard Powers, James Lawrence Radford, Ambrose Robinson, Charles W. Sanders, and William Radford Wharton. The treasurer was C. W. Sanders. The four trustees were Warner Justice Kenderdine, Aaron Jeffrey, William Francis Collins, and Charles W. Sanders.

The congregation supported each other and their rector when Rev. Goodwin's wife Maria died in the rectory at the age of forty-four on July 16, 1892. Rev. Goodwin thanked the parish ladies' society for their "remembrances to his wife". He resigned from his Radford Parish duties in September 1893.

Rev. Edward Lewis Goodwin led worship services at St. James' Episcopal Mission Chapel in the East Ward of Central Dept and at St. John's Episcopal Mission Chapel in New River Depot. Grace Episcopal Mission Chapel was built on Fourth Street in the West Ward of the Radford in 1892. Many parishioners of St. James' Episcopal Mission Chapel attended services both at St. James' and at Grace, often attending two worship services on the

245

same Sunday in order to participate as members of both congregations. Others chose one chapel and a rivalry of sorts grew.

Grace Episcopal Mission Chapel received new pews during 1891 or 1892 purchased by families of parishioners and an altar was donated by the Radford Land and Improvement Company, of which Episcopal parishioner Warner Justice Kenderdine was Superintendent. The first confirmation class was formed and confirmed that year, with Kenderdine's daughter Bess being a member of that first class.

Church services were advertised in the local newspaper, the Radford Advance, as follows.

> "EPISCOPAL CHURCH. Rev. E. L. Goodwin, rector. Services at St. James' church, Railroad Avenue, first and third and fifth Sundays at 11 o'clock a.m., on second, fourth Sundays at 7:30 o'clock p.m.; at Grace Chapel, fourth and Fairfax Streets, second and fourth Sundays at 11:00 o'clock a.m., first, third, and fifth Sundays at 7:30 o'clock p.m. Ushers will show strangers to seats. Sunday school every Sunday at the church at 9:30 a.m. Capt. A. Robinson, superintendent; at Grace Chapel, Sunday school and rector's bible class every Sunday at 8:30 p.m., Col. W. J. Kenderdine, superintendent."

Just as other denominations had allowed the Episcopal parishioners to use their church buildings prior to the erection of an Episcopal church building, so the Episcopal parishioners partnered with those of the Lutheran faith:

> "EVANGELICAL LUTHERAN CHURCH. Divine services will be conducted every 1st and 3rd Sunday at 11:00 o'clock a.m., in the Episcopal church. S. S. Rahn, pastor.

246

The Diocese of Virginia was again divided into two entities, one maintaining the designation of the Diocese of Virginia and the other being called the Diocese of Southern Virginia (of which Radford Parish was a part). The Rt. Rev. Alfred Magill Randolph became the first Bishop of the Episcopal Diocese of Southern Virginia in 1892.

Also in 1892, these early church leaders were among the first community leaders when the Town of Radford became the City of Radford. Eight of the twelve members of the first city council were members of the Episcopal congregations. Two of the first four appointed city officers were Episcopalians, as was the first President of the City Council and the first city physician.

Despite the financial crash of 1893, the Radford Episcopal Parish congregation worked tirelessly to raise money to pay the church debt and to pay the rector's salary. Rev. Goodwin was assisted by twenty-five female parishioners who were members of the Rector's Aid Society of Grace Chapel. They organized the Society on January 10, 1893 "to aid the Rector in the parish work, raise funds for the same, and cultivate good feeling, fellowship, and harmony in the Church".

They worked tirelessly to secure financial stability and purchase needed items the chapels. The ladies held "sociables" (more commonly referred to as "socials"), formal teas, suppers, ice cream sales, and bake sales to raise funds for the Chapel, as well as taking orders for "hand-sewn items". One project involved the creation and sale of a "comfortable" (i.e. "comforter"). Opening each meeting with a prayer, the ladies would discuss business and then "adjourn to devote the afternoon to sewing" with each member working on the project "for which they are best adapted, and most pleasing to themselves . . . crocheting, knitting, embroidery, fancy or plain sewing". They continued even when a March 1893 fire destroyed The Radford Inn, where a member of the Rector's Aid Society lived and held meetings and maintained the group's sewing materials. Those materials were lost in the 1893 fire. The women recouped their losses and continued to support their congregation. Proceeds from their many accomplishments were used to purchase church lamps, altar linens and cloths, and a memorial font for the Chapel, as well as contributing to the Chapel Fund.

The ladies of the parish raised funds to install lights at St. James' Chapel and Grace Chapel in 1894.

They also made it their role to extend acknowledgements and appreciation to those who performed certain services for the church, such as thanking Mr. J. G. Osborne for a donation of books, thanking "Mr. W. J. Kenderdine for the many kindnesses which he has extended to the Society", and, for "Mrs. Bibb", "a vote of thanks was tendered Mrs. Bibb for her kindness in presenting the Society with the linen for the Altar cloths for the Society". Their names were recorded by the Society secretary in elegant and formal script. The names of Married women were recorded in the society rolls and minutes as "Mrs." and the surname, it being inappropriate to record a matron's Christian name in the record. The names of unmarried ladies, however, were recorded as "Miss" followed by their Christian name and given surname.

Gentlemen of the church continued to tend to business and financial duties as members of the vestry. The 1893 Radford Parish Vestry included Allan J. Black, Frank L. Buck, William Wirt Darnell, Dr. R. Bruce James, Dr. Aaron Jeffrey, George T. Kearsley, Warner Justice Kenderdine, John G. Osborne, Charles W. Sanders, George A. Weisiger, and William Radford Wharton.

Rev. Edward Lewis Goodwin resigned his position as rector of Radford Episcopal Parish in September 1893. Mr. A. A. Pruden came to the parish as Deacon in Charge in 1894 after the resignation of Rev. Goodwin.

Frank L. Buck, William Wirt Darnell, Warner Justice Kenderdine, Dr. Aaron Jeffrey, and Charles W. Sanders continued to serve as vestrymen in 1894. Ambrose Robinson returned to the vestry after a one year break in service, as did James Lawrence Radford. John Andrew Wilson joined the vestry as a new member.

The ladies' Rector's Aid Society had been disbanded. It reorganized as the Ladies Chapel Fund Society a month after Rev. Pruden came to Grace. During his fifteen months of service, the Society raised money for new hangings for Grace Chapel, Easter flowers, an enclosure around the Chapel, a rectory fence, and for payment towards the Chapel Fund debt. The women of Grace held ice cream and cake sales, swept and dusted the church, sewed aprons and bonnets for sale by order, and, at Rev. Pruden's suggestion, pledged a penny a day as a Lenten donation based upon individually selected items or activities to deny oneself of during the season of Lent.

George T. Kearsley rejoined the vestry in 1895 both as a vestryman and as the treasurer. William Radford Wharton served on the vestry again that year after a two-year break in service and John G. Osborne returned after a one-year break in service. James Lawrence Radford continued to serve, as did Frank L. Buck, W. W. Darnell, Dr. Aaron Jeffrey, Warner Justice Kenderdine, Ambrose Robinson, and C. W. Sanders.

The 1895 Radford Parish vestry was comprised of a few returning members and many new members. Serving as vestrymen for the first time were J. D. Bibb, Lewis Washington Clark, Henry G. Pierce, John D. Smith, Bennett W. Taylor, and Ira W. Wilson. Continuing vestry service or returning for an additional term as vestrymen were Frank L. Buck, William Wirt Darnell, Dr. Aaron Jeffrey, George T. Kearsley, Warner Justice Kenderdine, John G. Osborne, James Lawrence Radford, Charles W. Sanders, and William Radford Wharton. George T. Kearsley was the treasurer. Dr. Aaron Jeffrey, Warner Justice Kenderdine, and Charles W. Sanders were also church trustees.

Rev. A. A. Pruden was ordained as a priest and became the rector of the Parish on May 18, 1895. He resigned his position at Radford Episcopal Parish on October 24, 1895. Rev. Pruden resigned his position on October 24, 1895. Rev. Frederick Goodwin Ribble accepted the call and served the parishioners of Radford Episcopal Parish July 1896 through December 1897.

The ladies of the church were active in 1895, holding an Anniversary Reception and Sociable along with "a silver offering at the Rector's rooms" in August of that year. Attendance at meetings of the Ladies Chapel Fund Society decreased during 1896 and 1897, but seemed to be on the increase as Autumn of 1897 began. Miss Anna Kenderdine, the secretary, recorded in the meeting minutes that the September 1897 meeting was "one of the largest and most interesting meetings of the Chapel Fund Society for the past year". They also distributed Lent Boxes to parishioners for the first time in 1898, sewed sun bonnets to order, made extra effort to collect past dues for the Society to use on materials for fund-raising efforts, and held an ice cream festival. When meeting attendance slacked off, they chose to assess each missing member a fine of five cents for each meeting the member did not attend.

Current vestry members continued to serve. No first-time vestrymen were tapped to serve from 1896 through 1897, according to church records. Members of the 1896 / 1897 vestry included Frank L. Buck, photographer William Wirt Darnell, George T. Kearsley, and Ambrose Robinson.

Rev. Floyd L. Kurtz came to the Radford Episcopal Parish during March 1898 as the country once again engaged in military conflict. He led his Episcopal flock through the anxieties of the Spanish-American War. He served his parishioners until Spring 1899. The parish was temporarily without a rector, Rev. Kurtz's departure being precipitated by a decrease in the number of parishioners coupled with the congregation's inability to pay a rector's salary. The congregation kept their chapel afloat through service and support. The Vestry continued to serve as new members came on aboard. Radford Carter Adams, son of Richard Henry Adams Jr., became an Episcopal vestryman in 1898 and served until 1902. The following year, 1899, John W. Wilson began his vestry duty which lasted from 1899 through 1902.

Illustration 49: Grace Episcopal Mission Chapel sanctuary. Courtesy of Glencoe Museum / Radford Heritage Foundation.

Illustration 50: Stained glass windows at Grace Episcopal Church offer tribute to early parishioners. Photos by Dr. Russell Davis of Radford.

THE FAMILIES OF GRACE
1888 THROUGH 1900

Information about the people who worshipped together and built a parish together is contained herein. This information has been culled from church records and, where possible, supplemented by local records including public records from the Virginia courthouses in Montgomery County and Radford City, articles from area newspapers, and information provided by family descendants.[79]

The Episcopal Bishops and Rectors 1888 Through 1900

St. James' Episcopal Mission Chapel was without a rector from 1888 through 1893, Episcopal services being provided by lay readers, neighboring and visiting rectors, and the Episcopal Bishop.

Goodwin, Edward L.
Circa 1856

Edward L. Goodwin was the son of the Rev. F. D. Goodwin, an Episcopal missionary priest. Rev. Edward L. Goodwin served as Episcopal clergy for Montgomery Parish from 1889 through 1891. He then took charge of the newly formed Radford Parish in 1892 and served through 1893.

---

[79] The author welcome readers to share additional information, including photos and personal narratives, regarding early rectors and parishioners of the Episcopal faith in southwest Virginia and the area now known as Radford City. Dr. Joanne Spiers Moche can be contacted at drjmoche@swva.net.

Rev. Edward L. Goodwin married Maria S. She was born around 1848. Mrs. Maria S. Goodwin was baptized at St. Thomas Church in Christiansburg, and confirmed in the Grace Episcopal parish in 1890. She died on July 16, 1892 at home in the Grace Episcopal rectory. Cause of death was not recorded in the church records. Rev. Goodwin did note that she was buried on July 17, 1892 in Wytheville. The Rev. Forsythe officiated. A baptismal font and communion vessels (paten, chalices and flagon) were donated to Grace Episcopal Mission Chapel in her memory.

Before the Goodwins came to Radford's Episcopal parish, Rev. Edward L. Goodwin's first parish was the Trinity Ascension / Emmanuel Episcopal Chapel in Rocky Mt., Virginia. He wrote about those early experiences in "Reflections of My First Parish: 1880 – 1885" and in "The Colonial Church of Virginia" (published 1927).

During their time at Grace Episcopal Parish, the Rev. Edward L. Goodwin and his wife Maria provided the Radford Parish with love, time, and energy. Rev. Goodwin was instrumental in the building of the Grace Episcopal rectory in Radford in 1890 (which was originally built on the site of the present Parish Center, renamed the Vest Center for retired Bishop Frank Vest in 2006). He and his wife were the first to live in the newly built rectory. Mrs. Maria Goodwin taught the first Grace Episcopal Mission Chapel Sunday school class in the rectory parlor.

He recorded into the church record four confirmations performed by the Rt. Rev. Alfred Magill Randolph when the chapel was without a rector in 1888. Rev. Goodwin officiated at twenty-four funerals between 1889 and 1893, twelve of which were for children between the ages of one hour and eight years. He led ten couples through their wedding vows, and baptized thirty-three parishioners. He also had the privilege of attesting to thirty-four confirmations, nine of which were performed by the Rt. Rev. F. M. Whittle and twenty-five of which were performed by the Rt. Rev. A. M. Randolph. Rev. Edward L. Goodwin resigned the parish in September 1893, about a year and a half after his wife died. The Rector's Aid Society expressed their sadness over his departure with a letter: "it was moved and carried that a letter be written to Mr. Goodwin thanking him for his many kindnesses toward us while he was here, and expressing our regret in losing him".

253

Lacy, T. H.
Circa 1849

Rev. T. H. Lacy was an evangelist of the Diocese of Southern Virginia during the late 1800s. Rev. Lacy traveled to locations throughout southwestern Virginia, visiting individual congregations two to three times a year. He helped newly forming congregations organize and held services for parishes without a rector. It was during a time when the Radford Episcopal Parish was without a rector that Rev. Lacy came to that community. May 1894, he performed two adult baptisms at St. James' Episcopal Mission Chapel in Radford.

When the 1880 Census was taken, Rev. Lacy and his family were residing in Lewis of Mason County, West Virginia. Their family information was reported as follows: Head of Household was a thirty-one year old white minister T. H. Lacy, his thirty-five year old wife M. B. Lacy, his five year old daughter M. G. Lacy, his four year old daughter E. L. Lacy, his one year old daughter F. E. Lacy, and a nineteen year old white cook from Ohio named Hannah Rairden.

Pruden, A. A.
Circa 1800s

The Rev. A. A. Pruden served as Episcopal clergy for Radford Parish from 1894 through 1895. He worked closely with the ladies of the church in their fundraising efforts to meet Episcopal Mission Chapel needs. The Rector's Aid Society disbanded and reorganized as the Ladies Chapel Fund Society a month after Rev. Pruden came to Grace. During his fifteen months of service, the Society raised money for new hangings for the Chapel, for payment towards the Chapel Fund, for Easter flowers, and for the purchases of an enclosure around the Chapel and a rectory fence. The women of Grace held ice cream and cake sales, swept and dusted the chapel, sewed aprons and bonnets for sale, and, at Rev. Pruden's suggestion, pledged a penny a day as a Lenten donation based upon individually selected items or activities to deny oneself of during the season of Lent.

Rev. A. A. Pruden entered into the church records five confirmations which were conducted by the Bishop F. M. Whittle and three baptisms conducted by the Bishop A. M. Randolph during 1894 when the parish was without a rector. During his time at the Radford parish, Rev. A. A. Pruden performed thirty-four baptisms, two marriage ceremonies, and attested to nineteen confirmations performed by the Rt. Rev. Alfred Magill Randolph. Rev. Pruden also conducted three burial services during 1895, one of which was for an infant and one of which was for a fifty-year old suicide victim.

Rev. Pruden may have held expectations which were too strict for the democratic body of parishioners who comprised the Grace Episcopal congregation, or perhaps there was lacking a personality match between the good reverend and his flock. At any rate, it appears that his service and his resignation came with some degree of sadness and mutual discontent. Vestry minutes hint to the rector's concerns, with Rev. Pruden reporting at one point that Lent services were "very well attended at St. James; not as well at Chapel as the rector thinks they ought to have been". Rev. Pruden bemoaned poor attendance at an additional meeting, with "congregations not so large as they should be, a great deal of indifference manifested on the part of some of the vestrymen and other leading members of the Church".

While one can not know through mere glimpses into the past what the true nature of relations were, a poignant thank-you to the vestry in July 1895 provides some indication that all had not been well: "The Rector desires to tender to the vestry, and through them to the congregations, his sincere thanks for the pleasant and beneficial vacation from which he has recently returned, and he desires to ask their prayers that he with them may be inspired with greater earnestness and zeal in the future than in the past".

As the summer of 1895 warmed the New River Valley, Rev. Pruden recommended that "Wilson + Wharton" be advised that St. John's, the mission church at New River, "serve as an Episcopal School or close the Church". He was able to report to the vestrymen by August 1895 that "the union Sunday School at St. John's was disbanded and in its place an Episcopal Sunday school organized, which is getting along fairly well with an attendance of about 30 pupils and 5 teachers".

In a September 1895 report to the Vestry, Rev. Pruden chastised the vestrymen in no uncertain terms when he reported that "On the 16th of August the Ladies of the Church held an Anniversary Reception and Sociable, with a silver offering at the Rector's rooms, which was pronounced by all to be a success both socially and financially, but the rector was much mortified that only two of his vestrymen were present".

Rev. A. A. Pruden resigned on October 24, 1895. His resignation letter read: "Gentlemen, After earnest prayerful consideration I have decided for various reasons, many of which are apparent to the vestry but which I do not see necessary to mention here, to resign this parish. I therefore, hereby, tender the vestry my resignation as rector of Radford Parish to take effect on Nov. 15th 1895. Yours very sincerely,   A. A. Pruden".

Ribble, Frederick Goodwin
Circa 1800s

The Rev. F. G. Ribble served as Episcopal Clergy for Radford Parish from 1896 through 1897. Like his predecessors, he was supported by the Ladies Chapel Fund. His wife, Mrs. Carrie M. Ribble, supported her husband both in his Wytheville parish and in his Radford parish. A "Mrs. Ribble" joined the Ladies Chapel Fund Society of Grace Church in October 1896.

Rev. Ribble had been active in the establishment of Episcopal churches. In 1868, he was one of two trustees supervising the construction of St. Paul's Chapel in Salem, Virginia. At some point, he and his wife may have moved to Wytheville. Their daughter Frances LeBaron Ribble was born in Wytheville in 1896 and baptized at Grace Episcopal in Radford two months later.

In the Radford Episcopal Parish, Rev. Ribble conducted three marriage ceremonies and five funeral services during 1896 and 1897. Two new parishioners were confirmed during 1898 by the Rt. Rev. Alfred M. Randolph as attested to by Rev. Ribble.

Carrie M. and Frederick Goodwin Ribble had at least one child: Frances LeBaron Ribble (1896). She was born in Wytheville, Virginia, on August 13, 1896. When she was two months old, she was baptized by her father at Grace Episcopal Mission Chapel in Radford. Her sponsors at the October 15, 1896 baptism were Warner Justice Kenderdine, L. Ribble, and "proxy for W. H. Ribble Jr.".

Kurtz, Floyd L.
Circa 1800s

The Rev. Floyd L. Kurtz served as clergy for Grace Episcopal Mission Chapel during 1898. He conducted two funerals and attested to three confirmations performed by the Rt. Rev. A. M. Randolph in 1898. The conclusion of Rev. Kurtz's time at Grace came about more from financial crisis within Grace than from any other concern. The congregation size had dropped significantly and, when a sister church pulled out of an agreement to share a rector (and the rector's salary), the Grace congregation was simply unable to pay the rector for his services.

Correspondence from the Rt. Rev. Randolph to Mr. Warner J. Kenderdine on February 13, 1899, indicates the Bishop's awareness of the troubles at Grace: "My dear Mr. Kenderdine, I have received your letter and sympathize with the Congregation in the conditions which you describe. Some time since I wrote to Mr. Kurtz with reference to the mobility of the Congregation and the probability of the necessity of his removal to another fold. I have placed him in correspondence with Bishop Spalding at Denver, Colorado and I am informed that he has a Mission Church there to which he is calling Mr. Kurtz." Rev. Kurtz left the Radford Episcopal Parish by the end of the year 1899.

The Episcopal Parishioners 1888 through 1900

Adams, Blanche
1854 – 1934

Miss Blanche Adams was born on November 19, 1854 in England. She came to the young United States of America and took a position as live-in tutor for the Eskridge family children. When the Eskridges were unable to pay for her services, she became governess and tutor for the Wharton children.

According to church records, Miss Blanche Adams was "an old communicant" who re-entered Radford Parish in 1895 and attended Grace Episcopal Mission Chapel. She dissented from the Church of England where she had been baptized and joined the Episcopal faith. "Miss Blanche" joined the Rector's Aid Society of Grace Parish Episcopal Chapel on July 14, 1900, the year the Society was formed, and participated with the group through 1902. She was a member of the Altar Committee, and served as both secretary and treasurer of the church women's group.

During the early 1900s, the Episcopal Diocese of Virginia established mission stations in the remote and mountainous areas of southwestern Virginia. These stations were staffed by unmarried women of the church who would live in the mission houses, conduct religious works on behalf of the Episcopal Church, and perform charity work for the congregations in those communities. These women were given the title of "Deaconess".

In 1908, Miss Blanche Adams accepted the call and became a deaconess for the church's first mission station. That station was located at a coal camp in Keokee, Lee County, Virginia. Deaconess Adams conducted Episcopal Sunday school classes in her station home, provided health care services to those in need, established a weekly Boys' Club, and offered sewing class for the women of Keokee. She also held prayer meetings and bible readings. Deaconess Blanche Adams died on July 1, 1934. A stained glass window depicting Mary anointing Jesus' feet was donated to Grace Episcopal Church of Radford in her memory.

Illustration 51: Deaconess Blanche Adams, "set apart" as Deaconess on March 30, 1908. Courtesy of Grace Episcopal Church, Radford, Virginia.

Adams, Radford Carter
1872-1937

Radford Carter Adams was born at the Arnheim estate in Montgomery County, Virginia on September 15, 1872. He was the son of Elizabeth Campbell Radford and Richard Henry Adams Jr. His first name, "Radford", was his mother's maiden surname. His middle name, "Carter", was his paternal great-grandmother's maiden surname.

He was baptized as an Episcopalian. In 1886, when he was about fourteen, his family moved from Radford, Virginia to Alabama. They returned to the Radford area and its Episcopal Church three years later in 1889. Radford Carter Adams was confirmed at St. James' Episcopal Mission Chapel on October 30, 1889 by the Rt. Rev. Francis M. Whittle, attested to by the Rev. Edward Lewis Goodwin.

Around 1908 he married Mancye Doyle, who was born on July 5, 1889 and died in 1990. She was the daughter of Minnie Pilkington Harris and L. W. Doyle. Mancye was a Baptist but, at the encouragement of her husband and the Rev. Robert Carter Jett (who would later become Bishop Jett), she attended the Episcopal chapel. She and her husband became life-long and active members of the Radford Episcopal Parish.

Radford Carter Adams became a vestryman and church trustee in 1898. He served on the vestry from 1898 through 1902. He also served on the vestry of Grace Episcopal Church (which was a merged congregation from St. James' Episcopal Mission Chapel and Grace Episcopal Mission Chapel) during the years 1912, 1913, 1930, and 1935 through 1936. During part of that vestry service he was also the Junior Warden. Church records indicate that he, his wife, his mother, and four of his children were living together in Radford and attending Grace Episcopal Church around 1906. The Radford Adams family transferred to Emmanuel Episcopal Church in Staunton, Virginia, during July 1909 and returned to Radford City by 1912[80].

Mancye was a member of the Radford Daughters of the Confederacy, a part of the United Daughters of the Confederacy. Her membership was based upon her lineage to John Thomas Harris.

---

[80] A notation in the church register lists Mancye Adams's transfer date from Emmanuel Episcopal to Grace Episcopal as February 18, 1936. Other notations in church records prove this date to be incorrect. Her husband was a member of the vestry in 1912-1913 and again in 1930. Their daughter Minnie was baptized at Grace Episcopal in 1912. Mancye was a member of the church choir at least by 1922.

Harris, Mancye's grandfather, was a soldier in the Surry Light Artillery of Surry County, Virginia in 1862 and served until the close of the Civil War. Mancye wrote in her membership application that her grandfather performed his duties as a private well, was never disciplined, "but a quiet, orderly, and respected soldier".

Mrs. Mancye Doyle Adams was an active member of the church ladies' societies. She was a member of the Grace Episcopal Church choir at least by 1922. She contributed a pew to Grace in memory of her mother Minnie Pilkington Harris Doyle, and contributed to the Parish Building Fund in memory of her mother and of her father L. W. Doyle. Mancye was also a member of the Grace Episcopal Church Planning Committee in 1956 for the establishment of an Episcopal Student Center to meet the fellowship needs of Episcopalians attending Radford University. She wrote about her fellow parishioners in an unpublished collection called "Personalities of Grace Church" in 1992 in honor of the church's centennial celebration.

Radford Carter Adams died from paralysis (likely a reference to a cerebral stroke) at the age of fifty-five on February 14, 1937, as recorded in the church register by Rev. James A. Figg and Rev. Charles W. Sydnor. He was buried at West View Cemetery. A pew was donated by his family in memory of vestryman Radford Carter Adams. Mancye continued to be an active member of Radford's Grace Episcopal Church and the Radford City community.

Mancye's personality was captured in a 1979 newspaper piece by Thora Jervey[81] titled "Mancye's baking is Christmas tradition". Mancye began baking six-pound pecan cakes from her mother's family recipe in 1920, giving as many as thirty-three cakes in one year as Christmas gifts for family and friends. She was still baking her Christmas cakes at the age of ninety, by which time she had become well known for her skills as bridge player, hostess, and, especially, as cook.

Mrs. Mancye Doyle Adams and Mrs. Sophie Sublette, friend and fellow Episcopal parishioner, had opened Radford High School's first cafeteria in 1928. Mancye was still in charge of the school lunch program when her son Lucien Doyle was the high school principal from 1932 through 1941. During that time and

---

[81] Thora Jervey is still capturing the personalities of Radford in her column, "Jervey's Jottings", which appears in the *Radford News Journal*.

later, she was helping with church bake sales and suppers, the annual Grace Episcopal Church St. Nicholas Shoppe, and preparing weekly dinners for the Rotary Club and the Kiwanis Club of Radford. The widow Mrs. Mancye Doyle Adams lived in Radford and attended Grace Episcopal Church until her death in 1990 at the age of one hundred years. Mancye Doyle and Radford Carter Adams had children:

1. Elizabeth Campbell Adams (1909), daughter of Mancye Doyle and Radford Carter Adams. She was born on January 20, 1909 at the Arnheim estate in Radford City. She became a communicant of Grace Episcopal Church on May 21, 1921 from Pilot, Virginia. Elizabeth Campbell Adams married artist Kenneth Frederick Small on January 14, 1932. Small's painting of Arnheim included his mother-in-law Mancye walking across the Arnheim lawn. The Smalls transferred to St. Mark's Episcopal Church in Jacksonville, Florida, on September 22, 1947. Mrs. Elizabeth Campbell Adams Small preceded her older sister Mickey in death (i.e. she died prior to 2006). Elizabeth Campbell Adams and Kenneth Frederick Small had children:

    a. Elizabeth Campbell Small (1933), daughter of Elizabeth Campbell Adams and Kenneth Frederick Small. She was born August 23, 1933 in Philadelphia, Pennsylvania. She first married Gordon D. Price; they had three children. She married second to William Barham. The children of Elizabeth Campbell Small and Gordon D. Price were as follows:

        i. Stephen O'Hara Price (1955), son of Elizabeth Campbell Small and Gordon D. Price. He was born on August 27, 1955.

        ii. David Price (1957), son of Elizabeth Campbell Small and Gordon D. Price.

        iii. Susan Elizabeth Price (1961), daughter of Elizabeth Campbell Small and Gordon D. Price.

b. Kenneth Hollingshead Small (1937), son of Elizabeth Campbell Adams and Kenneth Frederick Small. He was born on March 29, 1937.

2. Lucien Doyle Adams (1910), son of Mancye Doyle and Radford Carter Adams. He was born at the Arnheim estate in Radford, Virginia on November 17, 1910. He was confirmed and became a communicant of Grace Episcopal Church on May 20, 1923. On November 22, 1939, he married Eleanor Elizabeth Eakin. Called "Tommy", she was a student of high school teacher Lucien Doyle Adams. Tommy later attended Radford College. Lucien was a career educator. His career included positions of Industrial Arts teacher, principal of Radford High School, and Assistant Superintendent and Superintendent of Richmond City Schools. He was instrumental in the integration of Richmond City Public Schools. One notation in Grace Episcopal Church records reported that the Adams transferred to the Church of the Good Shepherd in Richmond in 1951. Another notation indicated that they were "removed to old D.M.I. Building, Danville, VA" and then in 1953 transferred to Richmond. Lucien served in the military during World War II. Tommy and Lucien Adams retired to Athens, West Virginia and Bradenton, Florida. Lucien Doyle Adams died on June 21, 2004. His family brought his cremains to the Radford Family Cemetery for interment on October 9, 2004. The service was performed by Episcopal priest Rev. Caroline Kramer (wife of Grace Episcopal Church rector B. Kris Kramer). A reception followed at Grace Episcopal Church. Eleanor Elizabeth Eakin and Lucien Doyle Adams had children:

a. John Gordon Adams (1944), son of Eleanor Elizabeth Eakin and Lucien Doyle Adams. He was born on January 1, 1944. He married first Ann Martin. He married second to Susan Robert. He and Ann Martin had at least one child: John Gordon Adams Jr. (1967).

b. Ann Carter Adams (1946), daughter of Eleanor Elizabeth Eakin and Lucien Doyle Adams. She was born on June 13, 1946.

c. Sally Taylor Adams (1956), daughter of Eleanor Elizabeth Eakin and Lucien Doyle Adams. She was born on February 1, 1956. She married Finn Duerr. They had children: Anna Radford Duerr (1982) and Taylor Phillip Duerr (1985).

3. Minnie Harris Adams (1912), daughter of Mancye Doyle and Radford Carter Adams. Minnie Harris Adams, also known as Mickey, was born on November 21, 1912 at the Arnheim estate in Radford, Virginia. She was baptized by the Rev. C. E. A. Marshall at Grace Episcopal Church. Her sponsors were Miss Anna Kenderdine and Mr. and Mrs. H. C. Karnes. Mickey was confirmed and became a communicant on May 20, 1923. She was a nurse in the United States Navy. Stationed in Norman, Oklahoma, her duties included the training and preparation of nurses for departure to the South Pacific during World War II. She later earned her Bachelors Degree in Education and became a teacher, teaching at Iowa State University and at Auburn High School in Montgomery County, Virginia. Her pride in her military service was only equaled by her pride in the publication of her family history book, The Radford Letters: History of a Virginia Family. Minnie Harris Adams married Robert Dancy Fitting on March 19, 1943 at the Radford home Arnheim. He was born in New York in July of 1917. They transferred to Trinity Episcopal Church in the Diocese of North Texas at Midland, Texas on April 26, 1947. Robert D. Fitting died prior to the year 2000. Mrs. Minnie Harris Adams Fitting died on July 21, 2006 at the age of ninety-three from complications related to a stroke. Her cremains were interred in the Radford Family Cemetery in Radford City with Grace Episcopal Church rector Father Kris Kramer officiating. Minnie "Mickey" Harris Adams and Robert Dancy Fitting had children:

a. Robert Eric Fitting (1946), son of Minnie Harris Adams and Robert Dancy Fitting. He was born on November 3, 1946. He married Maria (maiden surname not now known). Robert Eric Fitting predeceased his mother (i.e. he died before the year

2006). They lived in Flagstaff, Arizona. Maria and Robert Eric Fitting had at least one child: Jason Fitting (circa 1900s).

b. Richard Kent Fitting (1948), son of Minnie Harris Adams and Robert Dancy Fitting. He was born on November 10, 1948. He married Darlene (maiden surname not now known). They lived in Riner, Virginia. Darlene and Richard Kent Fitting had children, all three of whom lived in Texas. Those children were: Chris Fitting, Brad A. Fitting, and Betty J. Fitting. Chris Fitting (circa 1900s) married Stacey (maiden surname not now known). Brad A. Fitting (circa 1900s) may not have married. Betty J. Fitting (circa 1900s) married Meryl Walters.

4. Radford Carter Adams Jr. (circa 1922), son of Mancye Doyle and Radford Carter Adams. He was born on August 15, 1922 in Pilot, Virginia. He was a communicant of Grace Episcopal Church at least from 1936 through 1947. He married Jamie Elizabeth Bagwell on August 18, 1951 in Atlanta, Georgia. Radford Carter Adams Jr. served on a destroyer in the Navy during World War II. He became a chemical engineer and resided in North Carolina. He died prior to 2004, preceding his brother Lucien and his sister Minnie in death. Jamie Elizabeth Bagwell and Radford Carter Adams Jr. had children:

a. Rebecca Elizabeth Adams (1954), daughter of Jamie Elizabeth Bagwell and Radford Carter Adams Jr. She was born on February 24, 1954. She married Roy Ogle. They had children: Molly Elizabeth Ogle (1982) and Katherine Adams Ogle (circa 1900s).

b. Lucy Harrison Adams (1956), daughter of Jamie Elizabeth Bagwell and Radford Carter Adams Jr. She was born on June 22, 1956.

5. Mancye Prince Adams (1925), daughter of Mancye Doyle and Radford Carter Adams. She was born on March 22, 1925 in Radford, Virginia. She was baptized by the Rev. James A. Figg at Grace Episcopal Church on December 6,

1925. Her sponsors were Mrs. J. G. Osborne, Mrs. Bess Kenderdine Bullard, Mrs. W. R. Wharton, Mrs. J. C. Caldwell, and her father Radford Carter Adams. Mancye Prince Adams died at the age of four and a half on October 27, 1929 due to a congenital heart disease (church records state "blue baby"). She was buried at West View Cemetery on October 29, 1929. Her mother later contributed funds to Grace Episcopal Church for a stained glass window in her young daughter's memory. Electric candles were also donated to Grace Episcopal Church in memory of Mancye Prince Adams by her mother Mancye and her godmother Bess Bullard.

Baldwin, John M.
Circa 1800s

John M. Baldwin was a communicant of St. James' Episcopal Mission Chapel in 1895. He was confirmed at St. James' on May 18, 1895 with the Rt. Rev. Alfred M. Randolph D. D. officiating, attested to by Rev. A. A. Pruden. John M. Baldwin later transferred to the Galilee Episcopal Church in Virginia Beach, Virginia.

Bartelle, Albert Hugh
Circa 1800s

Albert Hugh Bartelle was a member of the St. James' Episcopal congregation during the early 1890s. He may have had a son: Robert Hugh Bartelle, described in church records as the son of "Mr. and Mrs. Bartelle", was born around 1890. He was baptized as an infant at his parents' home on July 4, 1892. The home baptism was, in the writing of Rev. Edward Lewis Goodwin, "Private – In extremis". The child died that same day of "membranous group". He was eighteen months old. Robert Hugh Bartelle was buried at "Radford Cemetery" (most likely a reference to Central Cemetery) on July 5, 1892.

266

Battle, John Anna Somerville
1851-1915

Mrs. John (called "Johnnie") Anna Somerville Battle was a parishioner of Grace Episcopal Mission Chapel at least by the mid-1890s. She was born on December 1, 1851 and died on July 1, 1915. Her husband was James Smith Battle.

Mrs. Johnnie Somerville Battle was a member of the Ladies chapel Fund Society of Grace Episcopal Chapel in 1896. She attended the first meeting held on January 29, 1896. Some of her activities included pursuit of a quote on the cost of two-piece and three-piece chapel hangings, as well as membership on the Entertainment Committee for Socials held as church fund-raisers. Her name was still on church rolls at the time of her death in 1915. A brass altar cross was donated to the church in her memory. A set of stained glass windows depicting the annunciation and birth of Jesus was also donated to Grace Episcopal Church in her memory. The windows were inscribed with her name, date of birth, and date of death.

John Anna Somerville and James Smith Battle had at least one child: Mary Dancy Battle (1874). She was born in Warrenton, North Carolina on July 24, 1874. She was a teacher at the Wadsworth Street School in Radford, Virginia, from 1896 through 1897. On October 18, 1897, she married United States Army Lieutenant William C. Rivers of Radford, Virginia. Friends and family witnessed the marriage ceremony held in the Radford Parish which was performed by the Rt. Rev. T. F. Gailor and Grace Episcopal Mission Chapel clergyman Rev. F. G. Ribble.

Battle, Maude Alston
Circa 1885

Maude Alston Battle was a member of the Radford Episcopal Parish congregation at least from 1895 through 1904. She was born around 1885. She was baptized in the Church, and was confirmed at St. John's Episcopal Mission Chapel in New River, Virginia, by the Rt. Rev. Alfred M. Randolph D.D. on May 18, 1895 as attested to by Rev. F. G. Ribble. At age nineteen, she married twenty-eight year old James Randal Kent Cowan. Both residents of Radford, they were married at Grace Episcopal Church with the Rev. Edwin R. Carter officiating on June 15, 1904. At some point, according to church records, they attended Christ Episcopal Church in Blacksburg, Virginia.

Bienkampen, Charles A.
Circa 1800s

Charles A. Bienkampen was a member of Grace Episcopal Mission Chapel in the early 1890s. He was also one of Radford City's first government officials in 1892, as were a good number of his Episcopal community. He served on that first city council along with Episcopal parishioners John Henry Washington, George T. Kearsley, Henrick Parsons Briggs, Robert Jackson Noell, Warner Justice Kenderdine, Harry Hazard Powers, William Radford Wharton, Mayor Hugh Caperton Preston, and Treasurer Ambrose Robinson. Charles A. Bienkampen was a representative for Radford's West Ward.

Black, Allan J.
Circa 1800s

Mr. and Mrs. Allan J. Black were Episcopal parishioners at least from 1888 through 1904. They were both confirmed on November 24, 1888 by the Rt. Rev. A. M. Randolph "when parish was without a rector" as noted in the St. James' Episcopal Mission Chapel register by Rev. Edward Lewis Goodwin. The Black family lived in the East Ward of Radford on Norwood Street. A Mrs. Saunders and a Miss Alma Saunders were listed as members of the Black family in the 1889 church records. The Blacks were described as chapel communicants on April 28, 1889.

Allan J. Black, a physician, was active in his community and in his church. An 1892 "Society Directory of Radford" in the *Radford Advance* newspaper listed A. J. Black as "W.M. of A.F. & A.M., Virginia May Lodge No. 88". Dr. Black served on his church vestry from 1890 through 1893. Mrs. Black was a member of the Woman's Guild of Grace Episcopal Mission Chapel in 1903. She was also a member of the Radford Chapter of the Virginia Daughters of the Confederacy around 1906.

Mr. and Mrs. Black transferred from St. James' Episcopal Mission Chapel of Radford to St. John's Episcopal Church of Roanoke, Virginia on November 21, 1904 according to church records.

Boothe, Charles
Circa 1800s

Charles Boothe was a communicant of St. James' Episcopal Mission Chapel by April 1891. He may have been a civil engineer. A map of the West Ward of Radford created around 1892 contains engineer inscriptions "R. H. Adams, Civil Engineer, Radford, VA" and "Chas. Boothe, C. E., Del.". A notation in church records states that Charles Boothe moved from the area, his "name removed without letters, September 1892" (i.e. moved without officially transferring membership to another church).

Boothe, Jessie
Circa 1800s-1892

Mrs. Jessie Boothe came to St. James' Episcopal Mission Chapel from "Canada, Kingston, Ontario" by 1892. She was a communicant from April 30, 1892 until her death on September 15, 1892. Another parishioner, Mrs. Helen Greaves, also came to the chapel from "Canada, Kingston, Ontario" and enrolled as a parishioner on April 30, 1892. Relationship between Mrs. Jessie Boothe and Mrs. Helen Greaves is unknown at this time.

Bowen, Alfred R.
Circa 1800s

Alfred R. Bowen and his wife, Mrs. Jennie E. Bowen, were communicants of St. James' Episcopal Mission Chapel from 1890 until they moved to Michigan in 1891. Additional information is not available at this time.

Branscom, John R.
Circa 1800s

John R. Branscom was a member of St. James' Episcopal Mission Chapel at least by the 1890s. He married Bertha Edna Likens on January 7, 1904[82]. She was an Episcopal parishioner at least from 1895 through 1920. At some point they left the area. A notation in church records states that John R. Branscom moved to Dilton, Virginia.

Bransford, Eugene
Circa 1800s

Eugene Bransford and his wife lived in Radford, Virginia at least in 1892. They chose the Episcopal faith for their son's burial service as follows: John Bransford (1892), son of Mr. and Mrs. Eugene Bransford, was born March 1892. He died at the age of seven months from "cathars of bowels" on October 11, 1892. He was buried on October 12, 1892 in Ingles Cemetery "temporarily", as recorded in the church register by Episcopal clergyman Edward Lewis Goodwin.

Briggs, Henrick Parsons
Circa 1845-1895

---

[82] *See* Radford City Marriage Register re: Likens-Branscom marriage of January 7, 1904.

Henrick Parsons Briggs was a member of Grace Episcopal Chapel during the 1890s. He also served on Radford's first city council. He and his family hailed from Massachusetts. According to the 1880 Census of Berkshire County, Massachusetts, Parsons was a white thirty-five year old woolen manufacturer who had been born in Vermont around 1845. His wife was white thirty-four year old Clara Briggs (maiden surname not now known). She was born in New York around 1846. They were living at the time with their young son. Also in the household was a fifteen year old domestic servant from Ireland named Lizzie Beahan. Briggs was a member of Radford's first city council in 1892. He served as a representative from the East Ward for three years, until his death. Henrick Parsons Briggs fatally "shot himself" on February 18, 1895, according to church records; it was not noted whether the shooting was an accident or a suicide. He was a fifty-year old resident of Radford at the time. He was buried in "Radford Cemetery" on February 22, 1895 with Episcopal clergyman A. A. Pruden officiating.

Clara and Hendrick Parsons Briggs had a child: Henrick Parsons Briggs, Jr. was born in Massachusetts and was one month old at the time of the 1880 Census.

Bryant, Mary L.
Circa 1800s

Miss Mary L. Bryant was a communicant of St. John's Mission Chapel in New River, Virginia in 1895. She was baptized as a Methodist, but later confirmed as an Episcopalian at St. John's on May 5, 1895 by the Rt. Rev. Alfred M. Randolph D.D., as attested to by Rev. F. G. Ribble.

Buck, Frank L.
Circa 1800s

Frank L. Buck was a member of St. James' Episcopal Mission Chapel in 1891, and was baptized there as an adult on October 25, 1891. Mr. J. S. Rudd and Captain Ambrose Robinson were his witnesses and sponsors. Frank was confirmed at St. James' six months later in 1892 by the Rt. Rev. A. M. Randolph as attested to by the Rev. Edward Lewis Goodwin. Frank L. Buck served on the parish vestry from 1893 through 1904.

Buckner, Charles B.
Circa 1822-1892

Charles B. Buckner (also spelled Bucknor) was born around 1822. He was a communicant of Grace Episcopal Mission Chapel in 1892. While a notation in one section of the church register states that he later moved to Florida, his 1892 death in Radford, Virginia was recorded in another section of the church register. The Honorable Judge Charles B. Buckner died on December 10, 1892 in Radford, Virginia at the age of seventy. Cause of death was listed as debility[83]. Judge Buckner was buried on December 11, 1892 in "Radford Cemetery", Rev. Edward Lewis Goodwin officiating.

Bullard, Clifford S.
Circa 1849

The family of Louisa and Clifford S. Bullard were living in Pulaski, Virginia and worshipping within the Radford Episcopal Parish by the late 1890s. At the time of the 1880 Census, the Bullards were living in the Hiwassee District of Pulaski County. Head of household was C. S. Bullard, a white thirty-one year old boot and shoe maker. He was born in Massachusetts, as were his parents. His wife was twenty-eight year old Louisa Bullard (maiden surname not now known). She was born in Virginia, as were her parents. They had five children at the time. Also in the home was Clifford Bullard's twenty-one year old unmarried sister Ella Bullard (born around 1859) and a single white nineteen year old mail carrier named Fred Pillows (born around 1861). A single

---

[83] The terms "debility" and "feebleness" were written in early church records in reference to stroke, dementia, or mental confusion.

seventeen year old mulatto cook named Ella Brown (born around 1863) was a member of the household as well.

Louisa and Clifford S. Bullard had children:

1. Julia Bullard (c. 1871), daughter of Louisa and Clifford S. Bullard. She was nine years old at the time of the 1880 Census.
2. Mary Bullard (c. 1873), daughter of Louisa and Clifford S. Bullard. She was seven years old at the time of the 1880 Census.
3. Grace Bullard (1875), daughter of Louisa and Clifford S. Bullard. She was five years old at the time of the 1880 Census. She was born in Pulaski, Virginia on March 1, 1875.
4. Truman Jefferson Bullard (1877), son of Louisa and Clifford S. Bullard. He was three years old at the time of the 1880 Census. He was born in Pulaski, Virginia on April 29, 1877.
5. Frank Bullard (c. 1878), son of Louisa and Clifford S. Bullard. He was one year old at the time of the 1880 Census.
6. Fred Sayles Bullard (1881), son of Louisa and Clifford S. Bullard. He was born in Pulaski, Virginia on February 8, 1881; of whom more. He married Bess Kenderdine.
7. Ella Bullard (1883), daughter of Louisa and Clifford S. Bullard. She was born in Pulaski, Virginia on June 15, 1883.
8. Maurice Bullard (1885), son of Louisa and Clifford S. Bullard. He was born in Pulaski, Virginia on October 4, 1885.
9. Eugene Bullard (1887), son of Louisa and Clifford S. Bullard. He was born in Pulaski, Virginia on October 4, 1887.
10. Bullard *son* (1890), son of Louisa and Clifford S. Bullard. He was born in Pulaski, Virginia on December 22, 1890. Birth records did not list his first name.
11. Dess Louise Bullard (1892), daughter of Louisa and Clifford S. Bullard. She was known as "Lou" and as "Dessie". She was born in Pulaski, Virginia on December 15, 1892 according to county birth records and on November 15, 1892 according to Episcopal church records. She was bap-

tized at Grace Episcopal Mission Chapel by Rev. Edwin R. Carter on November 29, 1903. Her sponsors were Abie Miles, Warner Justice Kenderdine, and Bess Kenderdine (daughter of Warner Justice Kenderdine and future sister-in-law of Dess Louise Bullard). Dess Louise Bullard married a Mr. Combitha. Mrs. Dess Bullard Combitha gave an oil painting of Madonna and Child to be hung in the Grace Episcopal Sunday School classroom.

Bullard, Fred Sayles
1881-1918

Fred Sayles Bullard and his wife Bess Kenderdine were communicants of St. James' Episcopal Mission Chapel, Grace Episcopal Mission Chapel, and, later, Grace Episcopal Church.

Fred was born in Pulaski, Virginia on February 8, 1881 to Louisa and Clifford S. Bullard. He was a parishioner of Grace Episcopal Mission Chapel along with his family by the 1890s and was living in Radford and attending the parish services by 1901. He was baptized on April 13, 1901 by Rev. John S. Alfriend. His sponsors were his sister Julia Bullard as well as Mrs. Mary Lytle Kenderdine and her husband Colonel Warner Justice Kenderdine. According to notes in the church records, Fred "enlisted in the Navy April 1902". He returned to the area and to the Episcopal church after his naval service.

Fred Sayles Bullard married Bessie Kenderdine on November 11, 1908; their marriage is recorded in the Radford City Marriage Register as well as in the church register.

Bess Kenderdine was the daughter of Mary Lytle and Warner Justice Kenderdine. She was born in 1880.

Fred Sayles Bullard died on October 8, 1918 from influenza during a national Spanish Flu epidemic. His widow honored his memory in many ways. The church parish house hosts a memorial plaque which states that the Parish House was made possible by gifts from his widow Bess and the women of Grace, noting that Fred Sayles Bullard was "baptized, confirmed, married in, and buried from Grace Church".

He and his wife Bess never had children, nor did she remarry. She devoted her life to service within the Radford Episcopal Parish, especially in the strengthening of the Sunday School programs for the children. She was the driving force behind much of the growth and construction of Grace Episcopal Church. Her generous service and donations led to projects including the purchase of stained glass windows for the vestibule and the sanctuary as well as the construction of a Parish House. She was fondly known by generations of church parishioners as "Miss Bess". Mrs. Bess Kenderdine Bullard died on March 10, 1968. The General William Campbell Chapter of the DAR and at least seventy-two friends and fellow parishioners made financial contribution to Grace Episcopal Church in her memory.

Other gifts to the Episcopal Church by or in honor of Mrs. Bess Kenderdine Bullard and her husband Fred Sayles Bullard included: stained glass windows depicting The Last Supper in memory of Fred Sayles Bullard, a credence table and white altar hanging made by Mrs. Buchanan Henry in memory of Fred Sayles Bullard, vestibule windows from Mrs. Bess Kenderdine Bullard and Mrs. Homer Jamison, a church organ donated by Mrs. Bess Kenderdine Bullard, church pews donated by Mrs. Bess Kenderdine Bullard and her sister Miss Anna Lytle Kenderdine, and an Eagle Lectern donated by Mrs. Bess Kenderdine Bullard in memory of her sister Miss Anna Lytle Kenderdine.

Illustration 52: Mrs. Bess Kenderdine Bullard. Courtesy of Grace
Episcopal Church.

Burton, Samuel William
Circa 1800s

Samuel William Burton was a member and communicant of St. James' Episcopal Mission Chapel by 1892. He was baptized as an adult at St. James' on April 3, 1892. Baptismal sponsors and witnesses were Dr. Allan J. Black and photographer W. W. Darnell with the Rev. Edward Lewis Goodwin officiating. Samuel was confirmed two days later, on Aril 5, 1892 with the Rt. Rev. A. M. Randolph officiating as attested to be the Rev. Edward Lewis Goodwin.

Samuel William Burton married Flora C. (maiden surname not now known). They were communicants of the Church until their names were removed from the roll of communicants in 1893. Also in 1893, records indicate that Samuel W. Burton may have been living with the Banks family. S. W. Burton was a member of the vestry in 1892.

Flora C. and Samuel W. Burton had at least one child: Cornelia May Burton (born circa 1800s). She was baptized at St. James' Episcopal Mission Chapel in Radford as an infant on October 20, 1892, six months after her father's baptism. Her parents were witnesses. Dr. Allan J. Black, who had been her father's baptismal sponsor, also acted as her baptismal sponsor. The Rev. Edward Goodwin officiated.

Burton, Mary
Circa 1800s

Mrs. Mary Burton, a parishioner of St. James' Episcopal Mission Chapel at least during the late 1890s, had two children:
1. Nora Eskridge Burton (circa 1800s), daughter of Mrs. Mary Burton. She was baptized at St. James' Episcopal Mission Chapel on November 10, 1895, as verified by Rev. A. A. Pruden "by proxy" (an indication that another minister served in his stead). Her sponsors were Mrs. Rosamond G. Eskridge and Miss Janie B. Taylor. Nora Eskridge Burton may have later moved away from the Radford area.

2. Nellie Gay Burton (circa 1800s), daughter of Mrs. Mary Burton. She was baptized at the same time and date as her sister Nora (i.e. November 10, 1895) with the same sponsors.

Butler, William J.
Circa 1800s

William J. Butler and his wife, Mollie B. (maiden surname not now known; she was also known as Mattie) came to St. James' Episcopal Mission Chapel during 1889 from Emmanuel Episcopal Church in Lynchburg, Virginia. They lived on Grove Avenue in Radford and were communicates of St. James' in 1889. At least one of their children was born in Radford. They moved to Roanoke, Virginia in 1897.

Church records reveal some contradictions as to the religious preference of Mrs. Mollie B. Butler. A notation in church records indicated that she was an "old communicant returned by letter from Methodist Pastor, 1893". Another note, written beside her name in the church register and then crossed out by a line through the sentence reads "degenerated to the Methodist April 14, 1895".

The children of Mollie B. and William J. Butler were:
1. Effie Belle Butler (circa 1800s), daughter of Mollie B. and William J. Butler.
2. William Henry Butler (circa 1800s), son of Mollie B. and William J. Butler.
3. Lula Linwood Butler (circa 1800s), daughter of Mollie B. and William J. Butler.
4. Sadie Rachel Butler (circa 1800s), daughter of Mollie B. and William J. Butler. She was baptized on October 25, 1891 as an infant by Rev. Edward Lewis Goodwin at St. James' Episcopal Mission Chapel in Radford. Her parents were her witnesses.
5. Beulah Pearl Butler (1893), daughter of Mollie B. and William J. Butler. While not listed in church records, the burial marker for this daughter of M. B. and W. J. Butler is found in Central Cemetery in Radford. Beulah Pearl

Butler was born on February 11, 1893 and died at the age of nine months on November 22, 1893.

6. Eugene Vernon Butler (1895), son of Mollie B. and William J. Butler. According to church baptismal records, he was born on November 6, 1895 in East Radford. He was baptized at age one and a half at his parents' home. Rev. F. G. Ribble officiated, with Eugene's father in attendance and Mr. and Mrs. Phillips acting as sponsors.

Campbell, Margaret Kirkwood
1880

Margaret Kirkwood Campbell, the daughter of Cornelia B. and E. Bertram Campbell, was baptized at the age of fifteen on August 4, 1895 at Grace Episcopal Mission Chapel in Radford. She was born on May 16, 1880 in Campbell County, Virginia. Her 1895 baptismal rites were administered by Rev. A. A. Pruden. Her sponsors were Mr. and Mrs. James D. Bibb, and M. M. and C. M. Woodson.

The 1880 population census conducted fifteen years before her baptism described the Campbell family as residing at Falling River in Campbell County, Virginia as follows: white thirty-three year old miller E. B. Campbell, his thirty-year old wife Cornelia "M." Campbell, his six year old daughter Cornelia Campbell, his four year old son John R. Campbell, and his one year old daughter Mary K. Campbell.

Clark, Lewis Washington
1866

Lewis Washington Clark and his family attended St. James' Episcopal Mission Chapel at least by 1889. They were living either on Railroad Avenue or Rock Road in the East Ward of Radford (both street addresses being listed in the church register). He was an area jeweler and optician. His painted business advertisement is still visible on the outside wall of the Radford City Florist building overlooking the parking lot that hosts the Radford Farmer's Market each summer.

Lewis Washington Clark was the son of Arthelia and Charles Clark. Local oral history holds that he was a descendant of William Clark and George Rogers Clark. According to church baptismal records, Lewis Washington Clark was born on February 22, 1866 and baptized at St. James' Episcopal Mission by Rev. A. A. Pruden as an adult on February 24, 1895. His sponsors were Colonel and Mrs. Warner J. Kenderdine and Captain Ambrose Robinson. Lewis W. Clark's wife Mollie was a witness. He was confirmed at Grace Episcopal Mission Chapel on May 17, 1895, three months after his baptism, with the Rt. Rev. A. M. Randolph officiating as attested to by the Rev. A. A. Pruden.

He married Mary Phoebe Finch, also known as "Mollie" and "May". Her name was written in church records as "Mollie (May) Clark", "Mrs. Mollie M. Clark", and "Mrs. Mollie B. Clark". She was baptized as an adult at St. James' Episcopal Mission Chapel on October 30, 1889 six years prior to her husband's baptism. The Rt. Rev. F. M. Whittle officiated, as attested to by the Rev. Edward Lewis Goodwin. Her sponsors were Captain Ambrose Robinson (who would later sponsor her husband) and Miss Banks Davies. It is interesting to note that the mother of Bishop McNeece was Mary Ann Davies (wife of Fortescue Whittle); relationship between Mrs. Mary Ann Davies Whittle, the Bishop Francis McNeece Whittle, and Miss Banks Davies, if any, is unknown at this time.

Lewis Washington Clark served on the Radford Episcopal Parish vestry in 1895. Mr. and Mrs. Clark and their children transferred from St. James' Episcopal Mission Chapel to Grace Episcopal Mission Chapel. They continued as members of the Episcopal congregation during May 1904 when St. James' Episcopal Mission Chapel and Grace Episcopal Mission Chapel merged to form Grace Episcopal Church. Mrs. Mary Phoebe Finch Clark was a member of the Woman's Guild of Grace Episcopal Mission Chapel in 1902. She served actively on many committees including her work to "ascertain whether a suitable room could be found in East Radford in which to hold the bazaar", a reference to the 1903 Christmas bazaar at which she hosted the "Fancy Table" with Mrs. Mary L. Kenderdine. Mary Phoebe Finch and Lewis Washington Clark had children:

1. Mabel Bruce Clark (circa 1800s), daughter of Mary Phoebe Finch and Lewis Washington Clark. She was baptized as an infant on November 1, 1891 at St. James' Episcopal Mission Chapel. The Rev. Edward Lewis Goodwin officiated. Mabel was sponsored by her mother and Mrs. L. W. Bruce. Mabel Bruce Clark was confirmed at St. James' six and a half years later in 1898 by the Rt. Rev. A. M. Randolph as attested to by the Rev. Floyd L. Kurtz. Mabel married J. M. Thomas and moved with him to St. John's Episcopal Church in Roanoke in 1949.

2. Lewis Edward Earle Clark (circa 1800s), son of Mary Phoebe Finch and Lewis Washington Clark. Called Earle, he was baptized at St. James' Episcopal Mission Chapel on November 1, 1891 with his sister Mabel by Rev. Edward Lewis Goodwin. Mrs. L. W. Bruce and Earle's mother Mrs. Mary Phoebe Finch Clark were his sponsors.

3. Kathleen Arthelia Clark (1892), daughter of Mary Phoebe Finch and Lewis Washington Clark. This third child of Mollie and L. W. Clark was born on September 10, 1892 in Radford, Virginia according to church baptismal records. She was baptized at St. James' Episcopal Mission Chapel in Radford when she was two and a half years old. Her father was baptized at the same time. Rev. A. A. Pruden conducted the baptismal service on February 24, 1895. Her sponsor was Miss Patty J. Taylor, with her parents as witnesses. Kathleen Arthelia Clark was later confirmed at Grace Episcopal Mission Chapel.

4. Charles Jacobs Clark (1896), son of Mary Phoebe Finch and Lewis Washington Clark. According to church baptismal records, this young man was born in East Radford on August 6, 1896. He was baptized on July 11, 1897, one month shy of his first birthday. The baptismal ceremony was held at St. James' Episcopal Mission Chapel and conducted by the Rev. F. G. Ribble. Witnesses and sponsors were his parents and Mr. Edward Jacob Fink. Charles Jacobs Clark may have later moved to Petersburg, Virginia.

Local oral history holds that the lineage of Lewis Washington Clark is shared with that of George Rogers Clark and William Clark. The definitive link has not been proved yet by this author. The lineage now known of explorer William Clark (who married a Radford family widow) is as follows: (John C. Clark > William Clark > John Clark > John Clark Jr. > Jonathan Clark > John Clark > William Clark).

1) John C. Clark 1st Generation (circa 1500s). John C. Clark was born in Kent County, England. He married Elizabeth Steed. They had at least one child:
    a) William Clark 2nd Generation (circa 1500s), son of Elizabeth Steed and John C. Clark. He was born in Kent County, England. He married Mary Culpepper, also of Kent County. They had at least one child:
    i) John Clark 3rd Generation (1625 - circa 1684), son of Mary Culpepper and William Clark. He was born in 1625 in England and died sometime after 1683. He married Mary Bird. They had at least one child:
    (1) John Clark Jr. 4th Generation (circa 1660-circa 1736), son of Mary Bird and John Clark. He was born around 1660 in Kent County, England or in Ireland. He died sometime after 1735. He immigrated to the American colonies. John Clark Jr. married Elizabeth Ann Lumkin, who was born in Virginia around 1667 and descended from English parents. They had at least one child:
    (a) Jonathan Clark 5th Generation (1695-1734), son of Elizabeth Ann Lumkin and John Clark Jr. He was born in Albemarle County, Virginia in 1695. He married twenty-five year old Elizabeth Ann (also called Nancy) Wilson around 1725; she was born in King and Queen

County, Virginia around 1700. They had children:

(i) John Clark 6th Generation (1724), son of Elizabeth Ann "Nancy" Wilson and Jonathan Clark. He was born in King and Queen County, Virginia on October 20, 1724. He died in 1799. John Clark married Ann Rogers, the daughter of John Rogers. She was born in King and Queen County on October 20, 1734. They had children:

1. Jonathan Clark 7th Generation (1750), son of Ann Rogers and John Clark. He was born on August 1, 1750 in Albemarle County, Virginia and died in 1816. He married Sarah Hite. They had children.

2. George Rogers Clark 7th Generation (1752), son of Ann Rogers and John Clark. He was born on November 19, 1752 in Albemarle County, Virginia.

3. Ann Clark 7th Generation (1755), daughter of Ann Rogers and John Clark. She was born on July 14, 1755 in Caroline County, Virginia and died in 1822. She married Owen Gwathmey in 1733. They had children.

4. John Clark Jr. 7th Generation (1757), son of Ann Rogers and John Clark. He was born on September 15, 1757 in Caroline County, Virginia.

5. Richard Clark 7th Generation (1760), son of Ann Rogers and John Clark. He was born on

July 6, 1760 in Caroline County, Virginia and died in 1784.

6. Edmund Clark 7th Generation (1762), son of Ann Rogers and John Clark. He was born on September 25, 1762 in Caroline County, Virginia and died in 1817 in Louisiana.

7. Lucy Clark 7th Generation (1765), daughter of Ann Rogers and John Clark. She was born on September 15, 1765 in Caroline County, Virginia. She married William Croghan. They had children.

8. Elizabeth Clark 7th Generation (1768), daughter of Ann Rogers and John Clark. She was born on February 11, 1768 in Caroline County, Virginia and died in 1795. She married Richard Clough Anderson. They had children.

9. William Clark 7th Generation (1770-1838), son of Ann Rogers and John Clark. He was born on August 1, 1770 in Caroline County, Virginia. He was an Episcopalian, and a member of the Freemasons. He first married Julia Hancock in 1808. She was born on November 21, 1791 in Fincastle County, Virginia. They had five children. After Julia's death, he married her widowed cousin Harriet Kennerly Radford (who had been married to John Radford, the uncle of John Blair Radford). She was born on July 25, 1788

in Fincastle, Virginia. They had three children. Explorers William Clark and Meriwether Lewis led the Lewis and Clark Expedition across the area of the Louisiana Purchase. Their exploration took them from the Missouri River to the Pacific Coast during 1804, 1805, and 1806. After holding public offices in Missouri, William Clark returned to the family lands in Virginia where he died in 1838. The children of William Clark were:

a. Meriwether Lewis Clark 8th Generation (1809), son of Julia Hancock and William Clark. He was born on January 10, 1809 in St. Louis, Missouri. He married Abby Churchill in 1834. She was born in Louisville, Kentucky on March 9, 1817. They had children:

   i. William Hancock Clark 9th Generation (1839), son of Abby Churchill and Meriwether Lewis Clark. He married Camilla Gaylord, who was born in 1848.

   ii. Samuel Churchill Clark 9th Generation (1843), son of Abby Churchill and Meriwether Lewis Clark.

   iii. Mary Eliza Clark 9th Generation (1845), daughter

of Abby Churchill and Meriwether Lewis Clark.

iv. Meriwether Lewis Clark Jr. 9th Generation (1846), son of Abby Churchill and Meriwether Lewis Clark. He married Mary Martin Anderson, who was born in 1852. He married second Julia Davidson. The children of Meriwether Lewis Clark Jr. were John Henry Churchill Clark (1874), and Carrie Anderson Clark (1876),

v. John O'Fallon Clark 9th Generation (1848), son of Abby Churchill and Meriwether Lewis Clark.

vi. George Rogers Clark 9th Generation (1850), son of Abby Churchill and Meriwether Lewis Clark.

vii. Charles Jefferson Clark 9th Generation (1852), son of Abby Churchill and Meriwether Lewis Clark.

b. William Preston Clark 8th Generation (1811), son of Julia Hancock and William Clark.

c. Mary Margaret Clark 8th Generation (1814), son of Julia Hancock and William Clark.

d. George Rogers Hancock Clark 8th Generation (1816), son of Julia Hancock and

William Clark. In 1841, he married Eleanor Ann Glasgow. They had children: Julia Clark (1842), Sarah Leonida Clark (1843), John O'Fallon Clark (1844), and Ellen Glasgow Clark (1846).

e. John Julius Clark 8th Generation (1818), son of Julia Hancock and William Clark.

f. Jefferson Kearny Clark 8th Generation (1824), son of Harriet Kennerly Radford and William Clark. He was born on February 29, 1824. He married Mary Susan Glasgow, who was born in 1828. They had children: Mary Susan Clark (1877), Evelyn Kennerly Clark (1882), and Edwinna Churchill Clark (1893).

g. Edmund Clark 8th Generation (1826), son of Harriet Kennerly Radford and William Clark. He was born on September 9, 1826 in St. Louis, Missouri.

h. Clark son 8th Generation (circa 1800s), son of Harriet Kennerly Radford and William Clark. There may have been a third child from the marriage of Harriet Kennerly Radford and William Clark.

10. Frances Elanor (or Eleanor) Clark 7th Generation (1773), daughter of Ann Rogers and John Clark. She was born on January 1, 1773 in Caroline

287

County, Virginia. She married James O'Fallon of Ireland. They had four children.

(ii) Benjamin Clark 6th Generation (circa 1730-1806), son of Elizabeth Ann "Nancy" Wilson and Jonathan Clark. He was born around 1730 near Culpeper, Virginia. He became a preacher. He married Elizabeth Lee. She was born around 1734. Records conflict as to whether Benjamin Clark's first wife was named Elizabeth Lee with a second wife named Greene (first name not now known), or whether he had only one wife, named Elizabeth Lee Greene. The children of Benjamin Clark were as follows:

1. John, or Jonathan, Clark 7th Generation (circa 1761), son of Elizabeth Lee [Greene?] and Rev. Benjamin Clark. He was born around 1761 in Virginia and died in Kentucky around 1806.

2. Marston Greene Clark 7th Generation (1771), son of Elizabeth Lee Greene and Rev. Benjamin Clark. He was born in Lunenberg, Virginia on December 12, 1771. He died in Indiana in 1846.

3. Benjamin Wilson Clark 7th Generation (circa 1773), son of Elizabeth Lee [Greene?] and Rev. Benjamin Clark. He was born near Lunenberg, Virginia around 1773. He married Frances Ragsdale. They had twelve children: Jonathan Clark (circa 1785), Elizabeth Clark (circa

1789) who married Alexander Beard, Joseph Clark (circa 1793) who married Patsy Greer, Frances Clark (circa 1797) who married John Y. Eses, Drewry Clark (circa 1800) who married first to a Miss Estes and second to , Lucy Clark (circa 1802) who married William Naylor, Sophia Clark (circa 1807) who married Otho Naylor, Patsy Clark (circa 1804) who married Alexander Naylor, Roderick Clark (circa 1800s) who married Elizabeth Naylor, Benjamin Clark (circa 1800s) who married Elizabeth Greer, William Clark (circa 1800s) who married Nancy Hardy, and Richard Clark (circa 1800s), who married Ann Richie.

4. William Clark 7th Generation (circa 1700s), son of Benjamin Clark. He married Elizabeth Mitchell.

5. Everard Clark 7th Generation (circa 1700s), son of Elizabeth Lee [Greene?] and Benjamin Clark. He married Lucinda Courts. They had one daughter.

6. Lucy Clark 7th Generation (circa 1700s), daughter of Elizabeth Lee [Greene?] and Benjamin Clark. She married John Poole. They had four children.

(iii) Elizabeth Clark 6th Generation (circa 1700s), daughter of Elizabeth Ann "Nancy" Wilson and Jonathan Clark.

(iv) Ann Clark 6th Generation (circa 1700s), daughter of Elizabeth Ann

"Nancy" Wilson and Jonathan Clark.

Colebaugh, George Franklin
Circa 1800s

George Franklin ("Frank") Colebaugh and his wife, Carrie Sanders, lived in the West Ward of Radford and were communicants of St. James' Episcopal Mission Chapel and Grace Episcopal Mission Chapel by 1890. Mrs. Carrie Sanders Colebaugh was baptized in the church and confirmed on October 4, 1890 by the Rt. Rev. A. M. Randolph as attested to by Rev. Edward Lewis Goodwin. She was a parishioner of Grace at least from 1890 through 1895.

Records are somewhat contradictory at this point. One note in the church register states that she moved to the MacJill Memorial Church in Pulaski, Virginia in 1895. She was again a communicant of Grace Episcopal Mission Chapel in Radford in 1898 and, according to the church register, may have transferred to Christ Episcopal Church in Pulaski at that time. A note in the church register by her husband Frank's name states that he transferred to Christ Church in Pulaski at some point after 1890.

George F. Colebaugh was the manager of the "Radford Inn" by 1892 and was also an N & W railroad depot agent. He and his wife resided at the Inn. On March 16, 1893, the Radford Inn caught fire; newspapers reported a total loss of the property. Mrs. Colebaugh was at the time about five months pregnant with the Colebaugh's first child.

Mrs. Carrie Sanders Colebaugh was a member of the Rector's Aid Society of Grace Parish Episcopal chapel at least from 1893 through 1895. She hosted Society meetings, chaired entertainment committees and, in 1894, served as President of the Rectors Aid Society. The last meeting she attended was held on March 6, 1895.

Rev. A. A. Pruden noted their move from the Radford area in his August 1895 report to the Grace Vestry: "During the last month we have lost from our parish Dr. Aaron Jeffrey, one of our vestrymen, and his charming wife. We have also sustained a great loss in the removal from our parish of Mr. and Mrs. G. F. Colebaugh, with their little ones. May God's blessing accompany them in their new homes."

Carrie Sanders and George Frank Colebaugh had children:

1. George Franklin Colebaugh Jr. (1891), son of Carrie Sanders and George Frank Colebaugh. According to church baptismal records, Frank Jr. was born on July 17, 1893. Two months later he was baptized at Grace Episcopal Mission Chapel in Radford. The Rev. Edward Lewis Goodwin conducted the September 24, 1893 service. His parents were witnesses. His sponsors were Mr. Rowland Colebaugh, Mrs. Anna Sanders, and Mrs. W. R. Clegg.

2. Charles William Colebaugh (1895), son of Carrie Sanders and George Frank Colebaugh Jr. According to church baptismal records, he was born in Radford, Virginia on April 5, 1895. He was christened (i.e. baptized) on May 19, 1895 at the age of one month. The baptismal rites were performed by Rev. A. A. Pruden "by proxy" at Grace Episcopal Mission Chapel. His parents were his witnesses. Mr. and Mrs. Warner Justice Kenderdine were his sponsors.

Colebaugh, Rowland Poinsett
1865

Rowland Poinsett Colebaugh was a son of Emma R. and Joel P. Colebaugh. According to church baptismal records, he was born on June 16, 1865 in Franklin, Philadelphia County, Pennsylvania. He was baptized as an adult at Grace Episcopal Mission Chapel on January 6, 1895 at the age of twenty-four. Sponsors and witnesses were Mrs. H. Y. Colebaugh and Col. Warner J. Kenderdine. Clergyman of record was the Rev. A. A. Pruden "by proxy". Rowland P. Colebaugh was confirmed at Grace Episcopal Mission Chapel on May 17, 1895, four months after his baptism, by the Rt. Rev. A. M. Randolph, attested to by the Rev. F. G. Ribble. A note in church records states that Rowland Poinsett Colebaugh later moved to Pulaski, Virginia.

Cowan, John F.
Circa 1841

At least two of the children of M. G. and John F. Cowan married parishioners of St. James' Episcopal Mission Chapel and Grace Episcopal Mission Chapel during the late 1800s. John F. Cowan was born in Virginia around 1841. His mother had been born in Virginia as well; his father was born in Pennsylvania. At the time of the 1880 United States Census, John was a thirty-nine year old farmer living in Blacksburg in Montgomery County, Virginia with his wife and three children. His wife was thirty-eight year old M. G. Cowan. She and her parents were all born in Virginia. The children of M. G. and John F. Cowan were:

1. Elizabeth "Lizzie" Kent Cowan (1870), son of M. G. and John F. Cowan. At the time of the 1880 United States Census, "L. K." Cowan was nine years old and attending school. She was born in Virginia. Elizabeth Kent Cowan married John Putnam Adams, son of Lottie Putnam and Richard Henry Adams.

2. M. C. Cowan (circa 1874), daughter of M. G. and John F. Cowan. At the time of the 1880 United States Census, she was six years old and attending school.

3. James Randal Kent Cowan (circa 1876), son of M. G. and John F. Cowan. At the time of the 1880 United States Census he was four years old. He married Maude Alston Battle at Grace Episcopal Church on June 15, 1905 (as recorded in church records and in the Radford City Marriage Register). She was a parishioner of St. James' Episcopal Mission Chapel and of Grace Episcopal Mission Chapel. Maude Alston Battle and James Randal Kent had at least one child: Margaret Kent Cowan. She was born on April 5, 1905. Margaret Kent Cowan was baptized at Grace Episcopal Church on June 4, 1905 by Rev. E. R. Carter. Her sponsors were Marion Battle, Bruce Carr, and Elizabeth Adams. Relationship between Marion Battle and Mrs. Maude Alston Battle Cowan (mother of Margaret Kent Cowan) is unclear. It is also unclear whether Margaret's baptismal sponsor was Mrs. Elizabeth Campbell Radford Adams (wife of Richard Henry Adams Jr. and step-

mother of Margaret's uncle John Putnam Adams) or Mrs. Elizabeth Kent Cowan Adams (paternal aunt of Margaret, i.e. sister of James Randal Kent Cowan, and wife of John Putnam Adams).

Cowan, Robert H.
Circa 1800s

Mary W. and Dr. Robert H. Cowan were members of the Radford Episcopal Parish congregation at least during the late 1800s and early 1900s. Mary W. transferred from St. John's Episcopal Mission Chapel in New River to St. James' Episcopal Mission Chapel in Radford in 1890. The date of her husband's transfer as a communicant of St. James' was not recorded in the church register. Dr. Robert H. Cowan was a surgeon for the N & W. Railroad.

They moved to Schoolers in Pulaski County, Virginia and their names were removed from the St. James' roster of communicants in 1897. However, the Cowan family again appears on the roster of Grace Episcopal Church, Radford, communicants during the early 1900s as "Robert H. Cowan, Mrs. J. R. H. Cowan, and Margaret Kent Cowan". The married woman referred to above may have been Mrs. J. R. K. Cowan (i.e. Mrs. Maude Alston Battle Cowan, wife of James Randal Kent Cowan and mother of Miss Margaret Kent Cowan) or to Mrs. R. H. Cowan (i.e. Mrs. Mary W. Cowan, wife of Dr. Robert H. Cowan). At any rate, church records further note that "Mrs. J. R. H. Cowan" transferred to Christ Church in Blacksburg, Virginia on June 5, 1964.

Richard Cruff
Circa 1857

Richard Cruff, born around 1857, was the son of Mary and Henry Cruff of Montgomery County, Virginia. He married Rosa Lee Kesterson at St. James' Episcopal Mission Chapel on August 1, 1895 as recorded in church records and in the Radford City Marriage Records. Rosa Lee Kesterson, born around 1873, was the daughter of Nannie and John M. Kesterson of East Radford, Virginia. At the time of their marriage, Rosa Lee was twenty-two and Richard was thirty-eight. They were both then living in East Radford. Rev. A. A. Pruden officiated at the marriage ceremony that was attended by "a large congregation at the Church".

According to the 1880 United States Census, an unmarried twenty-three year old white male named Richard Cruff was living with the family of Crocket Kinser in Central Depot and working as a laborer. This may have been the Richard Cruff who married Rosa Lee Kesterson in 1895. That same census described a Mary Cruff as a white forty-eight year old woman living with her mother, sixty year old Margaret Moore, and her two sons in the Auburn area of Montgomery County, Virginia. Those sons were a twenty-one year old farmer named James Cruff and a nine year old son named Giles W. Cruff. There was also a two year old white child named John Clayton Moore living with the family.

Darnell, William Wirt
Circa 1854-1934

William Wirt Darnell, born around 1854, was a photographer in East Radford during the late 1800s and early 1900s. He was a communicant of St. James' Episcopal Mission Chapel at least by 1891. He was a communicant of Grace Episcopal Mission Chapel by 1900 and continued as a communicant when the two chapels merged to form Grace Episcopal Church in 1904. He remained as a parishioner until his death in 1934.

During his time in the Radford Episcopal Parish, he served as a vestryman and as a Junior Warden of the Vestry. On June 8, 1891, he was elected to the vestry of the newly formed Radford Parish. He continued to serve on the vestry from 1891 through 1906. He was also active in his community both as a photographer and as a member of the Radford Wheelmen bicycle club.

Rev. James A. Figg recorded in the church register that Mr. W. W. Darnell was living in East Radford when he died at the age of eighty from "complications". He died on April 3, 1934 and was buried in "E. Radford" on April 7, 1934; this may have been a reference to Central Cemetery. William Wirt Darnell's family donated a stained glass window depicting The Crucifixion to Grace Episcopal Church in his memory and in honor of his service as a vestryman and junior warden.

Deal, John
Circa 1844-1897

John Deal of Radford, Virginia was born around 1844. He died in Radford on March 29, 1897 at age 53 from "paralysis" according to Rev. F. G. Ribble's entry in the Radford Episcopal Parish register. John Deal was buried on March 31, 1897 in the "Radford Cemetery", a reference either to Central Cemetery in the East Ward or to West View Cemetery in the West Ward.

Dixon, Elizabeth
Circa 1800s

Mrs. Elizabeth Dixon was a St. James' Episcopal Mission Chapel communicant in 1891. No additional information is available regarding this parishioner at this time.

Drake, C. L.
Circa 1800s

C. M. and C. L. Drake were parishioners of Grace Episcopal Mission Chapel in Radford at least from 1895 through 1897. Mrs. C. M. Drake joined the Ladies Chapel Fund society and attended its organizational meeting on January 26, 1896. Her participation was quite active, from hosting meetings in her home to helping plan society fund-raising events. The minutes of the March 2, 1897 meeting reported that "Mrs. Drake showed the society a very pretty sun bonnet. The Society agreed to make similar ones if orders were given". Also in 1897, Mrs. Drake served as Vice President of the church women's society.

C. M. and C. L. Drake chose Grace Episcopal Chapel in Radford, Virginia for the baptism of their son as follows: Stewart

Livingston Drake. According to church baptismal records, he was born in Roanoke, Virginia on May 4, 1894. He was baptized at Grace Episcopal Mission Chapel in Radford on November 10, 1895 at the age of one and a half. Rev. A. A. Pruden conducted the service, which was attended by his parents and sponsors Mrs. M. S. Moyer and Mrs. E. S. Drake.

Echols, R. M.
Circa 1800s

R. M. Echols was a communicant of Grace Episcopal Mission Chapel at least from 1890 through 1897, when he transferred to Christ Episcopal Church in Roanoke, Virginia. He came to the Radford area from Pulaski. R. M. Echols was baptized "in the Church" and was confirmed at Grace Episcopal Mission Chapel on October 4, 1890 by the Rt. Rev. Alfred M. Randolph, attested to by Rev. Edward L. Goodwin.

Edmonds, W. P.
Circa 1800s

W. P. Edmonds and his wife were communicants of St. James' Episcopal Mission Chapel at least by 1895, when they transferred from Trinity Episcopal Church in Pottsville, Pennsylvania. They later moved out of the Radford area. Additional information about these parishioners is not now known.

Eggleston, William
Circa 1821

Capt. William Eggleston and his wife, Maria L., were communicants of the Radford Episcopal Parish chapel from about 1890 through 1893. Mrs. Maria L. Eggleston was listed as a communicant from Giles County, Virginia in 1890. The family moved to Mississippi in 1893.

The family was living in Giles County, Virginia when the 1880 United States Census was compiled. They were described as a fifty-nine year old white farmer named William Eggleston living with his fifty-three year old wife M. L. Eggleston and their three children. Maria L. and William Eggleston had children:

1. I. B. Eggleston (circa 1852), daughter of Maria L. and William Eggleston. She was twenty-eight years old when the 1880 United States Census was compiled.
2. William M. Eggleston (circa 1857), son of Maria L. and William Eggleston. He was twenty-three years old when the 1880 United States Census was compiled.
3. Lewis T. Eggleston (1860), son of Maria L. and William Eggleston. His name was written as twenty year old "Louis" T. Eggleston in the 1880 United States Census report and as "Lewis" Eggleston in church records. Lewis T. Eggleston was born in 1860, confirmed in 1893, and died at the age of thirty-three on March 12, 1893. Rev. Edward L. Goodwin recorded in the church register that Lewis died in Eggleston's Springs, Giles County, Virginia of typhoid fever and was buried there on March 13, 1893.

Eskridge, Edgar Peyton
1862-1933

Edgar Peyton Eskridge, born on June 7, 1862, was the son of Mary Jane Smith Taylor and James Edgar Eskridge. He attended Virginia Military Institute in Lexington, Virginia at least during the year 1880.

When he was twenty-two, he married Rosamond Gwenllian[84] Terrell in September 1884 according to church records. Born in South Wales on December 15, 1869, she was the daughter of Isabella M. Sprye and Judge Terrell of London, England.

Rosamond and Edgar Peyton Eskridge were parishioners of Grace Episcopal Mission Chapel at least during the late 1800s. They and their children were listed in parishioner records as resid-

[84] Rosamond G. Terrell's middle name is spelled "Gwenllian" in the church register.

ing with Mary and James E. Eskridge in Pepper's Ferry in 1891. Mrs. Rosamond Eskridge was a Grace Episcopal Mission Chapel communicant on March 1, 1891, an "old communicant of St. John's, New River Depot". Another note in records states that she "made communion" at Grace on August 7, 1904. Edgar Peyton Eskridge died in 1933 and was buried in Central Cemetery. His marker reads "Edgar P. Eskridge, 1862-1933". Rosamond Gwenllian Terrell and Edgar Peyton Eskridge had children:

1. Edgar Henry Terrell Eskridge (1883), son of Rosamond Gwenllian Terrell and Edgar Peyton Eskridge. Called Harry, he was born on June 29, 1883. According to church records, he passed away on February 14, 1893 from diphtheria[85] at the young age of "seven and a half years". He was buried in Eskridge Cemetery[86] on February 17, 1893 with clergyman Edward L. Goodwin officiating. His grave marker in Radford City's Central Cemetery reads "Edgar Henry Terrell Eskridge, only son of E. P. and R. T. Eskridge, June 29, 1883, Feb. 14, 1893". According to his grave marker, Harry was nine and a half years old when he died.

2. Mary Alice Eskridge (1886), daughter of Rosamond Gwenllian Terrell and Edgar Peyton Eskridge. She was born on November 4, 1886. When she was four, she and two of her sisters were baptized as children at their parents' home in Montgomery County, Virginia on November 5, 1890. Her sponsor was her grandmother, "Mrs. Eskridge Sr.", whose full name was Mrs. Mary Jane Smith Taylor Eskridge. Her mother was in attendance as a witness. The Rev. Edward L. Goodwin officiated. She was a parishioner of Grace Episcopal Mission Chapel at least from 1890 through 1894.

3. John McCanless Taylor Eskridge (1888), son of Rosamond Gwenllian Terrell and Edgar Peyton Eskridge. She

---

[85] Diptheria, a highly infectious disease which can result in fever, breathing difficulty, swallowing difficulty, heart failure, and paralysis of breathing muscles, was also called croup, spotted fever, ship fever jail fever and putrid fever in early records.

[86] Church records listing a family cemetery often referred to a family plot within a public cemetery. Note reference to "Eskridge Family Cemetery" as burial site for E. H. T. Eskridge who was buried in the public "Central Cemetery".

was born on February 2, 1888 and died October 4, 1888. A marker in Radford's Central Cemetery reads "Infant son of Edgar P. and Rosamond Eskridge, Feb. 2, 1888, Oct. 4, 1888, age 8 mo. 2 days".

4. Anne Rebecca Wharton Eskridge (1889), daughter of Rosamond Gwenllian Terrell and Edgar Peyton Eskridge. She was born on March 16, 1889. She was baptized at the Eskridge home on November 5, 1890 when she was one and a half years old. Rev. Edward L. Goodwin conducted the baptism, with her grandmother Mrs. Eskridge Sr. serving as sponsor and her mother as witness. Anne Rebecca Wharton Eskridge was a parishioner of Grace Episcopal Mission Chapel at least from 1890 through 1894, and again from 1902 through 1904. She was confirmed on April 7, 1905 at the church, renamed Grace Episcopal Church. She married a Pritchard. Mrs. A. R. W. E. Pritchard donated books from the family collection to Radford University library in 1933, the year of her father's death.

5. Isabella Terrell Eskridge (1890), daughter of Rosamond Gwenllian Terrell and Edgar Peyton Eskridge. She was born on August 31, 1890. She was baptized two months later on November 5, 1890 with the Rev. Edward L. Goodwin officiating. Her witness was her mother Rosamond Eskridge and her sponsor was her paternal grandmother. The service was held at the Eskridge family home. Isabella Terrell Eskridge was a parishioner of Grace Episcopal Mission Chapel at least from 1890 through 1894. She married an Englishman named Arthur Richard Davis. At some point, they moved to California. Upon their deaths, they were both buried in Radford's Central Cemetery. Their markers read "Isabella Eskridge Davis, Radford, VA, San Francisco, CA, Feb. 1969" and "Arthur Richard Davis, London, England, Daville, CA, April 1976".

6. Rosamond Blanche Eskridge (1894), daughter of Rosamond Gwenllian Terrell and Edgar Peyton Eskridge. She was born on January 8, 1894. She was baptized at Grace Episcopal Mission Chapel in Radford by the Rev. E.

Sterby Gunn of "Clresmont", Virginia on November 11, 1894.

7. Margaret Peyton Eskridge (1903), daughter of Rosamond Gwenllian Terrell and Edgar Peyton Eskridge. She was born on June 4, 1903. She was baptized at Pepper, Virginia on December 31, 1903 as entered into church records by Rev. E. R. Carter. Margaret Peyton Eskridge's sponsors were Lilly P. Kearsley, Julia Kohlhousen (wife of Theodore F. Kohlhousen), and Theophilus H. Kohlhousen.

Fink, Jacob
Circa 1800s

Amanda and Jacob Fink lived in East Radford of Montgomery County, Virginia at least by 1889 and were Episcopal parishioners. They had children:

1. Florence B. Fink (circa 1861), daughter of Amanda and Jacob Fink. She was born around 1861. She was twenty-eight years old when she married twenty-seven year old John B. R. Cameron. John B. R. Cameron, born around 1862, was the son of Virginia G. and G. W. Cameron of Mercer County, West Virginia. The Fink-Cameron wedding was held in Radford on October 9, 1889 with the Episcopal clergyman Rev. Edward Lewis Goodwin officiating and family and friends in attendance. Nine years earlier, at the time of the 1880 United States Census, seventeen year old white male John B. Cameron was living in Roanoke County, Virginia with his forty year old mother Virginia Cameron.

2. Edward Jacob Fink (1870), son of Amanda and Jacob Fink, of whom more.

Fink, Edward Jacob
1870-1956

Edward Jacob Fink and his wife Irene Robinson were residents of East Radford, Virginia and parishioners of St. James' Episcopal Mission Chapel and Grace Episcopal Mission Chapel at least from 1889 through the early 1900s. They continued their Episcopal communicant status when the two chapels merged to form the Grace Episcopal Church. The family was listed on Grace Episcopal Church rolls as Edward Fink, Irene Fink, Ambrose Fink, Mary Margaret Fink, Edward Fink Jr., and Lewis Clark Fink. Mrs. Irene Fink still attended the Church and played the organ during church services at least into the 1920s. The Finks purchased a pew for Grace Episcopal Church.

Edward Jacob Fink, the son of Amanda and Jacob Fink, was born on February 2, 1870. He was baptized at St. James' Episcopal Mission Chapel on April 10, 1898 by the Rev. Floyd L. Kurtz. His sponsors were Mrs. L. W. Clark (i.e. Mrs. Mary Phoebe Finch Clark) and Captain Ambrose Robinson. Edward Jacob Fink was also confirmed at St. James' by the Rt. Rev. A. M. Randolph, attested to by Rev. Floyd L. Kurtz, on May 10, 1898. As a young man, Edward Fink invented the railroad car derailer.

On May 26, 1897, he married Irene Robinson as documented by church records and by Radford City Marriage Records. The Rev. F. G. Ribble officiated, with family and friends in attendance at St. James' Episcopal Mission Chapel. Irene, the daughter of Mary and Ambrose Robinson, was born on March 8, 1876.

Irene Robinson Fink died at the age of seventy-six. Her marker in Radford's Central Cemetery reads "Irene R. Fink, March 8, 1876, May 24, 1952". Edward Jacob Fink died at the age of eighty-six. His marker in Radford's Central Cemetery reads "Edward J. Fink, Feb. 12, 1870, May 16, 1956".

Irene Robinson and Edward Jacob Fink had children:
1. Ambrose Franklin Fink (circa 1899), son of Irene Robinson and Edward Jacob Fink. He was born in Radford, Virginia and baptized at St. James' Episcopal Mission Chapel "as an infant" by the Rev. Floyd L. Kurtz on May 10, 1899. His sponsors were Captain Ambrose Robinson (his maternal grandfather) and Mrs. L. W. Clark. A note in the

church register states that Ambrose Franklin Fink may have passed away in Portsmouth, Virginia on January 18, 1957. Ambrose Franklin Fink, his mother Mrs. Irene Robinson Fink, and his father Edward Jacob Fink gave a Litany Desk to the Church in memory of Frank Stringfellow Wilson, his brother and their son.

2. Mary Margaret Fink (1901), daughter of Irene Robinson and Edward Jacob Fink. A marker in Central Cemetery reads "Mary M. Fink Wilson, Oct. 20, 1901, June 11, 1998". She was ninety-six years of age when she died.

3. Lewis Clark Fink (circa 1900s), son of Irene Robinson and Edward Jacob Fink.

4. Edward Jacob Fink Jr. (1904), son of Irene Robinson and Edward Jacob Fink. He was born on March 2, 1904 and was baptized at the age of four months on July 31, 1904. The baptismal ceremony was conducted by Rev. Edwin Royall Carter. Edward's baptismal sponsors were Lewis Washington Clark, Captain Ambrose Robinson, and Miss Blanche Adams. A grave marker in Radford's Central Cemetery reads "Edward J. Fink Jr., Mar. 21, 1904, Jan. 11, 1933. He was twenty-nine when he died.

5. Alva Duval Fink (1905), may have been a son of Irene Robinson and Edward Jacob Fink. A marker in Central Cemetery reads "Alva Duval Fink, VA. PVT US Army, World War II, Sept. 20, 1905, Feb. 6, 1959".

Fitzgerald, Peter
Circa 1800s

Mary L. and Peter Fitzgerald attended St. John's Mission Chapel in New River, Virginia, in 1895. They had a daughter: Veda Massie Fitzgerald. According to church baptismal records, she was born on September 5, 1888. She was baptized at St. John's Episcopal Mission Chapel in New River, Virginia on July 28, 1895 when she was seven years old. Her sponsors were Mrs. W. C. Hodge (i.e. Mrs. Weurginia Anne Hodge) and Veda Massie's mother Mrs. Mary L. Fitzgerald. The baptism was recorded by Rev. A. A. Pruden "by proxy". Veda Massie Fitzgerald attended St. John's Episcopal Mission Chapel and then St. James' Episcopal Mission Chapel. She may have moved out of the area at some point.

Franklin, Sarah E.
Circa 1809 - 1889

Mrs. Sarah E. Franklin was born around 1809. She was living in Radford, Virginia, when she died on March 29, 1889, cause of death in church records being listed as "burnt". She was eighty years old. She was buried on March 30, 1889 at Central Cemetery. Episcopal clergyman Edward L. Goodwin officiated, although Sarah's religious denomination was listed as Methodist.

French, John Pettus
1856-1917

John Pettus French and his family lived in the East Ward of Radford on Seventh Street at least by 1889. His wife Mrs. Susan "Susie" Roberts French "re-entered as a communicant" of Grace Episcopal Mission Chapel on September 9, 1890, according to church records. Meeting minutes from the Rectors Aid Society of Grace Parish Episcopal Chapel state that "Mrs. French and her sister" (name not recorded) joined the Aid Society during March of 1902.

John French was living in Central Depot with his mother and his siblings when the 1880 Census was taken. The family was described as being composed of a white twenty-five year old railroad employee named John French, his fifty-six year old mother named Susan French, his twenty-seven year old brother and railroad employee Henry French, and his twenty-two year old unmarried sister Ella French.

Upon their deaths, Mr. and Mrs. John Pettus French were both buried at Radford's Central Cemetery. Her grave marker reads "Susie Roberts French, 1863-1915". He died two years later. His marker reads "John Pettus French, 1856-1917".

Susan Roberts and John Pettus French had children:

1. Sophia Roberts French (circa 1800s), daughter of Susan Roberts and John Pettus French. She was a parishioner and communicant of Grace Episcopal in 1898.
2. Robert Bruce French (circa 1889), son of Susan Roberts and John Pettus French. He was born around March 1889. He died at the age of fifteen months on June 25, 1890 from "summer complaint". He was buried June 26, 1890 at Central Cemetery, as recorded by Rev. E. L. Goodwin.
3. Hugh French (circa 1900s), may have been a son of Susan Roberts and John Pettus French. A marker in Radford's Central Cemetery reads "Hugh R. French, VA. CORP 116 INF 24 DIV, Aug. 27, 1937".

Fry, Worley M.
Circa 1853

Worley M. Fry and his wife A. Belle were members of the St. James' Episcopal Mission Chapel congregation in 1886. They may have moved away from the Radford area sometime after 1895.

Worley M. Fry was born around 1853. His wife A. Belle was born around 1859. The 1880 United States Census recorded the Fry family as living in Central Depot, Montgomery County, Virginia with three sons. The family members were described as twenty-seven year old white railroad fireman Worley Fry, his twenty-one year old wife Belle Fry, their four year old son William Fry, their two year old son "Center" Fry, and their one year old son Roy Fry. By 1887, A. Belle and Worley M. Fry had eight children, all of whom were baptized as members of the St. James' Episcopal Mission Chapel congregation. The baptisms were performed by Rev. J. E. Hammond on September 29, 1887, which was St. Michael's Day and All Angels' Day. Their sponsor was Captain Ambrose Robinson. Belle and Worley Fry had children:
1. William Risk Fry (1876), son of A. Belle and Worley M. Fry. Called William, he was born on May 4, 1876. He was four years old at the time of the 1880 Census. He was ten years and four months of age when baptized in 1887.
2. John Centre Fry (1877), son of A. Belle and Worley M. Fry. Called Centre, he was born on August 18, 1877. He

was two years old at the time of the 1880 Census. He was nine years old when baptized in 1887.

3. Charles W. Roy Fry (1879), son of A. Belle and Worley M. Fry, was born on February 17, 1879. Roy was one year old when the 1880 Census was taken. He was eight and a half years old when the Fry children were baptized.

4. Ambrose Gill Fry (1881), son of A. Belle and Worley M. Fry. He was born on February 5, 1881. He was six and a half years of age when the Fry children were baptized in 1887.

5. Carrie Myrtleday Fry (1882), daughter of A. Belle and Worley M. Fry. Called Myrtle, she was born on February 26, 1882. She was five and a half years of age when the Fry children were baptized in 1887. Heth Fry (1884), son of A. Belle and Worley M. Fry. He was born on September 4, 1884. He was three years of age when the Fry children were baptized in 1887. He died at the age of eight years on November 10, 1891 from "concussion of the brain". He was buried on November 12, 1891 at the "Radford Cemetery", according to church records entered by Rev. Edward L. Goodwin.

6. Robert Gregory Fry (1886), son of A. Belle and Worley M. Fry. He was born on June 1, 1886. He was one year and three months of age when the Fry children were baptized in 1887.

7. Lena Mabell Fry (1887), daughter of A. Belle and Worley M. Fry. She was born on March 20, 1887. She was five months old when the Fry children were baptized in 1887.

Galway, William Henry
Circa 1858-1939

William Henry Galway and his wife, Mrs. Lydia Harris Galway, of Radford were members of Grace Episcopal Mission Chapel at least during the late 1800s and early 1900s.

Lydia Harris Galway was a parishioner of Grace Episcopal Mission Chapel and a member of the Rector's Aid Society of Grace Parish Episcopal Chapel in 1894. She served in many ways, including membership on the entertainment committee for Society fund-raisers. She does not appear to have attended any Society meetings from December 1894 through June 1900. However, she rejoined the Society in July 1900 and continued to participate through 1902. She assumed roles such as engaging cleaners for the church and in 1902 was the society President. The Galways supported their church throughout their lives. As one example of their financial and other support, Mr. and Mrs. William Henry Galway presented a pew to Grace Episcopal Church.

Lydia Harris Galway died in 1938. Her husband William H. Galway died the following year. They were both buried in Radford's West View Cemetery. Church records as entered by Rev. Charles W. Sydnor in 1938 read "Mrs. Lydia Harris Galway (W. H.). Female. Age 71. Last residence: Radford. Died Jan. 27, 1938 of paralysis. Buried Jan. 29, 1938. West View." A second entry by Rev. Sydnor in 1939 reads "Mr. William H. Galway. Male. Age 81. Last residence: Radford. Died Jan. 3, 1939 of old age. Buried Jan. 4, 1939. West View."

Many gifts were made to Grace Episcopal Church in memory of the Galways. A financial gift was given to Grace in memory of the Galways by their daughter Mrs. W. T. Baldwin (i.e. Mrs. Marie Louise Galway Baldwin). A missal stand was also given to the church in memory of Lydia Harris Galway and William Henry Galway by their children Mrs. Marie Louise Galway Baldwin and Stanley Harris Galway. Lydia and W. H. Galway had children:

1. Marie (also called Mary) Louise Galway (circa 1800s), daughter of Lydia Harris and William Henry Galway. She was attending Grace Episcopal Mission Chapel with her family at least by 1900. She married William Thomas Baldwin Jr., son of Alice Cummings Field and William Thomas Baldwin Sr. W. T. Baldwin Sr. was a veteran of the Civil War, having served in the Fourth Virginia Regiment of the Wythe County Grays of Stonewall's Brigade. A professional in his community after the War, he was a member of the Sovereign Grand Lodge of Odd Fellows, a representative to the Virginia State Lodge meeting three times and one time Grand Master, a member of the Lodge of Ancient and Accepted Masons, and first Chairman of the Board of Trustees of the Radford Normal School. The

Baldwins lived in East Radford. Mrs. Marie Louise Galway Baldwin and William Thomas Baldwin Jr. had children, including Calvin B. Baldwin Sr. He married Louise Delp, daughter of Sally Clark and Mayor William Delp of the Delp Hotel in West Radford.

2. Stanley Harris Galway (circa 1800s), son of Lydia Harris and William Henry Galway. He was attending Grace Episcopal Mission Chapel with his family at least by 1900. He married Mary Clay Roby on June 9, 1920 (as recorded in the Radford City Marriage Register).

Garking, William Henry
1871-1948

William Henry Garking, his wife Mrs. Florence "Alice"[87] Yardley Crangle Garking, and their children were parishioners and communicants of Grace Episcopal Mission Chapel and then Grace Episcopal Church by the late 1890s or early 1900.

William Henry Garking was born in London, England on November 3, 1871. He was confirmed by the Archbishop of Canterbury. W. H. Garking learned the tailoring trade in London and immigrated to the North American continent. He married Florence Yardley Crangle of Canada. Florence was born in Toronto, Canada on November 3, 1871. Florence Yardley Crangle and William Henry Garking were married by or around Spring 1891. The young couples' first two children were born in Toronto. The family moved to Bedford, Virginia sometime between March 1897 and August 1898; the Garking's third child was born in Bedford in 1898. By 1900 the family moved to Radford, Virginia, where William H. Garking operated a tailoring business and made suits for students enrolled at the prestigious St. Alban's School for Boys across the river from Radford. The Garking's oldest son, Wallace Albert, later attended St. Alban's School. The Garking's last three children were born in Radford.

---

[87] Mrs. Garking's name was written as Florence Alice Garking in church records and as Florence A. Garking on the stained glass church window in her memory.

The Garking family was active in the Grace Episcopal Mission Chapel community. Mrs. Florence Alice Garking was a member of the Rector's Aid Society of Grace Parish Episcopal Chapel at least in 1900 and 1901. Mr. William Henry Garking went to church early every Sunday morning to start the fire so the church would be warm for morning service until central heat was installed at Grace. He was Senior Warden of the Vestry late in life until his death in 1948.

Florence Alice Garking died in 1914. Church records by the Rev. C. E. A. Marshall state the following: "Mrs. W. H. Garking, Female, Age 44, of Radford, died on April 21[88], 1914". Official church records state that she was buried on April 24, 1914 in the "West Radford Cemetery", a reference to West View Cemetery in Radford. William Henry Garking Sr. died from angina on May 20, 1948. He too was buried at West View Cemetery, the Garking Family Plot adjoining that of the Sutcliffe family.

Numerous gifts were made to Grace Episcopal Church by and in memory of the Garkings. W. H. Garking Sr. presented the church with a pew and a hymnal cross. The Family donated to the church a stained glass window depicting "Jesus Enters Jerusalem" in memory of Mrs. Florence A. Garking and Wallace A. Garking Jr. Mr. W. H. Garking Sr. gifted the church with carillonic bells in memory of his wife and son[89]. Two small alms basins were given to the church in memory of W. H. Garking. Florence Alice and William Henry Garking had children:

1. Wallace Albert Garking (1892), son of Florence Yardley Crangle and William Henry Garking. Wallace Albert Garking was born in Toronto, Canada on April 3, 1892. As a boy, he attended St. Alban's School for Boys, a prestigious preparatory school in the Radford area. He was twenty-two when his mother died. He died on February 15, 1922 from pneumonia; he was twenty-nine years old.

---

[88] Florence Yardley Crangle Garking died from cancer on April 14, 1914 (not April 21 as written in church records), according to descendant and Grace Episcopal Church parishioner Mrs. Iris Elizabeth "Betty" Ritenour Wright. William Henry Garking Sr. was her grandfather. Betty's great-grandson was the sixth generation to be baptized at Grace Episcopal in Radford.

[89] The church Red Book of Remembrances list the carillonic bells in memory of Mrs. Florence A. Garking, Wallace A. Garking, W. H. Garking Jr. and William H. Garking.

2. Clarence Sinclair Garking (1897), son of Florence Yardley Crangle and William Henry Garking. Clarence Sinclair Garking was born in Toronto, Canada on February 15, 1897. He died on December 28, 1977 from multiple health challenges.

3. William Henry Garking Jr. (1898), son of Florence Yardley Crangle and William Henry Garking. William Henry Garking Jr., known as "Willie", was born in Bedford, Virginia on August 25, 1898. He was confirmed at Grace Episcopal Church on April 7, 1905. He died at the age of sixteen on December 1, 1914, eight months after his mother's death. A note in church records states that he was buried at "Central Cemetery". This is incorrect. He was buried in the Garking family plot at West View Cemetery.

4. Florence Alexandra Garking (1903), daughter of Florence Yardley Crangle and William Henry Garking. Called "Girlie" by her family, she was born in Radford, Virginia on October 18, 1903. She was baptized at Grace Episcopal Mission Chapel on October 17, 1903 by Rev. Edwin R. Carter, according to church records (Note: her birth date and her baptism date are in conflict; it is likely she was baptized during November of 1903. Her sponsors were Sam Sutcliffe, Anna D. Stevens, and Martha J. Sutcliffe. She married a Mr. Ritenour. Mrs. Florence Alexandra Garking Ritenour died of cancer on June 23, 1991 at the age of eighty-eight. Her daughter Iris Elizabeth Ritenour was also baptized in Grace Episcopal. She married Mr. Wright. Their daughter, Mrs. Rebecca Wright Markert, was baptized at Grace Episcopal. Additional descendants Jason and Kyla Wickline were also baptized at Grace Episcopal.

5. Crangle Royal Garking (1907), son of Florence Yardley Crangle and William Henry Garking. He was born in Radford, Virginia on March 16, 1907. At some point, he moved out of state. He died on June 20, 1960 at the age of fifty-three years; cause of death not now known.

6. Lydia Henrietta Garking (1910), daughter of Florence Yardley Crangle and William Henry Garking. Called

"Dollie", she was born in Radford, Virginia on July 24, 1910. She died from multiple health problems on December 12, 2000 at the age of eighty-nine.

Illustration 53: The Garking family, 1914. Back row: Florence Alexandria Garking, Clarence Sinclair Garking, and their father William Henry Garking. Front row: Crangle Royal Garking and Lydia Henrietta Garking. Courtesy of Garking descendant Mrs. Bette R. Wright.

Gibbs, M. C.
Circa 1800s

Minnie Gross and her husband M. C. Gibbs were communicants of Grace Episcopal Mission Chapel in 1891. Frank Gross, the brother of Mrs. Minnie Gross Gibbs, lived with them in Radford, Virginia until they moved to North Carolina. Her name was "removed without letters" in August 1892.

Goldsmith, James
Circa 1800s

James Goldsmith came to the Radford area from Warrenton, Virginia. He and his wife were communicants within the Radford Episcopal Parish at least from 1892 through 1895. At some point after 1895, their names were removed the church membership roster.

Greaves, Helen
Circa 1800s

Mrs. Helen Greaves entered the Radford Episcopal Parish from Kingston, Ontario, Canada on April 30, 1892. She enrolled as a communicant on the same date that Mrs. Jessie Boothe joined the parish from Kingston, Ontario, Canada. Her name was removed from the roster of communicants during September 1892, as was that of Charles Boothe. Additional information about early Episcopal communicants Charles Boothe, Mrs. Jessie Boothe, and Mrs. Helen Greaves is not now known.

Green, James K.
Circa 1800s

James K. Green and his wife, Mrs. L. C. Green, were parishioners of St. James' Episcopal Mission Chapel in 1892, having transferred from St. John's Episcopal Church in Roanoke, Virginia. They were parishioners of St. James' at least from 1892 through 1895. L. C. and James K. Green had children:

1. Susan Green (circa 1800s), daughter of L. C. and James K. Green. Called Susie, she transferred from St. John's Episcopal Church in Roanoke, Virginia to St. James' Episcopal Mission Chapel in Radford in April 1892.

2. Gertrude Belle Green (circa 1800s), daughter of L. C. and James K. Green. This 1892 communicant of St. James' Episcopal Mission Chapel married Alfred Perkins Page on November 4, 1893. She moved to Norfolk, Virginia soon after her marriage. A notation in church records indicates she may have died soon thereafter.

3. Mary C. Green (circa 1800s), daughter of L. C. and James K. Green. She was baptized "in the Church", according to St. James' Episcopal Mission Chapel records, and was confirmed at St. James' on May 12, 1893. The Rt. Rev. A. M. Randolph performed the confirmation rite as attested to by Rev. Edward Lewis Goodwin.

4. Hellen James Green (1881), daughter of L. C. and James K. Green. According to church baptismal records, she was born on April 6, 1881 in Little Washington, Virginia. She was baptized four years later at St. James' Episcopal Mission Chapel in Radford. Rev. A. A. Pruden performed the baptismal service, with sponsors Mr. O. H. Kohlhousen, Miss Patty J. Taylor, and Miss Susan Green in attendance. Hellen was a St. James' communicant from 1895 until 1947 when she transferred to St. John's Episcopal Church in Waynesboro, Virginia.

Haldeman, Charles
Circa 1800s

Charles Haldeman and his wife, Emily Wilson, were parishioners of St. James' Episcopal Mission Chapel at least from 1891 through 1897. Her name appears on the church rosters as a communicant from Columbia, Pennsylvania in 1891. His name appears with hers the following year, in 1892.

They lived in the West Ward of Radford. They were living at the Radford Inn when it was destroyed by fire in March 1893.

Mrs. Emily Wilson Haldeman was baptized at St. James' Episcopal Mission Chapel. She was an active member of the Rector's Aid Society of Grace Parish Episcopal Chapel from 1894 through 1896, when the Society was re-established as the Ladies Chapel Fund Society. She had served as President of the Rector's Aid Society in 1895, and was President of the Ladies Chapel Fund Society in 1896. Emily and Charles Haldeman had children:

1. Louise Haldeman (1891), daughter of Emily Wilson and Charles Haldeman. According to church baptismal records, she was born on March 6, 1891. She was baptized at Grace Episcopal Mission Chapel on September 2, 1894 at the age of three years. With Rev. A. A. Pruden officiating, her sponsors were John S. Wilson (by proxy), Catherine A. Wilson (by proxy), and her mother Emily Wilson Haldeman.

Harkness, Robert P.
Circa 1800s

Mary L. and Robert P. Harkness lived in Radford and were members of Grace Episcopal Mission Chapel in Radford Episcopal Parish at least between 1890 through 1893. At some point following the 1892 death of their daughter Helen, they moved to Cincinnati, Ohio.

A "Miss Harkness" was a member of the church women's organizations including the Rector's Aid Society of Grace Parish Episcopal Chapel at least from 1891 through 1893. She was a public school teacher who served as the church society treasurer for two years before resigning in February 1893. There is no record that she attended any meetings after her resignation. Her first (i.e. Christian name) is not given, although it is likely that this young woman was either Josephine or Mary Harkness.

Mary L. and Robert P. Harkness had children:

1. Sallie C. Harkness (circa 1869), daughter of Mary L. and Robert P. Harkness. At the age of twenty-one, she married Harvey E. Hannaford on December 24, 1890 at her par-

ents' home in Radford. Harvey E. Hannaford, the son of Phoebe and Sam C. Hannaford of Cincinnati, Ohio, was born around 1857. He came to the Radford Episcopal Parish from Cincinnati and married Sallie C. Harkness when he was twenty-three years of age. The December 24, 1890 wedding ceremony was performed by Rev. Edward Lewis Goodwin with family and friends in attendance.

2. Elizabeth Vail Harkness (circa 1800s), daughter of Mary L. and Robert P. Harkness. She was baptized as a child by Grace Episcopal Mission Chapel rector Edward Lewis Goodwin at her family home on May 29, 1892. Her sponsors were her mother Mrs. Mary L. Harkness (by proxy) and her sister Miss Josephine M. Harkness. Her sister Helen was baptized at the same time.

3. Helen Dorcas Harkness (circa 1884), daughter of Mary L. and Robert P. Harkness. She was eight years old when she was baptized at the Harkness home on May 29, 1892 one month before her death. Rev. Edward Lewis Goodwin performed the baptismal rites for Helen and for her sister Elizabeth with her mother Mrs. Mary L. Harkness (by proxy) and her sister Miss Josephine M. Harkness as sponsors. Helen's parents chose the Grace Episcopal Mission Chapel for her funeral service when died at the young age of eight years. Helen Dorcas Harkness died on June 13, 1892 from endocarditis. She was buried on June 14, 1892 in Cincinnati, Ohio according to church records entered by clergyman Edward Lewis Goodwin.

4. Josephine M. Harkness (circa 1800s), daughter of Mary L. and Robert P. Harkness. She is listed in court records as an Episcopal communicant at least in 1891, having come to the parish from Winton Place, Ohio. Records also state that she moved to Cincinnati, Ohio during September 1894.

5. Mary S. Harkness (circa 1800s), believed to have been a daughter of Mary J. and Robert P. Harkness. She is listed in church records as a communicant at least in 1891, having come to the parish from Winton Place, Ohio and moving to Cincinnati, Ohio during September 1894.

Harless, Allen I.
Circa 1819

Allen I. Harless and his wife M. Ann were members of the Radford Episcopal Parish during the late 1800s. Mrs. M. Ann Harless came to St. James' Episcopal Mission Chapel from Christiansburg, Virginia. Church records note that she was baptized at St. James'.

Allen I. Harless was born around 1819. Mrs. M. Ann Harless was born around 1842. When the United States Census of 1880 was taken, the Harless family was living in the Blacksburg district of Montgomery County, Virginia. They were a farming family. Allen Harless was sixty-one years of age in 1880. His wife was thirty-eight. Their children ranged in age from four years to seventeen years old. Mr. and Mrs. Harless, their parents, and their seven children were all born in Virginia.

According to advertisements in the 1892 issues of the *Radford Advance*, Allen I. Harless was an attorney practicing with Judge W. D. Vaughan in the firm of Vaughan & Harless Attorneys-at-Law; Harless would have been seventy-three years of age. Their offices were located in Rooms 4 and 5 of the Briggs' Building in East Radford. Ann and Allen Harless had seven children:

1. F. A. Harless (circa 1863), son of M. Ann and Allen Harless. He was a seventeen year old farm laborer when the 1880 United States Census data was recorded.
2. J. A. Harless (circa 1867), son of M. Ann and Allen Harless. He was a thirteen year old farm laborer when the 1880 United States Census data was recorded.
3. J. C. R. Harless (circa 1869), son of M. Ann and Allen Harless. He was an eleven year old farm laborer when the 1880 United States Census data was recorded.
4. M. E. Harless (circa 1872), daughter of M. Ann and Allen Harless. She was eight years old when the 1880 United States Census data was recorded.
5. J. M. Bittle Harless (circa 1873), son of M. Ann and Allen Harless. He was seven years old when the 1880 United States Census data was recorded.

315

6. Edmonia N. Harless (circa 1874), daughter of M. Ann and Allen Harless. She was six years old when the 1880 United States Census data was recorded.
7. Margie Harless (circa 1876), daughter of M. Ann and Allen Harless. She was four years old when the 1880 United States Census data was recorded.

Hayhoe, George
Circa 1800s

Mr. and Mrs. George Hayhoe (spelled "Hayhoe" in church records and "Hayhole" in Radford City marriage records) of England were living in Radford, Virginia with their daughter Mary by 1892. Mary I. Hayhoe was born in Sunderland, England around 1872, as reported in the City of Radford Marriage Register Book One Page Two. When she was twenty years old, she married twenty-five year old Radford resident Henry Edward Tear.

Henry Edward Tear was working as a bricklayer at the time of his marriage. The son of Rose and Fred K. Tear, he was born in London, England around 1867. Episcopal clergyman Rev. Edward L. Goodwin performed the marriage ceremony in Radford on August 24, 1892. The wedding was held at Grace Episcopal Mission Chapel with friends of the bridge and groom in attendance.

Hodge, William C.
Circa 1800s

William C. Hodge and his wife Weurginia Anne were parishioners of Grace Episcopal Mission Chapel from New River Depot in 1891. He was employed as a contractor.

Mrs. Weurginia Hodge, who was born on February 11, 1861, was listed in church records as an "old communicant of St. John's Church, New River Depot", and a communicant of Grace Episcopal Mission Chapel. She was a member of the Rector's Aid Society of Grace Parish Episcopal Chapel during 1893 and 1894. She attended her last meeting on July 11, 1894. Prior to that, she participated in the many sewing activities of the Society. One such activity, the sewing of aprons to offer for sale, was an idea presented by Weurginia and agreed upon by the ladies of the group.

William C. Hodge, his wife Weurginia Ann Hodge, and their daughter Agnes Laura Hodge were still listed in church records as communicants from New River in 1903. An additional undated note in church records states that Mrs. Weurginia A. Hodge and Miss Agnes L. Hodge "left communion".

Weurginia Anne Hodge died on March 9, 1915. A stained glass window depicting "In the Garden" was donated to Grace Episcopal Church during the 1930s in her memory. It was inscribed "Weurginia Anne Hodge 1861-1915, Mother of Mrs. Homer Jamison". Vestibule windows were also presented to the Church by Mrs. Bess K. Bullard and Mrs. Agnus Laura Hodge Jamison (i.e. Mrs. Homer Jamison).

Weurginia Anne and William C. Hodge had children:

1. Agnes Laura Hodge (1883), daughter of Weurginia Anne and William C. Hodge. She was born on July 23, 1883 at New River, Virginia according to church baptismal records. She was baptized at St. John's Episcopal Mission Chapel in New River on March 31, 1895. the twelve year old received the baptismal rites from Rev. A. A. Pruden. Her sponsors were W. J. Kenderdine and his wife M. L. Kenderdine. Agnes Laura Hodge was confirmed at St. John's by the Rt. Rev. A. M. Randolph as attested to by Rev. A. A. Pruden. She married Homer J. Jamison.

2. Hodge *son* (circa 1885), may have been the son of Weurginia Anne and William C. Hodge. According to church records, "the infant son of Mr. Hodge and his wife" died of "cholera infantum"[90] on August 25, 1885. The family resided in New River, Virginia, and their son was buried near New River on August 26, 1885. The Rev. J. E. Hammond officiated at the burial service.

3. Anna Virginia Hodge (circa 1890), may have been the daughter of Weurginia Anne and William C. Hodge. According to church records, she died on July 15, 1890 at the age of seven months from "summer complaint", a term

---

[90] Cholera infantum referred to a disease contracted by infants from contaminated milk. Cholera was also contracted from contaminated water or food and was often fatal due to the severe dehydration resulting from symptoms of the illness.

which described any childhood illness characterized by severe diarrhea which occurred during high seasonal temperatures, i.e. summer months. Her family was then residing in New River. Episcopal clergyman Edward Lewis Goodwin did not record in church records the names of her parents. Anna Virginia Hodge was buried on July 16, 1890 at "Morgan's Cemetery" in Pulaski County.

Howe, Minnie Stuart
1883-1930

Minnie Stuart Howe was a parishioner of St. James' Episcopal Mission Chapel and Grace Episcopal Mission Chapel at least by 1895. She was a member of the Woman's Guild of Grace chapel in 1902, hosted the candy table at the 1903 Christmas bazaar, and was a communicant of Grace Episcopal Church in 1904 along with family member "Pollie Howe" (who may have been her sister Sallie DeJarnette Howe). Minnie was a member of the church choir at least during the 1920s. She was also a member of the Radford Chapter of the Virginia Daughters of the Confederacy, of the United Daughters of the Confederacy.

Minnie Stuart Howe, the daughter of Sallie DeJarnette and Captain John T. Howe, was born on January 22, 1883. She died on September 8, 1930 at the age of forty-seven from "tonsil operation and enemia" [a misspelling in church records for the word "anemia"] according to church records. She was buried on September 9, 1930 at Central Cemetery in East Radford. Her marker reads "Minnie Stuart Howe, Jan. 22, 1883, Sept. 8, 1930". Her family donated a stained glass window depicting "Feed the Lamb" to Grace Episcopal Church in her memory.

Howe, Virginia Preston
1878-1897

Virginia Preston Howe was a Grace Episcopal Mission Chapel communicant in 1895 who had been baptized as a "Campbellite", according to church records. She moved from Radford to

Norfolk, Virginia around 1896 where she attended Christ Episcopal Church. She returned to Radford at least by Autumn 1897. She was confirmed at St. James' Episcopal Mission Chapel two years before her 1897 death. The 1895 confirmation rites were performed by the Rt. Rev. A. M. Randolph, attested to by Rev. A. A. Pruden.

She was also a member of the Radford Chapter of the Virginia Daughters of the Confederacy, of the United Daughters of the Confederacy.

Miss Virginia Preston Howe, daughter of Sallie DeJarnette and Captain John T. Howe, was born on March 29, 1878. She died at the age of nineteen on November 12, 1897 from "apoplexy", according to church records as recorded by Rev. F. G. Ribble. She was buried in "Radford Cemetery" (i.e. Central Cemetery") on November 14, 1897. Her marker in Central Cemetery reads "Virginia Preston Howe, beloved daughter of J. T. and S. DeJ. Howe, Mar. 27, 1878-Nov. 12, 1897".

The detailed paternal lineage[91] of Minnie Stuart Howe and Virginia Preston Howe is as follows (Joseph Howe > Daniel Howe > John Dunbar Howe > John Thomas Howe > Minnie Stuart Howe & Virginia Preston Howe).

1) __Joseph Howe__ 1st GENERATION (circa 1729-1794), son of James Howe (born circa 1703) of England. Joseph Howe was born in England around 1729 and immigrated to the American colonies around 1737. He married a Scottish woman named Eleanor Dunbar. They lived in Massachusetts prior to moving to Virginia's New River Valley during the 1750s. They settled in a section of Montgomery County that would become a part of Pulaski County, Virginia. Joseph served as a Major in the colonial militia. Major Joseph Howe died March 1794 in Pulaski County. Eleanor Dunbar and Joseph Howe had children as follows.

[91] Lineage of Hoge, Howe, and Tyler families has been presented by researchers including Johnston in 1906, L. G. Tyler in 1915, J. H. Tyler as published posthumously in 1927, Bruce in 1929, Howe in 1961, and Kegley in 1980 and 2003.

a) <u>Joseph Howe Jr.</u> 2nd GENERATION (circa 1749), may have been a son of Eleanor Dunbar and Joseph Howe.

b) <u>Rebecca Howe</u> 2nd GENERATION (circa 1751), daughter of Eleanor Dunbar and Joseph Howe. She married John Day.

c) <u>John William Howe</u> 2nd GENERATION (circa 1752), son of Eleanor Dunbar and Joseph Howe. He married Mary Ann Waggoner, also known as Polly. They had eight children: Joseph Howe (circa 1700s), Rebecca Howe (circa 1700s), Eleanor Howe (circa 1700s, John Nelson Howe (circa 1700s), Sarah Howe (circa 1700s), William Howe (circa 1700s), Daniel Lyman Howe (circa 1700s), James Howe (1774) who married Martha Hood, and Eleanor Howe (circa 1755) who married George Pearisof Back Creek (who was the brother of Robert Pearis and Matilda Pearis). Eleanor's sister-in-law Matilda Pearis married Samuel Pepper, who came to the New River Valley around 1770 and established Pepper's Ferry in Montgomery County in 1780. Eleanor's brother-in-law Robert Pearis married her sister Anne Howe.

d) <u>Ann Howe</u> 2nd GENERATION (circa 1756), daughter of Eleanor Dunbar and Joseph Howe. She married Robert Pearis, her sister's brother-in-law, in 1772. Robert's sister Matilda Pearis married Samuel Pepper, the founder of Pepper's Ferry.

e) <u>Ellen Howe</u> 2nd GENERATION (circa 1761), may have been a daughter of Eleanor Dunbar and Joseph Howe.

f) <u>Elizabeth Howe</u> 2nd GENERATION (circa 1763), daughter of Eleanor Dunbar and Joseph Howe. She married James Hoge Jr., the son of Agnes Crawford and James Hoge. James Hoge Sr., born in 1706, was descended from Scottish ancestry. James Hoge Jr. was born in 1742 and died in 1812. Elizabeth Howe and James Hoge settled in the Back Creek area of present-day Pulaski County, Virginia and created an estate. Their home was called "Hayfield" and was built on the site where a brick home was built in 1826; that home was named Belle Hampton by their grandson James Hoge Tyler in honor of his two daughters Belle Norwood Tyler and Sue Hampton Tyler. James Hoge Jr. and Elizabeth Howe had children.

i) James Hoge III 3rd GENERATION (circa 1788), son of Elizabeth Howe and General James Hoge Jr. He married Eleanor Howe, the daughter of his mother's brother Daniel Howe. They had children.

g) Daniel Howe 2nd GENERATION (1758-1838), son of Eleanor Dunbar and Joseph Howe. He was born in Montgomery County, Virginia on September 20, 1758. The family lived in the Back Creek section of Montgomery County (Back Creek later becoming a part of Pulaski County). Daniel Howe died in Back Creek at the age of eighty on January 2, 1838. He was a Major and a Lieutenant in the colonial militia during the Revolutionary War. He applied for a military pension in 1832 based upon his service in the Virginia militia. Daniel Howe married Nancy Heavin (also spelled Haven) of New River on August 28, 1790. The daughter of Ruth Hall and Howard Heavin, she was born on January 8, 1771 and died at the age of fifty-nine years of age on March 4, 1830, eight years before her husband's death. Nancy Haven and Daniel Howe had eleven children: Elizabeth Howe, Julia Howe, Ruth Howe, Joseph H. Howe, Lucretia Howe, Daniel Webster Howe, Nancy Howe, Luemma Howe, William H. Howe, Eleanor Howe, and John Dunbar Howe as follows.

i) Elizabeth Howe 3rd GENERATION (circa 1790), daughter of Nancy Haven and Daniel Howe. She married George Neeley Pearis.

ii) Julia Howe 3rd GENERATION (circa 1794), daughter of Nancy Haven and Daniel Howe. Also called July or Julie, she married Zacharia Cecil.

321

iii) Rutha Howe 3rd GENERATION (circa 1796), daughter of Nancy Haven and Daniel Howe. Also called Ruth, she married Thomas Kirk.

iv) Joseph Howard Howe 3rd GENERATION (circa 1798), son of Nancy Haven and Daniel Howe. He married Margaret Feely.

v) Lucretia H. Howe 3rd GENERATION (circa 1802), daughter of Nancy Haven and Daniel Howe. She married William Thomas.

vi) Daniel Webster Howe 3rd GENERATION (circa 1804), may have been a son of Nancy Haven and Daniel Howe.

vii) Nancy Howe 3rd GENERATION (circa 1806), daughter of Nancy Haven and Daniel Howe. She married Harvey Deskins.

viii) William Henry Howe 3rd GENERATION (1810-1896), son of Nancy Haven and Daniel Howe. He was born in Back Creek of present Pulaski County on March 15, 1810. He married Mary Margaret Fisher of Christiansburg in 1836. She was born in Virginia around 1814. They had nine children.

(1) Nancy Deskins Howe 4th GENERATION (circa 1837), daughter of Mary Margaret Fisher and William Henry Howe.

(2) Isabella Howe 4th GENERATION (circa 1839), daughter of Mary Margaret Fisher and William Henry Howe. She married Dr. Charles T. Pepper.

(3) Mary Elizabeth Howe 4th GENERATION (circa 1840), daughter of Mary Margaret Fisher and William Henry Howe.

(4) Daniel Kirk Howe 4th GENERATION (circa 1843), son of Mary Margaret Fisher and William Henry Howe.

(5) William Grayson Howe 4th GENERATION (circa 1845), son of Mary Margaret Fisher and William Henry Howe.

(6) Augusta Virginia Howe 4th GENERATION (circa 1847), daughter of Mary Margaret Fisher and William Henry Howe.

(7) Eleanor Howe 4th GENERATION (circa 1849), daughter of Mary Margaret Fisher and William Henry Howe.

(8) Sarah Margaret Howe 4th GENERATION (circa 1851), daughter of Mary Margaret Fisher and William Henry Howe.

(9) Alice Howe 4th GENERATION (circa 1853), daughter of Mary Margaret Fisher and William Henry Howe.

ix) Luemma F. (or P.) Howe 3rd GENERATION (circa 1812), daughter of Nancy Haven and Daniel Howe. She married a Dr. Jackson.

x) Eleanor Howe 3rd GENERATION (1792-1856), daughter of Nancy Haven and Daniel Howe. She was born on December 1, 1792 in Montgomery County, Virginia. She married General James Hoge III. He was born around 1788 and died in 1861. They made their home in a section of Montgomery County that would later be a part of Pulaski County. They had ten children: Helen Mary Hoge, James Robert Hoge, Eliza Hoge, Senah Ann Hoge, Joseph Crockett Hoge, Ellen Hoge, Oscar Hoge, Samuel Sayers Hoge, Willie Sue Hoge, and John T. Hoge as follows.

(1) Helen Mary Hoge 4th GENERATION (circa 1800s), daughter of Eleanor Howe and James Hoge III.

(2) James Robert Hoge 4th GENERATION (circa 1800s), son of Eleanor Howe and James Hoge III.

(3) Eliza Hoge 4th GENERATION (circa 1815), daughter of Eleanor Howe and James Hoge III. She may have been born around 1815. She married George Tyler[92], who was also

---

[92] George Tyler, father of Governor James Hoge Tyler, may have been born on December 13, 1817.

born during the early 1800s (around 1817). George Tyler had first married Jane Coleman DeJarnette; they had two daughters. Mrs. Jane Coleman DeJarnette was born on December 26, 1820 and died on January 5, 1841. George Tyler married second to Eliza Hoge. Mrs. Eliza Hoge Tyler died from childbirth complications in 1846, about two weeks after the birth of their only child James Hoge Tyler (a future governor of Virginia). George Tyler married third to Jane Coleman Quesenberry (or Quisenberry), who was born on March 15, 1830 and died on February 25, 1859; they had two children. The three-time widower George Tyler died on November 6, 1889, when his son was forty-three. George Tyler was a member of the lineage of President John Tyler as per the 1896 book The Letters and Times of the Tylers by Lyon Gardiner Tyler, President Tyler being one of the "Tylers of York, James City and Charles City Counties" and George Tyler being one of the "Essex and Caroline Tylers" of Virginia. George Tyler, himself a State Legislator from Caroline County from 1859 through 1865, was the son of Lucinda Coleman and Henry Tyler and the grandson of Revolutionary War veteran Captain George Tyler. Captain George Tyler was the son of William Tyler of Caroline County, Virginia, and the grandson of Susannah and Richard Tyler. Children of George Tyler as follows:

(a) Tyler daughter 5th GENERATION (circa 1800s), may have been a daughter of George Tyler and a first wife named Jane Coleman DeJarnette, who died in 1841. This daughter of DeJarnette and Tyler married James Armistead Otey.

(b) Tyler daughter 5th GENERATION (circa 1800s), may have been a daughter of George Tyler and Jane Coleman DeJarnette, who died in 1842.

(c) James Hoge Tyler 5th GENERATION (1846-1925). The only son of Eliza Hoge and George Tyler, James Hoge Tyler was born on August 11, 1846 at the family home called "Blenheim" in Caroline County. He joined the Confederate army at the age of sixteen and became a Major by the end of the War. J. Hoge Tyler married Susan Montgomery Hammet. She was the daughter of Clementina Venable Craig and Colonel Edward Hammet, sister of Mrs. Isabella Hammet Heth and sister-in-law of Captain Stockton Heth. Susan, called Sue, was born in 1845 and died in 1927. James Hoge Tyler inherited his great-grandfather's estate in Back Creek of present Pulaski County. He named the estate "Belle Hampton" in honor of two his daughters, Belle Norwood Tyler and Sue Hampton Tyler. James Hoge Tyler, his wife Sue Hammet Tyler, their children, his half-brother George W. Tyler (a teacher), and three servants (George Burke, Miss Malinda Carter, and Miss Jennie Deane) were living in the Tyler home in the Dublin District of Pulaski County, Virginia, when the 1880 United States Census was recorded. Tyler developed a coal vein on his Pulaski County lands as well as agricultural interests. Sue and J. Hoge Tyler established a home in eastern Radford, Virginia built from handmade bricks around 1890 or 1891, and named it "Halwyk". The Tyler home became a no-

325

table landmark in Radford, both as the home of one of Virginia's Governors and as the home where William Jennings Bryan was a guest during his 1900 presidential campaign stop in southwest Virginia. Halwyk was built on a hilltop overlooking the New River; that original entrance is now the back of the house, with a semi-circle driveway on the opposite side leading up to the house from Tyler Avenue, named for Governor Tyler. James Hoge Tyler was a member of the Virginia State Senate representing Giles County, Pulaski County, Bland County, and Tazewell County from 1877 through 1879, a Lieutenant Governor, and then Governor of Virginia from 1897 through 1902. He served on the Board of Visitors of Blacksburg College, was a member of the State Agricultural Society, and an elder in the Presbyterian church. He was also the President of the Radford Development Company, of the Virginia Mutual Building and Loan Association, and of the Radford Building and Investment Association. J. Hoge Tyler died in 1925 and was buried in the Tyler plot in West End Cemetery of Radford[93]. His tombstone reads "James Hoge Tyler, Aug. 11, 1846, Jan. 3, 1925". A stone memorial in his honor reads "James Hoge Tyler, Born "Bleinheim" Caroline County, VA Aug. 11, 1846. Died "Halwick" East Radford, VA Jan. 3, 1925. Soldier. Christian.

[93] In addition to the thirteen Tyler grave markers in the Tyler plot of the West End Cemetery in Radford VA is a marker that reads "Rev. David J. Williams Chorister, Born in Wales, Died 1922, I WAS A STRANGER AND YE TOOK ME IN".

Statesman. Holding all men as God's children and loving them Without respect to race or creed. He was beloved likewise by all mankind. A devoted member of the Presbyterian Church for thirty years, entrusted with many of its highest missions. A Confederate soldier at seventeen. State senator 1877-70. Lieut. Governor 1898-1894. Governor of Virginia 1890-1902. Faithful unto death". Governor Tyler's wife died two years after his death. Mrs. Susan Montgomery Hammet Tyler's West View Cemetery marker reads "Sue Montgomery Hammet, wife of James Hoge Tyler, July 16, 1845-Apr. 24, 1927". Susan Montgomery Hammet and James Hoge Tyler had children:

(i) Edward Hammet Tyler 6th GENERATION (1869), son of Susan Montgomery Hammet and Governor James Hoge Tyler. He was a ten year old student at the time of the 1880 Census. He attended Virginia Agricultural and Mechanical College in Blacksburg, was a farmer and a well-known member of the community in Pulaski County. He belonged to a local guard company called the Radford Rifles during the late 1890s. His grave marker in West View Cemetery reads "Edward Hammet Tyler, Dec. 15, 1869, Mar. 22, 1939".

(ii) James Hoge Tyler Jr. 6th GENERATION (1871), son of Susan Montgomery Hammet and Governor James Hoge Tyler. He was eight years old at the time of the 1880 Census. He married Evelyn (maiden

327

surname not now known). He attended the Virginia Agricultural and Mechanical College in Blacksburg and Hampton-Sidney College. His grave marker in West View Cemetery, Radford, reads "James Hoge Tyler Jr., Dec. 12, 1871, Feb. 27, 1937".

(iii) Stockton Heth Tyler 6th GENERATION (1874), son of Susan Montgomery Hammet and Governor James Hoge Tyler. He was five years old at the time of the 1880 Census. He was born in Pulaski, Virginia, on September 13, 1874. He attended Virginia Polytechnic State University in Blacksburg, Virginia, Hampden-Sidney College, and Washington and Lee University where he received his B. L. degree in 1895. Stockton Heth Tyler married Miss Nellie Serpell in 1904. He was a lawyer who became the Mayor of Norfolk, Virginia, and the Director of the Seaboard National Bank. He served his country curing the Spanish-American War as a Major and an Addl. Paymaster for the U. S. Volunteers, S. A. W. He was a member of the Presbyterian faith. Stockton Heth Tyler was living in Norfolk, Virginia, when his biography appeared in a 1927 Edition of Who's Who in the South published by the Mayflower Publishing Company. Stockton Heth Tyler was a delegate to the Democratic National Convention in 1940. Nellie and Stockton Heth Tyler had children:

1. Goldsborough Serpell Tyler 7th GENERATION (circa 1907), son of Nellie Serpell and Stockton Heth Tyler.
2. James Hoge Tyler 7th GENERATION (circa 1911), son of Nellie Serpell and Stockton Heth Tyler.
3. Sue Hammet Tyler 7th GENERATION (circa 1915), daughter of Nellie Serpell and Stockton Heth Tyler.
4. Nellie Serpell Tyler 7th GENERATION (circa 1916), daughter of Nellie Serpell and Stockton Heth Tyler.
5. Stockton Heth Tyler Jr. 7th GENERATION (circa 1918), son of Nellie Serpell and Stockton Heth Tyler.
6. Gulielma Tyler 7th GENERATION (circa 1922), daughter of Nellie Serpell and Stockton Heth Tyler.

(iv) Belle Norwood Tyler 6th GENERATION (1876), daughter of Susan Montgomery Hammet and Governor James Hoge Tyler. She was four years old at the time of the 1880 Census. She married Frank Percy McConnell, a Radford banker and businessman. Upon their deaths, they were both buried in the Tyler family plot in West View Cemetery. Her grave marker reads "Belle Norwood Tyler, wife of Frank Percy McConnell, Mar. 9, 1876-Feb. 4, 1955". His marker reads "Frank Percy McConnell, July 1, 1870, Sept. 21, 1941". An additional marker in the Tyler plot of Radford's

West View Cemetery may mark the burial of Frank Percy McConnell's sister; it reads "Lena McConnell, wife of Capt. Clifton L. Sitton, Sept. 3, 1877, Feb. 23, 1944".

(v) Sue Hampton Tyler 6th GENERATION (1877), son of Susan Montgomery Hammet and Governor James Hoge Tyler. She was born on the Back Creek estate. She was three years old at the time of the 1880 Census. She married Robert Ware Jopling. Her marker reads "Sue Hampton Tyler, wife of Robert Ware Jopling, Apr. 9, 1877, Apr. 24, 1949". His marker in the Tyler plot reads "Robert Ware Jopling, May 11, 1865, June 8, 1944". Two additional Jopling markers in the Tyler plot would appear to be laid for their children as follows:

1. Sue Tyler Jopling 7th GENERATION (1916), daughter of Sue Hampton Tyler and Robert Ware Jopling. Her grave marker reads "Sue Tyler Jopling, Nov. 4, 1916, Oct. 8, 1979".

2. James Robert Jopling 7th GENERATION (1918), may have been a son of Sue Hampton Tyler and Robert Ware Jopling. His grave marker reads "James Robert Jopling, Aug. 10, 1918, Aug. 11, 1920".

(vi) Henry Clement Tyler 6th GENERATION (1878), son of Susan Montgomery Hammet and Governor James Hoge Tyler. Called Hal, he was born at the "Belle Hampton" estate in Pulaski County on December

330

10, 1878. He was listed as a one year old at the time of the 1880 Census. Hal Tyler attended St. Albans School for Boys (also known as St. Albans Academy) under Colonel Miles, later attended the University of Virginia, and became an attorney. He was appointed and then elected to be Radford City's Commonwealth Attorney at least from 1906 through 1912. In 1902, he was secretary for the Southwest Virginia Livestock Fair in Radford. His grave marker in the Tyler plot of the West End Cemetery in Radford reads: "Henry Clement Tyler, Dec. 10, 1878, Dec. 1, 1941".

(vii)   Lily Tyler 6th GENERATION (circa late-1800s), daughter of Susan Montgomery Hammet and Governor James Hoge Tyler. Lily Tyler, whose formal Christian name was Eliza, married Henry H. Wilson. Wilson graduated from Virginia Agricultural and Mechanical College and became a civil engineer. At some point they may have made their residence in Richmond, Virginia. They had children.

1. James Hoge Tyler Wilson 7th GENERATION (circa 1800s), son of Lily Tyler and Henry H. Wilson. He graduated from the University of Virginia, served during World War II as an army pilot, and returned to the area to become an instructor at Virginia Tech and an attorney.

2. Lily Norwood Tyler Wilson 7TH GENERATION (circa 1800s),

331

daughter of Lily Tyler and Henry H. Wilson.

(d) <u>Nannie Brown Tyler</u> 5th GENERATION (circa 1800s), may have been son of George Tyler and a third wife named Jane Coleman Quesenberry; in which case he would have been born after 1852.

(e) <u>George William Tyler</u> 5th GENERATION (1857), son of George Tyler. His mother was the third wife of George Tyler, believed to have been Jane Coleman Quesenberry. George William Tyler was born on February 9, 1857. According to the U. S. Census of 1880, George William Tyler was at that time a twenty-three year old teacher living in the home of his half-brother James Hoge Tyler. George William Tyler married Mary Stuart Carter.

(4) <u>Senah (or Sarah) Ann Hoge</u> 4th GENERATION (circa 1849), daughter of Eleanor Howe and James Hoge III.

(5) <u>Joseph Crockett Hoge</u> 4th GENERATION (circa 1851), son of Eleanor Howe and James Hoge III.

(6) <u>Ellen Hoge</u> 4th GENERATION (circa 1853), daughter of Eleanor Howe and James Hoge III.

(7) <u>Oscar Hoge</u> 4th GENERATION (circa 1855), son of Eleanor Howe and James Hoge III.

(8) <u>Samuel Sayers Hoge</u> 4th GENERATION (circa 1856), son of Eleanor Howe and James Hoge III.

(9) <u>Willie Sue Hoge</u> 4th GENERATION (circa 1858), daughter of Eleanor Howe and James Hoge III.

(10) <u>John T. Hoge</u> 4th GENERATION (circa 1861), son of Eleanor Howe and James Hoge III.

xi) John Dunbar Howe 3rd GENERATION (1801-1885), son of Nancy Haven and Daniel Howe. He married Sarah (also spelled "Sara") Boyd Logan Shepherd in 1830. She was born in 1815 and died in 1859. Sarah B. Shepherd and John Dunbar Howe had nine children: Agnes Howe, Margaret Howe, Susan Howe, Eliza Jane Howe, Ellen Mary Howe, Samuel S. Howe, Willie Howe, Haven B. Howe, and John Thomas Howe as follows.

(1) Agnes Howe 4th GENERATION (circa 1800s), daughter of Sarah Boyd Logan Shepherd and John Dunbar Howe. She was born in Pulaski County, Virginia. She married Eugene G. DeJarnette. Mrs. Agnes Howe DeJarnette was a member of the Daughters of the American Revolution (DAR), member #127203, as a granddaughter of Revolutionary War veteran Lt. Daniel Howe.

(2) Margaret Howe 4th GENERATION (circa 1800s), daughter of Sarah Boyd Logan Shepherd and John Dunbar Howe. She married George Shannon.

(3) Susan Howe 4th GENERATION (circa 1800s), daughter of Sarah Boyd Logan Shepherd and John Dunbar Howe. She married J. M. Thomas.

(4) Eliza Jane Howe 4th GENERATION (circa 1800s), daughter of Sarah Boyd Logan Shepherd and John Dunbar Howe. She married Charles J. Matthews.

(5) Ellen Mary Howe 4th GENERATION (circa 1800s), daughter of Sarah Boyd Logan Shepherd and John Dunbar Howe. She married J. G. Kent.

(6) Samuel S. Howe 4th GENERATION (circa 1800s), son of Sarah Boyd Logan Shepherd and John Dunbar Howe.

(7) <u>Willie Howe</u> 4th GENERATION (circa 1800s), son of Sarah Boyd Logan Shepherd and John Dunbar Howe.

(8) <u>Haven B. Howe</u> 4th GENERATION (1847-1912), son of Sarah Boyd Logan Shepherd and John Dunbar Howe. In 1873, he married as his first wife Katherine M. Cloyd. Called Kate, she was born in 1852 and died in 1895. Katherine M. Cloyd and Haven B. Howe had children, including:

(a) <u>Mary Howe</u> 5th GENERATION (circa 1800s), daughter of Katherine Cloyd and Haven B. Howe. She was born in Pulaski County, Virginia. She married Thomas F. Farrow. She was a member of the Daughters of the American Revolution (DAR), member #127692, as a great-granddaughter of Revolutionary War veteran Lt. Daniel Howe.

(b) <u>Emma Howe</u> 5th GENERATION (circa 1874), daughter of Katherine Cloyd and Haven B. Howe. She was living with her parents in the Newbern District of Pulaski County, Virginia at the time of the 1880 Census.

(c) <u>David C. Howe</u> 5th GENERATION (circa 1876), son of Katherine Cloyd and Haven B. Howe. He was living with his parents in the Newbern District of Pulaski County at the time of the 1880 Census.

(d) <u>Lucy Howe</u> 5th GENERATION (circa 1879), daughter of Katherine Cloyd and Haven B. Howe. She was living with her parents in the Newbern District of Pulaski County at the time of the 1880 Census.

(9) <u>John Thomas Howe</u> 4th GENERATION (1842-1909), son of Sarah Boyd Logan Shepherd and John Dunbar Howe. He was

334

born on April 21, 1842 in Pulaski County, Virginia. He served in the Confederate Army during the Civil War. He married Sallie Lewis DeJarnette. They were living in the Blacksburg District in Montgomery County, Virginia at the time of the 1880 Census. The family was described as: thirty-seven year old farmer John T. Howe, his wife thirty-seven year old Sallie Lewis DeJarnette (although her birth year was 1848, making her age at the time of the 1880 Census to be thirty-two), and their five sons and one daughter. Mrs. Sallie Lewis DeJarnette Howe was born in 1848 and died in 1897 at the age of forty-nine. Her husband John Thomas Howe died in 1909 at the age of sixty-seven. Sallie and John T. Howe later lived in Radford and, upon their deaths, were buried at Central Cemetery. Their shared marker reads "John T. Howe, Father, C.S.A., CAPT. CO E 4th VA INF, Apr. 21, 1842, Mar. 3, 1909" and "Sallie DeJarnette Howe, Mother, Feb. 10, 1848, Nov. 12, 1897".

(a) Robert DeJarnette Howe 5th GENERATION (circa 1867), son of Sallie Lewis DeJarnette and John Thomas Howe. He was thirteen at the time of the 1880 United States Census.

(b) Samuel Sheppard Howe 5th GENERATION (circa 1870), son of Sallie Lewis DeJarnette and John Thomas Howe. He was eleven at the time of the 1880 United States Census.

(c) Bessie Howe 5th GENERATION (circa 1871), daughter of Sallie Lewis DeJarnette and John Thomas Howe. She died as a toddler around 1874.

(d) Ellen Dunbar Howe 5th GENERATION (circa 1872), daughter of Sallie Lewis DeJarnette and John Thomas Howe.

(e) John Thomas Howe Jr. 5th GENERATION (circa 1874), son of Sallie Lewis DeJarnette and John Thomas Howe. He was six at the time of the 1880 United States Census.

(f) George Shannon Howe 5th GENERATION (1876), son of Sallie Lewis DeJarnette and John Thomas Howe. He was four at the time of the 1880 United States Census. His grave marker in Central Cemetery reads "George Shannon Howe, A Disciple of Christian Social Justice, May 8, 1876, Oct. 9, 1938".

(g) Virginia Preston Howe 5th GENERATION (1878-1897), daughter of Sallie Lewis DeJarnette and John Thomas Howe. She was born on March 29, 1878. She was two years old at the time of the 1880 United States Census. She was a parishioner of Grace Episcopal Mission Chapel in Radford. Miss Virginia Preston Howe died on November 12, 1897.

(h) Elliott Hampton Howe 5th GENERATION (1880-1918), son of Sallie Lewis DeJarnette and John Thomas Howe. He was three months old at the time of the 1880 United States Census. His marker in Central Cemetery reads "Elliott Hampton Howe, 1st Lieutenant Company M, 116th Infantry 29th Div, son of Capt. Jno. & Sallie DeJarnette Howe, May 21, 1880. Killed Oct. 11, 1918 in the Argone, East of the Meuse, France".

(i) Minnie Stuart Howe 5th GENERATION (1883-1930), daughter of Sallie Lewis DeJarnette and John Thomas Howe.

She was a parishioner of Grace Episcopal Mission Chapel.

(j) <u>Charles Kent Howe</u> 5th GENERATION (circa 1886), son of Sallie Lewis DeJarnette and John Thomas Howe.

(k) <u>Daniel Dunbar Howe</u> 5th GENERATION (circa 1888), son of Sallie Lewis DeJarnette and John Thomas Howe.

(l) <u>Sallie DeJarnette Howe</u> 5th GENERATION (circa 1890), daughter of Sallie Lewis DeJarnette and John Thomas Howe. A Howe family member called "Polly" was listed as a parishioner with Minnie Stuart Howe during the early 1900s. "Polly" may have been a nickname for "Sallie".

Ingles, Walter
1876-1949

Walter Ingles and his new bride, Mrs. Mary Melton Farmer Ingles, were living in Radford, Virginia, and attending the Radford Parish Episcopal Church at least by 1897.

Walter Ingles was born on July 25, 1876. He was the son of Ellen Ora Brewster and Elijah McClanahan Ingles of Pulaski County, Virginia. The United States Census of 1880 reported this Pulaski County family as follows: head of household Elijah Ingles was a thirty-nine year old white farmer living with his thirty-nine year old wife Ellen, their fourteen year old daughter Kate Ingles, their eleven year old daughter Fanny Ingles, their eight year old son Brewster Ingles, and their four year old son Walter Ingles.

Walter Ingles was residing in East Radford when he married Mary "Mamie" Milton (or Melton) Farmer of East Radford. She was the daughter of Mrs. Flora E. Welch Farmer and Dr. John W. Farmer of East Radford. The Farmer-Ingles wedding was held on December 8, 1897 at the Farmer home with the Rev. F. G. Ribble officiating as documented both in church records and in the Radford City Marriage Register. Witnesses included the bride's father

337

Dr. John W. Farmer, the bride's brothers, and Captain Ambrose Robinson.

Walter Ingles died on August 9, 1949. He was buried in the Ingles family plot in West View Cemetery in Radford. His parents' grave markers are in a line preceding a marker which reads "Annie Harless, wife of Walter Ingles, Aug. 1876, Mar. 5, 1948". Her marker is followed by one which reads "Walter Ingles, July 25, 1876, Aug. 9, 1949", which is followed by a marker that reads "Ollie Patterson, wife of Walter Ingles, Sept. 11, 1873, Feb. 13, 1938". No marker for Mrs. Mary Milton Farmer Ingles is found in the Ingles family plot. One additional marker reads "Henrietta Ingles, Infant daughter of Walter & Ollie P. Ingles, June 7, 1917, September 1917".

No additional Episcopal records have been found pertaining to Mrs. Mary Milton Farmer Ingles and her husband Walter Ingles.

A more detailed lineage of Walter Ingles, including discussions of lineal relationships to other family members and other prominent area families, is as follows (Thomas Ingles > William Ingles > John Ingles > Thomas Ingles > Elijah McClanahan Ingles > Walter Ingles):

1) Thomas Ingles 1st GENERATION (circa 1600s). Thomas Ingles was a merchant from Dublin, Ireland who immigrated to London, England and then to America sometime after 1730. He and his wife (name not now known) had at least three children: Matthew Ingles, John Ingles, and William Ingles as follows.
   a) Matthew Ingles 2nd GENERATION (circa 1700s), son of Mr. and Mrs. Thomas Ingles.
   b) John Ingles 2nd GENERATION (circa 1700s), son of Mr. and Mrs. Thomas Ingles.
   c) William Ingles 2nd GENERATION [94](1729-1782), son of Mr. and Mrs. Thomas Ingles. He was born

[94] William Ingles, Revolutionary War veteran, was the great-great grandfather of DAR member Mrs. Mary McClellan O'Hair, member #127167. Note: Mrs. O'Hair reported that William Ingles was born in Ireland; other sources give his country of birth as England.

in London, England in 1729. He married Mary Draper at Draper's Meadow, Virginia in 1750. Mary, daughter of George and Eleanor Hardin Draper, was born in Philadelphia, Pennsylvania in 1732. The Ingles and the Draper families moved to and established Draper's Meadow near present-day Blacksburg in 1748. William worked tirelessly to find his wife Mary after she was kidnapped by Shawnee warriors in 1755. Mary escaped and found her way home after many months of captivity and hardship. William founded the Ingles Ferry settlement in Montgomery County, Virginia near present-day Radford. He operated a licensed ferry in Pulaski County by 1762. He was a Revolutionary War veteran, serving as a Major during the Battle of Point Pleasant and as a Colonel of the Montgomery County, Virginia militia. William died in 1782; Mary died in 1815. They were buried on Ingles property in unmarked graves. A marker in Radford's West View Cemetery commemorating William Ingles reads "William Ingles, Colonial VA Troops, REV. WAR, 1782". Mary Draper and William Ingles had children[95]: Thomas Ingles, George Ingles, John Ingles, Mary Ingles, Susan Ingles, and Rhoda Ingles as follows.

i) Thomas Ingles 3rd GENERATION (1751), son of Mary Draper and William Ingles. He was kidnapped by the Shawnee in 1755 along with his mother and his brother George. Thomas was located almost thirteen years later and ransomed back by his family. He returned home at the age of seventeen. Thomas married Ellinor (also spelled Elenor) Grills of Albemarle County, Virginia. They moved with their children to the westward edges of the Eastern colonial settlement frontier as that frontier ex-

---

[95] Some oral history holds that Mary Draper Ingles may have been pregnant and given birth to a daughter at the time of her captivity. No mention of a daughter or of a pregnancy is included in the written history of her experience as recorded by her son John Ingles.

panded. In 1781, his two children were killed and his wife was injured in an Indian raid.

ii) George Ingles 3rd GENERATION (1752), son of Mary Draper and William Ingles. He was kidnapped by the Shawnee in 1755 along with his mother and his brother Thomas. George Ingles died in captivity as a child.

iii) John Ingles 3rd GENERATION (1766-1836), son of Mary Draper and William Ingles. He was born at Ingles Ferry in Montgomery County, Virginia on June 18, 1766. He was sixteen years old when his father died. John Ingles made his home at the Ingles Ferry settlement and, around 1790, built his estate called "Ingleside". Ingleside was intended to be a new home for his mother, but it is said that Mrs. Mary Draper Ingles would spend days at Ingleside and return to her old cabin home in the evenings. John Ingles married Margaret Crockett on April 22, 1794. Margaret was born around 1776, and died on October 26, 1810. After Margaret's death, John married Elizabeth Saunders on January 27, 1814. She died on August 4, 1834. John Ingles died on July 16, 1836 and was buried near the Ingles Ferry settlement. Margaret Crockett and John Ingles had nine children: William Ingles, Mary Ingles, Samuel Ingles, Crockett Ingles, Malinda Ingles, Lockey Ingles, John Ingles Jr., Margaret Ingles, and Thomas Ingles as follows.

(1) William Ingles 4th GENERATION (circa 1700s), son of Margaret Crockett and John Ingles.

(2) Mary Ingles 4th GENERATION (circa 1700s), daughter of Margaret Crockett and John Ingles.

(3) Samuel Ingles 4th GENERATION (circa 1800s), son of Margaret Crockett and John Ingles.

(4) <u>Crockett Ingles</u> 4th GENERATION (circa 1800s), son of Margaret Crockett and John Ingles.

(5) <u>Malinda Ingles</u> 4th GENERATION (circa 1800s), daughter of Margaret Crockett and John Ingles.

(6) <u>Lockey Ingles</u> 4th GENERATION (circa 1800s), son of Margaret Crockett and John Ingles.

(7) <u>John Ingles Jr.</u> 4th GENERATION (1805-1849), son of Margaret Crockett and John Ingles. He became a physician and established a medical practice at "Ingleside". Dr. John Ingles was born on August 3, 1805, died on August 3, 1949, and was buried at the Ingles family plot in Radford's West View Cemetery. He married Agnes L. McClanahan. She was born in 1812, died in 1888, and was also buried at the Ingles family plot in Radford's West View Cemetery. Agnes L. McClanahan and Dr. John Ingles had four children: William Ingles, John Ingles, Agnes L. Ingles, and McClanahan Ingles as follows.

(a) <u>William Ingles</u> 5th GENERATION (circa 1800s), son of Agnes L. McClanahan and John Ingles. He died as an infant. A shared marker in Radford's West View Cemetery reads "William Ingles, John Ingles, Agnes L. Ingles, Infant children of Dr. John Ingles and Agnes L. McClanahan".

(b) <u>John Ingles</u> 5th GENERATION (circa 1800s), son of Agnes L. McClanahan and John Ingles. He died as an infant. A shared marker in Radford's West View Cemetery reads "William Ingles, John Ingles, Agnes L. Ingles, Infant children of Dr. John Ingles and Agnes L. McClanahan".

(c) <u>Agnes L. Ingles</u> 5th GENERATION (circa 1800s), daughter of Agnes L. McClanahan and John Ingles. He died as an infant. A shared marker in Radford's West View Cemetery reads "William Ingles, John Ingles, Agnes L. Ingles, Infant children of Dr. John Ingles and Agnes L. McClanahan".

(d) <u>McClanahan Ingles</u> 5th GENERATION (1847-1907), son of Agnes L. McClanahan and John Ingles. He was born in 1847, died in 1907, and was buried at the Ingles family plot in Radford's West View Cemetery. He married Angeline "Angie" Harvey. She was born in 1853, died in 1934, and was buried at the Ingles family plot in West View Cemetery. Angie Harvey and McClanahan Ingles had three children: James Lewis Ingles, Nathaniel Harvey Ingles, and John Ingles as follows.

(i) <u>James Lewis Ingles</u> 6th GENERATION (1876), son of Angeline Harvey and McClanahan Ingles. He was born in 1876, died in 1936, and was buried at West View Cemetery. He married Gertrude Virginia Venable. The daughter of Laura Milles and Marcellus Venable, she was born in 1880, died in 1940, and was buried at West View Cemetery.

(ii) <u>Nathaniel Harvey Ingles</u> 6th GENERATION (1878), son of Angeline Harvey and McClanahan Ingles. He was born on January 6, 1878, died on September 1, 1949, and was buried at West View Cemetery. He married Minnie Jurey. She was born on February 10, 1879, died on

December 22, 1931, and was buried at Radford's West View Cemetery. Minnie Jurey and Nathaniel Harvey Ingles had two children: Robertson Jurey Ingles and Paul Ingles as follows.

1. Robertson Jurey Ingles 7th GENERATION (1912), son of Minnie Jurey and Nathaniel Harvey Ingles. He was born on March 22, 1912, died on April 29, 1961, and was buried at Radford's West View Cemetery.

2. Paul Ingles 7th GENERATION (1906), son of Minnie Jurey and Nathaniel Harvey Ingles. He was born on May 25, 1906, died on November 9, 1952, and was buried at Radford's West View Cemetery.

(iii) John Ingles 6th GENERATION (1874), son of Angie Harvey and McClanahan Ingles. He was born on September 24, 1874, died on August 7, 1947, and was buried at Radford's West View Cemetery. John Ingles married Elizabeth Graham Robinson. She was born on Sept. 11, 1883, died on Dec. 9, 1955, and was buried at West View Cemetery. Elizabeth Robinson and John Ingles had three children: Betty Ingles, Angelyn Harvey Ingles, and John Thomas Ingles.

1. Betty Ingles 7th GENERATION (1909), daughter of Elizabeth Robinson and John Ingles. She was born on September 29, 1909, died on December 22, 1997, and buried at Radford's

West View Cemetery. She married a Mr. Roosevelt (first name not now known).

2. Angelyn Harvey Ingles 7th GENERATION (1912), daughter of Elizabeth Graham Robinson and John Ingles. She was born on January 22, 1912, died on November 12, 1987, and was buried at Radford's West View Cemetery. Her grave marker commemorates her as the "family historian".

3. John Thomas Ingles 7th GENERATION (1920), son of Elizabeth Robinson and John Ingles. He was born on July 6, 1920. A monument in the Ingles family plot of West View Cemetery commemorates his life and World War II military service as a First Lieutenant "missing in action over Germany October 9, 1943".

(iv) Laura Ingles 6th GENERATION (1881), daughter of Angie Harvey and McClanahan Ingles. She was born on January 6, 1881, died on June 5, 1971, and was buried at West View Cemetery. She married David Cloyd Barton. He was born on April 11, 1877, died on August 14, 1949, and was buried at Radford's West View Cemetery. Laura Ingles and David Cloyd Barton had three children: David Cloyd Barton Jr., John Ingles Barton, and Robert Rittenhouse Barton.

1. David Cloyd Barton Jr. 7th GENERATION (1913), son of

Laura Ingles and David Cloyd Barton. He was born on October 2, 1913, died on July 24, 1924, and was buried at Radford's West View Cemetery.

2. John Ingles Barton 7th GENERATION (1918), son of Laura Ingles and David Cloyd Barton. He was born on October 14, 1918, died on December 7, 1998, and was buried at Radford's West View Cemetery.

3. Robert Rittenhouse Barton 7th GENERATION (1921), son of Laura Ingles and David Cloyd Barton. He was born on January 22, 1921, died on December 17, 1998, and was buried at West View Cemetery.

(8) Thomas Ingles 4th GENERATION (1810), son of Margaret Crockett and John Ingles. He was born on May 3, 1810, died on May 13, 1852, and was buried in the Ingles family plot in Radford's West View Cemetery. Thomas Ingles married Catherine McClanahan, who was born on January 27, 1817, died on December 21, 1887, and was buried in the Ingles plot at West View Cemetery in Radford. Thomas Ingles built a covered bridge across New River near Ingles Ferry between 1840 and 1842. It was destroyed by retreating southern troops during the Civil War to prevent the passage of Union forces seeking to pursue the Confederate soldiers into Central Depot. Catherine McClanahan and Thomas Ingles had at least three children: Elijah McClanahan Ingles, Andrew Lewis Ingles, and William Ingles as follows.

345

(a) Elijah   McClanahan   Ingles   5th
GENERATION (1840), son of Catherine
McClanahan and Thomas Ingles. He
was born on December 25, 1840, died
on October 1, 1924, and was buried in
the Ingles family plot at Radford's West
View Cemetery. He married Ellen Ora
Brewster. She was born in Georgia on
May 3, 1840, died on November 28,
1928, and was also buried in the Ingles
family plot at Radford's West View
Cemetery. Elijah Ingles served as a
Confederate Captain during the Civil
War. He was living in the Newbern Dis-
trict of Pulaski County, Virginia with
his wife, children, and servants at the
time of the 1880 United States Census.
Ellen   Ora   Brewster   and   Elijah
McClanahan Ingles had seven children,
as follows.

(i) Kate   Ingles   6th   GENERATION
(1866), daughter of Ellen Ora Brew-
ster and Elijah McClanahan Ingles.
She was born in Pulaski County,
Virginia during November 1866.
She was fourteen years old and liv-
ing with her parents when the 1880
United States Census was taken.

(ii) Fannie Ingles 6th   GENERATION
(1869), daughter of Ellen Ora Brewster and Elijah McClanahan Ingles.
Although her name was not found
in Pulaski County, Virginia birth records as a child of Ellen O. Brewster
and Elijah M. Ingles, her name did
appear as their eleven year old
daughter "Fanny" when the 1880
United States Census was taken. A
marker at the Ingles family plot in
Radford's   West   View   Cemetery

346

reads "Fannie Ingles Melton, Apr. 15, 1869, Nov. 22, 1960".

(iii) <u>Hugh   Brewster   Ingles</u>   6th GENERATION (1871), son of Ellen O. Brewster and Elijah M. Ingles. He was born in Pulaski County, Virginia on June 17, 1871. He was listed as Brewster Ingles, the eight year old son of Ellen O. Brewster and Elijah M. Ingles, in the 1880 United States Census; his name was not located in the Pulaski County birth records as a son of Ellen and Elijah. Brewster Ingles married Fannie Miller. H. Brewster Ingles died on March 12, 1943 and was buried in the Ingles family plot at West View Cemetery. Mrs. Fannie Miller Ingles was born on May 12, 1872, died on September 8, 1950, and was buried in the Ingles family plot at West View Cemetery.

(iv) <u>Thomas Ingles</u> 6th GENERATION (1873), son of Ellen O. Brewster and Elijah M. Ingles. He was born on March 14, 1873 according to Pulaski County birth records, although his name was not listed as a member of the Elijah Ingles' household on the 1880 United States Census.

(v) <u>Ellen   Ingles</u>   6th   GENERATION (1874), twin daughter of Ellen O. Brewster and Elijah M. Ingles. According to Pulaski County birth records, Ellen Ingles and her twin brother E. M. Ingles were born on July 27, 1874. One of the twins may have died at or shortly after birth. Neither Ellen Ingles nor E. M.

347

Ingles were listed as members of the Elijah Ingles' household at the time of the 1880 United States Census.

(vi) E. M. Ingles 6th GENERATION (1874), twin son of Ellen O. Brewster and Elijah M. Ingles. He may have been named for his father (i.e. Elijah McClanahan Ingles). E. M. Ingles and his twin sister Ellen Ingles were born on July 27, 1874. One of the twins may have died at or shortly after birth. Neither E. M. Ingles nor Ellen Ingles were listed as members of the Elijah Ingles' household at the time of the 1880 United States Census.

(vii) Walter Ingles 6th GENERATION (1876), son of Ellen O. Brewster and Elijah M. Ingles. He was born on July 25, 1876 in Pulaski County, Virginia and died on August 9, 1949. According to Episcopal church records, this son of Ellen O. and Elijah M. Ingles married Mary "Mamie" Milton (or Melton) Farmer on December 8, 1897. The daughter of Flora E. Welch (born around 1849) and Dr. John W. Farmer (born 1843) of East Radford, she was born around 1878.

(b) Andrew Lewis Ingles 5th GENERATION (1846), son of Catherine McClanahan and Thomas Ingles. He had a twin brother, William Ingles. He was born on February 16, 1846, died August 25, 1924, and was buried in the Ingles plot at West View Cemetery in Radford. His grave marker reads "He fulfilled well and faithfully the duties of all the relations of life". He and his twin brother

348

William joined the Confederate Army at age sixteen during the Civil War. Andrew Lewis Ingles married Julia Harvey. Mrs. Julia Harvey Ingles was born on March 3, 1851, died on March 30, 1940, and was buried in the Ingles plot at West View Cemetery in Radford. Her grave marker reads "Her children arise up and call her blessed". Julia Harvey and Andrew Lewis Ingles had eight children, as follows.

(i) Thomas Ingles 6th GENERATION (1875), son of Julia Harvey and Andrew Lewis Ingles. He was born on August 1, 1875 in Pulaski County, died in 1934, and was buried at Radford's West View Cemetery. He married Margaret Jordan in 1900.

(ii) William Ingles 6th GENERATION (1877), son of Julia Harvey and Andrew Lewis Ingles. He was born on November 27, 1877 in Pulaski County, died on April 20, 1966, and was buried at Radford's West View Cemetery. William Ingles married Sallie Harris, the daughter of Roberta Drummond and Frederick J. Harris. Sallie was born on February 13, 1887, died on November 10, 1979, and was buried at West view Cemetery. Her grave marker reads "Great is thy faith". William was a local banker. William inherited the "La Riviere" estate from his uncle William Ingles. In fact, Sallie and William Ingles moved into "La Riviere" in 1920 to care for his aunt Mrs. Minnie Snow Ingles. Sallie Harris and William Ingles had children as follows.

349

1. Andrew Lewis Ingles Sr. 7th GENERATION (1909), son of Sallie Harris and William Ingles. He was born on May 27, 1909, died on April 20, 1989, and was buried in West View Cemetery.

2. Mary Lewis Ingles 7th GENERATION (1914), daughter of Sallie Harris and William Ingles. She was born on November 8, 1919, died on August 22, 2004, and was buried at West View Cemetery. Mary Lewis Ingles married Melville Lewis Jeffries. They lived at "Ingleside". He was born on September 21, 1902, died on August 14, 1987, and was buried in West View Cemetery. Mary Lewis Ingles and Melville Lewis Jeffries had children:

   a. Lewis "Bud" Ingles Jeffries 8th GENERATION (1942), son of Mary Lewis Ingles and Melville Lewis Jeffries. He was a career military officer in the United States Army. Colonel Jeffries retired and returned to "Ingleside" with his wife Ann Deirs around 1991. They had children: John Travis Jeffries and Mary Jennifer Jeffries.

3. Roberta Harris Ingles 7th GENERATION (1919), daughter of Sallie Harris and William Ingles. She was born on November 8, 1919, died on August 22, 2004, and was buried in West View Cemetery. Her grave

350

marker reads "Whatsoever things are true". She was an Ingles family historian. Roberta Harris Ingles married Paul Steele. They were married at "La Riviere" and, in 1977, moved into "La Riviere" to take care of her mother Mrs. Sallie Harris Ingles. They continued to live at "La Riviere" until Roberta's death in 2004 and Paul's subsequent move to Roanoke, Virginia. Roberta Harris Ingles and Paul Steele had a son, Robert Steele. He lived in Roanoke, Virginia with his wife and son.

(iii) <u>Mary Draper Ingles</u> 6th GENERATION (1879), daughter of Julia Harvey and Andrew Lewis Ingles. She was born on August 16, 1879 near Ingles Ferry in Pulaski County, died on January 30, 1981, and was buried at West View Cemetery. She was a teacher. She also helped raise her widowed brother's children after the death of his wife.

(iv) <u>Elrica Harvey Ingles</u> 6th GENERATION (1881), daughter of Julia Harvey and Andrew Lewis Ingles. She was born on May 17, 1881 in Pulaski County, died on January 30, 1961, and was buried at West View Cemetery.

(v) <u>Minnie Mary Ingles</u> 6th GENERATION (1890), daughter of Julia Harvey and Andrew Lewis Ingles. She was born on April 15, 1890 in Pulaski County, died on February 6, 1974, and was buried

351

in West View Cemetery. Her grave
marker reads "She lived for others".

(vi) <u>Andrew Lewis Ingles Jr.</u>, 6th
GENERATION (1883), son of Julia
Harvey and Andrew Lewis Ingles.
Andrew L. Ingles was born in Pulaski County on July 22, 1883 and
died on February 28, 1900 at the
age of 16. He was buried at Radford's West View Cemetery.

(vii) <u>Julia Harvey Ingles</u> 6th
GENERATION (1889), daughter of
Julia Harvey and Andrew Lewis Ingles. She was born on March 30,
1889. She married Walter Budwell.

(viii) <u>Katherine McClanahan Ingles</u>
6th GENERATION (circa 1800s), may
have been a daughter of Julia Harvey and Andrew Lewis Ingles. She
married William Palmer Hill.

(c) <u>William Ingles</u> 5th GENERATION (1848),
son of Catherine McClanahan and
Thomas Ingles. He had a twin brother,
Andrew Lewis Ingles. He was born on
February 16, 1848, died on April 14,
1920, and was buried in the Ingles plot
at West View Cemetery in Radford as
was his wife. His grave marker reads
"He lived and died for good. Be that his
fame." William, nicknamed "Captain
Billy", fought for the Confederacy along
with his sixteen year old twin brother
Andrew during the Civil War. As a
young man after the War, he became a
civil engineer and worked for the railroad. He also maintained an interest in
architecture, designing and having
built a Queen Anne-style home completed with castle-like tower in 1892.
He named his home "La Rivere"; today

it is a Virginia state and a national Historic Landmark. William Ingles married Minnie Snow. She was born on May 13, 1850, died on October 14, 1926 and was buried at West View Cemetery. Her grave marker reads "Her lips did speak no guile".

(9) Margaret Ingles 4th GENERATION (circa 1800s), daughter of Margaret Crockett and John Ingles.

iv) Mary Ingles 3rd GENERATION (circa 1700s), daughter of Mary Draper and William Ingles. She married John Grills.

v) Susan Ingles 3rd GENERATION (circa 1700s), daughter of Mary Draper and William Ingles. She married Abraham Trigg. The Trigg family was one of the early families who settled in southwest Virginia. At one time the Triggs owned the land on the north side of New River that later became the site of Radford's Bissett Park.

vi) Rhoda Ingles 3rd GENERATION (1762-1829), daughter of Mary Draper and William Ingles. In 1781, she married Byrd Smith. They had children, including:

(1) Juliet Smith 4th GENERATION (1804-1885), daughter of Rhoda Ingles and Byrd Smith. In 1824 she married W. B. McClellan. He was born in 1804 and died in 1880. They had children, including:

(a) W. R. McClellan 5th GENERATION (1846), son of Juliet Smith and W. B. McClellan. In 1866, he married Louisa E. Ratliff. She was born in 1845. They had children, including:

(i) Mary McClellan 6th GENERATION (circa 1800s), daughter of Louisa E. Ratliff and W. R. McClellan. She was born in Washington County, Texas. She married H. J. O'Hair.

353

Mrs. Mary McClellan O'Hair was a member of the Daughters of the American Revolution, member #127167, based upon the Revolutionary War service of her great-great-grandfather William Ingles.

Illustration 54: Monument in memory of Mrs. Mary Draper Ingles, erected at West View Cemetery in Radford, Virginia. Photo by Joanne Spiers Moche.

James, R. Bruce
Circa 1800s

Dr. R. Bruce James came from Lexington, Virginia at least by 1891 and became a Grace Episcopal Mission Chapel communicant. Dr. James was elected on June 8, 1891 to serve on the first vestry of the new Radford Parish. He was again elected for vestry service on April 18, 1892, and was a delegate to the Episcopal Diocesan Council of 1892. Dr. James continued to serve on the vestry during 1893. His name was later removed from the church roster of communicants.

Jamison, Homer J.
Circa 1800s-1968

Homer J. Jamison attended St. John's Episcopal Mission Chapel, St. James' Episcopal Mission Chapel, and then Grace Episcopal Mission Chapel at least from 1891 through 1895.

He married Agnes Laura Hodge during the early 1900s. The daughter of Weurginia Ann and William C. Hodge, she was born on July 23, 1883 in New River, Virginia. Agnes (also spelled Agnus) was baptized at St. John's Episcopal Mission Chapel in New River on March 31, 1895. Her sponsors were Mrs. Mary Lytle Kenderdine and Colonel Warner Justice Kenderdine. Agnes was confirmed at St. John's by the Rt. Rev. A. M. Randolph as attested to by Rev. A. A. Pruden. In 1903, Agnes's name was listed as a member of the Hodge household, i.e. William C. Hodge, Weurginia A. Hodge, and Agnes L. Hodge of New River, Virginia.

In 1908, Mrs. Agnes Laura Hodge and members of the congregation donated a new organ to Grace Episcopal Church. This organ, the second for the congregation, replaced an old organ previously purchased by Mrs. E. S. Jones and Colonel Warner Justice Kenderdine for Grace Episcopal Mission Chapel. Mrs. Jamison also donated a pew to the church. Homer J. Jamison died on January 6, 1968. Gifts were given to the church in his memory from the Kiwanis Club of Radford and at least twenty-six other mourners. Miss Bess Kenderdine and Mrs. Homer Jamison donated vestibule windows in his memory.

Jeffrey, Aaron
Circa 1800s

Dr. Aaron Jeffrey, a physician, and his wife Maimie Luck came to the Episcopal parish in Radford either from Fredericksburg, Virginia or from Grace Episcopal Church in Richmond, Virginia. In 1890 they lived in the West Ward of Radford on Eighth Street. The family surname was spelled "Jeffery" in parishioner records and "Jeffrey" in church vestry records.

Dr. Jeffrey was a member of the Montgomery Episcopal Parish vestry from 1890 through 1891. In 1891, he was a member of the building committee for a new church "west of Connally's Branch". He was a member of the first vestry of Radford Parish in 1891 and continued to serve through 1895. He was also one of four church trustees at least from 1892 through 1895.

Dr. and Mrs. Aaron Jeffrey moved in 1895 to Newport News, Virginia. Rev. A. A. Pruden noted their moved from the Radford area in his August 1895 report to the Grace Episcopal Mission Chapel as follows: "During the month we have lost from our parish Dr. Aaron Jeffery *[sic]*, one of our vestrymen, and his charming wife".

Mamie Luck and Aaron Jeffrey had children:
1. Richard Fitzgerald Jeffrey (1893), son of Mamie Luck and Aaron Jeffrey. According to church baptismal records, he was born on January 16, 1893 in Radford, Virginia. He was baptized on July 9, 1893 at the age of six months. The baptismal service was conducted by Rev. Edward Lewis Goodwin at Grace Episcopal Mission Chapel. His sponsors were Firth D. Luck and Miss Margaret L. Goodwin.

Jenkins, J. Fredell
Circa 1800s

J. Fredell Jenkins came to the Radford Episcopal Parish from Richmond, Virginia. He was a communicant of Grace Episcopal

Mission Chapel in 1891. In 1892, he moved back to Richmond and transferred to St. Paul's Episcopal Church.

Jennings, Charles H.
Circa 1800s

Charles H. Jennings came to the Montgomery Episcopal Parish from Abingdon, Virginia. He was a communicant of St. James' Episcopal Mission Chapel in 1890 and was either living in the Radford home of Mrs. Fred Daly on Clement Street or Mrs. George Smith on Railroad Avenue; both addresses appear in the church register.

Jones, Edmund Sanford
1864-1929

Edmund Sanford Jones and his wife were parishioners of Grace Episcopal Mission Chapel during the late 1880s. Edmund Sanford Jones was born on July 19, 1864 and died on September 1, 1929. Additional information on Mrs. E. S. Jones is not now known. It is known that she shared the purchase of the Chapel's first organ with Colonel W. J. Kenderdine; that organ was first used in Randolph Hall jointly by the Episcopalians and the Methodist congregations.

A stained glass window depicting John the Baptist baptizing Jesus was donated to Grace Episcopal Church, Radford, in memory of Edmund Sanford Jones.

Kearsley, George Tali
Circa 1800s

George Tali Kearsley was a member of Montgomery Episcopal Parish congregation and then the Radford Episcopal Parish congregation at least from 1889 through 1892, a member of the parish vestries, and a member of the Radford City Council. He was a member of the Montgomery Episcopal Parish vestry in

1890, then a member of the Radford Episcopal Parish vestry at least from 1891 through 1893 and again from 1895 through 1902. In 1891, he was a member of the building committee to have a new church built "west of Connally's Branch" according to vestry minutes. In addition to continuing vestry service, he was the vestry treasurer in 1895. He was also a member of the first Radford City Council in 1892.

George Tali Kearsley married Lily A. P. (maiden surname not now known). According to church records, she was baptized as an Episcopalian in Staunton, Virginia. Mrs. Lily A. P. and George Tali Kearsley were living in the East Ward of Radford on Grove Avenue and were communicants of Grace Episcopal Mission Chapel at least by 1889. Mrs. Kearsley was a member of the Woman's Guild of Grace Episcopal Mission Chapel in 1902. She helped plan social and fund-raising activities including her suggestion that the Guild provide "entertainment with assistance of Mr. Lee, an elocutionist" for a 1902 Guild function. A note in the church register states that Mrs. Kearsley transferred to Christ Episcopal Church in Roanoke, Virginia in 1920.

Lily A. P. and George Tali Kearsley had children:
1. Imogen Patton Kearsley (circa 1800s), daughter of Lily A. P. and George Tali Kearsley. She was baptized at St. James' Episcopal Mission Chapel in Radford as an infant on October 25, 1891. The Rev. Edward Lewis Goodwin performed the baptismal rites, with sponsors Dr. Aaron Jeffrey and Miss Dora McPherson in attendance.
2. George William Tali Kearsley (circa 1800s), son of Lily A. P. and George Tali Kearlsey. He was baptized at St. James' Episcopal Mission Chapel in Radford as an infant on November 20, 1892. The Rev. Edward Lewis Goodwin performed the baptismal rites, with sponsor Colonel William Ingles in attendance. George William Tali Kearsley was also confirmed at St. James'.
3. Edward Patton Kearsley (circa 1800s), son of Lily A. P. and George Tali Kearsley.
4. Rebecca Kearsley (circa 1800s), daughter of Lily A. P. and George Tali Kearsley. She was born in Radford. She was baptized by the Rt. Rev. Alfred M. Randolph and

Rev. Floyd L. Kurtz. Her sponsors were Mrs. John H. Washington and Mrs. Patton.

Kello, Richard Henry
Circa 1800s

Richard Henry Kello and his family lived in North Radford in 1891. He was a communicant of Grace Episcopal Mission Chapel at least by 1893, being an "old communicant restored". Richard Henry, known as R. H., married Myrtle (maiden surname not now known). They may have been living in Pulaski County by 1894. The Kello family moved from the area to eastern Virginia at some point. Myrtle and Richard Henry Kello had children:

1. Sallie Anne Kello (circa 1800s), daughter of Myrtle and Richard Henry Kello. She was baptized at Grace Episcopal Mission Chapel as an infant on July 9, 1893. Her sponsor was Mrs. Carrie Hart. The ceremony was performed by Rev. Edward Lewis Goodwin. Her sister Margaret was baptized at the same time.

2. Marguerite Belches Kello (circa 1800s), daughter of Myrtle and Richard Henry Kello. She was called Margaret. She was baptized at Grace Episcopal Mission Chapel as an infant on July 9, 1893, as was her sister Sallie. Mrs. Carrie Hart was the baptismal sponsor for both Sallie Anne Kello and for Margaret Kello.

3. Richard Henry Kello Jr. (1894), son of Myrtle and Richard Henry Kello. According to church baptismal records, he was born on December 15, 1894 in Pulaski County, Virginia. He was baptized at the age of six months at Grace Episcopal Mission Chapel in Radford. Church records read that Rev. A. A. Pruden officiated "by proxy", indicating that another rector likely performed the baptismal rites in Rev. Pruden's absence. Richard Henry Kello Jr.'s sponsors were Mrs. Lucy C. Taylor and Miss Alma Saunders.

Kemp, Joseph R.
Circa 1866

Joseph R. Kemp and Mary Elizabeth Collins were married in an Episcopal ceremony at St. James' Episcopal Mission Chapel in front of the church congregation on December 23, 1890. The Rev. Edward Lewis Goodwin officiated. Joseph R. Kemp, born around 1866, was the son of Mrs. B. C. Kemp and Mr. T. E. Kemp of Radford, Virginia. He was twenty-four years old at the time of his 1890 marriage. Mary Elizabeth Collins, called Lizzie, was the daughter of Mary J. and William Francis Collins of Radford. She was born in 1872 and was baptized "in the church", according to church records. She was eighteen years old at the time of her 1890 marriage.

Lizzie and Joseph Kemp lived in the West Ward of Radford on First Street at least in 1891; a notation in the church record by Joseph's name reads "Campbelites". Lizzie was confirmed at St. James' Episcopal Mission Chapel on April 5, 1892 by the Rt. Rev. A. M. Randolph as attested to by Rev. Edward Lewis Goodwin. At some point they lived on Third Avenue with "Mr. Collins", likely a reference to her father. A notation in church records by Mrs. Lizzie Collins Kemp's name lists her as a communicant from 1892 through 1897.

Mary Elizabeth Collins and Joseph R. Kemp had at least one child: Kemp *infant* (1891). According to church records, the infant daughter of Mr. and Mrs. Joseph R. Kemp of Radford passed away one hour after her birth from "luamition". Her date of birth was listed as November 2, 1891; her date of death was listed as November 3, 1891. She was buried on November 3, 1891 at the "Radford Cemetery" with clergyman Edward Lewis Goodwin officiating.

Kenderdine, Anna Lytle
1876-1955

Miss Anna Lytle Kenderdine, the oldest of the two daughters of Mary Lytle and Warner Justice Kenderdine, was born on May 25, 1876 and died on December 18, 1955. She devoted her life to the children of Radford, Virginia both as a public school teacher and as a Sunday school teacher at Grace Episcopal Church. "Miss Anna" was described by church parishioners as a quiet and modest woman who lived with her sister "Miss Bess" (i.e. Mrs. Bess Kenderdine Bullard) for the improvement of the Radford Episcopal Parish.

Anna Kenderdine was baptized "in the Church". She was confirmed on April 5, 1892 by the Rt. Rev. Alfred Magill Randolph as attested to by Rev. Edward Lewis Goodwin. She joined her mother in participation in the Rector's Aid Society of Grace Parish Episcopal chapel from 1893 through 1895, continuing her membership when the Society first reorganized as the Ladies Chapel Fund Society in 1896 and as the Rector's Aid Society in 1900. In 1897, Anna was secretary for the church women's society. She continued her activities as a member of the Woman's Guild of Grace Chapel in 1902. She participated in the work of a number of committees, although her great love was the Sunday School program. She proudly reported to the church vestry on a high Sunday School enrollment and attendance, and told of the special activities such as church picnics for the children. Anna was chairwoman of the Sunday School committee in 1903 when she reported an enrollment of forty-one children. She played the church pedal organ at services at least by 1922.

Anna and Bess presented a pew to Grace Episcopal Church. Following her 1955 death, her sister Bess donated an eagle lectern to Grace Episcopal Church in Anna's memory.

Kesterson, John M.
1836-1917

John[96] M. Kesterson, the son of Mary and William Kesterson, was born in 1836. Mary and William were both born around 1807. They were living with their son and his wife and children in Central Depot, Virginia by 1880.

John married Nancy, known as "Nannie" and "Nanie"; maiden surname not now known. She was born around 1835. The Kestersons lived in Bath County, Virginia before moving to the eastern section of Central Depot in 1870. They lived north of the railroad tracks on the west side of Harrison Street and, at some point, in the Haven house on Plum Creek.[97]

The 1880 United States Census lists the Kesterson family, living in Central Depot of Montgomery County, Virginia as follows: Head of Household was a white, forty-five year old carpenter named John M. Kesterson, living with his forty-five year old wife Nancy Kesterson, his nineteen year old son Henry Kesterson who was employed as a laborer, his sixteen year old daughter "Georganna" Kesterson, his thirteen year old daughter Mary E. Kesterson, his nine year old daughter Rosa L. Kesterson, his seventy-three year old mother Mary Kesterson, and his seventy-three year old father William Kesterson who was also a carpenter.

John M. Kesterson was baptized as a Lutheran but was confirmed as an Episcopalian at St. James' Episcopal Mission Chapel on May 18, 1895. The Rt. Rev. Alfred Magill Randolph performed the rites of confirmation, attested to by Rev. A. A. Pruden. The Kesterson family members were parishioners of St. James' Episcopal Mission Chapel and of Grace Episcopal Mission Chapel.

John M. Kesterson died in 1917 or 1918. His family donated a church pew to Grace Episcopal Church in his memory.

Nancy and John M. Kesterson had children:

---

[96] Church and census records list this individual as "John" M. Kesterson. The Radford City Marriage Register Book One, Page 4, incorrectly listed his first name as "James" in the recording of his daughter Georgianna's 1897 marriage.

[97] Information on the Kesterson families residences was based upon an interview of Mrs. Georgianna Kesterson Likens by Daniel Dunbar Howe for his 1963 book Lovely Mount Tavern.

1. Henry Robertson Kesterson (circa 1861), son of Nancy and John M. Kesterson, of whom more.
2. Georgianna[98] Kesterson (1864), daughter of Nancy and John M. Kesterson, was born on February 29, 1864. She was baptized as a Methodist but confirmed as an Episcopalian at St. James' Episcopal Mission Chapel along with her father on May 18, 1895. Rev. A. A. Pruden attested to the confirmation performed by the Rt. Rev. Alfred Magill Randolph. Georgianna Kesterson, called Georgie, married James William Likens in Radford on August 7, 1897 as recorded in church records and in the Radford City Marriage Register. Will Likens was born on November 18, 1852. He was employed by the railroad company at the time of their marriage. Mrs. Georgianna Kesterson Likens and James William Likens were both buried in Central Cemetery. Her date of death was not recorded. His date of death was March 28, 1933.
3. Mary E. Kesterson (circa 1867), daughter of Nancy and John M. Kesterson.
4. Rosa Lee Kesterson (circa 1873), daughter of Nancy and John M. Kesterson. She was born around 1873, according to church records. She married Richard Cruff, a thirty-eight year old mechanic from East Radford, at St. James' Episcopal Mission Chapel on August 1, 1895. The ceremony was performed by Rev. A. A. Pruden in front of "a large congregation at the Church". Richard Cruff, the son of Mary and Henry Cruff, was born in Montgomery County, Virginia around 1857.
5. Mollie Kesterson (circa 1800s). Nancy and John M. Kesterson may have had a daughter named Mollie.

[98] The first name of Mrs. Georgianna Kesterson Likens appears in records both as "Georgianna" and "Georgiana". Her grave marker in Central Cemetery spells her first name with two "n"s, i.e. "Georgianna".

Illustration 55: John M. Kesterson's 1895 Confirmation certificate from St. James's Episcopal Mission Chapel. Courtesy of Grace Episcopal Church, Radford, Virginia.

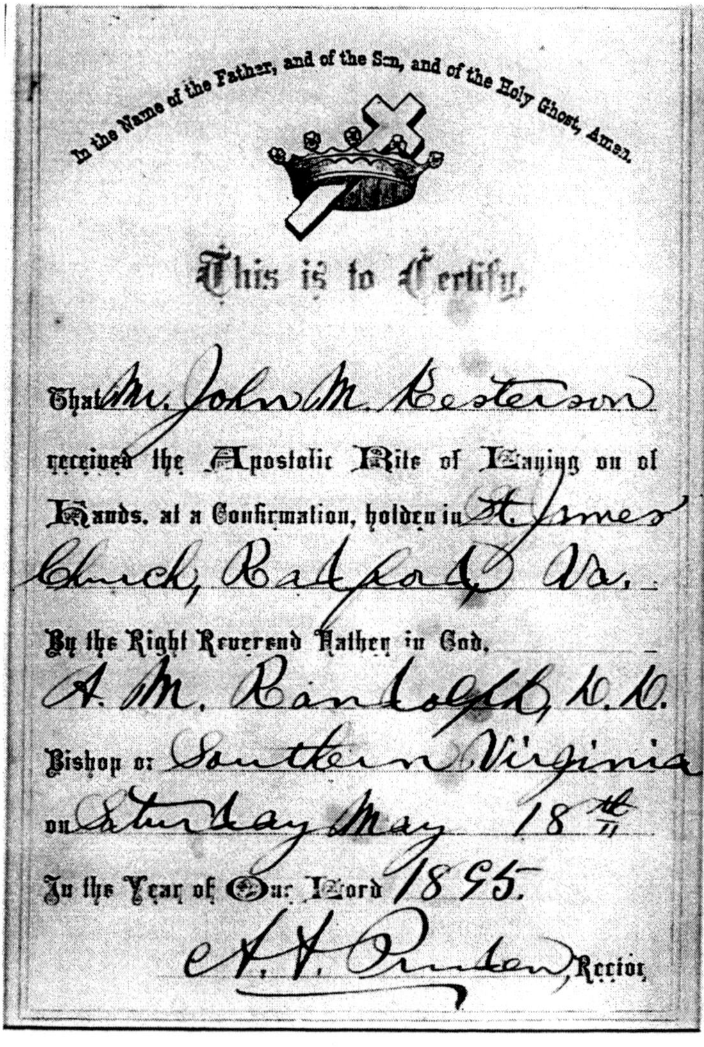

Kesterson, Henry Robertson
Circa 1861-1940

Henry Robertson Kesterson, the son of Nancy and John M. Kesterson, was born around 1861. He married Luvenia V.[99]; maiden surname not now known. She was born around 1862. The Kestersons attended St. James' Episcopal Mission Chapel and Grace Episcopal Mission Chapel.

Mrs. Luvenia V. Kesterson died in Vickers, Virginia at the age of sixty-six on July 18, 1928. According to church records entered by Rev. James A. Figg, cause of death was "general breakdown and heart failure". She was buried on July 19, 1929 at the "Family Cemetery near Vickers".

Henry Robertson Kesterson died in Radford at the age of eighty, according to church records entered by Rev. James A. Figg and Rev. Charles W. Sydnor. Cause of death was reported as "old age". He died on February 6, 1940 and was buried at West View Cemetery in Radford on February 8, 1940.

Luvenia V. and Henry Robertson Kesterson had children:

1. Guy William Kesterson (1889). This son of Luvenia and Henry R. Kesterson was born on October 29, 1889 in Radford, Virginia according to Episcopal church records. He was baptized at St. James' Episcopal Mission Chapel by Rev. A. A. Pruden on May 26, 1895 when he was five and a half years old. His sponsors were John M. Kesterson (his grandfather), Miss Georgianna Kesterson (his paternal aunt), and Mrs. Flora E. Farmer. Guy William Kesterson married Ethel Mills. They had at least one child: Mamie Alice Kesterson, born on August 22, 1913 in Vickers, Virginia. She was baptized at Grace Episcopal Church in Radford on May 13, 1928 and confirmed one week later on May 20, 1928.

2. Pearl K. Kesterson (1891). This daughter of Luvenia and Henry R. Kesterson was born on July 30, 1891 and died on March 21, 1894 from cholera infantum. She was buried

---

[99] Mrs. Luvenia Kesterson's name appears in church records both as "Luvenia B." , "Luvenia V.", and "L. V." Her initials on her daughter Perlie's tombstone in Central Cemetery are "L. V.".

on March 22, 1894[100] at the "Radford Cemetery", according to Episcopal church records as recorded by Rev. A. A. Pruden. Her tombstone marker in Central Cemetery, Radford, Virginia reads "Perlie K. Kesterson, daughter of H. R. and L. V. Kesterson, July 30, 1891 – March 21, 1894".

3. Clara May Kesterson (1893). This daughter of Luvenia and Henry R. Kesterson was born on August 26, 1893 in Radford, Virginia according to Episcopal church records. She was baptized with her brother Guy William Kesterson at St. James' Episcopal Mission Chapel by Rev. A. A. Pruden on May 26, 1895 when she was one and a half years old. She had the same sponsors as did her brother: John M. Kesterson (her grandfather), Miss Georgianna Kesterson (her paternal aunt), and Mrs. Flora E. Farmer.

4. Lena Rivers Kesterson (1895). This daughter of Luvenia and Henry R. Kesterson was born on August 6, 1895, three months after her older siblings Guy William and Clara May were baptized. Lena was baptized at St. James' Episcopal Mission Chapel three months after her birth. Rev. A. A. Pruden officiated at the baptismal ceremony held at the Kesterson family's private residence in Radford, Virginia. Her sponsors were Miss Patty J. Taylor, Miss Georgianna Kesterson, and Miss Lilly Likens. Lena Rivers Kesterson married Fred Litton.

5. Mary Catherine Kesterson (circa 1896), may have been a daughter of Luvenia and Henry R. Kesterson. Mary Catherine Kesterson was born around 1896 and died in 1928. Rev. James A. Figg recorded in Grace Episcopal Church records that Miss Mary Catherine Kesterson was thirty-two years of age and living in Vickers, Virginia when she died of "heart failure". She died on May 13, 1928 and was buried on May 14, 1928 at the "Family Cemetery near Vickers, Virginia". The names of her parents were not listed in the church records.

---

[100] Episcopal church records erroneously recorded Pearl K. Kesterson's year of burial as 1895; the correct year being 1894.

Kimball, George A.
Circa 1800s-1905

George A. Kimball[101] and his wife, Mrs. Nancy L. Kimball, were parishioners of St. James' Episcopal Mission Chapel and living in the West Ward of Radford on Eighth Street at least in 1891. They were both baptized in New Berlin, New York prior to moving to the Radford area and becoming Episcopal communicants. They continued as members of St. James' Episcopal Mission Chapel and then of Grace Episcopal Church through 1905.

Mrs. Kimball was very active in the Rector's Aid Society of Grace Parish Episcopal Chapel in 1893, hosting meetings and serving as treasurer until it was announced that a new treasurer would need to be elected to replace her (meeting minutes stating "Mrs. Kimball being compelled to resign on account of leaving Radford"). The Kimball family apparently returned to the Radford area by 1895. Mrs. Kimball resumed her activities with the church women's groups, being a member of the Ladies Chapel Fund Society in 1896 and continuing that membership when the Society reorganized as the Rector's Aid Society in 1901 and the Woman's Guild of Grace Chapel in 1902 and 1903.

George A. Kimball died in December 1905. Church records note that his widow, Nancy L. Kimball, moved out of the area.

Nancy L. and George A. Kimball had children:
1. Laura L. Kimball (circa 1871), daughter of Nancy L. and George A. Kimball. When she was thirty-two, she married Clyde Miller. Clyde was then twenty-three and hailed from Wayne, West Virginia. Laura and Clyde were married on June 10, 1903 at Grace Episcopal Mission chapel with the Rev. John S. Alfriend officiating.
2. George A. Kimball Jr. (circa 1800s), son of Nancy L. and George A. Kimball.

---

[101] The surname Kimball was also spelled Kimble in church records.

Kolfage, _____
Circa 1800s

Mrs. Nancy Ella Fry Kolfage and her husband were Episcopal parishioners of the Radford Parish during the late 1800s. Mrs. N. E. Fry Kolfage later moved to Tampa, Florida. Additional information is not now known about this family.

Kowuslar, Randolph
Circa 1800s

Randolph Kowuslar and his wife were communicants of the Radford Episcopal Parish and living in the Radford area at least in 1890 and 1891. Mrs. Kowuslar was baptized at Grace Episcopal Church in Berryville, Virginia. The Kowuslars transferred to Christ Episcopal Church in Roanoke, Virginia in 1892.

Landers, Charles W.
Circa 1800s

Charles W. Landers was one of three Montgomery Episcopal Parish church trustees when the deed to property on which to build Grace Episcopal Mission Chapel was obtained. Additional information on this parishioner is not now known.

Lasell, Laura
Circa 1800s

Miss Laura Lasell was a parishioner of Grace Episcopal Mission Chapel and an active member of the church women's groups at least from 1893 through 1897. She joined the Rector's Aid Society of Grace Parish Episcopal Chapel in 1893, serving as Secretary, Vice President, and then President. Meeting minutes of August 9, 1893 express "regrets by the society that Miss Lasell is leaving". She either did not leave the Radford area or left and returned. Her name again appears on the church parishioner rolls on January 17, 1894. Miss Lasell continued her participation when the group reorganized as the Ladies Chapel Fund Society in 1896; she was treasurer of that group in 1897.

Lawrence, Clayton Lyle
1863-1930

Clayton Lyle Lawrence, son of Gertrude and Frank Lawrence of Radford, Virginia married Eliza Baylis, daughter of Eliza and Thomas Baylis of Troy, New York at the Grace Episcopal Mission Chapel rectory on July 12, 1893. The bride was twenty-two and the groom was thirty years of age. The wedding ceremony was performed by Rev. Edward Lewis Goodwin and attended by friends of the couple.

Eliza Baylis was born on October 17, 1869 and died on August 13, 1939. At the time of the 1880 Census, the Baylis family (spelled "Balis") was living in Troy, New York. The parents, Eliza and Thomas Baylis, were both born in England. Their children were all born in New York. The Baylis family was described as follows: fifty-four year old brick mason Thomas Baylis, his forty-seven year old wife Eliza Baylis, their twenty-six year old daughter Sarah Baylis, their twenty-three year old son Thomas Baylis, their twenty year old son William Baylis, their seventeen year old son George Baylis, their fifteen year old daughter Libbie Baylis, their twelve year old daughter Eliza "Lizzie" Baylis, and their eight year old daughter Henvia Baylis.

Clayton Lyle Lawrence was born on July 7, 1863 and died on January 21, 1930. Mrs. Eliza Baylis Lawrence and Mr. Clayton Lyle Lawrence were both buried at Central Cemetery in Radford City. Eliza Baylis and Clayton Lyle Lawrence had children:
1. Elsie May Lawrence (1894), daughter of Eliza Baylis and Clayton Lyle Lawrence. According to church baptismal records, she was born on March 31, 1894 in Radford. She was baptized when she was eight months old on November 11, 1894 at St. James' Episcopal Mission Chapel. The Rev. A. A. Pruden recorded the baptismal rite as being performed by the Rt. Rev. M. P. Logan D.D. Her sponsors

were John Stafford, her grandmother Mrs. Eliza Baylis, and Miss Lottie Collins. Elsie May Lawrence either later moved away from the area and/or adopted the Methodist faith.

2. Hattie Lawrence (circa 1800s), daughter of Eliza Baylis and Clayton Lyle Lawrence.

Leffler, Mary C.
Circa 1800s

Miss Mary C. Leffler was baptized as a Methodist and confirmed as an Episcopalian at Grace Episcopal Mission Chapel in Radford. The Rite of Confirmation was performed on May 12, 1893 by the Rt. Rev. Alfred Magill Randolph as attested to by Rev. Edward Lewis Goodwin.

She was a member of the Rector's Aid Society of Grace Parish Episcopal Chapel from 1893 through 1895. She continued that participation in 1896 when the society reorganized as the Ladies Chapel fund Society. The last meeting that Miss Mary C. Leffler attended was held on January 29, 1896.

Likens, James M.
Circa 1800s

Mr. and Mrs. James M. Likens were communicants of St. James' Episcopal Mission Chapel and then of Grace Episcopal Mission Chapel. The name of James M. Likens' wife was Mary K.; her maiden surname is not now known. Mrs. Mary K. Likens was born on April 16, 1826. She died at the age of seventy-three on October 30, 1895 from "paralysis" according to church records. Rev. A. A. Pruden officiated at the funeral service on November 1, 1895. Mary K. Likens was buried at "the Radford cemetery". Her marker reads "Mary K. Likens, April 16, 1826, November 1, 1895". Mary K. and James M. Likens had a child, J. Henry Likens (1854), of whom more.

Likens, J. Henry
1854

J. Henry Likens was the son of Mary K. and James M. Likens. According to church baptismal records, he was born on March 3, 1854 in Central Depot, Virginia. He was baptized at St. James' Episcopal Mission Chapel as an adult on November 3, 1895 when he was forty-one years old. The baptismal rites were administered by Rev. A. A. Pruden. His baptismal sponsors were Col. Bennett Taylor, A. L. Woodley, and Miss Irene Robinson.

He married Josephine; maiden surname not now known. She was born around 1856. The 1880 United States Census lists J. H. Likens (misspelled as "Likeings") as a white twenty-three year old carpenter residing in Central Depot with his twenty-four year old wife "Josephin Likeings" and their one-month old son.

Josephine and J. Henry Likens had children:

1. Likens *son* (circa 1880). He was one month old when the Census of 1880 was taken; this child's Christian name was not given.

2. Lilly Likens (1882). She was born in Central, Virginia on February 2, 1882. She was baptized by a visiting rector ("Rev. A. A. Pruden by proxy") at Grace Episcopal Mission Chapel on July 28, 1895. Lilly Likens' baptismal sponsors were Mrs. L. C. Taylor and Miss Alma Saunders. Lilly married a Mr. Price. At some point they moved to Roanoke, Virginia, where they attended Christ Church.

3. Bertha Edna Likens (1885). This daughter of Josephine and Henry Likens was born on February 15, 1885. When she was ten years old, she was baptized along with her siblings Romeo Farmer Likens and Lafonza Burke Likens at St. James' Episcopal Mission Chapel by the Rev. A. A. Pruden. Her sponsors at the November 10, 1895 baptism were her father Henry Likens, Miss Patty J. Taylor, W. W. Darnell, and Miss Georgianna Kesterson (who would marry James William Likens). Bertha Edna Likens married John R. Branscom on January 1, 1904 according to Radford City marriage records. At some point they moved to Dilton, Virginia.

4. Romeo Farmer Likens (1888). This son of Josephine and J. Henry Likens was born on June 24, 1888 and was baptized at St. James' Episcopal Mission Chapel on November 10, 1895, along with his sister Bertha Edna Likens and his brother Lafonza Burke Likens. Romeo was seven years old when he was baptized by the Rev. A. A. Pruden. His sponsors were Henry Likens, Miss Patty J. Taylor, W. W. Darnell, and Miss Georgianna Kesterson. Romeo Farmer Likens moved to Roanoke, Virginia at some point.
5. Lafonza Burke Likens (1891). This son of Josephine and J. Henry Likens was born on December 4, 1891 and was baptized at St. James' Episcopal Mission Chapel on November 10, 1895, along with his sister Bertha Edna Likens and his brother Romeo Farmer Likens. Lafonza was four years old when he was baptized by the Rev. A. A. Pruden. His sponsors were Henry Likens, Miss Patty J. Taylor, W. W. Darnell, and Miss Georgianna Kesterson. Lafonza Burke Likens moved to a location near Roanoke, Virginia at some point.

Likens, James William
1852-1933

James William Likens of Central Depot, Virginia attended the St. James' Episcopal Mission Chapel and the Grace Episcopal Mission Chapel. He was employed by the railroad and lived near Heth's Grove.

He married Georgianna Kesterson. The daughter of Nancy and John M. Kesterson, she was born around 1864. The Kesterson family moved from Bath County to Central Depot in 1870. Georgianna, called Georgie, was confirmed at St. James' Episcopal Mission Chapel in 1895. James William Likens, called Will, and Georgie Kesterson were married on August 7, 1897, as documented in the Radford City Marriage Register Book One Page Four.

James William Likens died in 1933. His grave marker in Central Cemetery reads "James W. Likens, November 18, 1852, March 28, 1933". Mrs. Georgianna Kesterson Likens was interviewed by Daniel Dunbar Howe, author of the 1963 book <u>Lovely Mount Tavern</u>, when she was a ninety-three year old widow still residing in the area. Mrs. Georgianna Kesterson's date of death was not recorded. The Likens marker in Central Cemetery is a shared marker for her and her husband James William. Her side of the marker has her name and date of birth only: "Georgianna Likens, February 29, 1864".

Likens, Andrew Lewis
Circa 1857

Andrew Lewis Likens, called Andy, was born around 1857 in Vickers, Virginia. He died of tuberculosis in 1926.

Lineberry, Edward S.
Circa 1861

Edward S. Lineberry, son of B. A. and L. C. Lineberry of Durham, North Carolina was born around 1861. When he was twenty-nine, he married Mary K. Campbell of Virginia. Mary K. Campbell was born around 1866 and was twenty-four when she wed in 1890. The Episcopal wedding ceremony took place on December 17, 1890 at the Radford home of Colonel Barclay, with the Rev. E. L. Goodwin officiating and family and friends in attendance. The couple may have moved to Norfolk, Virginia, according to church records.

Longstreth, Joseph
Circa 1800s

Joseph Longstreth was baptized at St. Luke's Chapel in Philadelphia, Pennsylvania. By 1893, he was a communicant of St. James' Episcopal Mission Chapel in Radford, Virginia. He and his wife, Eliza Konax, were living in Radford's West Ward on Sixth Street by 1893. She too was a St. James' communicant.. Eliza had been baptized in Germantown, Philadelphia County, Pennsylvania.

Mrs. Longstreth was a member of the Rector's Aid Society of Grace Parish Episcopal Chapel during 1893 and 1894. The last meeting which she attended was held on October 24, 1894. At some point after October 1894, the Longstreth family moved from the Radford Episcopal Parish to Kenova, West Virginia.

Eliza Konax and Joseph Longstreth had at least one child: Alice Stokes Longstreth. According to church baptismal records, she was born in Radford, Virginia on July 7, 1894. She was baptized at Grace Episcopal Mission Chapel on September 9, 1894 when she was two months old. The rite of baptism was conducted by Rev. A. A. Pruden, with Miss Sarah M. Stokes serving as baptismal sponsor.

Lovell, Pocahontas
Circa 1835

Pocahontas Lovell of Radford, Virginia was born around 1835. She died on May 20, 1893 at the age of fifty-eight from typhoid fever[102]. Pocahontas Lovell was baptized as a Presbyterian but had an Episcopal funeral service conducted by Rev. Edward Lewis Goodwin. She was buried on May 21, 1893 in Danville, Virginia.

Luck, Firth DeFord
1871

Firth DeFord Luck was baptized in the Episcopal faith as an adult on October 25, 1891. Rev. Edward Lewis Goodwin performed the baptismal service at St. James' Episcopal Mission Chapel in Radford, Virginia. Firth DeFord Luck's baptismal sponsors were Mrs. Maimie Luck Jeffrey and her husband Dr. Aaron Jeffrey. Firth was confirmed and became a communicant one year later. The Rt. Rev. Alfred Magill Randolph performed the confir-

---

[102] Typhoid fever was also known as camp diarrhea, camp fever, and enteric fever.

mation on April 5, 1892 as attested to by Rev. Edward Lewis Goodwin.

Madison, Margaret
Circa 1800s

Mrs. Margaret Madison was a communicant of St. James' Episcopal Mission Chapel as of April 30, 1892. Her name was removed from the roster of communicants September 1893, without letters. No additional information about this parishioner is known at this time.

Malin, Jeanette I.
Circa 1800s

Miss Jeanette I. Malin, called "Nette", was a St. James' Episcopal Mission chapel communicant as of September 10, 1895. She came to the parish from Baltimore, Maryland where she had been "active in the Presbyterian tradition".

Miss Malin was a member of the Rector's Aid Society of Grace Parish Episcopal Chapel from 1893 through 1895, and continued that membership when the society reorganized as the Ladies Chapel Fund Society in 1896. With the exception of a period of absence between May 1, 1895 and August 2, 1895, she faithfully attended to her duties as a Society office holder and as a member of the Entertainment Committee. At some point during or after 1896, she moved back to Baltimore.

Marshall, Charles E. A.
Circa 1800s

Mrs. Charles E. A. Marshall was listed as a St. James' Episcopal Mission Chapel communicant, having come from Wytheville, Virginia on January 1, 1893. She transferred to Charlottesville, Virginia effective November 11, 1895. Additional information is not known about this parishioner at this time.

Matherly
Circa 1800s

Mr. and Mrs. Matherly of Radford, Virginia chose Grace Episcopal Mission Chapel for the funeral service of their infant son. The child died at the age of three months on October 23, 1891. His cause of death was not recorded. He was buried in the "Radford Cemetery" on October 24, 1891 with the Rev. Edward Lewis Goodwin officiating.   ·

Neville, Frederick
Circa 1800s

Mr. and Mrs. Frederick Neville were communicants of Grace Episcopal Mission Chapel by 1891. Mrs. Neville was born around 1856 and died on December 20, 1891 in Radford, Virginia. She was thirty-five when she died from "consumption" (i.e. tuberculosis). She was buried in the "Radford Cemetery" on December 21, 1891. The Rev. Edward L. Goodwin officiated. Frederick Neville was listed on church rolls as a communicant of Grace Episcopal Mission Chapel as of April 30, 1892. His name was "removed, without letters, January 1893".

Noell, Robert Jackson
Circa 1800s - 1956

Irene and Robert Jackson Noell were members of St. James' Episcopal Mission chapel and residing in the East Ward of Radford by 1891. Irene was baptized as an adult at St. James' on October 25, 1891 by Rev. Edward L. Goodwin. Her baptismal sponsors were Mrs. Pocahontas Lovell and Dr. R. Bruce James. The Rt. Rev. Alfred Magill Randolph confirmed her, as attested to by Rev. Edward L. Goodwin, on May 12, 1893 at St. James'.

Robert Jackson Noell (also spelled Noel) was one of Radford City's first government officials in 1892, as were a good number of his Episcopalian community. He was also a businessman in the community. Robert Jackson Noel, his son Randolph A. Noell, and associates purchased the Radford Trust Building on First and Harvey Streets, known locally as the Old Delp Hotel. A deed dated April 7, 1930 states that the Radford Investment Corp. sold this property to Robert J. Noell, Randolph A. Noell, N. H. Webb, and Ted Dalton (as per Radford City Deed Book 31, page 296). Ted Dalton, trustee, conveyed the property with interests as follows: Robert J. Noell 2/8s, Randolph A. Noell 3/8s, N. H. Webb 1/8, and Ted Dalton 2/8s. The hotel property was transferred at a June 23, 1932 meeting.

Robert J. Noell later bought out Dalton and Webb. Robert J. Noell owned the property jointly with his son Randolph A. Noell. Randolph inherited the building when his father died in 1956. The Noells sold the property in 1981 to The New River Bank Inc. In 1983, the property was returned to the Noells for satisfaction of debt, remaining in the family until it was purchased in 1984 by Chuckatuck Corporation. Irene and R. J. Noel had children:

1. Mollie James Noell (circa 1800s), daughter of Irene and Robert Jackson Noell.

2. John James Noell (1890), son of Irene and Robert Jackson Noell. According to church records, he was born on June 22, 1890 and was baptized as an infant on June 4, 1893 at St. James' Episcopal Mission Chapel. Rev. Edward L. Goodwin performed the baptism. Dr. R. Bruce James served as baptismal sponsor.

3. Richard Bruce Noell (1892), son of Irene and Robert Jackson Noell. He was baptized as an infant on June 4, 1893 at St. James' Episcopal Mission Chapel by Rev. Edward L. Goodwin. Dr. R. Bruce James was his sponsor. Richard Bruce Noell died eighteen days later, at the age of ten months, from "summer complaint". He was buried two days after his death, on June 24, 1893, in Christiansburg, Virginia with the Rev. Edward L. Goodwin officiating.

4. William Wilson Noell (1894), son of Irene and Robert Jackson Noell. He was born on July 10, 1894 in Radford, Virginia. He was baptized at his parents' "private residence" in Radford by Rev. A. A. Pruden on February 10, 1895. His sponsors were Mrs. N. J. Tinsley "by proxy",

377

Dr. R. Bruce James "by proxy", and Dr. W. Ambrose Wilson.

5. Julian Rorer Noell (1896), son of Irene and Robert Jackson Noell. He was born in East Radford on December 2, 1896. He was baptized "at home" by St. James' Episcopal Mission Chapel rector Rev. F. G. Ribble. Mrs. Hugh Preston and Mrs. Bennett Taylor were his sponsors at the July 23, 1897 baptismal service.

6. Randolph A. Noell (circa 1800s), son of Irene and Robert Jackson Noell. At some point he transferred to Christ Episcopal Church in Blacksburg, Virginia. He went into business with his father in 1930 as partial owner of the Radford Trust Building (which had housed the Delp Hotel). He inherited ownership from his father in 1956. He married. He and his wife had at least one child: Irene Noell. She married a Mr. Turner.

Omohundra, John Burwell
1816-1898

John Burwell Omohundra was born in Albemarle County, Virginia on November 23, 1816, according to church records. He lived on Fourth Street in Radford's West Ward at least in 1895 and was a communicant of Grace Episcopal Mission Chapel. His name was dropped from the roster of communicants in 1898.

According to the 1880 United States Census, J. B. Omohundra was a sixty-three year old white farmer living in Fluvanna County, Virginia with his thirty-eight year old wife "Margret" A. Omohundra (born around 1842) and their thirteen year old son Malvern H. Omohundra.

John Burwell Omohundra was baptized as an Episcopalian at his private residence in Radford, Virginia on January 13, 1895 when he was seventy-nine years of age. The baptismal ceremony was recorded in church records by Rev. A. A. Pruden. His sponsors were Mrs. Nina D. Washington "by proxy" and Mrs. C. van Allen. He was confirmed four months later at Grace Episcopal Mission Chapel by the Rt. Rev. Alfred Magill Randolph as attested to by Rev. A. A. Pruden.

Margaret A. and John Burwell Omohundra had a child: Malvern H. Omohundra (circa 1867). He married Margaret (maiden surname not now known). The child of Margaret and Malvern H. Omohundra was Julia Elizabeth Omohundra. She was born on July 14, 1893 in Roanoke, Virginia. She was baptized along with her paternal grandfather when she was one and a half years old. The baptismal service recorded by Rev. A. A. Pruden was held at John Burwell Omohundra's private residence in Radford on January 13, 1895. Her baptismal sponsors were Mrs. Nina D. Washington "by proxy" and Mrs. C. van Allen.

Osborne, John Godolphine
1851-1938

Captain John Godolphine Osborne was a communicant of Grace Episcopal Mission Chapel and living on Second and Randolph Streets in Radford's West Ward at least by 1891. Living with him in his home were a Mr. M. M. Osborne and three members of the Stevens family: Mr. Edward D. Stevens, Mrs. Annie D. Stevens, and Arthur Leigh Stevens. They were still on parishioner rolls in 1903. Captain Osborne was a member of the church vestry during 1893, 1895, and 1898 through 1907.

John G. Osborne came to Radford, then known as Central Depot, in 1883 as the Superintendent of the Radford Division of the N & W (Norfolk & Western) Railroad. He was confirmed as an Episcopalian at Grace Episcopal Mission Chapel on May 17, 1895. The confirmation rite was performed by the Rt. Rev. Alfred Magill Randolph as attested to by Rev. A. A. Pruden.

Osborne married Virginia Perrow Bailey in 1923. She was a parishioner and a member of the church choir at least by 1922.

Captain John Godolphine Osborne died in 1938. A stained glass rose window was given to the church in his memory: John Godolphine Osborne, 1851-1938, Vestryman and Sr. Warden. His widow contributed to the Parish House Building Fund in his memory.

Osborne, T. A.
Circa 1800s

T. A. Osborne became a communicant of Grace Episcopal Mission Chapel in Radford from St. John's Episcopal Church in Scottsville, Virginia in 1898. Additional information about this parishioner is not known at this time.

Owens, James E.
Circa 1800s

James E. Owens and his wife Mary lived in New River, Virginia. They were communicants of the St. John's Episcopal Mission congregation and then of Grace Episcopal Mission Chapel by 1891. They joined the Grace congregation as "old communicants of St. John's Church, New River Depot".

Mary and James E. Owens had children:

1. John T. Owens (circa 1867), son of Mary and James E. Owens. He was born around 1867. He was living in New River Depot, Virginia when he was twenty-three and married Leona Newly of Pulaski County. Leona, born around 1866, was twenty-four when she married John. The wedding took place on November 12, 1890 in front of family and friends with the Rev. Edward L. Goodwin officiating.

2. Adeline D. Owens (circa 1800s), daughter of Mary and James E. Owens. She was baptized as a Methodist but was confirmed in the Episcopal faith at St. John's Episcopal Mission Chapel on May 18, 1895 by the Rt. Rev. Alfred Magill Randolph as attested to by Rev. A. A. Pruden.

3. Annie Belle Owens (1884), daughter of Mary and James E. Owens. She was born in New River on January 20, 1884. She was baptized at age eleven on March 31, 1895 at St. John's Episcopal Mission Chapel by the Rev. A. A. Pruden. Her godmother was Mrs. I. W. Wilson.

Page, Alfred Perkins
Circa 1800s

Alfred Perkins Page of Cambridge, Massachusetts married Gertrude Belle Green of Radford, Virginia in an Episcopal ceremony at the bride's home on November 4, 1893. Gertrude was the daughter of L. C. and James K. Green. The Rev. Dr. William H. Meade of Roanoke, Virginia performed the wedding ceremony at the Green home with friends of the families in attendance.

Gertrude had been a communicant of St. James' Episcopal Mission Chapel at least by 1892. She and her husband Alfred P. Page were St. James' parishioners during 1892 and 1893. They moved to Norfolk, Virginia. A note in church records indicates that Mrs. Gertrude Belle Green Page may have died in Norfolk during May 1953.

Pamplin, Byra Louise
Circa 1878

Byra Louise Pamplin, daughter of Mary E. and John L. Pamplin, was born around 1878. She was a parishioner of St. James' Episcopal Mission Chapel at least by 1898. Byra Louise Pamplin was baptized as an adult at St. James' Episcopal Mission Chapel. Rev. Floyd L. Kurtz conducted the baptismal service on April 17, 1898. Her baptismal sponsors were Susan Green and George T. Kearsley. She was confirmed at St. James' one month later, on May 10, 1898, by the Rt. Rev. Alfred Magill Randolph as attested to by Rev. Floyd L. Kurtz.

Byra Louise Pamplin was living with her parents and siblings in Central Depot, Virginia at the time of the 1880 United States Census. The family information was recorded as follows: thirty-six year old white railroad employee John L. Pamplin (born around 1844), his twenty-seven year old wife Mollie Pamplin (born around 1853), their nine year old son William J. Pamplin (born around 1871), their seven year old daughter Mildred L. Pamplin (born around 1873), their four year old daughter Maude H. Pamplin (born around 1876; she was a member of the Radford Chapter of the United Daughters of the Confederacy in 1906), and their two year old daughter "Bira A." Pamplin. Also in the home was a black thirty-nine year old housekeeper named Rosana Carson (born around 1841)

Peter, John Custis
1867-1952

John Custis Peter, son of L. and J. P. C. Peter of Culpepper, Virginia was born on December 4, 1867. He came to St. James' Episcopal Mission Chapel from St. Stephens Church in Culpepper. He became a communicant of St. James' Episcopal Mission Chapel in 1891 and, by 1900, of Grace Episcopal Mission Chapel in Radford.

He married Gertrude Landon Pile. The daughter of Annie Roper and David Landon Pile of East Radford, Gertrude was born on December 24, 1874. Episcopal clergyman Rev. A. A. Pruden performed the September 18, 1895 wedding ceremony for the twenty-seven year old groom and the twenty year old bride in front of a large congregation at the St. James' Episcopal Mission Chapel in East Radford.

Mrs. Gertrude Landon Pile Peter had come to the Radford Episcopal Parish from Bristol, Virginia. She became a communicant of Grace Episcopal Mission Chapel. She also joined the Radford Chapter of the United States Daughters of the Confederacy on September 29, 1915 based upon the service of her grandfather William Edward Black, who was a member of the Washington Mountain Riflemen and of the D Company of the First Virginia Cavalry under Commander William E. Jones.

Mrs. Gertrude Landon Pile Peter died on July 13, 1934 at the age of sixty. She was buried in Central Cemetery in Radford. Her husband John Custis Peter died eighteen years later, on January 14, 1952, at the age of eighty-five. He too was buried in Central Cemetery. A pew was donated to Grace Episcopal Church in memory of "Mrs. G. C. Peter". A kneeler bench was donated to the church in memory of "John Custis Peter 1868-1952 and

Gertrude Pile Peter 1875[103]-1934, in loving memory of Father and Mother". Gertrude and John Custis Peter had children:

1. Gertrude Custis Peter (1896), daughter of Gertrude Landon Pile and John Custis Peter. She was born on July 7, 1896 in Radford. When she was three months old, she was baptized at Grace Episcopal Mission Chapel by Rev. F. G. Ribble. Her sponsors for the October 25, 1896 baptism were Mrs. Moyer and Colonel W. J. Kenderdine.

2. Eleanor Custis Peter (circa 1800s), daughter of Gertrude Landon Pile and John Custis Peter. Eleanor, also spelled Elanor, Custis Peter may have died sometime between 1900 and 1906, according to church records.

3. John Park Custis Peter (1898), son of Gertrude Landon Pile and John Custis Peter. He was born on December 23, 1898. He was baptized at Grace Episcopal Mission Chapel by the Rev. John S. Alfriend on December 16, 1900. His sponsors were Radford Carter Adams, Warner Justice Kenderdine, and Mrs. Fanny Miles. He died in 1953 at the age of fifty-five. A pew was donated to Grace Episcopal Church in memory of "our brother John Park Custis Peter 1898-1953".

4. Anna Lucy Peter (1901), daughter of Gertrude Landon Pile and John Custis Peter. She was born on September 1, 1901. She was baptized at Grace Episcopal Church in Radford by the Rev. Edwin Royall Carter along with her younger brother James Beverly Peter on October 8, 1905. Her sponsors were Warner Justice Kenderdine, Anna Lytle Kenderdine, and Bessie Kenderdine.

5. James Beverly Peter (1904), son of Gertrude Landon Pile and John Custis Peter. He was born on april 27, 1904. He was baptized at Grace Episcopal Church in Radford by Rev. Edwin Royall Carter on October 8, 1905. His sponsors were Warner Justice Kenderdine, "W. J." Parker (likely a reference to parishioner John William Parker), and Mary K. Walters.

---

[103] Church records list Mrs. Gertrude Pile Peter's birth year as 1874; a kneeler bench donated to the church in her memory lists the year as 1875.

Pierce, Henry G.
1862

Henry G. Pierce, called "Gee", was the son of Elizabeth H. and William Pierce. He was born on November 29, 1862 in Pittsfield, Massachusetts. He was baptized as an adult at the Grace Episcopal Mission Chapel in Radford, Virginia on November 18, 1894 when he was thirty-two. The Rev. A. A. Pruden officiated. Gee Pierce's baptismal sponsors were E. Z. Moyer and Mr. and Mrs. Warner Justice Kenderdine. Pierce was confirmed at Grace Episcopal Mission Chapel six months later by the Rt. Rev. Alfred Magill Randolph as attested to by Rev. A. A. Pruden. Henry G. Pierce served as a vestryman in 1895.

Powers, Harry Hazard
Circa 1800s

Harry Hazard Powers and his wife Bettie were members of the Montgomery Episcopal Parish congregation and then of the Radford Episcopal Parish congregation at least from 1889 through 1893. Church records list the Powers family as residing in Christiansburg, Virginia and then, during June 1893, Central Depot.

Harry H. Powers was an alternate Montgomery Episcopal Parish delegate to the Diocesan convention in 1889, as elected by the Episcopal churches of Blacksburg and Christiansburg and agreed upon by the St. James' Episcopal Mission Chapel congregation. He was a member of the Montgomery Episcopal Parish from 1890 through 1891 and served on the Radford Episcopal Parish during 1891 and 1892. In 1890 and 1891, he was a member of the church committee working with the Radford Land and Improvement Company to obtain land on which a new church building (i.e. the planned Grace Episcopal Mission Chapel) could be constructed "west of Connally's Branch". He was also a member of the church committee which petitioned the Episcopal Diocese to draw new boundary lines dividing the Montgomery Parish into two separate parishes: the Montgomery Episcopal Parish and the Radford Episcopal Parish.

Harry Hazard Powers was one of Radford City's first government officials in 1892. He was a member of the first City Council. Bettie and Harry Hazard Powers had children:

1. Harry Hazard Powers Jr. (circa 1800s), son of Bettie and Harry Hazard Powers. He was baptized as an infant on September 4, 1892. The Rev. W. D. Powers, assisted by the Rev. Edward Lewis Goodwin, performed the baptismal rites at Grace Episcopal Mission Chapel in Radford, Virginia. The child's sponsors were Mrs. S. H. Hoge and Mr. J. F. Tilly.

2. Leslie Powers (circa 1800s), daughter of Bettie and Harry Hazard Powers.

Preston, Hugh Caperton
1856-1905

Hugh Caperton Preston and his family were Episcopal parishioners who lived in the East Ward of the Radford by 1891. He was Radford City's first mayor in 1892.

Hugh Caperton Preston, son of Sarah Ann Caperton and James Francis Preston, was born on September 5, 1856. At the time of the 1880 United States Census, he was described as a twenty-three year old farmer living in the Blacksburg District of Montgomery County with his fifty-four year old mother S. A. Preston (born in 1826), his twenty-one year old brother William B. Preston (born in 1858), and his twenty-one year old wife Cary B. Preston (born in 1858).

He was baptized as a Presbyterian but confirmed as an Episcopalian at St. James' Episcopal Mission Chapel on May 23, 1894. The Rite of Confirmation was performed by the Rt. Rev. A. M. Randolph when the Radford Episcopal Parish was without a rector; the confirmation was recorded in the church register by Rev. A. A. Pruden.

H. C. Preston married Caroline Baldwin, daughter of Caroline Marx Barton and Dr. Robert Frederick Baldwin. Known as Cary, she was born on September 10, 1858. Church records list Mrs. Cary Baldwin Preston as becoming a communicant of St. James' Episcopal Mission Chapel on April 29, 1892, having come from

Christ Episcopal Church in Blacksburg, Virginia. She was baptized "in the Church" and was confirmed by the Rt. Rev. A. M. Randolph on May 18, 1895, as attested to by Rev. F. G. Ribble.

The Preston family members were listed as St. James' Episcopal Mission Chapel parishioners by 1903 as follows: "Hugh Caperton Preston, (Mrs.) Carey *[sic]* Baldwin Preston, John Macky Preston (adopted), Robert Baldwin Preston, Cary Baldwin Preston, Sarah Caperton Preston, William Ballard Preston, Hugh Caperton Preston Jr., Katherine Stuart Preston". Hugh Caperton Preston, his wife Mrs. Cary Baldwin Preston, and their daughter Sarah Caperton Preston of East Radford transferred from St. James' Episcopal Mission Chapel on April 1, 1904, according to one notation in church records. However, that daughter as well as her brother William Ballard Preston were confirmed at Grace Episcopal Church in 1905.

Hugh Caperton Preston was one of Radford City's first government officials in 1892. He was a member of the first city council and served as Mayor of the City of Radford. Mrs. Cary Baldwin Preston was a member of the Radford Chapter of the United Daughters of the Confederacy in 1906. A stained glass window was given to Grace Episcopal Church in memory of the Prestons. The engraving on the window, which depicts "Healing of Jarius' Daughter", reads "Cary Baldwin Preston 1858-1935, Hugh Caperton Preston 1856-1905".

Caroline Baldwin and Hugh Caperton Preston had children:

1. James Francis Preston (1879), son of Caroline Baldwin and Hugh Caperton Preston. He was born on November 31, 1879.
2. Robert Baldwin Preston (1881), son of Caroline Baldwin and Hugh Caperton Preston. He was born on May 12, 1881.
3. Hugh Caperton Preston Jr. (circa 1800s), son of Caroline Baldwin and Hugh Caperton Preston. He was baptized at St. James' Episcopal Mission Chapel as an infant on June 4, 1893. Rev. Edward Lewis Goodwin performed the baptismal rites. Witnesses and sponsors were Mr. J. Hoge Tyler, Miss Louisa Myers, and Mrs. Richard Norris.
4. Sarah Caperton Preston (circa 1800s), daughter of Caroline Baldwin and Hugh Caperton Preston. She became a

communicant of St. James' Episcopal Mission Chapel on April 7, 1905.

5. William Ballard Preston (circa 1800s), son of Caroline Baldwin and Hugh Caperton Preston. He became a communicant of St. James' Episcopal Mission Chapel on April 8, 1905.

6. Cary Baldwin Preston (circa 1800s), daughter of Caroline Baldwin and Hugh Caperton Preston. At least one notation in church records lists her name as Miss Cary M. Preston. She was a St. James' Episcopal Mission Chapel communicant on September 10, 1895. She married Hartwell Henry Gary. They later moved to Norfolk, Virginia.

7. Kathryne Stewart Preston (circa 1800s), daughter of Caroline Baldwin and Hugh Caperton Preston. Her name was written in census records as "Katherine Stuart" Preston.

8. John Macky Preston (circa 1800s), son of Caroline Baldwin and Hugh Caperton Preston. Church records list this male child as the adopted son of Caroline Baldwin and Hugh Caperton Preston.

Ragland, Waverly Nathaniel
Circa 1848

Waverly Nathaniel Ragland married Lavinia Cargill Blow. They were parishioners of Grace Episcopal Mission Chapel at least during the late 1890s and early 1900s. By 1900, they were described in church records as: "Waverly N. Ragland, Mrs. Lavinia Cargill Ragland, William Nevison Ragland, Louisa Cargill Ragland, Emma B__ [104] Ragland, Lucy Regrave Ragland, and Cargill Blow Ragland".

Mrs. L. C. Ragland was a member of the Rector's Aid Society of Grace Parish Episcopal Church from 1900 through 1902. She attended her first meeting on June 18, 1900 and was the first Society secretary. She was a member of the Church Chancel Committee in 1900. In 1902, she was a member of the Woman's

---

[104] The spelling of Emma Ragland's middle name is illegible in church records. It appears to read "Black _ _ _ _".

Guild of Grace Chapel and again served as Secretary. She was a member of the 1903 committee for a reception to be held for the "St. Albans boys" and helped to host the Christmas Bazaar table selling handkerchiefs and aprons.

A stained glass window was given to Grace Episcopal Church in memory of Waverly Nathaniel Ragland, Lavinia Cargill Blow Ragland, and their son Rene Chastaine Ragland. The window depicted "Jesus Calls His Disciples". Lavinia Cargill Blow and Waverly Nathaniel Ragland had children:

1. William Nevison Ragland (circa 1800s), son of Lavinia Cargill Blow and Waverly Nathaniel Ragland.
2. Louisa Cargill Ragland (circa 1800s), daughter of Lavinia Cargill Blow and Waverly Nathaniel Ragland. She became a communicant of Grace Episcopal Mission Chapel on April 7, 1905.
3. Emma B. Ragland (circa 1800s), daughter of Lavinia Cargill Blow and Waverly Nathaniel Ragland.
4. Lucy Regrave Ragland (circa 1900s), daughter of Lavinia Cargill Blow and Waverly Nathaniel Ragland.
5. Cargill Blow Ragland (1902), son of Lavinia Cargill Blow and Waverly Nathaniel Ragland. He was born on May 7, 1902 and baptized at Grace Episcopal Mission Chapel on November 29, 1903. The baptism was performed by the Rev. E. R. Carter. His baptismal sponsors and witnesses were his father Waverly Nathaniel Ragland, his rector Rev. Edwin R. Carter, Miss Anna Kenderdine, and Miss Belle Pilcher.
6. Rene Chastaine Ragland (circa 1900s), son of Lavinia Cargill Blow and Waverly Nathaniel Ragland. He died at a young age.
7. Ragland child (circa 1900s). Lavinia Cargill Blow and Waverly Nathaniel Ragland may have had a seventh child.

Richardson, Bessie
Circa 1800s

Mrs. Bessie Richardson moved to Radford, Virginia from Wytheville, Virginia, where she had attended St. John's Episcopal Church, at least by April 29, 1892. She became a communicant of Grace Episcopal Mission Chapel. She may have left the Episcopal faith and joined the Presbyterian Church during May 1894.

Roberts, Sophia A.
Circa 1800s

Sophia A. Roberts was a communicant of Grace Episcopal Mission Chapel by August 1895. Additional information is not known about this parishioner at this time.

Roby, Charles Johnson
1860-1941

Charles Johnson Roby and his wife Beulah Boyd Garrett were Episcopal parishioners of the Radford Parish at least by 1889. Mrs. Roby's name is written in church records as Mrs. Beula Boyd Roby, Mrs. Bulah Boyd Roby, and as Mrs. Beaula Garrett Roby. Her name is written on her grave marker as "Beulah Garrett Roby".

Charles Johnson Roby was baptized as an adult on October 30, 1889 at St. James' Episcopal Mission Chapel in Radford, Virginia. His witnesses and his sponsors were John Andrew Wilson and William Radford Wharton. Charles was confirmed that same day by the Rt. Rev. Francis McNeece Whittle as attested to by clergyman Edward Lewis Goodwin. By 1904, they were attending Grace Episcopal Church. Mrs. Roby was involved in community activities as well. She was a member of the Radford chapter of the Virginia Daughters of the Confederacy during the early 1900s.

According to church records entered by Rev. Charles W. Sydnor, Beulah died at the age of fifty-nine from "paralysis" on December 11, 1935. She was buried on December 12, 1935 at

Central Cemetery. Her husband Charles died of "old age" at the age of eighty-one years on January 24, 1941. He was buried on January 26, 1941 at Central Cemetery. Their shared grave marker reads "Beulah Garrett Roby, Mother, 1876, 1935" and "Chas. Johnson Roby, Father, 1860, 1941". A pew was given to Grace Episcopal Church in memory of Mr. and Mrs. Charles Roby. An iron railing was purchased for the church in memory of Mr. and Mrs. Charles Roby and Charles Roby Jr.

Beulah Boyd Garrett and Charles Johnson Roby had children:

1. Thomas Garrett Roby (1904), son of Beulah Boyd Garrett and Charles Johnson Roby. He was born on June 24, 1904 and baptized by Rev. E. R. Carter at Grace Episcopal Church on December 25, 1904. His sponsors were Ambrose Robinson, his father Charles Roby, and Mrs. Lily P. Kearsley.

2. Charles Johnson Roby Jr. (1910), son of Beulah Boyd Garrett and Charles Johnson Roby. He was born on September 26, 1910 and died at the young age of thirty-two from "suffocation in fire; burns and concussion" according to an entry in church records by Rev. Charles W. Sydnor and Rev. Wilfred E. Roach. He died on September 14, 1943. Charles Johnson Roby Jr. was buried at Central Cemetery on September 17, 1943.

Rogers, Arthur
Circa 1800s

Arthur Rogers was a communicant of Grace Episcopal Mission Chapel in Radford at least by March 18, 1892. Church records note that he had previously been an Episcopal communicant in Lunenberg County, Virginia. His name was removed as a Grace Episcopal Mission Chapel communicant "without letters" in June 1892.

Rudd, John S.
Circa 1800s

John S. Rudd was baptized in the Episcopal faith. He was confirmed at Grace Episcopal Mission Chapel in the Town of Radford, also known as Central Depot and Central City, on October 30, 1889 by the Rt. Rev. Francis McNeece Whittle and attested to by Rev. Edward Lewis Goodwin. John Rudd later moved to Waynesboro, Virginia.

Sanders, Charles W.
Circa 1800s

Charles W. Sanders and his wife Carrie were communicants of Grace Episcopal Mission Chapel in 1890. They had moved to the Town of Radford from Wytheville, Virginia where they were communicants of St. John's Episcopal Church. The Sanders were living on Eighth Street in the West Ward of Radford by 1890. They were communicants of Grace Episcopal Mission Chapel at least through 1892. At some point, they moved to Roanoke, Virginia.

Charles W. Sanders was a member of the Episcopal vestry of Montgomery Parish and then Radford Parish from 1890 through 1891. He was the vestry secretary in 1890 and the vestry assistant clerk in 1891. He served as a member of the committee to work with the Radford Land and Improvement Company to secure land on which to build a new church "west of Connally's Branch".

He also worked with fellow church committee members in 1891 to petition the Episcopal Diocese to establish boundary lines for the division of the Montgomery Parish into two parishes: the Montgomery Parish and the Radford Parish. When the Radford Episcopal Parish was established, C. W. Sanders was elected to be a member of its new vestry. He served as vestryman, vestry registrar, and vestry treasurer during 1891 and 1892. He was an alternate delegate to the Episcopal Diocesan Council in 1892. He was a church trustee at least from 1892 through 1898 and continued to serve on the Radford Parish vestry during the years 1893, 1894, and 1895.

Mrs. Carrie B. Sanders was baptized as a Methodist but confirmed at Grace Episcopal Mission Chapel on April 5, 1892 by the Rt. Rev. Alfred Magill Randolph. The confirmation was attested to by Rev. Edward Lewis Goodwin. She lived at the Grace Episcopal Mission Chapel Rectory during the tenure of Rev. E. L. Goodwin. She was a member, office holder, and hostess for the Rector's Aid Society of Grace Parish Episcopal Mission Chapel and, on June 28, 1893, was elected to serve as the society's secretary but "being obliged to decline" did not hold that office. The last meeting she attended was held on August 15, 1894.

Carrie B. and Charles W. Sanders had children:

1. Richard Keenen Sanders (1894), son of Carrie B. and Charles W. Sanders. He was born on July 2, 1894 and was baptized at Grace Episcopal Mission Chapel in Radford, Virginia at the age of one month. The baptism was performed by Rev. A. A. Pruden on August 26, 1894. His sponsors were Warner Justice Kenderdine, Dr. Aaron Jeffrey, and Miss Mary Sutton.

2. Infant Sanders (circa 1800s), child of Carrie B. and Charles W. Sanders. Church burial records contain the report that the infant child of Carrie B. and C. W. Sanders of Radford, Virginia passed away on either October 7 or November 7, 1892 and was buried that same day. Cause of death was listed as "luamition"[105]. The infant was "temporarily" buried in "Radford Cemetery". Clergyman Edward L. Goodwin officiated at the funeral service.

Saunders, Alma
Circa 1800s

Mrs. Saunders and Miss Alma Saunders lived with the family of A. J. Black in the East Ward of the Town of Radford on Norwood Street in 1889. They were parishioners of St. James' Episcopal Mission Chapel. Additional information is not known regarding this family at this time.

---

[105] Church records on the Sanders infant were difficult to decipher, especially the month of the child's death and the cause of death.

Smith, Bettie Lou
Circa 1800s

Bettie Lou Smith, daughter of Bettie B. and N. H. Smith, was baptized as an adult by Rev. Edward Lewis Goodwin at St. James' Episcopal Mission Chapel in the Town of Radford on September 11, 1889. Her witnesses and sponsors were Captain Ambrose Robinson, "Mrs. Tyler", and Miss Banks Davies. Bettie Lou Smith was confirmed the following month, on October 30, 1889, by the Rt. Rev. Francis McNeece Whittle as attested to by Rev. Edward Lewis Goodwin. She married R. J. Dunahoe during October of 1894.

Smith, John D.
Circa 1800s

Mr. and Mrs. John D. Smith were communicants of St. James' Episcopal Mission Chapel in Radford in 1895. They came to Radford from Christ Episcopal Church in Roanoke, Virginia. John served on the church vestry in 1895. They moved to Richmond, Virginia in 1897.

Smith, J. H.
Circa 1800s

Dr. J. H. Smith designed a sacristy presented to Grace Episcopal by the women of the church. Additional information is not known about this parishioner at this time.

Stevens, Edward D.
Circa 1800s

Edward D. Stevens, his wife Anna, and their son were living with Captain J. G. Osborne and Mr. M. M. Osborne at Capt. Osborne's home at least in 1891. The residence was located in the West Ward of Radford on Second and Randolph Streets.

Edward D. Stevens was born in Portsmouth, Ohio. His date of transfer to Grace Episcopal Mission Chapel was not listed in church records. However, records indicate that Mrs. Anna D. Stevens transferred from St. John's Episcopal Church in Roanoke, Virginia and became a communicant of Grace Episcopal Mission Chapel on April 18, 1895. They may have moved back to Roanoke sometime between 1895 and 1903; church records list a second transfer date from St. John's Episcopal Church in Roanoke to Grace Episcopal Mission Chapel on November 23, 1903.

Mrs. A. D. Stevens, also known as Annie, was briefly a member of the Rector's Aid Society of Grace Parish Episcopal Chapel and elected to be the society president during January 1893. Her last attended meeting was held on February 28, 1893. Mrs. W. J. Kenderdine presented a letter of resignation from Mrs. Stevens at the March 7, 1893 meeting of the Rector's Aid Society.

Anna D. and Edward D. Stevens had at least one child: Arthur Stevens. He was confirmed at Grace Episcopal Church on April 7, 1905. He may have later moved to Shreveport, Louisiana.

Stewart, Wallace B.
Circa 1800s

Wallace B. Stewart of West Radford, Virginia, married Hattie R. Davis of Radford in an Episcopal ceremony on October 23, 1892. He was the son of A. B. and Joseph H. Stewart of Louisiana. She was the daughter of M. J. and Charles M. Davis of Monroe County, West Virginia. Hattie Davis was twenty-three years old when she married Wallace Stewart at the Radford home of Captain Ambrose Robinson. Rev. Edward L. Goodwin conducted the marriage ceremony with friends of the couple in attendance.

Taylor, Bennett W.
Circa 1800s

Bennett W. Taylor served as a vestryman for the first time in 1895. Additional information is not known about this gentleman at this time.

Veily, Philip
1845-1893

Philip Veily, his wife Freida, and their three children were members of the Radford Episcopal Parish at least from 1891 through 1898. Philip Veily (also spelled Phillip Veily and Philip Veilly) was born in 1845. He was a Grace Episcopal Mission Chapel parishioner and lived with his family in the West Ward of Radford in 1891. He was later "removed by letter to Philadelphia", Pennsylvania.

At some point prior to 1893, the family returned to the Radford area. According to an entry in church records by Rev. Edward Lewis Goodwin, Philip Veily died in Radford, Virginia from "softening of the brain" at the age of forty-eight on June 1, 1893. His death occurred one month before the baptism of his son George Grover Veily. Philip Veily was buried in the "Radford Cemetery", according to church records, on June 3, 1893. This may have been a reference to the Radford City public cemetery in the West Ward of Radford which was called "West View Cemetery".

Mrs. Freida Veily (maiden surname not now known) was briefly a member of the Rector's Aid Society of Grace Parish Episcopal Chapel in 1894. She last attended a Society meeting on October 31, 1894. Mrs. Freida Veily was still listed in church records as a Grace Episcopal Mission Chapel communicant in 1898.

Freida and Philip Veily had children:
1. Mary Veily (circa 1800s), daughter of Freida and Philip Veily.
2. Radford Veily (circa 1800s), son of Freida and Philip Veily. Radford Veily was baptized as an infant on March 23, 1890. The Episcopal baptism, held at the Veily home in Radford, was performed by Rev. Edward Lewis Good-

win. His sponsors were Mr. L. P. Ashmead, Mr. Joseph I. Doran, and Mrs. Elizabeth Campbell Radford Adams.

3. George Grover Veily (1892), son of Freida and Philip Veily. George Grover Veily was born in Radford, Virginia on December 14, 1892, six months before his father's death. He was baptized on July 9, 1893, one month after his father's death. George Grover Veily's baptism was recorded by Rev. Edward Lewis Goodwin as having been performed "at home, Radford (sick)". His mother was a witness and Mrs. A. D. Stevens was his sponsor. George Grover Veily may later have transferred to Philadelphia, Pennsylvania, according to church records.

Washington, John Henry
1836-1918

John Henry Washington and his family lived in the West Ward of Radford on Third and Preston Streets at least by 1891. The Washington family attended Grace Episcopal Mission chapel from around 1891 through 1904.

John Henry Washington was a fourth cousin to the first United States President, President George Washington. Born in Fauquier County, Virginia, J. H. Washington was the son of Hannah Fairfax Whiting and Perrin Washington. He was born in 1836[106]. His wife Selina "Nina" Dulaney was born in 1843.

The Washington family data was listed in the 1880 United States Census for Fauquier County, Virginia, as follows: forty-one year old dry goods merchant John H. Washington, his thirty-three year old wife Selina Washington, his nine year old daughter Sophia Washington, his seven year old son William D. Washington, his five year old daughter Mary B. Washington, his two year old daughter Hannah F. Washington, his seventy-five year old widowed mother Hannah F. Washington, and three servants: a single black twenty-one year old servant named Maria Braxton (circa 1859), a married black thirty year old laborer named Jeffer-

---

[106] John Henry Washington's birth year has been listed in sources as 1822, 1836, and 1839. It is listed as 1836 on the dedication panel of a stained glass window at Grace Episcopal Church in Radford.

son Woodson (circa 1850), and his wife described as a twenty-five year old servant named Amelia Woodson (circa 1855).

By 1891 they were living in the West Ward of Radford, Virginia. John Henry Washington was active in his church and in his community, including serving on Radford's first city council in 1892. They purchased land in Radford. William Ingles bought land from J. H. Washington in 1893 and from Nina Washington in 1895 and in 1900.

Mrs. Nina Dulaney's name appeared on the roster of Grace Episcopal Mission Chapel communicants, entering from "The Plains, Fauquier County, VA", at least from 1891 through 1904; J. H. and Nina D. Washington with five of their children were named on the church membership rolls in 1900. A notation in church records states that the family transferred to Birmingham, Alabama effective February 16, 1904. John Henry Washington died in 1918. Mrs. Selina Dulaney Washington died three years later, in 1921.

Selina Dulaney and John Henry Washington had children:

1. Sophia Carter Washington (1873), daughter of Selina Dulaney and John Henry Washington. Sophia, also called Sophie, was born in Virginia and August 12, 1873 and died at the age of eighty on December 21, 1953. She was baptized "in the Church" and was confirmed at Grace Episcopal Mission Chapel on May 12, 1893. Her confirmation rites were conducted by the Rt. Rev. Alfred M. Randolph as attested to by Rev. Edward Lewis Goodwin. Sophie became an Episcopal communicant in 1893 and was a member of the Grace Episcopal Rector's Aid Society and Ladies Chapel Fund from 1893 through 1902. She was also a member of the Radford Chapter of the United Daughters of the Confederacy.

2. William Dodge Washington (1875), son of Selina Dulaney and John Henry Washington. He was born in Virginia in 1875 and died at the age of forty-seven in 1922.

3. Mary Welby Washington (1877), daughter of Selina Dulaney and John Henry Washington. She was born in Virginia in 1877 and died at the age of eighty-nine in 1966. She was baptized "in the church" and was confirmed with her sisters Sophie and Hannah at Grace Episcopal Mission Chapel in Radford on May 12, 1893. The Rt. Rev. Alfred

M. Randolph officiated, as attested to by Rev. Edward Lewis Goodwin. She was an unmarried public school teacher at the Wadsworth Street School in Radford during the 1896-1897 school year. Mary Welby Washington married George Clay. They were both members of St. James' and Grace Episcopal Mission Chapel. Although the church register indicates that she moved to Plainfield, New Jersey at some point, she is listed as an unmarried member of the Rector's Aid Society of Grace Parish Episcopal Church in 1900. Mary was appointed and later elected to be the first treasurer of that group. She continued her participation as a member and an office holder of the Woman's Guild of Grace Chapel in 1902. At some point Mary W. and George Clay moved to Plainfield, New Jersey. A notation in the Episcopal church register indicates that the Washington family moved to Birmingham, Alabama in 1904. Mrs. Mary Welby Washington Clay died in 1966.

4. Hannah Fairfax Washington (1879), daughter of Selina Dulaney and John Henry Washington. She was born in Virginia in 1879 and died at the age of eighty-four in 1963. Her grandmother Mrs. Hannah Fairfax Washington was her namesake. Young Hannah was baptized "in the church" and was confirmed with her sisters Sophia and Mary on May 12, 1893 at Grace Episcopal Mission Chapel in Radford. The Rt. Rev. Alfred M. Randolph performed the confirmation rites as attested to by Rev. Edward Lewis Goodwin. Hannah Fairfax Washington became a communicant of Grace Episcopal Mission Chapel in 1893, and was a member of the Rector's Aid Society of the church by 1900.

5. Fannie Scott Washington (circa 1800s), daughter of Selina Dulaney and John Henry Washington. This Washington daughter was not named on the 1880 United States Census as a Washington family member, but was listed as a member of the Washington family on the Grace Episcopal Mission Chapel membership roster in 1900.

6. John Henry Washington Jr. (circa 1800s), son of Selina Dulaney and John Henry Washington. This son of the Washington's was neither listed on the 1880 United States

398

Census nor on the roster of Radford Episcopal Parish members through 1904.

A detailed lineage of John Henry Washington is as follows (John Washington > Lawrence Washington > John Washington > Warner Washington > Warner Washington Jr. > Perrin Washington > John Henry Washington).

1) <u>John Washington</u> 1st GENERATION (circa 1632 – circa 1677), son of Lawrence Washington; his mother may have been Amphilis Twigden. Both of his parents were born in England around 1602. John Washington was born in England around 1632 and immigrated to the Virginia Colony in the Americas in 1656. He was a colonel in the colonial militia in Virginia and the great-grandfather of the first United States President, George Washington. He married Ann Pope (who was born around 1635 and died in 1668). After her death, he married Anne Brett. After Anne Brett's death, Frances Appleton became John Washington's third wife. Ann Pope and John Washington had five children: Lawrence Washington, John Washington, Ann Washington, and two children who died young.

   a) <u>Child#1 Washington</u> 2ND GENERATION (circa 1600s), child of Ann Pope and Colonel John Washington. This child may have died before 1676.

   b) <u>Daughter [Child#2] Washington</u> 2ND GENERATION (circa 1600s), child of Ann Pope and Colonel John Washington. Her married name may have been Mrs. Lewis. She may have died before 1676.

   c) <u>John Washington Jr.</u> 2ND GENERATION (1663), son of Ann Pope and Colonel John Washington. He was a captain in the colonial militia. He married Ann Wickliffe. They had children:

     i) <u>Lawrence Washington</u> 3RD GENERATION (circa 1600s), son of Ann Wickliffe and John Washington Jr. He married Elizabeth (maiden surname not now known). They had children.

(1) John Washington 4TH GENERATION (circa 1700s), son of Elizabeth and Lawrence Washington.

(2) James Washington 4TH GENERATION (circa 1700s), son of Elizabeth and Lawrence Washington.

(3) Thomas Washington 4TH GENERATION (circa 1700s), son of Elizabeth and Lawrence Washington.

ii) John Washington III 3RD GENERATION (circa 1600s), son of Ann Wickliffe and John Washington Jr. His father willed the home plantation to his mother, to be willed to John Washington III upon the death of both of his parents.

iii) Nathaniel Washington 3RD GENERATION (circa 1600s), son of Ann Wickliffe and John Washington Jr. He married Mary (maiden surname not now known).

iv) Henry Washington 3RD GENERATION (1694-1748), son of Ann Wickliffe and John Washington Jr. Known as Captain Henry Washington, he married Mary Bailey. They had children.

(1) John Washington 4TH GENERATION (circa 1700s), son of Mary Bailey and Captain Henry Washington. In 1759 he married Katherine Washington. Born around 1741, she was the daughter of Mary and Captain John Washington. Katherine and John Washington had twelve children, including:

(a) Henry Washington 5TH GENERATION (1760), son of Katherine Washington and John Washington. He first married Mildred Pratt. He married second to Ann Quarles.

(b) Ann Washington 5TH GENERATION (1761), daughter of Katherine Washington and John Washington. She married Thomas Hungerford.

400

(c) <u>Nathaniel Washington</u> 5TH GENERATION (1762), son of Katherine Washington and John Washington.

(d) <u>Mary Washington</u> 5TH GENERATION (1764), son of Katherine Washington and John Washington.

(2) <u>Henry Washington Jr.</u> 4TH GENERATION (circa 1700s), son of Mary Bailey and Captain Henry Washington. He married Elizabeth Storke in 1743, two years before his death and five years before his father's death.

(3) <u>Nathaniel Washington</u> 4TH GENERATION (1726-1745), son of Mary Bailey and Captain Henry Washington.

(4) <u>Bailey Washington</u> 4TH GENERATION (1731), son of Mary Bailey and Captain Henry Washington. In 1749 he married Catherine Storke. They had children, including:

    (a) <u>William Washington</u> 5TH GENERATION (circa 1700s), son of Catherine Storke and Bailey Washington. He served at the Battle of Cowpens as a Virginia Colonel during the Revolutionary War.

d) <u>Ann Washington</u> 2ND GENERATION (circa 1600s), daughter of Ann Pope and John Washington. She married Major Francis Wright. They had at least one child:

    i) <u>John Wright</u> 3RD GENERATION (circa 1600s), son of Ann Washington and Francis Wright.

e) <u>Lawrence Washington</u> 2ND GENERATION (1659-1698), son of Ann Pope and Colonel John Washington and grandfather of future President George Washington. Lawrence Washington was born in Westmoreland County, Virginia in 1659. He was a major in the colonial militia. He inherited land from his father which included a section that would be known as Mt. Vernon. Major Lawrence Washington married Mildred Warner (who was born in 1671 and died in 1747). They had three children: John, Augustine, and Mildred.

i) <u>Mildred Washington</u> 3RD GENERATION (1686-1747), daughter of Mildred Warner and Major Lawrence Washington. She was both the aunt and the godmother of George Washington, the first President of the United States. She first married Roger Gregory. After his death, she married Colonel Henry Willis who was the founder of Fredericksburg, Virginia. Mildred Washington and Roger Gregory had three daughters. Those three daughters married three brothers by the name of Thornton.

ii) <u>John Washington</u> 3RD GENERATION (1692-1743), son of Mildred Warner and Major Lawrence Washington. He married Catherine Whiting, who was born in 1694. They had children, including: Warner Washington, Catherine Washington, Elizabeth Washington, Henry Washington and Warner Washington.

  (1) <u>Catherine Washington</u> 4TH GENERATION (circa 1700s), daughter of Catherine Whiting and John Washington. She was the first wife of Colonel Fielding Lewis.

  (2) <u>Elizabeth Washington</u> 4TH GENERATION (circa 1700s), daughter of Catherine Whiting and John Washington. She never married, and died as a young adult.

  (3) <u>Henry Washington</u> 4TH GENERATION (circa 1718), daughter of Catherine Whiting and John Washington. He married Anne Thacker. They had children.

    (a) <u>Elizabeth Washington</u> 5TH GENERATION (circa 1700s), daughter of Anne Thacker and Henry Washington.

    (b) <u>Catherine Washington</u> 5TH GENERATION (circa 1700s), daughter of Anne Thacker and Henry Washington.

(c) <u>Ann Washington</u> 5TH GENERATION (circa 1700s), daughter of Anne Thacker and Henry Washington.

(d) <u>Thacker Washington</u> 5TH GENERATION (circa 1740-1763), daughter of Anne Thacker and Henry Washington. He married Harriet Peyton.

> (i) <u>Henry Thacker Washington</u> 6TH GENERATION (circa 1700s), son of Harriet Peyton and Thacker Washington. He married Amelia Stith, the daughter of Mary Townshend (or Townsend) Washington and Robert Stith. Amelia Stith and Henry Thacker Washington had children.
>
> > 1. <u>Henry Thacker Washington Jr.</u> 5TH GENERATION (1802-1855), son of Amelia Stith and Henry Thacker Washington. He married Virginia Grymes (1812-1855). They had children.
> >
> > > a. <u>William Henry Washington</u> 6TH GENERATION (circa 1800s), son of Virginia Grymes and Henry Thacker Washington Jr. He married Rosalie Catlett. They had children.
> > >
> > > b. <u>John Peyton Washington</u> 6th GENERATION (circa 1800s), son of Virginia Grymes and Henry Thacker Washington Jr.
> >
> > 2. <u>Cecelia Peyton Washington</u> 5TH GENERATION (circa 1800s-1841), daughter of Amelia Stith and Henry Thacker Washington. She married Edwin B. Burwell in 1822. She later married John W. Owen. She died in 1841 at

403

Woodland in Clarke County, Virginia.

3. Amelia Stith Washington 5TH GENERATION (1810-1831), daughter of Amelia Stith and Henry Thacker Washington. In 1826, she married Dr. Mann P. Nelson.

4. Putnam Stith Washington 5TH GENERATION (circa 1800s), son of Amelia Stith and Henry Thacker Washington.

5. daughter Washington 5TH GENERATION (circa 1800s), may have been a daughter of Amelia Stith and Henry Thacker Washington. This daughter's Christian (i.e. first) name is not now known. Her married named was Mrs. William P. Floyd.

(ii) Warner Washington 6TH GENERATION (circa 1700s), son of Harriet Peyton and Thacker Washington. He married Ariana (maiden surname not now known) in 1805. They had children.

1. Francis Whiting Washington 7TH GENERATION (circa 1800s), son of Ariana and Warner Washington.

2. John Stith Washington 7TH GENERATION (circa 1800s), son of Ariana and Warner Washington. He lived in Alabama.

3. Henry Thacker Washington 7TH GENERATION (circa 1800s), son of Ariana and Warner Washington.

4. Harriet Ann Washington 7TH GENERATION (circa 1800s), son

404

of Ariana and Warner Washington. She married William Garrett Jr. They lived in Montgomery, Alabama.

(4) Warner Washington 4TH GENERATION (c. 1715-1792), son of Catherine Whiting and John Washington. He was born around 1715. He married first Elizabeth Macon, who was born around 1729. In 1765, after her death, he married second to Hannah Fairfax. Hannah Fairfax was born in 1742 and died in 1804. The children of Warner Washington were as follows.

(a) Fairfax Washington 5TH GENERATION (circa 1700s), son of Hannah Fairfax and Warner Washington. He married Sarah Armistead.

(b) Elizabeth Washington 5TH GENERATION (circa 1700s), daughter of Hannah Fairfax and Warner Washington. In 1795, she married George Booth.

(c) Mildred Washington 5TH GENERATION (circa 1700s), son of Hannah Fairfax and Warner Washington. In 1785, she married a Mr. Throckmorton.

(d) Louisa Washington 5TH GENERATION (circa 1700s), son of Hannah Fairfax and Warner Washington. She may have married Thomas Fairfax in 1798.

(e) Catharine Washington 5TH GENERATION (circa 1700s), son of Hannah Fairfax and Warner Washington. In 1789, she married John Nelson.

(f) Hannah Fairfax Washington 5TH GENERATION (circa 1767-1828), daughter of Hannah Fairfax and Warner Washington. She was born around 1767 and died in 1828. In 1788 she married Peter Beverly Whiting. He was born around 1762 and died around 1811. Hannah Fairfax Washington and Peter Beverly Whiting had children.

   (i) Hannah Fairfax Whiting 6TH GENERATION (1799), daughter of Hannah Fairfax Washington and Peter Beverly Whiting. She married Perrin Washington, a son Mary Whiting and Warner Washington Jr. (her paternal uncle).

(g) Whiting Washington 5TH GENERATION (circa 1700s), son of Elizabeth Macon and Warner Washington. He married Rebecca Smith in Frederick County, Virginia in 1804.

(h) Warner Washington Jr. 5TH GENERATION (1751-circa 1829), son of Elizabeth Macon and Warner Washington. He was born in 1751. He married Mary Whiting in 1770. She was born in 1754. Mary Whiting and Warner Washington Jr. had children. She died in 1794. In 1795, he married Sarah Warner Rootes. They had children. Warner Washington Jr. died around 1829. Children of Warner Washington Jr. were as follows.

   (i) Reade Washington 6TH GENERATION (circa 1700s), son of Warner Washington Jr. and either Mary Whiting or Sarah Warner Rootes.

   (ii) Fairfax Washington 6TH GENERATION (circa 1700s), son of Warner Washington Jr. and either Mary Whiting or Sarah Warner Rootes.

   (iii) Hamilton Washington 6TH GENERATION (circa 1700s), son of Warner Washington Jr. and either

Mary Whiting or Sarah Warner Rootes.

(iv) Elizabeth W. Washington 6TH GENERATION (circa 1700s), daughter of Warner Washington Jr. and either Mary Whiting or Sarah Warner Rootes.

(v) Warner Washington III 6TH GENERATION (circa 1700s), son of Warner Washington Jr. and either Mary Whiting or Sarah Warner Rootes.

(vi) Perrin Washington 6TH GENERATION (1790-1857), son of Mary Whiting and Warner Washington Jr. He was born on February 7, 1790 in Virginia and died in 1857 in Washington D. C. He married Hannah Fairfax Whiting, daughter of his aunt Hannah Fairfax Washington (i.e. Mrs. Peter Beverly Whiting). Hannah Fairfax Whiting was born in 1799 and died in Virginia in 1878. They had children, including John Henry Washington.

1. John Henry Washington 7TH GENERATION (1836), son of Hannah Fairfax Whiting and Perrin Washington. He was born in Fauquier County, Virginia in 1836. He married Selina Dulaney. Called Nina, she was born in 1843. Selina Dulaney and John Henry Washington had children.

a. Sophia Carter Washington 8TH GENERATION (1873), daughter of Selina Dulaney and John Henry Washington. She was born on August

407

12, 1873 and died on December 21, 1953.

  b. Mary Welby Washington 8TH GENERATION (1877), daughter of Selina Dulaney and John Henry Washington. She was born in 1877. She married George Clay. She died in 1966.

  c. William Dodge Washington 8TH GENERATION (1875), son of Selina Dulaney and John Henry Washington. He was born in 1875 and died in 1922.

  d. Hannah Fairfax Washington 8TH GENERATION (1879), daughter of Selina Dulaney and John Henry Washington. She was born in 1879 and died in 1963.

  e. John Henry Washington Jr. 8TH GENERATION (circa 1800s), son of Selina Dulaney and John Henry Washington.

  f. Fannie Scott Washington 8TH GENERATION (circa 1800s), daughter of Selina Dulaney and John Henry Washington.

iii) <u>Augustine Washington</u> 3RD GENERATION (1694-1743), son of Mildred Warner and Major Lawrence Washington. Augustine was the father of George Washington, the first President of the United States. Augustine Washington married first Jane Butler, they had four children. She died in 1728. Augustine Washington married Mary Ball in 1731; they had six children. The children of Augustine Washington were as follows.

(1) Lawrence Washington 4TH GENERATION (circa 1717), son of Jane Butler and Augustine Washington.

(2) Augustine Washington Jr. 4TH GENERATION (1720-1762), son of Jane Butler and Augustine Washington. He was born in 1720 and died in 1762. He fought in the Revolutionary War. Known as Austin, he married Ann Aylett in 1743. She died at Wakefield in 1774. After her death, he married Jane Ashton and lived with her at the Wakefield estate. Children of Augustine Washington Jr. were as follows.

  (a) Ann Washington 5TH GENERATION (1752), daughter of Augustine Washington Jr. Known as Nancy, she was born in 1752 and died in 1777. In 1768, she married Burdett Ashton.

  (b) Elizabeth Washington 5TH GENERATION (1749-1814), daughter of Ann Aylett and Augustine Washington Jr. She married Alexander Spotswood in 1769. She was known as Betsey and as Eliza. Elizabeth Washington and Alexander Spotswood had children.

    (i) Mary Randolph Spotswood 6th GENERATION (1775-1803), daughter of Elizabeth Washington and Alexander Spotswood. She married Francis Taliaferro Brooke in 1791. They had children.

      1. Robert Spotswood Brooke 7TH GENERATION (1800-1851), son of Mary Randolph Spotswood and Francis Taliaferro Brooke. He married Elizabeth Smith in 1828. She was born in 1810 and died in 1834. They had children.

409

a. <u>Elizabeth Brooke</u> 8TH GENERATION (1833-1891), daughter of Elizabeth Smith and Robert Spotswood Brooke. In 1856 she married James Cochran. He was born in 1830 and died in 1897. They had children.

    i. <u>Elizabeth Cochran</u> 9TH GENERATION (circa 1800s), daughter of Elizabeth Brooke and James Cochran. She was born in Augusta County, Virginia. She married Lionel S. Rawlinson. Mrs. Elizabeth Cochran Rawlinson was a member of the Daughters of the American Revolution (DAR member #127205) based upon her lineage to Augustine Washington Jr.

(c) <u>Jane Washington</u> 5TH GENERATION (circa 1700s), daughter of Augustine Washington Jr. She married John Thornton.

(d) <u>William Augustine Washington</u> 5TH GENERATION (1757-1810), son of Ann Aylett and Augustine Washington Jr. He inherited Wakefield plantation and built the Blenheim plantation. He married first Jane Washington, the daughter of John Augustine Washington, He married second to Mary Lee, the daughter of Richard Henry Lee. He married third to Sally Tayloe (also seen written as "Tayhoe"). He fathered children as follows.

410

(i) <u>Augustine Washington</u> 6TH GENERATION (1778), son of William Augustine Washington. He was born at Wakefield in 1778. Dr. Augustine Washington became a Professor of Philosophy at William and Mary College in Williamsburg, Virginia.

(ii) <u>George Corbin Washington</u> 6TH GENERATION (1789-1854), son of William Augustine Washington. He inherited Wakefield, later selling it in 1813 to John Gray. He married first Eliza Beall in 1807. He married second Ann Thomas Peter (i.e. widow Beall). He fathered children, including Lewis W. Washington.

1. <u>Lewis William Washington</u> 7TH GENERATION (circa 1800s), son of George Corbin Washington. He lived at Beallair. Colonel Lewis W. Washington married first to Mary Ann Barroll. He married second to Ella M. Bassett. Lewis William Washington fathered children.

a. <u>James Barroll Washington</u> 8TH GENERATION (circa 1800s), son of Mary Ann Barroll and Lewis William Washington. He was a major in the Confederate Army during the Civil War. He married Jane Bretney Lanier. They had at least one child: William Lanier Washington.

i. <u>William Lanier Washington</u> 9TH GENERATION (1865-1933), son of Jane Bretney Lanier and

411

James Barroll Washington. He was born in Alabama on March 30, 1865. He first married to Mary Bruce Brennan in 1906. He married two additional times as a widower.

b. 1st daughter Washington 8TH GENERATION (circa 1800s), daughter of Mary Ann Barroll and Lewis William Washington.

c. 2nd daughter Washington 8TH GENERATION (circa 1800s), daughter of Mary Ann Barroll and Lewis William Washington.

d. William De Hertburn Washington 8TH GENERATION (circa 1800s), son of Ella M. Bassett and Lewis William Washington. He was born in Virginia at the Bassett estate Clover Lea in 1863. He died in 1914.

(iii) Sarah Tayloe Washington 6TH GENERATION (1800-1866), daughter of Sally Tayloe and William Augustine Washington. She married her cousin Lawrence Washington. They had children.

1. Robert James Washington 7TH GENERATION (circa 1800s), son of Sarah Tayloe Washington and Lawrence Washington. He was a military colonel. He married Bessie Payne Wirt.

2. Lloyd Washington 7TH GENERATION (circa 1800s), son

of Sarah Tayloe Washington and Lawrence Washington. He lived in Westmoreland County, Virginia.

3. <u>Mary West Washington</u> 7TH GENERATION (circa 1800s), daughter of Sarah Tayloe Washington and Lawrence Washington. She married Dr. Walker Washington of Westmoreland County, Virginia.

(iv) <u>William Augustine Washington Jr.</u> 6TH GENERATION (circa 1700s), son of Sally Tayloe and William Augustine Washington.

(3) <u>Jane Washington</u> 4TH GENERATION (1722-1735), daughter of Jane Butler and Augustine Washington.

(4) <u>Butler Washington</u> 4TH GENERATION (1724), son of Jane Butler and Augustine Washington. He died as an infant.

(5) <u>George Washington</u> 4TH GENERATION (1732-1799), son of Mary Ball and Augustine Washington. He was born at the Wakefield estate in Westmoreland County, Virginia on February 22, 1732. George Washington married a widow by the name of Martha Dandridge Custis in 1759. The daughter of Frances Jones and Colonel John Dandridge, she was born in Virginia on June 2, 1731. She married first Daniel Parke Custis. She married second George Washington. He fought in the Revolutionary War and became the first President of the United States of America. President George Washington died at Mt. Vernon in Virginia on December 14, 1799. Mrs. Martha Dandridge Custis Washington died at Mt. Vernon in 1802. She had at least two children by Daniel Parke Custis: John

413

Parke Custis and Martha Custis. She had
no children by George Washington.

(6) Elizabeth Washington 4TH GENERATION
(1733-1797), daughter of Mary Ball and
Augustine Washington. Known as Betty,
she married Colonel Fielding Lewis.

(7) Samuel Washington 4TH GENERATION
(1734-1781), son of Mary Ball and
Augustine Washington. He was born at the
Wakefield estate in 1734. He was married
five times. Samuel Washington died at the
Harewood estate in 1781.

(8) John Augustine Washington 4TH
GENERATION (1736-1787), son of Mary
Ball and Augustine Washington. He was
born on January 13, 1736. He married
Hannah Bushrod. They made their home
both at Mt. Vernon and at Bushfield. Hannah Bushrod and John Augustine had
children.

(a) Jane Washington 5TH GENERATION
(1758), daughter of Hannah Bushrod
and John Augustine Washington.

(b) Mildred Washington 5TH GENERATION
(1760), daughter of Hannah Bushrod
and John Augustine Washington.

(c) Bushrod Washington 5TH GENERATION
(1762), child of Hannah Bushrod and
John Augustine Washington.

(d) Corbin Washington 5TH GENERATION
(1765-1800), son of Hannah Bushrod
and John Augustine Washington.

(9) Charles Washington 4TH GENERATION
(1738-1799), son of Mary Ball and
Augustine Washington. He married Mildred Thornton.

(10) Mildred Washington 4TH
GENERATION (1739-1740), daughter of
Mary Ball and Augustine Washington.

Waskey, Joseph
Circa 1859-1897

Joseph Waskey's 1897 funeral service was performed by the Rev. F. G. Ribble, the rector of St. James' Episcopal Mission Chapel and Grace Episcopal Mission Chapel. Joseph Waskey, born around 1859, was living in Radford, Virginia when he was killed in a railroad engine explosion on May 31, 1897. He was thirty-eight years of age. Waskey was buried at "Radford Cemetery", according to church records.

Weisiger, George A.
Circa 1800s

George A. Weisiger and his wife Bessie were parishioners of Grace Episcopal Mission Chapel during the late 1800s. Beside George's name in church records is the note "old communicant from St. John's; name re-entered". George A. Weisiger was a member of the Radford Episcopal Parish vestry in 1893, and was a Grace communicant at least from 1891 until he moved with letters either to Amelia County, Virginia or to Richmond, Virginia.

Wharton, William Radford
1864-1918

William Radford Wharton was a lifelong member of the Radford Episcopal Parish, as were his parents. He married Susan Hammet Heth, also a lifelong member of the Episcopal congregation.

William Radford Wharton, son of Anne Rebecca Radford and Gabriel Colvin Wharton, was born on June 11, 1864. He married Susan Hammet Heth, also known as Sue and Susie, on October 1, 1890 according to church records. Born on August 23, 1868, Sue was the daughter of Isabelle Hammet Heth and Stockton Heth. She was the niece of Mrs. Susan Hammet Tyler and Governor James Hoge Tyler. She was also the great-niece of Methodist minister

Rev. William Hammet, who was chaplain of the University of Virginia and the chaplain of the United States Congress. Susan Hammet Heth was baptized and confirmed at St. James' Episcopal Mission Chapel, although she was not carried as a communicant until 1891.

At the time of their marriage, William was twenty-six and Sue was twenty-two years of age. The wedding was held with their families in attendance at Norwood, the Heth family home in Radford. Rev. Edward Lewis Goodwin performed the wedding ceremony. The young couple shared a home on Wadsworth Street with William Radford's widowed father at least in 1891. They lived at Glencoe by the early 1900s. Descendants continued to use Glencoe as a summer home until the early 1960s.

William Radford Wharton was active in his community and in his church. He was an attorney practicing both in Montgomery and Pulaski County courts during the early 1890s. His office was located on Norwood Street in Radford.

The Whartons were active parishioners of the Grace Episcopal Mission Chapel. On June 8, 1891, W. R. Wharton proposed to the Radford Episcopal Parish vestry a resolution that each congregation in the have its own vestry. Those congregations were the St. James' Episcopal Mission Chapel and the Grace Episcopal Mission Chapel congregations. That proposal was defeated by the standing vestry in a vote of five for and seven against the vestry division. The new parish vestry then held member elections. W. R. Wharton was elected to the parish vestry but declined to serve. His father G. C. Wharton was elected to serve "in his stead".

Mrs. Susan Hammet Heth Wharton was a member of the Ladies Chapel Fund Society of Grace Episcopal Parish at least by 1896. She was also a member of the Radford Chapter of the Virginia Daughters of the confederacy of the United Daughters of the Confederacy based upon her lineage to both her father Captain Stockton Heth and to her father-in-law General Gabriel Colvin Wharton.

William Radford Wharton died on May 16, 1918 at the age of fifty-four. The church register contained a listing that William Radford Wharton, male, age fifty-four, whose last residence was Los Angeles, California, died on May 16, 1918 from "heart trouble". He was buried on June 30, 1918 at the "Family grave yard, Radford, VA".

His widow Mrs. Susan Hammet Heth Wharton lived to be ninety. She was still living at Glencoe when she passed away on Saturday, May 17, 1958 after some period of illness. One of Mrs. Wharton's four grandchildren, Mrs. Sally Fits van Solkema, was living with her at Glencoe at the time. The funeral service was conducted at Grace Episcopal Church with the Rev. Wilfred Roach officiating. The service was followed by her burial at the private Radford family cemetery. Her pallbearers were Henry Heth, Dr. Ernest Merrill, Richard P. Adams, Frank Y. Caldwell, and Andrew Lewis Ingles.

The grave markers for the Whartons read "William Radford Wharton, Captain U.S.A., June 11, 1864, May 16, 1918, He that believeth in me hath everlasting life" (Wharton having served as a Captain during the Spanish-American War) and "Sue Heth Wharton, Aug. 23, 1868-May 17, 1958, Loving wife of William Radford Wharton, Beloved mother of Heth, Ann and William". Mr. and Mrs. William Radford Wharton Jr. donated to the Parish House Building fund in memory of his parents, Mr. and Mrs. William Radford Wharton St.

Susan Hammet Heth and William Radford Wharton had children:

1. Stockton Heth Wharton (1892), son of Susan Hammet Heth and William Radford Wharton, was born on April 18, 1892. He was called Heth. He was baptized at Norwood, the home of his namesake and maternal grandfather Captain Stockton Heth. Stockton Heth Wharton was two years old when the baptismal rites were performed by the Rt. Rev. Alfred M. Randolph on May 23, 1894. His eleven year old uncle, Clement Craig Heth, and his sister Anne Rebecca Radford Wharton were baptized at the same time. Their witnesses and sponsors were Mrs. Susan Hammet Heth Wharton, Captain Stockton Heth, and Mrs. Richard Henry Adams Jr. A note in church records states that, at some point, Stockton Heth Wharton "left town". He was living in Los Angeles, California at the time of his mother's 1958 death.

417

2. Anne Rebecca Radford Wharton (1894), daughter of Susan Hammet Heth and William Radford Wharton, was born on April 3, 1894. She was called Anne. She was baptized along with her brother Stockton Heth Wharton and her uncle Clement Craig Heth on May 23, 1894. She was one month old. The baptismal rites were performed by the Rt. Rev. Alfred M. Randolph, with Susan H. H. Wharton, Stockton Heth, and Mrs. R. H. Adams Jr. as witnesses and sponsors. Anne married Hugo Swaen von Poederoyen and was living in Van Nuys, California at the time of her mother's 1958 death.

3. William Radford Wharton Jr. (1904), son of Susan Hammet Heth and William Radford Wharton, was born on March 3, 1904. He was called William. He married Evelyn (maiden surname not now known). W. R. Wharton Jr. and his family were living in White Plains, New York at the time of his mother's 1958 death. He died on May 27, 1990. His grave marker reads: "William Radford Wharton Jr., Mar. 3, 1904 – May 27, 1990, Beloved husband of Evelyn, Loving father of Sally and Sue". Evelyn and William Radford Wharton Jr. had children:

a. Sue Wharton (circa 1900s), daughter of Evelyn and William Radford Wharton Jr. A note in church records states that she moved to Washington D.C. in 1902.

b. Sally Wharton (circa 1900s), daughter of Evelyn and William Radford Wharton Jr. She married Frith van Solkema.

Wilson, John Andrew
1849-1910

Mary Catherine Lock and her husband John Andrew Wilson were communicants of St. James' Episcopal Mission Chapel and living in the East Ward of Radford by 1885. They transferred to Grace Episcopal Church on April 1, 1904. The Wilson continued as members of the Radford Episcopal Parish until their deaths.

John Andrew (incorrectly written as "Archer" in church records) Wilson Sr. was born on February 12, 1840. His wife was Mary Catherine Lock, daughter of Wilhemina and Fred Lock. She was born on February 21, 1855.

When the 1880 United States Census was taken, they were living in Central Depot with their three daughters and a son as follows: thirty-one year old white railroad employee John A. Wilson, his twenty-seven year old wife Mary C. Wilson, their six-year old daughter Ethel R. Wilson, their four year old son Frederick M. Wilson, their two year old daughter Carrie L. Wilson, and a two month old daughter whose Christian name was not listed.

John Andrew Lock was active in his church. He was a vestryman and the vestry treasurer of St. James' Episcopal Mission Chapel in 1885. He was elected to be a parish delegate to the Episcopal Diocese Council on May 18, 1887. In 1889, John A. Lock was a member of the committee which included John Lawrence Radford to work with Captain Heth and the Radford Land Company to find a lot for a new Episcopal rectory.

John Andrew Wilson died on April 14, 1910 and was buried in Central Cemetery. His grave marker includes the inscription "Woodmen of the World". Mrs. Mary Catherine Lock Wilson died on April 29, 1933. According to church records entered by Rev. James A. Figg, she was then a seventy-eight year old resident of East Radford who died from "old age". She too was buried in Central Cemetery, described in church records as "East Radford", on May 1, 1933. Stained glass windows depicting "Mary and Christ in the Temple" were purchased for Grace Episcopal Church in their memory. A priest chair was presented in her memory by the Parish Aid Society in 1934.

Hugo L. Wilson was listed as a member of John Andrew Wilson's family in the 1904 church records; relationship was not noted. Also, a church pew was given to the church in memory of "Henry Harrison Wilson, 1882-1933"; relationship to the family of John Andrew Wilson was not noted.

Mary Catherine Lock and John Andrew Wilson had children:
1. Ethel R. Wilson (1873), daughter of Mary Catherine Lock and John Andrew Wilson. She was born on September 4, 1873, became a communicant of St. James' Episcopal Mission Chapel on May 18, 1895, and died on April 19,

1901. She was buried in Central Cemetery. Brass vases for the altar flowers were given to the church by the Junior Altar Guild in memory of Mary Ethel Wilson; it is not known if this was the Ethel listed here.

2. Frederick M. Wilson (circa 1876), son of Mary Catherine Lock and John Andrew Wilson. He was baptized "in the church" and was confirmed along with his brothers John Andrew Wilson Jr. and Robert Lilburn Wilson on May 18, 1895. Called Fred, he may later have moved to Gulfport, Mississippi. He may have died in 1953, according to a notation in church records.

3. Carrie Louisa Wilson (circa 1878), daughter of Mary Catherine Lock and John Andrew Wilson. Called Louise, she was baptized "in the church" and was confirmed on May 12, 1893. The Rt. Rev. A. M. Randolph performed the Rite of Confirmation as attested to by Rev. Edward Lewis Goodwin. Carrie Louise Wilson married Edward Deming Lucas on November 21, 1900 as recorded in the Radford City Marriage Register. They later transferred to Christ Church in Petersburg, Virginia in 1938.

4. Wilson daughter (circa 1880), daughter of Mary Catherine Lock and John Andrew Wilson. Her name may have been Susan U. Wilson.

5. John Andrew Wilson Jr. (1882), son of Mary Catherine Lock and John Andrew Wilson. He had a twin brother named Robert Lilburn Wilson. They were born on October 4, 1882. He was baptized at the age of two and a half along with his brother Robert at St. James' Episcopal Mission Chapel in Central, Virginia on May 14, 1885. Their sponsor was Mrs. Wilhemina Lock. Rev. J. E. Hammond officiated. The boys were confirmed at St. James' Episcopal Mission Chapel ten years later, on May 18, 1895, by the Rt. Rev. A. M. Randolph and attested to by Rev. A. A. Pruden. John Andrew Wilson Jr., called John, became an Episcopal preacher. Rev. Wilson conducted his sister-in-law Epsie's first confirmation class while he was on leave from teaching at Boone University in Honan, China. His younger brother Ambrose and Ambrose's wife Epsie made a donation to the Building Fund for the new Parish

Hall in memory of Rev. J. A. Wilson Jr. A purple pall was also given to the church in his memory.

6. Robert Lilburn Wilson (1882), son of Mary Catherine Lock and John Andrew Wilson and twin brother of John Andrew Wilson Jr. Called Robert, he was born on October 4, 1882. He was baptized at the age of two and a half along with his brother John at St. James' Episcopal Mission Chapel in Central, Virginia on May 14, 1885. The boys were confirmed at St. James' Episcopal Mission Chapel ten years later, on May 18, 1895. Robert married Ellie Shepherd. Robert Lilburn Wilson died on January 29, 1964 and was buried in Central Cemetery in Radford. Friends and family gave gifts to Grace Episcopal Church in his memory. Ellie Shepherd and Robert Lilburn Wilson had at least one child:

   a. Robert Lilburn Wilson Jr. (1904), son of Ellie Shepherd and Robert Lilburn. He was born on September 5, 1904. He was baptized at Grace Episcopal Church on March 12, 1905. His sponsors were John A. Wilson, Edward Deming Lucas, and Mrs. Carrie Louise Wilson Lucas.

7. Henry Rudolph Wilson (1885), son of Mary Catherine Lock and John Andrew Wilson. Called Rudolph, he was born on November 7, 1885. He was baptized by Rev. J. E. Hammond at St. James' Episcopal Mission Chapel in Central, Virginia. Mrs. Wilhemina Lock was his sponsor at the May 2, 1886 baptism for the seven-month old child.

8. Frank Stringfellow Wilson (1889), son of Mary Catherine Lock and John Andrew Wilson. Called Frank, he was born on April 5, 1889. He was confirmed at the same service during which his brothers Lewis and Ambrose were baptized, on May 23, 1894 at St. James' Episcopal Mission Chapel. Five-year old Frank S. Wilson was confirmed by Episcopal Evangelist Rev. T. H. Lacy. Frank Stringfellow Wilson died in 1959. His grave marker in Radford City's Central Cemetery reads "Frank S. Wilson, Virginia, U.S. Army, World War I, Apr. 5, 1889, June 3, 1959". A Litany Desk was given to Grace Episcopal Church by Mr.

and Mrs. E. J. Fink and Mr. Ambrose Fink in memory of Frank Stringfellow Wilson.

9. Lewis Lock [also spelled Locke] Wilson (1891), son of Mary Catherine Lock and John Andrew Wilson. Called Lewis, he was born on March 31, 1891. He was baptized at the age of three by Rev. T. H. Lacy at St. James' Episcopal Mission Chapel on May 23, 1894.

10. Ambrose Wilson (1893), son of Mary Catherine Lock and John Andrew Wilson. Ambrose was born on September 6, 1893. He was baptized at St. James' Episcopal Mission Chapel at the age of eight months by the Rev. T. H. Lacy on May 23, 1894. Ambrose was the proprietor of "Idle Hour", a restaurant and bar in downtown Radford. In 1922 he married Epsie Rike (also spelled Reich), the daughter of Roella Blizzard and Samuel McKindrey Rike. She was born on February 25, 1898, on a farm in Randolph County, North Carolina. In 1918, she graduated from the North Carolina Normal and Industrial College. She and her husband made their home in Radford. Mrs. Epsie Rike Wilson joined and was confirmed at Grace Episcopal Church, became a member of the church choir as well as sharing her skills as a pianist, and was co-teacher with Mrs. Bess Kenderdine Bullard (i.e. "Miss Bess") of the church Sunday school kindergarten class. Epsie was the first woman to serve on the church vestry. She and her husband ran a drug store, an office supply store, and she also was an insurance agent. Ambrose died in 1970. His marker in Radford City's Central Cemetery reads "Ambrose Wilson, VA, CPL 115 Field Hospital, WWI, Sept. 6, 1893, Feb. 22, 1970". Epsie was still living at the age of 110 in the year 2008, residing at Wheatland Hills Retirement Community in Pulaski County across the bridge from Radford City and honored as the oldest person in Virginia. Epsie Rike and Ambrose Wilson had one child: Elizabeth Agnes Wilson, adopted in 1946.

11. Estelle Ross Wilson (1894), daughter of Mary Catherine Lock and John Andrew Wilson. Called Stella, she was born on January 6, 1894. She died in 1970. Her grave

marker in Radford City's Central Cemetery reads "Stella Ross Wilson, Jan. 6, 1894, Apr. 22, 1970".

12. Edward Wilson (circa 1800s), may have been a child of Mary Catherine Lock and John Andrew Wilson. Called Edward, he was listed in church records as a member of the family of John Andrew Wilson.

Wilson, John W.
Circa 1848

The family of John W. Wilson may have been communicants of St. James' Episcopal Mission Chapel. Lucy Wilson was listed on church rolls as a member of the family of John A. Wilson of Central Depot (later called East Radford). However, Lucy Wilson is listed in the 1880 United States Census as a daughter of John W. Wilson of Montgomery County's Auburn District (later called West Radford).

John W. Wilson, born around 1848, was described in the 1880 Census as a white thirty-two year old farmer. His wife Mary D., born around 1849, was then thirty-one. They were living in the Auburn District with their three children. Also in the home was Miss Pattie E. Wilson, born around 1851 and a sister of John W. Wilson, who was described as a thirty-nine year old unmarried school teacher. Mary D. and John W. Wilson had children:

1. Lucy C. Wilson (circa 1875), daughter of Mary D. and John W. Wilson. She was five years old at the time of the 1880 United States Census.
2. Robert D. Wilson (circa 1877), son of Mary D. and John W. Wilson. He was three years old at the time of the 1880 United States Census.
3. Frederick B. Wilson (circa 1879), son of Mary D. and John W. Wilson. He was one year old at the time of the 1880 United States Census.

Winters, Ernest E.
Circa 1861

Ernest E. Winters and An Gabrielle Roby were married in an Episcopal wedding ceremony conducted by Rev. J. E. Hammond on June 1, 1887. An Gabrielle (spelled "Grabrielle" in church records) Roby was born around 1863. She was the daughter of Mr. and Mrs. T. W. Roby of Montgomery County, Maryland. She was a twenty-four year old resident of Central, Virginia, at the time of her 1887 wedding. Ernest E. Winters, born around 1861, was the son of Mrs. A. Winters and Mr. A. W. Winters of Baltimore, Maryland. He was twenty-six and living in Central, Virginia when the wedding took place. The marriage ceremony was held at "Glencoe", the home of General Gabriel Colvin Wharton. Witnesses listed were James Lawrence Radford and C. W. Fisher.

Woodley, A. L.
Circa 1800s

A. L. Woodley was a communicant of St. James' Episcopal Mission Chapel in 1894. She was baptized "in the church" and confirmed at St. James' Episcopal Mission Chapel on May 23, 1894. According to an entry by Rev. A. A. Pruden in church records, she was confirmed by the Rt. Rev. A. M. Randolph "when the parish was without a rector".

Woodson, M. M.
Circa 1800s

Mrs. C. M. Woodson and Mr. M. M. Woodson were parishioners of Grace Episcopal Mission Chapel in 1892. They transferred from St. Paul's Episcopal Church in Salem, Virginia. They were living in the West Ward of Radford on Randolph Street by 1892, and became Episcopal communicants in 1895.

Mr. M. M. Woodson was baptized as a Methodist. He was confirmed as an Episcopalian at Grace Episcopal Mission Chapel on May 17, 1895 by the Rt. Rev. A. M. Randolph as attested to by

Rev. A. A. Pruden. C. M. and M. M. Woodson had children: Kirrkwood Campbell Woodson (circa 1800s) and Lillian Page Woodson (1890). He was born on August 21, 1890. She was baptized by Rev. A. A. Pruden on September 2, 1894 when she was four years old. Mrs. Mary Lytle Kenderdine and Warner Justice Kenderdine were Lillian Page Woodson's baptismal sponsors.

Worth, S. I.
Circa 1800s

Mrs. S. I. Worth and her daughter Summers J. Worth became communicants of Grace Episcopal Mission Chapel on June 19, 1892. They transferred from Christ Episcopal Church in Henry County, Virginia. While in Radford, they lived in the West Ward on Third Street. Miss Summers J. Worth was a member of the Rector's Aid Society of Grace Parish Episcopal Chapel from 1893-1894. Mrs. S. I. Worth was a member of the Ladies Chapel Fund Society as of January 29, 1896. They may have moved to Baltimore, Maryland during October 1896.

Wysong, Rufus C.
Circa 1861

Rufus C. Wysong and his wife Mary (maiden surname not now known) were living in Central Depot, Virginia and were communicants of Grace Episcopal Mission Chapel by October 10, 1887. Mrs. Mary E. Wysong transferred into the Radford Episcopal Parish from St. John's Episcopal Chapel in Charleston, South Carolina. One notation in the church register indicates that they may have moved to Newport News, Virginia; another notation by Mrs. Wysong's name reads "removed May 1889 without taking letters".

Rufus Wysong was the son of Mrs. Elenor Wysong. Elenor was listed as the Head of Household in the 1880 United States Census from the Central Depot District. Household information was as follows: white fifty-six year old Elenor Wysong (born circa 1824), her twenty-year old son William Wysong (born circa 1856) who was a railroad engineer, her twenty-two year old daughter-in-law and wife of William named Kath Wysong (born circa 1858), her seven-month old grandson and child of Kate and William Wysong named Francis L. Wysong (born circa 1880), her twenty-three year old son and railroad fireman named James L. Wysong (born circa 1857), her seventeen year old daughter-in-law and wife of James named Mattie Wysong (born circa 1863), her nineteen year old unmarried son named Rufus Wysong (born circa 1861), her seventeen year old son and farmer named Coatz Wysong (born circa 1863), and her seven-year old granddaughter Ella Wysong (born circa 1873).

Yancey, William T. Jr.
Circa 1847

William T. Yancey Jr., his wife Mary McCanless Radford, and Mrs. Eugenie Yancey were living in Radford and attending Grace chapel by April 1, 1885. Mrs. Mary McCanless Radford Yancey, a daughter of Elizabeth Campbell Taylor and John Blair Radford, had been a member of the church congregation throughout her life.

Mary McCanless Radford Yancey's name is often written in church records as "Mary C.", the letter "C" being used as an initial for McCanless. She was born on April 28, 1851. She inherited a section of "Rockford", the family home of her grandfather John McCanless Taylor. She died on December 7, 1885 from typhoid fever and was buried in the private Radford Family Cemetery on December 9, 1885. Rev. J. E. Hammond officiated.

William T. Yancey Jr., born around 1847, was baptized "in the church" and confirmed as an adult on September 15, 1886 at the age of thirty-nine. The Rt. Rev. F. M. Whittle performed the Rite of Confirmation as attested to by Rev. J. E. Hammond. Mrs. Eugenie Yancey was still listed as a communicant in 1889. An undated notation in church records by the Yancey family name reads "removed to Lynchburg", Virginia. A notation by Mrs. Eugenie Yancey's name was "removed without taking letters; dropped name September 1890.

CHAPTER SEVEN: UNPUBLISHED EPISCOPAL CHURCH RECORDS 1865 THROUGH 1899

As European colonization efforts resulted in the birth of a new nation, the church underwent expansion and re-creation as well. It was against this historical backdrop that the Episcopal Diocesan Missionary Society began to look at expanding the church within and beyond the Montgomery County Parish. The progress of the church in the area that would become Radford City was documented in the church register by Episcopal rectors as well as in meeting minutes carefully maintained by vestrymen and members of the ladies societies.

"Progress of the Church in Central Depot" 1856 through 1887 as Recorded in the Church Register by the Rev. J. E. Hammond

Episcopal rector and church historiographer Rev. J. E. Hammond[107] recorded this church history in the church register of St. James' Episcopal Mission Chapel and Grace Episcopal Mission Chapel as follows.[108]

Parish Record – embracing families - communicants and etc. – connected with Saint James Church, Central Depot, Va.

From the first efforts to establish Montgomery parish – from the time, at least, that Rev. H. Melville Jackson came into the parish in 1873 – till the date on which Rev.

---

[107] Rev. J. E. Hammond served as Episcopal clergy in Central Depot, Virginia from 1885 through 1887. He recorded the history of the Church in the register. This previously unpublished history is transcribed verbatim herein. This register was located at Grace Episcopal Church, Radford, Virginia.

[108] Copied verbatim, including Hammond's usage of dashes, lines, abbreviations, and spellings.

J. E. Hammond became Rector – April 1st 1885 – the official record of St. James Church was kept in connection with that of Christ's Church Blacksburg ___ That record, however, is most imperfect, and in attempting to get a correct statement of the progress of the church of Central Depot, I have had to rely mainly upon the remembrances of some of the older citizens of the place.

J. E. H.   April 1st 1885

Having obtained definite information as to the earlier history of the church in Montgomery County I prefix to what my ancestors having written the following notes.

In December 1856 the Diocesan Missionary Society commissioned the Rev. F. D. Goodwin to visit South West Virginia with a view to the extension of the Church in this section. At that time there was no minister, and but one completed church building west of Roanoke. The result of this visit was that Mr. Goodwin settled in Wytheville in January 1857, and gave two Sundays in each month to Christiansburg, Montgomery County. He preached occasionally in Blacksburg and at Central Depot; as also in Pulaski, Tazewell, and Smyth Counties when opportunity offered.

At the Diocesan Convention of 1859 "privilege was granted . . . to the friends of the Protestant Episcopal Church in Montgomery County to organize a new parish". And in the convention of 1860 Dr. John B. Radford was an accredited Lay Delegate for Montgomery Parish. (Vide Dashull Digest of Virginia Councils). It was therefore a reorganization of the Parish that was effected in 1871.

Owing to the distractions incident to the Civil War, and to the difficulties in travelling [sic], Mr. Goodwin resigned the Parish in January 1862.

From that time nothing was done until Mr. Ingle interested himself in the Parish at the close of the war.

The first Vestry of Montgomery Parish consisted of Rev. F. D. Goodwin, Rector, Mr. Jeremiah Kyle, Mr. Alex.

Eskridge, Dr. Jno. B. Radford, Mr. Geo. Anderson, Hon. Wm B. Preston. Elected July 19, 1858.

1866

St. James Church, Central Depot, Va. Of Montgomery Parish, little is recorded. (See Bishop Meade's Old Families + Churches). The Rev. Ed. H. Ingles [sic] says: "In 1866, when I was a Deacon at Abingdon, there was but one parish ___ Wytheville, between Big Lick (now Roanoke), and Abington where we had a church or a clergyman ___ the churches of Salem, Blacksburg, Central Depot, New River, Pulaski, Dublin, Marion, + so on ___ all being since established".

In the spring of this year (1866) Mr. Ingle visited Blacksburg, Christiansburg, + Central Depot, and further says: "I held a Service in the dining room of the hotel at Central Depot, + obtained subscriptions from the people at all three points for the support of a clergyman to minister to them". Aid was then obtained from the Diocesan Missionary Society, and from the Convocation. Rev. Lyman B. Wharton now took charge of the work with headquarters at Central Depot. He remained about six months, and then left to take charge of a vacant parish. After this, occasional Services were held at Central Depot by different clergymen of the Convocation of South West Va ___ especially Rev. J. A. Wharton of Liberty.

1871

In 1871 – Rev. Mr. Ingle was instrumental in organizing Montgomery Parish ___ at a meeting held at Christiansburg Depot. The following married gentlemen were elected. Vestrymen: Dr. Jno. B. Radford ___ J. H. Kipps ___ Alex. P. Eskridge ___ R. H. Adams ___ + Wm. F. Tallant.

1872

429

In May, 1872, Dr. John B. Radford attended the Council at Norfolk Va, but efforts to obtain a clergyman failed until the establishment of the Virginia Agricultural College at Blacksburg ___ which gave additional strength to the young parish.

1873 to 1875

In August, 1873, Rev. H. Melville Jackson took charge of the work, but resigned in the fall of 1875 – going to Greenville S. C.

1877 to 1880

August, 1877, Mr. Dame remained a little more than three years ___ resigning in Sept. 1880 ___ removing to West River, Md.

1882 + 1883

Precisely when the Rev. Wm M. Walton became Rector of Montgomery Parish is uncertain. At Christ's Church, Blacksburg, he records one or two baptisms, Oct. 1882 ___ and his ministry extended through the year 1883. Mr. W. went to Michigan about the beginning of the year 1884.

A Church Building

The first church building attempted in Central was a brick structure. This was in 1877. After being covered in ___ a storm blew it down. The present one on the same site ___ constructed of timber, was consecrated by Bishop Whittle in [sentence unfinished; year not given].

Radford Parish

The Rev. J. E. Hammond took charge of the parish April 1st 1885. Resigned 1887.

"Progress of the Church in Central Depot" 1888 through 1900 as Recorded in the Church Register by the Revs. Edward L. Goodwin, A. A. Pruden, F. G. Ribble, and Floyd L. Kurtz

Episcopal rectors succeeding Rev. J. E. Hammond at the Radford Parish Episcopal chapels continued the historical narratives of the growth of the Church in that area. Rev. E. L. Goodwin continued the history from 1889 through 1893 as follows:

Rev. Edward L. Goodwin took charge Jan 1st 1889. On May 22, 1891, Radford Parish, including parts of Montgomery and Pulaski counties, was erected and admitted into union with the Council of the Diocese of Virginia, with metis and bounds as follows.

Metis[109] and Bounds

Beginning at the mouth of Walls Creek on New River, thence by a straight line to Christman's Mill on N. + W. R. R. Thence to Beane Shop on the old Christiansburg Turnpike. Thence to a point on Little River opposite the village of Snowville. Thence down Little River to New River, together with all of Pulaski County East of a line running due north + south through Morgan's Cut on N. + W. R. R. (See Journal Va Council 1891).

Rectory

In the Spring of 1890 a Rectory was built on 4th St. near Fairfax St. West Ward.

Chapel

---

[109] Narrative copied using Rev. Goodwin's language, spelling, punctuation, etc. Note the word "metis" above, also written as "metes" and "mètis".

And in the Spring of 1892 Grace Chapel was built near the same site. It was occupied for Divine service May 8, 1892.

Rev. E. L. Goodwin resigned the Parish September 30, 1893.

Episcopal rectors succeeding Rev. J. E. Hammond at the Radford Parish Episcopal chapels continued the record with dates of service.

Rev. A. A. Pruden took charge of the Parish as Deacon in Charge August 10th 1894. Was ordained Priest + accepted the rectorship of the Parish May 18th 1895. Rev. A. A. Pruden resigned the Parish Nov. 15th 1895.

Rev. F. G. Ribble took charge of this Parish July 15, 1896. Resigned Dec. 15 1897.

Rev. Floyd L. Kurtz took charge of the Parish March 1st 1898.

Rev. F. L. Kurtz served the Radford Parish until 1900.

Unpublished Minutes, Vestry, Montgomery Episcopal Parish, St. James' Episcopal Mission Chapel, April 6, 1874 and April 6, 1885 through June 8, 1891

The first page of history of the vestry of St. James' Episcopal Mission Chapel was written as transcribed below. The writer of the narrative detailing the events of April 6, 1874 was not identified.

At a meeting of the congregation at Central Depot held on the Church on Easter Monday (April 6th, 1874), S. Heth, R. H. Adams secretary, A. Robinson treasr., R.

T. Elliott[110] were elected local vestrymen of the Parish. Vestry then met and elected Mr. Ed C. Minor lay delegate to Convention with Capt. C. A. Calhoun as Alternate. Gen. ___ Lang was elected Parish Registrar. Balance of funds in the hands of Rector belonging to this congregation was appropriated to S. School papers. Mr. C. L. C. Minor was elected Senior and Capt. A. Robinson Junior Wardens of the Parish. Capt. Stockton Heth was elected General Treas. of Parish.

The second page of history of the vestry of St. James' Episcopal Mission Chapel was recorded by J. L. Radford, secretary pro tem, detailing the vestry meeting of April 6, 1885. The vestry minutes continued through May 4, 1899 as transcribed on the following pages.

On Easter Monday April 6th 1885 the congregation of St. James Church, Central Depot Va. assembled for the purpose of electing a vestry for the ensuing year. After prayer the Rev. J. E. Hammond was called to the chair and Mr. J. L. Radford was requested to act as Secty. After an exchange of views upon the subject, it was resolved that the vestry be chosen consist of five members, Messrs. Jno A. Wilson, Ambrose Robinson, Stockton Heth, J. L. Radford, and Wm F. Collins were then nominated and elected. The congregation was then dismissed and a meeting of the vestry took place. The Rev. J. E. Hammond, J. L. Radford, Stockton Heth, and A. Robinson being present. Mr. Ambrose Robinson was chosen Junior Warden. W. F. Collins Secty. and Jno A. Wilson Tr. On motion the warden was directed to engage a sexton and instruct him as to his duties. On motion the Treasurer was authorized to collect monthly the minister's salary. On motion it was resolved that the regular meetings of the vestry of St. James' Church shall be on Tuesday after the First (1st) Sunday in each month. No other business offering, the vestry then adjourned.

J. L. Radford, Secty. Protem

---

[110] R. T. Elliott, also spelled R. T. Ellett.

Tuesday, April 21st 1885 a called meeting of the vestry, St. James Church, Central Depot Va. Present A. Robinson, W. F. Collins, Stockton Heth and J. A. Wilson. On motion 1st Resolved that the warden of St. James Church, Central Depot, Va. and Christ Church, Blacksburg inform the Bishop of the Diocese that the Rev. J. E. Hammond has been duly chosen Rector of Montgomery Parish and that the Rector entered upon his duties April 1st 1885. Resolved 2nd that the missionary committee of the Diocese of Virginia be petitioned to grant Two Hundred Dollars ($200.00) per annum to supplement to the four hundred and fifty Dollars ($450.00) raised by the Vestry towards maintaining the services of St. James Church, Central Depot and Christ Church, Blacksburg, Montgomery Parish. On motion the secty. was directed to purchase a blank book for the use of the vestry of St. James Church. No other business offering, on motion this vestry adjourned.   Wm. F. Collins, Secty.

Tuesday, May 12th 1885. Called meeting of the Vestry of St. James Church, Central Depot, Va. Present: A. Robinson, S. Heth, J. A. Wilson, W. F. Collins and Capt. R. H. Adams as proxy for J. L. Radford. A. Robinson in the chair. The object of the meeting as stated by the chair – an election of a delegate to the Council to be held at Richmond May 20th 85. Nominations now in order. R. T. Ellett was nominated as the delegate and Capt. R. H. Adams as alternate. Elected unanimously. The time of services was discussed, and decided to let remain as at present viz 1st + 3rd Sundays. Secty. was requested to notify Dr. R. T. Ellett at an early day of his election + request him to attend. There being no other business on motion the vestry adjourned.   Wm. F. Collins, Secty.

April 28th, 1886. In accordance with the canons of the Diocese the congregation of St. James Church Central Va. was called to meet at the church on Monday afternoon April 28th 86 at 4 o'clock. For the purpose of electing vestrymen for the coming year. After prayer by the

Rector, Motion to elect a vestry to consist five. Nominations in order, the following persons nominated + elected as vestrymen for the following year. J. A. Wilson, A. Robinson, S. Heth, J. L. Radford + W. F. Collins. Motion that the treasurer make a report for the year past. Trs. J. A. Wilson makes the following report.

By amount subscribed to Rectors salary being	<u>266.00</u>
To amount having been collected + paid over	258.00
+ a balance subscribed not yet collected	<u>8.00</u>
	266.00

Of which every reason to believe will be paid soon.
Motion for election of officers in order. Motion that the old officers be re-elected viz. Jno. A. Wilson Trs. + W. F. Collins Secty. Motion to elect delegates to the Council at Charlottesville 3rd Wednesday in May. Dr. R. T. Ellett of Blacksburg nominated + elected delegate + Capt. S. Heth of Central as alternate. Motion for steps to be taken for better heating the church the coming winter for with the following committee – appointed. Jno. A. Wilson to solicit subscription for a new stove. W. F. Collins, S. Heth, + A. Robinson to raise funds to purchase a terra cotta pipe. A committee consisting of Rev. Mr. Hammond, J. L. Radford + N. T. Yancey [sic] to open a back gate + level the grounds. The Trs. Gave motion that there are some back dues which be wished settled. Not having the accounts in hand no action deffinate [sic] could be taken. Motion was made for a called meeting at an early day to attend to the matter. No other business offering, the meeting adjourned.   Wm. F. Collins, Secty.

May 4th 1886. Called meeting of the vestry St. James Church, held at office of W. F. Collins. Present: Rev. J. E. Hammond Rector, J. A. Wilson, J. L. Radford + W. F. Collins. The Trs. J. A. Wilson presented account outstanding against the church to the amount of 12.23 the amount of which he was authorized to settle out of the contingent fund. No other business meeting adjourned.
                    Wm F. Collins, Secty

435

At a meeting of the vestry of St. James Church Central Depot Va. Dec. 20th 1886. The committee appointed to secure the proper heating of the church building reported its work completed. The Treasurer reported money in hand as follows.

Special Collections	$18.00
Proceeds of Festival (Mrs. J. W. Turner)	31.25
	49.75

Bills submitted for stove, fixtures, terra cotta pipe + work putting of same amounting to $35.36. The Trs. was instructed to pay the same leaving in his hands of the above collection 14.39. Trs. was instructed to purchase a church register. Adjourned.

Wm. F. Collins, Secty.

Called meeting of the vestry St. James Church Central Va. January ___ 1887. Present A. Robinson, Jno. A. Wilson + W. F. Collins. A request for the Rev. J. E. Hammond Rector was submitted asking leave in such of health until Feb. 20th 87. This was granted + Secty instructed to so advise the Rector, and to also state that in the judgement [sic] of the vestry he had best remain in the Sanct. during March.   Wm F. Collins, Secty

A meeting of the congregation of St. James Church Central Depot, Va. to elect vestrymen took place in the Church building April 18th 1887. Notice to this effect having been given at a public service on Sunday the 17th April. Prayer was said by the Rector + the order of business then announced. Rev. J. E. Hammond was called to the chair + Mr. J. A. Wilson appointed Secty. Messrs. J. L. Radford, W. F. Collins, A. Robinson, Jno. A. Wilson + S. Heth were then nominated + elected as the vestry of the parish for one year or until their successors shall have been duly elected + qualified. The meeting then adjourned.   John A. Wilson, Secty.

At a meeting of the vestry of Montgomery parish held in A. Robinson store Central April 27th 1887. Mr. Jno. A. Wilson was elected a delegate to Council of the Diocese to assemble in Alexandria Va. May 18th. On motion it was resolved that the vestry meet Mr. Wilson's expenses. That portion of the vestry representing Christ Church Blacksburg having referred the matter to St. James Church Central. There being no other business on motion the vestry adjourned.

Wm F. Collins, Secty.
Rev. J. Hammond in the chair.

Meeting of the vestry St. James Church Radford Va. 1889. In the chair Rev. E. L. Goodwin Rector. Present A. Robinson, S. Heth, Jno. A. Wilson, J. L. Radford + W. F. Collins. The matter of salary of the present Rector was satisfactorly [sic] arranged and he Call accepted, Discussion to provide ways + means for the erection of a rectory. Each member of the vestry was requested to act as committee to solicit subscription re to this end. No other business, adjourned.   W. F. Collins Secty.

(A. Robinson's Hall)

Meeting of the vestry – St. James Ch. In the Church 1889. In the chair E. L. Goodwin Rector. Present A. Robinson, S. Heth, J. L. Radford, J. A. Wilson + W. F. Collins. Business to assertain [sic] what has been done toward raising funds to build the rectory. Nothing having been accomplished by any member, they were all requested to look farther [sic] to this end. Also to select suitable spot upon which to erect the same. No other business. Adjourned.   W. F. Collins Secty.

Meeting of the vestry St. James Church Radford April 24th 89. In the chair Rev. E. L. Goodwin. Present A. Robinson, J. L. Radford, Jno. A. Wilson + W. F. Collins. The Chair explained that this meeting was to select a delegate to Council, stating that the churches of Blacksburg + Christiansburg had selected Dr. R. T. Elliott as delegate + H. H. Power alternate. There being no objection to these gentlemen they were declared to be the choices of Montgomery Parish. The Chair explained that the council would be expected to vote on a clause of the canons to so

437

revise them to read writ the word being while [white?] a sence [?] of this body, for the clause to be voted upon with the above being while [white?] added[111]. Report asked for in regard to Rectory re nothing deffinate [sic] to report. Committee of 2, J. L. Radford + Jno. A. Wilson appointed to correspond with Radford Land Impr. Co. and confer with Capt. S. Heth as to lot for rectory and to report at a vestry meeting appointed for Monday Apr. 29th 89. There having been no congregation meeting for election of vestry + officers the old vestry + officers requested to hold over another year or until altern. successors are elected. No other business the meeting adjourned to meet Apr. 29 89.   W. F. Collins, Secty.

Meeting of the vestry St. James' Church at Robinson Hall May 27th 89. In the chair Rev. E. L. Goodwin. Present S. Heth, A. Robinson, J. L. Radford, Jno. A. Wilson, & W. F. Collins. Report of Treasurer Jno. A. Wilson submitted as follows, that 167.50 had been collected and paid over on 1st + 2nd quarter salary of Rector, 28.95 in hand belonging to the contingent fund. Rectory Fund on hand 5.00. Board of Trustees was elected for the Rectory: S. Heth, A. Robinson, and J. A. Wilson. No other business, adjourned.   W. F. Collins, Secty.

Meeting of Vestry St. James Church held in Robinson's Hall June 26st [sic] 89. In the Chair Rev. E. L. Goodwin Rector. Present S. Heth, J. L. Radford, A. Robinson, Jno. A. Wilson + W. F. Collins. Contracts were read for lost for Church and also for Rectory of the Radford Land Impr. Co. Motion that the contract be signed by the Trustees carried. Motion that the Vestry as a whole constitute a building committee with A. Robinson as Chairman carried. No other business, adjourned to meet again at call of chairman.   W. F. Collins, Secty.

Vestry meeting Aug. 26, 1889 at Robinson Hall. Rev. E. L. Goodwin in the Chair. Present – Robinson, Heth, Rad-

[111] See Vestry minutes page 15, April 24th 89. Some handwritten notes illegible.

ford + Wilson. Opened with prayer by the Rector. Resolved that the building committee shall not exceed $1800.00 in cash in letting the contract for the rectory. Carried. Resolved that Mr. Radford be authorized to borrow $1000 and that the vestry obligates themselves, individually, collectively to secure the same by giving a joint bond when it is needed. Carried. No other business. Adjourned. W. F. Collins, Secty.

Vestry meeting Robinson Hall Dec. 30th 1889. Rev. E. L. Goodwin in the Chair. Opened with prayer by the Rector. Present, Heth, Radford, Robinson, Collins + Wilson. Resolved that Mr. Radford call on Bishop Randolph in regard to his $200 toward the Rector's salary. Carried. Meeting was adjourned.
W. F. Collins, Secty.

Vestry meeting held in Robinson Hall Apr. 14, 1890. Rev. E. L. Goodwin in the Chair. Opened with prayer by the Rector. Present, Robinson, Heth, + W. O. Tyler elected + qualified. Business in reference to rector's salary was transacted. Mrs. Goodwin + Tyler appointed a committee to secure envelopes + introduce the envelopes system of collections as far as they find it expedient. No other bus., adjourned. W. F. Collins, Secty.

At a meeting of Episcopalians of Radford, Va. held December 1st 1890 for the purpose of taking some steps towards building a Church. It was moved and carried that a committee be appointed to correspond with Mr. Doran, president of the Radford Land and Improvement Company with reference to exchanging lots near the Rectory corner of Fourth and Fairfax Streets which had been given the Church by said Radford Land + Improvement Company for lots on corner of Third and Walker Streets adjoining the private semetary [sic] of the Radford family. Mssrs. H. H. Powers, J. L. Radford, and C. W. Sanders were appointed on said committee.
E. L. Goodwin, Chairman
C. W. Sanders, Secty.

439

At a meeting of the congregation of St. James' Church of Radford, Va. held Monday, January 12th 1891. Rev. E. L. Goodwin was called to the chair and C. W. Sanders was appointed secretary. Mr. Goodwin stated the object of the meeting to be to take steps looking to a division of the parish and read the cannon under which the meeting was called. Mr. H. H. Powers moved that a committee by appointed to petition Council to divide the parish and said committee to designate the boundary lines of the new parish. The motion was duly carried and the chair names as members of said committee Capt. R. H. Adams, Capt. A. Robinson, Gen. G. C. Wharton, Mr. H. H. Powers, + C. W. Sanders. Mr. Powers moved that the new parish be called "Radford Parish". The motion was seconded by Capt. R. H. Adams and was carried. Mr. Goodwin suggested that the vestry of St. James' Church appoint a committee to look after the building of a church in the new part of the town as the authority to do such building is in the Vestry. Dr. Aaron Jeffrey offered the following resolution "Resolved that the vestry of St. James' Church be requested to appoint a committee to consist of J. L. Radford, Ambrose Robinson, W. J. Kenderdine, R. H. Adams, G. T. Kearsley, H. H. Powers, C. W. Sanders and the Rector who shall be empowered to act for the vestry and congregation in building a new church west of "Connally's Branch". On motion the name of Dr. A. Jeffrey was added to the committee. Suggested. It was moved and carried that a committee be appointed to ascertain what amount can be raised for the salary of the Rector of the New parish. The following constitute said committee H. H. Powers chairman, Dr. R. B. James, G. T. Kearsley, J. S. Rudd and C. W. Sanders.

C. W. Sanders, Secretary

A meeting of the vestry St. James Church was held at the residence of Capt. A. Robinson for the purpose of hearing the report of committee appointed to find out what amount could be raised for salary of Rector of New Parish of Radford. Mr. Powers chairman of committee reported that so far the amount of six hundred and eighty (680) dollars had been subscribed and that the committee had not finished its work. It was moved by Capt. Robinson, seconded by Mr. Radford, that Mr. Goodwin be called at a salary of one thousand (1000) dollars and more if it could be raised. Mr. Goodwin expressed his willingness to accept on the conditions that the salary be made $1200 if it could be raised and if more was subscribed that he was willing to apply the excess to the payment of the debt on Rectory. It was moved and carried that Messrs. Kenderdine, Adams, Kearsley, Powers, Jeffrey, W. R. Wharton, James, + Sanders be elected as provisional members of Vestry until the parish be divided and a canoned [?] vestry elected.

C. W. Sanders, Sect pro tem

A meeting of the Vestry of St. James Church, together with the committee appointed to look after the building of a new Church, was held in office of Sanders Jones & Co. February 25th 1891. The Rector Mr. Goodwin called the meeting to order and after prayer the minutes of the last meeting were read and approved. It was moved by Mr. Powers and seconded by Capt. R. H. Adams that the salary of the Rector be fixed at $1200 per annum. The motion was carried. On motion a finance committee consisting of three members - ___ [ward'n?], Treas., a member, ex-officer, was appointed whose duty shall be the ordinary duties of a finance committee together with raising necessary funds for the minister's salary and all other church expenses. The Chairman appointed on above committee Capt. Ambrose Robinson, Mr. H. H. Powers, Mr. C. W. Sanders. It was moved and carried that a committee of five be appointed on the Rectory and Rectory debt whose duty it shall be to attend to paying the Rectory debt and to any repairs that may be needed. The following gentlemen were appointed W. J. Kenderdine, R. H. Adams, A. Robinson, Stockton Heth, + W. R. Wharton. It was further moved and carried that a committee of nine be appointed whose duty it shall be to take all steps necessary for the building of a new church in

Radford on the lots to be secured for that purpose. The following were appointed:

J. L. Radford	C. W. Sanders
Ambrose Robinson	Dr. Aaron Jeffrey
W. J. Kenderdine	Dr. R. B. James
R. H. Adams	W. R. Wharton
H. H. Powers	Rev. E. L. Goodwin
Geo. T. Kearsley	

The following committee was appointed on music:

H. H. Powers	The Rector
C. W. Sanders	G. T. Kearsley

The following were appointed to assist warden in East Radford in such duties as he may request.

Mr. J. S. Rudd and Dr. R. B. James

A committee of three was appointed to look after the services in Randolph Hall as follows:

W. J. Kenderdine	Dr. Aaron Jeffrey
C. W. Sanders	

At the suggestion of the Rector, C. W. Sanders was elected assistant clerk of Vestry. It was resolved that the Vestry hold monthly meetings on first Wednesday afternoon in each month at half past three o'clock.

C. W. Sanders, Ast. Clerk

A regular monthly meeting of the Vestry was held on Wednesday April 1st 1891. Present – The Rector, Capt. Stockton Heth, J. S. Rudd, H. H. Powers, G. T. Kearsley, Dr. Aaron Jeffrey, Capt. R. H. Adams, and C. W. Sanders. Mr. Powers moved that Treas. be instructed to make full report of those who are behind on their subscription on minister's salary. Carried. It was moved by Dr. James + Capt. Adams that the Warden and the committee appointed to assist him be authorized to spend what money is in the treasury to repair the fence and church of St. James'. It was agreed that the fifty dollars which was assumed to be paid by Mr. Goodwin on rectory debt be applied by him to putting fence around Rectory.

C. W. Sanders, Asst. Clerk

A called meeting of the Vestry was held in St. James Church Monday April 27th 1891. After prayer the Rector explained the object of the meeting to be first the election of a delegate to Council. Mr. Powers nominated Mr. Pelton of Christiansburg as delegate and Capt. Stockton Heth as alternate. And Mr. Goodwin was authorized to cast the vote of this vestry for said gentlemen in meeting of vestry of Montgomery Parish to be held in Christiansburg. The Rector then stated that another object of the meeting was the consideration of resolutions passed by committee of Convocation looking to division of diocese. Mr. Powers introduced the following resolution which was passed. "Resolved 1st That the Vestry of St. James Church, Radford are heartily in favor of the proposed division of the Diocese namely making a new Diocese as agreed upon in the Convocation of South West Virginia held in Lynchburg Va. on April 21st 1891. Resolved 2nd That this vestry will guarantee from this church a sum not less than seventy-five dollars per annum if necessary for the support of said New Diocese. Resolved 3rd That our delegate in Council be requested to sign such papers as are necessary to promote said division."

C. W. Sanders, Asst. Clerk

According to notice duly given a meeting of parishioners was held in St. James Church, Radford Va. June 8th for the purpose of electing a vestry for Radford Parish which was formed by Council in recent session. The Rector Mr. Goodwin read the canon setting forth the manner of holding said election. Mr. W. R. Wharton claimed that the parish was composed of more than one congregation and that each such congregation should elect its own separate vestry. There was quite a discussion on this point whereupon Mr. Wharton introduced the following resolution. "Resolved That the Radford Parish consists of at least two congregations". The resolution was defeated.

443

Mr. Wharton then called for a registered vote on the subject which was granted him.

Those present voting as follows –

Capt. Ambrose Robinson	no	
Capt. Stockton Heth		yes
Mr. H. H. Powers	no	
Dr. Aaron Jeffrey	no	
Dr. R. B. James	no	
Dr. A. J. Black		yes
Capt. R. H. Adams	no	
Mr. J. L. Radford		yes
W. R. Wharton		yes
W. Weiseger		yes
G. T. Kearsley	no	
C. W. Sanders	no	
	7	5

Mr. Wharton expressed his desire to enter a protest.
The meeting then proceeded to elect twelve vestrymen.
The following were elected:

Capt. Ambrose Robinson	W. J. Kenderdine
Capt. Stockton Heth	W. R. Wharton
H. H. Powers	G. T. Kearsley
Aaron Jeffrey	W. W. Darnell
Rich H. Adams	R. B. James
J. L. Radford	C. W. Sanders

Mr. W. R. Wharton having declined to serve, Gen'l. G. C. Wharton was elected in his stead. Adjourned.

C. W. Sanders, Secty.

The Rector called meeting of the Vestry immediately upon adjournment of above meeting for the purpose of electing officers. Capt. Adams nominated Capt. A. Robinson Senior Warden and Mr. W. J. Kenderdine Junior Warden. The gentlemen were elected by acclamation. C. W. Sanders was elected registrar and also Treasurer. Capt. Adams moved that a committee of three be appointed to examine the treasurers books to ascertain the amount of the deficiency on Rector's salary and report to Vestry. The Chairman named Capt. Ambrose Robinson, Capt. R. H. Adams, and Capt. Stockton Heth as said committee. The same committee was instructed to settle with the retiring treasurer and turning over whatever funds that may be in his hands to the new treasurer. The following resolutions were passed at a former meeting of Vestry but were omitted from minutes. "Resolved That the Vestry gratefully acknowledge the assistance heretofore given to this church by the Diocesan Missionary Society." "Resolved That the secretary be requested to inform the Executive Committee of the Society that this church has become self-supporting and has secured the services of a Rector as an independent ___ [cure?], and that we relinquish all claim upon the Society and upon any share in any appropriation they may make to the other churches in Montgomery Parish." "Resolved That we request the Society to continue the appropriation formerly made to the Parish to the churches at Blacksburg and Christiansburg so that they may not be weakened seriously by our withdrawal from the parochial union previously existing between us."

C. W. Sanders, Registrar

"Who we are, how we conduct ourselves, our personality, and what we ultimately become, depends in large measure on the root structure from which we grow.

Thus, it is of considerable importance and interest to learn from whence we come, and document that information for the generations yet to follow.

William Neal Hurley, Jr.
(1924-2003),
Genealogist &
Author.

Sources and Resources

Adams, Jennifer S. Gemmell. "Descendants of Colin Mor Campbell" in Family Tree Maker, http://family treemakergenealogy.com/Jennifer-S-Gemmelladams.txt (accessed November 7, 2007).

Anderson, Annie Sue. *The History of Radford*. Radford, VA: The 9 to 5 Secretaries Club, unpublished, May 1963.

Anderson, Carole. "Some History of Craig Cemetery." *Journal of the New River Historical Society* 6 (1993): 11-12.

Bailey, Ann. "Celebrating Lewis Miller's 200th Birthday." *Journal of the New River Historical Society* 10 (1997): 5-8.

Barton, John I. "Pulaski County's Battleground – 1864." *Journal of the New River Historical Society* 6 (1993): 4-8.

Baumgartner, Dawn. "Fotheringay: More than 200-year old home visited by Washington, Jackson". *New River Newspapers*, February 28, 2001, Section Sights & Sites, Progress 2001, p. 6, Radford News Journal, Radford, VA, Edition.

Baur, Carolyn Ann Niemantsverdriet and Baur, James L. "The Clark Family of Revolutionary Fame" in Our Genealogy Page, http: //www.manorweb.com/genea/genea.html (accessed 2001 and August 17, 2007).

Bell, Heather. "Going back in time with the old West End Hotel". *New River Newspapers*, February 28, 2001, Section Sights & Sites, Progress 2001, p. 7, Radford News Journal, Radford, VA, Edition.

Bell, Heather. "Alleghany was one of several grand hotels: It was originally called Hotel Shere". *New River Newspapers*, February 28, 2001, Section Sights & Sites, Progress 2001, p. 9, Radford News Journal, Radford, VA, Edition.

Bockstruck, Lloyd DeWitt. *Virginia's Colonial Soldiers*. Baltimore, MD: Genealogical Publishing Company Inc., 1988.

Booty, John E. *The Church in History*. New York, NY: The Seabury Press, 1979.

Brydon, George MacLaren. *Religious Life of Virginia in the Seventeenth Century: The Faith of Our Fathers*. Williamsburg, VA: Virginia 350th Anniversary Celebration Corporation; Jamestown 350th Anniversary Historical Booklet Number Ten, 1957.

Buchanan, William T. Jr. *The Trigg Site: City of Radford, Virginia*. Richmond, VA: unpublished report, Archeological Society of Virginia, 1984.

Bruce, Philip Alexander. *Virginia: Rebirth of the Old Dominion, Volumes I through V*. Chicago, IL: The Lewis Publishing Company, 1929.

Callahan, Charles H. *Washington: The Man and the Mason*. Published by the George Washington Masonic National Memorial Association. Washington, DC: Press of Gibson Bros., 1913.

Carter, Sarah Elizabeth. "Carter finds connections in family". *New River Newspapers,* February 28, 1996, Section F Progress '96: Tapping the Roots of our Family Tree, Radford News Journal, Radford, VA, Edition.

Carter, Sarah Elizabeth. Interviews with author, September 2005, February 2008.

Central Cemetery. *Grave markers and tombstones*. Radford, Virginia.

Chitwood, W. R. *Death and Marriage Notices from the South-West Virginia Enterprise April 17, 1870 to Dec. 28, 1881*. Wytheville, VA: Kegley Books, 1984.

Clark, Gary. "Clark Page: From Scotland to Ireland to America" in Gary Clark's Home Page, http://www.gclark.com/content/geneal/index.htm (accessed 2001 and August 17, 2007).

Coffey, E. Allen. "A Brief History of the Diocese of Virginia" in The Episcopal Diocese of Virginia, http://www.thediocese.net/diocese/history.shtml (accessed 2001 and August 17, 2007).

Darst, H. Jackson. "Dublin Depot." *Journal of the New River Historical Society* 1 (1988): 11-13.

Daughters of the American Revolution. *Lineage Book, National Society of the Daughters of the American Revolution, Volume CXXVIII, Membership Numbers 127001-128000, 1916.* Washington D.C.: Press of Judd & Detweiler Inc., National Society of the Daughters of the American Revolution, Amy Cresswell, DAR Historian General, 1932.

Davis, Betsy Naff. *History of the Episcopal Church in Radford, VA: Grace Episcopal Church Centennial 1992.* Radford, VA: Commonwealth Press Inc., 1992.

Dickens, Helen. Interview with author, February 2008.

Dickenson, Kathy. "Landmark house still 'just home': La Riviere." *Roanoke Times & World News,* September 11, 1994, New River Current, Roanoke, VA Edition.

Dickenson, Richard W. "Some Freedmen Identities." *Virginia Appalachian Notes,* October 1978, Community Development Study, VPI, 1978.

Dickenson, Richard W. "1867 Freedmens Bureau Census Excerpt." *Virginia Appalachian Notes,* February 1989, Southwestern Virginia Genealogical Society, Roanoke, VA.

Dickenson, Richard W. "1867 Freedmens Bureau Census Excerpt." *Virginia Appalachian Notes,* May 1989, Southwestern Virginia Genealogical Society, Roanoke, VA.

Dickenson, Richard W. "1867 Freedmens Bureau Census Excerpt." *Virginia Appalachian Notes*, August 1989, Southwestern Virginia Genealogical Society, Roanoke, VA.

Dorman, John Frederick. *The Prestons of Smithfield and Greenfield in Virginia.* Louisville, KY: The Filson Club Incorporated & General Printing Company, 1982.

Douthat, James L. *Montgomery County Deed Book A, 1773-1789.* Signal Mountain, TN: Mountain Press, 1987.

Egloff, Keith & Woodward, Deborah. *First People: The Early Indians of Virginia.* Charlottesville, VA: University Press of Virginia & Richmond, VA: The Virginia Department of Historic Resources, 1992.

Evans, Clement A., ed. *Confederate Military History: A library of Confederate States History, in Thirteen Volumes, Written by Distinguished Men of the South and Edited by Gen. Clement A. Evans of Georgia: Volume Three, Virginia.* Secaucus, NJ: The Blue and Grey Press, 1962.

Evans, Jean, ed. "St. Albans." *Journal of the New River Historical Society* 12 (1999): 21-24.

"Family Trees of Thomas Jefferson and Other Famous Americans" http://www.ishipress.com/ pafg63.htm (accessed 8/21/2007).

Farrar, Emmie Ferguson & Hines, Emilee. *Old Virginia Houses: The Mountain Empire.* Charlotte, NC: Delmar Publishing, 1978.

Fitting, Minnie Adams. *The Past is Never Lost.* Radford, VA: unpublished manuscript, 2002.

Fitting, Minnie Adams. *The Radford Letters: History of a Virginia Family.* Blacksburg, VA: Commonwealth Press, 2002.

450

Freeman, Douglas Southall. *George Washington: A Bibliography, Volumes One through Four.* New York, NY: Charles Scribner's Sons, 1951.

Gibson Cemetery. *Grave markers and tombstones.* Radford, Virginia.

Gokbudak, Tilly. "Radford African-American faces challenges in tracing roots". *New River Newspapers,* February 28, 1996, Section F Progress '96: Tapping the Roots of our Family Tree, Radford News Journal, Radford, VA, Edition.

Goodwin, Edward L., ed. *The History of Truro Parish in Virginia as written by Rev. Philip Slaughter D. D.* Philadelphia, PA: George W. Jacobs & Company, 1907.

Goodykoontz, Alf (1949). "Collapse of Bluestone Bridge Recalls Like Accident Here." Saturday April 30, 1949. West Virginia: newspaper article; newspaper name / corporation unknown, 1949.

Grace Episcopal Church. *Church Register 1885-1898 for St. James' Episcopal Mission Chapel and Grace Episcopal Mission Chapel.* Radford, VA: unpublished, 1898. Grace Episcopal Church. Microfilmed, Virginia State Library, Archives Division, Camera Operator T. Smith, Reel No. P1, date October 7, 1987.

Grace Episcopal Church. *Minutes, Grace Episcopal Parish Vestry, 1883-1891.* Radford, VA: Unpublished. Grace Episcopal Church, 1905.

Grace Episcopal Church. *Grace Episcopal Church Memorial Garden Interment Plaque.* Radford, VA, 2007.

Grant, Charles. *An Appalachian Portrait: Black and White in Montgomery County, Virginia, Before the Civil War.* Blacksburg, VA: Thesis submitted to the Faculty of the Virginia Polytechnic Institute and State University in partial fulfillment of the requirements for the degree of Master of Arts in History, May 1987.

Hale, John P. *Trans-Allegheny Pioneers*. Raleigh, NC: Derreth Printing Company, 1886, as edited by Harold J. Dudley, 1971.

Hammet Family Cemetery. *Grave markers and tombstones*. Radford, VA.

Hancock, Randolph S. "The Man Buried Sitting Up: Legend of Col. George Hancock's Weird Interment Substantiated by Fotheringay Owner's Exploration of the Vault." *Richmond Times-Dispatch*, April 28, 1935.

Heth Family Cemetery. *See* Hammet Family Cemetery.

Historic Publications. *George Washington's Relations and Relationships in Fredericksburg, Virginia*. Fredericksburg, VA: Historic Publications of Fredericksburg, 1981.

Historic Smithfield & Association for the Preservation of Virginia Antiquities (APVA Preservation Virginia). "Are you Related to the Prestons of Historic Smithfield?" in Blacksburg Electronic Village http://civic.bev.net/smithfield/preston.html (accessed August 18, 2007).

Holmberg, James J. *Dear Brother: Letters of William Clark to Jonathan Clark*. New Haven, CT: Yale University Press, 2002.

Howe, Daniel Dunbar. *Listen to the Mockingbird*. Boyce, VA: Carr Publishing Co., 1961.

Howe, Daniel Dunbar. *Lovely Mount Tavern: The Birth of a City and Something of the Early New River Settlers*. Boyce, VA: Carr Publishing Company, 1963.

Jeffries, Lewis Ingles. Interviews with author, September 2005, February 2008.

Jervey, Thora. "Jervey's Jottings: Mancye's baking is Christmas tradition". *Radford News Journal*, November 12, 1979, Radford, VA.

Jervey, Thora. "Relatively Speaking: Tyler Mansion Memories." *Radford News Journal*, August 22, 2007, New River Valley edition, Christiansburg, VA.

Johnson, David E. *A History of the Middle New River Settlement and Contiguous Territory.* Huntington, WV: Standard Printing and Publishing Co., 1906; *see also* War, WV: in Kinyon Digital Library, http://www.kinyon.com/westvirginia/midnewriver/ contents.htm (accessed 2001 and August 17, 2007).

Johnson, Elmer D. *Radford Then and Now: A Pictorial History for the American Revolution Bicentennial commission of Radford, Virginia.* Radford, VA: The American Revolution Bicentennial Commission of Radford, Virginia, 1975.

Johnson, Patricia Givens. *William Preston and the Allegheny Patriots.* Blacksburg, VA: Walpa Publishing, 1976, reprinted 1992.

Johnson, Patricia Givens. *The New River Early Settlement.* Blacksburg, VA: Walpa Publishing, 1983.

Johnson, Patricia Givens. *Kentland at Whitethorne.* Blacksburg, VA: Walpa Publishing, 1995.

Kegley, Mary B. & Kegley, Frederick Bittle. *Early Adventures on the Western Waters, Volume I, The New River of Virginia in Pioneer Days 1745-1800.* Orange, VA: Green Publishers Inc., 1980.

Kegley, Mary B. *Early Adventures on the Western Waters, Volume II, The New River of Virginia in Pioneer Days 1745-1800.* Wytheville, VA: Kegley Books, 2003.

Kenderdine, Thaddeus Stevens. *The Kenderdines of America.* Doylestown, PA: Doylestown Publishing Company, Printers, 1901.

Kestenbaum, Lawrence. "The Political Graveyard" http://politicalgraveyard.com/bio and http://political graveyard.com/bio/tyler.html (accessed 2001 and August 22, 2007)

Killen, Linda. *The Whartons' Town: New River Depot, 1870-1940.* Radford, VA: Radford University, 1993.

Killen, Linda. "The Whartons". *Journal of the New River Valley Historical Society* 8 (1995):1-6.

Killen, Linda. *Making Their Mark: Black Families of New River Depot, 1870-1940.* Radford, VA: Radford University, 1994.

Killen, Linda. *Radford's Early Black Residents 1880-1925.* Radford, VA: Radford University, Belspring, VA Books, 1995.

Latter Day Saints [LDS]. Family Research at www.familysearch.com (accessed 2002, 2008).

Lee, Ida J. "The Heth Family" in *Genealogies of Virginia Families, Volume IV.* Baltimore, MD: Genealogical Publishing Co., 1981.

MacCammond, A. Fraser. "History of St. Thomas' Episcopal Church, Christiansburg, Virginia," St. Thomas' Episcopal Church in Blacksburg Electronic Village http://www.civic.bev.net/stthomas; *see also* "St. Thomas Episcopal Church" at http://www.stecc.org/ (accessed 2001 and August 19, 2007).

Main Street Newspapers Inc. "Obituary Notices." *Radford News Journal.* Christiansburg, VA: Radford News Journal.

Martha Washington Inn. "Martha Washington Inn: Hotel History" at http://www.marthawashingtoninn.com (accessed 2006 and November 12, 20007).

Matthews, Geraldine M., ed. "Flag Presentation – 1861, William Mosely Radford." *Journal of the New River Historical Society* 6 (1993): 9-10.

Matthews, Lloyd. "The Battle of Cloyd's Farm." *Southwest Times*, 1993, in series "Looking Back with Lloyd Matthews", Pulaski, VA; see compilation Newbern, VA: Wilderness Road Regional Museum.

Mayflower Publishing Company. "Stockton Heth Tyler". In *Who's Who in the South*, 734. Washington D.C.: The Mayflower Publishing Company Inc., 1927.

Meacham, Jon. *American Gospel: God, the Founding Fathers, and the Making of a Nation.* New York, NY: Random House, 2006.

Meade, William. *Old Churches, Ministers, and Families of Virginia, Volumes I and II.* Philadelphia, PA: J. B. Lippincott Company, 1857, reprint 1906.

Miller Center of Public Affairs. "John Tyler (1841-1845), 10th President of the United States," Charlottesville, VA: Miller Center of Public Affairs, University of Virginia http://www.millercenter.virginia.edu/americanpresident/tyler and http://www.AmericanPresident.org (accessed 2001 and August 17, 2007).

Miller Center of Public Affairs. "John Tyler (1790-1862)", Miller Center http://www.millercenter.virginia.edu/academic/Ameri-can president/tyler (accessed August 21, 2007).

Miller, Charles. Radford, Virginia City Directory, Vol. I, 1942-1943. July 1942.

Moche, Joanne Spiers. "Within the Circle of Founders: Richard Henry Adams of Radford, Virginia", *Journal of the New River Historical Society* 18 (2005): 1-9.

Montgomery County Courthouse. *Public Records: Land Deeds, Marriage Registers, and Wills.* Christiansburg, VA: Montgomery County VA Courthouse.

Montgomery County Courthouse. *Minutes, Montgomery County Board of Supervisors.* Christiansburg, VA: Montgomery County VA Courthouse.

Morgan Cemetery. *Grave markers and tombstones.* Radford, VA.

Mountain View Cemetery. *Grave markers and tombstones.* Radford, VA.

Murray, J. Ogden. *The Immortal Six Hundred.* Winchester, VA: The Eddy Press Corporation, 2001, and Dahlonega, GA: The Confederate Reprint Company, 1905.

Nagel, Hanns Peter. "La Riviere, a hidden treasure revisited." *Radford News Journal*, February 23, 2008, Radford, VA, p. 2.

National Governors Association. "Virginia Governor James Hodge[112] Tyler (1846-1925)" in Governor's Information at http://www.nga.org/portal/site/nga (accessed on August 24, 2007).

National Governors Association. "Virginia Governor John Tyler (1747-1813)" in Governor's Information at http://www.nga.org/portal/site/nga (accessed on August 24, 2007).

National Governors Association. "Virginia Governor John Tyler (1790-1862)" in Governor's Information at http://www.nga.org/portal/site/nga (accessed on August 24, 2007).

New Democrat newspaper, circa 1891. Radford,VA.

New Mount Olive United Methodist Church. *Brief History of the New Mount Olive United Methodist Church, 1889-1976.* Radford, VA: printed by church, unpublished, 1976.

Newman, Jeffrey. "Murder and Scandal at VPI: A research project about The Murder of Stockton Heth, Jr. Submitted by Jeffrey

---

[112] The National Governors Association website incorrectly listed this Virginia Governor's name as "James Hodge Tyler". His name was "James Hoge Tyler", Hoge being his middle name and his mother's maiden name.

Newman for History 4004: Murder in America." *Journal of the New River Historical Society* 14 (2001): 1-20.

Norfleet, Philip C. "The Campbells of Southwest Virginia," http://philnorf.tripod.com/campbell.htm (accessed 2001 and August 18, 2007).

Norfleet, Philip C. "Norfleet, Campbell, Mayfield, Mortier, Cory and Mason Ancestors of Phil Norfleet," MyFamily.com and wysiwyg.colvin/Scottish.htm (accessed 2001.

Norfleet, Philip C. "The Scottish Migration to Northern Ireland," http://philnorf.tripod.com/scottish.htm (accessed 2001 and August 18, 2007).

Norfleet, Philip C. "Scotch-Irish Migration to Virginia," MyFamily.com and wysiwyg.colvin/Scottish.htm (accessed 2001).

Pilcher, Margaret Campbell. *Historical Sketches of the Campbell, Pilcher and Kindred Families*. Nashville, TN: Marshall & Bruce Co. Press, 1911.

Pritchett, John W. (2004). "Ancestry of John W. Pritchett", www.virginians.com/topics/topics_f.htm (accessed 2004 and August 18, 2007).

Pulaski County Courthouse. *Public Records: Land Deeds, Marriage Registers, and Wills*. Pulaski, VA: Pulaski County VA Courthouse.

Radford Advance (1892). Assorted advertisements. *Radford Advance Semi-Weekly Newspaper*, November 4, 1892, Radford, VA.

Radford Advance (1892). "Radford Directory: City Council," *Radford Advance Semi-Weekly Newspaper*, November 4, 1892, Radford, VA.

Radford City Chamber of Commerce. *The New River City: Radford, Virginia*. Radford, VA: pamphlet, Radford City VA Chamber of Commerce, 2003.

Radford City Courthouse. *Public Records: Land Deeds, Marriage Registers, and Wills*. Radford, VA: Radford City VA Courthouse.

Radford City Government. *Charter and General Ordinances of the City of Radford, Compiled by Ordinance Committee, By Order of Council*. Radford, VA: The Enterprise Printing Co., 1892.

Radford Development Company. *Land Sales Ledger Book No. 239, 1890-1892*. Radford, VA: unpublished, 1892.

Radford City. *Charter and General Ordinances of the City of Radford, Compiled by Ordinance Committee by Order of Council*. Radford, VA: The Enterprise Printing Company, 1892.

Radford Land and Improvement Company. *City Maps, Maps of Plans A. through H; Subdivisions*. 1888, & Circa mid- and late 1880s; subdivisions 1890.

Radford Family Cemetery. *Grave markers and tombstones*. Radford, VA.

Radford News Journal. "Obituary Notices." *Radford News Journal*, 2006 through present, New River Valley section, Radford VA edition.

St. Thomas' Episcopal Church. "Church Register." Christiansburg, VA: unpublished.

Schunk, John F., Editor. *1810-1820-1830 U. S. Census Montgomery County, Virginia*. Wichita, KS: S-K Publications, 2007.

Schunk, John F., Editor. *1850 U. S. Census Montgomery County, Virginia*. Wichita, KS: S-K Publications, 2007.

Schunk, John F., Editor. *1850 U. S. Census Montgomery County, Virginia.* Wichita, KS: S-K Publications, 2007.

Schunk, John F., Editor. *1850 U. S. Census Montgomery County, Virginia.* Wichita, KS: S-K Publications, 2007.

Schunk, John F., Editor. *1850 U. S. Census Montgomery County, Virginia.* Wichita, KS: S-K Publications, 2007.

Slaughter, Philip [as edited and revised by Rev. Edward L. Goodwin]. *The History of Truro Parish in Virginia.* Philadelphia, PA: George W. Jacobs & Company, 1907.

Slemp, C. Bascom. *Addresses of Famous Southwest Virginians.* Bristol, TN: The King Printing Company, 1940.

Smith, Conway Howard. *The Land that is Pulaski County.* Pulaski, VA: Pulaski County Library Board, 1981.

South-West Virginia Enterprise. *Birth, Death, and Marriage Announcements.* Wytheville, VA: Southwest Virginia Enterprise, 1880.

Sparks, Sadie Greening & Baugh, Judy. "Some Descendants of William Mallory Swepson". Swepson Home Page, 2000; *see also* Richmond, VA: Library of Virginia, Heth Family Papers.

Spillman, Betty. "Three Burned Bridges." *Journal of the New River Historical Society* 13 (2000): 15-16.

Steele, Roberta Ingles & Ingles, Andrew Lewis. *Escape from Captivity: The Story of Mary Draper Ingles and son Thomas Ingles as told by John Ingles Sr.* Radford, VA: self-published, 1969.

Streitmatter, Marles & Streitmatter, Rodger. *A History of the Stained Glass Windows of Grace Episcopal Church.* Radford, VA: self published, 1976.

Thom, James Alexander. *Follow the River*. New York, NY: Random House, Ballantine Publishing Company, 1981.

Thornton, Tim. "Honoring Virginia's Oldest Resident: I'm Too Old for Parties [Epsie Wilson]." *The Roanoke Times*, New River Valley Current section, February 26, 2008, Roanoke, VA, p. 1, 3-4.

Times-World Corp. "Obituary Notices." *Roanoke Times & World News*, 2006 through present, Virginia section, New River Valley edition.

Trausneck, Donald. "New River Valley Volunteers Answer Virginia's Call." *Journal of the New River Historical Society* 4 (1991): 14-16.

Trigg, Angela Adelaide. *A Romantic Adventurer Comes of Age: The Life of Daniel Trigg of Abingdon, VA*. Atlanta, GA: masters thesis, Georgia State University, 1997.

Tyler, Lyon Gardiner. *The Letters and Times of The Tylers, Volume II*. Williamsburg, VA: 1896; Salem, MA: Higgins Book Company, reprint.

Tyler, Lyon Gardiner. *The Letters and Times of The Tylers, Volume III*. Williamsburg, VA: 1896; Salem, MA: Higgins Book Company, reprint.

Tyler, Lyon Gardiner. "Henry Clement Tyler." *Encyclopedia of Virginia Biography*. Harvard University / Lewis Historical Publishing Company, 1915: 284-286.

United Daughters of the Confederacy (2003). *Manuscript Journal, Radford Journal, Virginia Daughters of the Confederacy, 1896-1909*, in CD-Rom from The History Broker: Goldenage Virtual Book, www.historybroker.com/cds/cd65.htm (accessed 2002 and August 18, 2007).

United States Bureau of the Census. *Heads of Families at the First Census of the United States Taken in the Year 1790, Records of the State Enumerations 1782 to 1785: Virginia.* Washington D.C.: Bureau of the Census, Department of Commerce and Labor, United States of America, 1790.

United States Bureau of the Census. *United States Population Census of 1810.* Washington D.C.: Bureau of the Census, United States of America, 1810; see also Schunk, John F.

United States Bureau of the Census. *United States Population Census of 1820.* Washington D.C.: Bureau of the Census, United States of America, 1820; see also Schunk, John F.

United States Bureau of the Census. *United States Population Census of 1830.* Washington D.C.: Bureau of the Census, United States of America, 1830; see also Schunk, John F.

United States Bureau of the Census. *United States Population Census of 1840.* Washington D.C.: Bureau of the Census, United States of America, 1850; see also Schunk, John F.

United States Bureau of the Census. *United States Population Census of 1850.* Washington D.C.: Bureau of the Census, United States of America, 1850; see also Schunk, John F.

United States Bureau of the Census. *United States Population Census of 1880.* Washington D.C.: Bureau of the Census, United States of America, 1880; see also Latter Day Saints / LDS.

United States Bureau of the Census. *United States Population Census of 1920.* Washington D.C.: Bureau of the Census, United States of America, 1920.

Virginia General Assembly. *Acts and Joint Resolutions Passed by the General Assembly of the State of Virginia During the Session of 1874.* Richmond, VA: Baughman Bros. Printing / A. R. Micou, Superintendent of Public Printing. 1874.

Virginia General Assembly. *Acts and Joint Resolutions Passed by the General Assembly of the State of Virginia During the Session of 1885- '86*. Richmond, VA: Baughman Bros. Printing / A. R. Micou, Superintendent of Public Printing. 1886.

Virginia General Assembly. *Acts and Joint Resolutions Passed by the General Assembly of the State of Virginia During the Session* of 1887. Richmond, VA: Baughman Bros. Printing / A. R. Micou, Superintendent of Public Printing. 1886.

Virginia General Assembly. *Acts and Joint Resolutions Passed by the General Assembly of the State of Virginia During the Session of 1889*. Richmond, VA: Baughman Bros. Printing / A. R. Micou, Superintendent of Public Printing. 1890.

Virginia General Assembly. *Acts and Joint Resolutions Passed by the General Assembly of the State of Virginia During the Session of 1890*. Richmond, VA: Baughman Bros. Printing / A. R. Micou, Superintendent of Public Printing. 1891.

Virginia General Assembly. "Chap. 85. – An Act to incorporate the city of Radford. Approved January 22, 1892.", p. 131-150. *Acts and Joint Resolutions Passed by the General Assembly of the State of Virginia During the Session of 1891-1892*. Richmond, VA: Baughman Bros. Printing / A. R. Micou, Superintendent of Public Printing. 1892.

Virginia General Assembly. "Chap. 109. – An Act to establish a corporation court for the city of Radford, in Montgomery county. Approved January 29, 1892.", p. 195-197. *Acts and Joint Resolutions Passed by the General Assembly of the State of Virginia During the Session of 1891-1892*. Richmond, VA: Baughman Bros. Printing / A. R. Micou, Superintendent of Public Printing. 1892.

Virginia General Assembly. "Chap. 132. – An Act to extend the time for commencing the construction of the Radford and Little River railroad company, and completing its main line. Approved February 2, 1892.", p. 222-223. *Acts and Joint Resolutions Passed by the General Assembly of the State of Virginia During the Session of 1891-1892.* Richmond, VA: Baughman Bros. Printing / A. R. Micou, Superintendent of Public Printing. 1892.

Virginia General Assembly. "Chap. 144. – An Act to amend and re-enact the 8th section of an act, entitled "an act to establish a corporation court for the city of Radford, in Montgomery county, approved January 29, 1892". Approved February 2, 1892.", p. 234-235. *Acts and Joint Resolutions Passed by the General Assembly of the State of Virginia During the Session of 1891-1892.* Richmond, VA: Baughman Bros. Printing / A. R. Micou, Superintendent of Public Printing. 1892.

Virginia General Assembly. "Chap. 158. – An Act to incorporate the Montgomery Club of Radford, Virginia. Approved February 4, 1892.", p. 247-248. *Acts and Joint Resolutions Passed by the General Assembly of the State of Virginia During the Session of 1891-1892.* Richmond, VA: Baughman Bros. Printing / A. R. Micou, Superintendent of Public Printing. 1892.

Virginia General Assembly. "Chap. 290. – An Act to incorporate the Radford water and light company. Approved February 16, 1892.", p. 477-479. *Acts and Joint Resolutions Passed by the General Assembly of the State of Virginia During the Session of 1891-1892.* Richmond, VA: Baughman Bros. Printing / A. R. Micou, Superintendent of Public Printing. 1892.

Virginia General Assembly. "Chap. 459. – An Act to allow Grace Episcopal church, Radford, Virginia, to borrow money. Approved February 29, 1892.", p. 759. *Acts and Joint Resolutions Passed by the General Assembly of the State of Virginia During the Session of 1891-1892.* Richmond, VA: Baughman Bros. Printing / A. R. Micou, Superintendent of Public Printing. 1892.

Virginia General Assembly. "Chap. 541. – An Act to incorporate the Radford street railway company. Approved March 1, 1892.", p. 858-860. *Acts and Joint Resolutions Passed by the General Assembly of the State of Virginia During the Session of 1891-1892.*

Richmond, VA: Baughman Bros. Printing / A. R. Micou, Superintendent of Public Printing. 1892.

Virginia General Assembly. "Chap. 543. – An Act to authorize the clerk of Radford school board to take a census of Radford division. Approved March 1, 1892.", p. 861. *Acts and Joint Resolutions Passed by the General Assembly of the State of Virginia During the Session of 1891-1892.* Richmond, VA: Baughman Bros. Printing / A. R. Micou, Superintendent of Public Printing. 1892.

Virginia General Assembly. "Chap. 594. – An Act to amend the charter of the city of Radford, approved January 22, 1892. Approved March 2, 1892.", p. 926-934. *Acts and Joint Resolutions Passed by the General Assembly of the State of Virginia During the Session of 1891-1892.* Richmond, VA: Baughman Bros. Printing / A. R. Micou, Superintendent of Public Printing. 1892.

Virginia General Assembly. "Chap. 713. – An Act to amend and re-enact sections 7 and 12 of an act entitled an act to establish a corporation court for the city of Radford, in Montgomery county, approved February 2, 1892. Approved March 4, 1892.", p. 1098-1099. *Acts and Joint Resolutions Passed by the General Assembly of the State of Virginia During the Session of 1891-1892.* Richmond, VA: Baughman Bros. Printing / A. R. Micou, Superintendent of Public Printing. 1892.

Virginia General Assembly. "Chap. 744. – An Act to incorporate the Radford wheelmen. Approved March 4, 1892. *Acts and Joint Resolutions Passed by the General Assembly of the State of Virginia During the Session of 1891-1892.* Richmond, VA: Baughman Bros. Printing / A. R. Micou, Superintendent of Public Printing. 1892.

Virginia General Assembly. *Acts and Joint Resolutions Passed by the General Assembly of the State of Virginia During the Session of 1897.* Richmond, VA: Baughman Bros. Printing / A. R. Micou, Superintendent of Public Printing. 1898.

Virginia General Assembly. *Acts and Joint Resolutions Passed by the General Assembly of the State of Virginia During the Session of 1898*. Richmond, VA: Baughman Bros. Printing / A. R. Micou, Superintendent of Public Printing. 1899.

Virginia General Assembly. *Acts and Joint Resolutions Passed by the General Assembly of the State of Virginia During the Session of 1899*. Richmond, VA: Baughman Bros. Printing / A. R. Micou, Superintendent of Public Printing. 1900.

Virginia General Assembly. *Acts and Joint Resolutions Passed by the General Assembly of the State of Virginia During the Session of 1900*. Richmond, VA: Baughman Bros. Printing / A. R. Micou, Superintendent of Public Printing. 1901.

Virginia Military Institute. "Archives: Richard Henry Adams Jr. Civil War Papers 1862-1866," Preston Library, in Online Manuscripts Guide www.vmi.edu/archives (accessed 2005 and August 18, 2007).

Virginia Tech. "Adams, Elizabeth Kent Collection (Papers 1813-1987)," Virginia Polytechnic Institute & State University, in Imagebase www.lib.vt.edu (accessed 2005 and August 18, 2007).

Virginia Tech. "Southwest Virginia: Kentland Farm, Montgomery County, Virginia," Virginia Polytechnic Institute & State University, in Imagebase www.lib.vt.edu (accessed 2005 and August 18, 2007).

Wallace, Amy Judith. *A History of the Heth Family*. Radford, VA: manuscript, 1996.

Wayland, John W. *The Washingtons and Their Homes*. Berryville, VA: Virginia Book Company, 1944, Facsimile Reprint 1973.

Weaver, Jeffrey C. & Moore, Robert III. "Virginia Civil War Biographies", in Virginia Civil War Home Page http://members.aol.com/jweaver300/grayson/vacwhp.htm (accessed 2001 and August 18, 2007).

Webb, Kerry. "A Civil War Circuit", in U. S. Civil War Generals http://sunsite.utk.edu/civil-war/generals.html (accessed 2004 and August 18, 2007).

West View Cemetery. *Grave markers and tombstones*. Radford, VA.

Wilson, Epsie Reich. *Meditation – Reflections – Cherished Memories – Grace Church 1922-1977*. Radford, VA: unpublished, 1977.

Yates, Robert Somerville Radford Sr. *A History of William Radford of Richmond, Virginia*. Decorah, IA: Anundsen Publishing Company, 1986.

Zion Hill Baptist Church. *The Seventy-Fourth Anniversary of the Zion Hill Baptist Church, Radford, Virginia, 1889-1983*. Radford, VA: unpublished, 1963.

Index

468

469

470

471

472

473

474

476

477

478

483

486

487

488

District, Ellen *Mrs.* (c. 1855)
See ____, Ellen *Mrs. W. District* (c. 1855)
District, Emma *Mrs.* (c. 1855)*See* ____, Emma *Mrs. J. District* (c. 1855)
District, Emma *Mrs. E. Franklin* (c. 1880)....... 107
District, Harvey (c. 1890) 107
District, James (c. 1800s)101
District, James (c. 1862) 102, 103
District, John (c. 1847) .. 102
District, Julia *Miss* (1864) 103
District, Laura *Miss* (c. 1878) 102
District, Lena Dean *Mrs.* (c. 1800s)See Dean, Lena *Mrs. H. District* (c. 1800s)
District, Lila *Miss* (c. 1858) 103
District, Lydia Cox *Mrs.* (c. 1900s)See Cox, Lydia *Mrs. W. District* (c. 1900s)
District, Mary *Miss* (c. 1879) 106
District, Maud *Mrs. E. Taylor* (c. 1894) 107
District, Millie *Miss* (c. 1844) 102
District, Minnie *Mrs. A. P. Armstrong* (c. 1894).... 107
District, Nancy Palmer *Mrs.* (c. 1817)*See* Palmer, Nancy *Mrs. W. District* (c. 1817)
District, Pocahantus *Miss* (c. 1855)......................... 103
District, Polina Fields *Mrs.* (c. 1859)See Fields, Polina *Mrs. E. District* (c. 1859)
District, Sherman (c. 1897) 107
District, Tucrla (c. 1858) . *See* District, Lila (c. 1858)
District, William (c. 1786)101

District, William (c. 1850)102
District, William (c. 1852)102
District, Willie (c. 1899) .. 107
Dixon, Elizabeth *Mrs.* (c. 1800s)*See* ____, Elizabeth *Mrs. Dixon* (c. 1800s)
Dobbins, Catherine Innes Adams *Mrs.* (c. 1800s) See Adams, Catherine Innes *Mrs. W. B. Dobbins* (c. 1800s)
Dobbins, Maria *Mrs. A. Mitchell* (c. 1800s)....... 114
Dobbins, Wilson B. (c. 1800s)........................ 161
Doran, Joseph I. (c. 1800s) 132, 396, 439
Doyle, L. W. (c. 1800s)....260
Doyle, Mancye *Mrs. R. C. Adams* (1889)78,   153, 201, 260
Doyle, Minnie Pilkington Harris *Mrs.* (c. 1800s). *See* Harris, Minnie Pilkington *Mrs. L. W. Doyle* (c. 1800s)
Drake, C. L. (c. 1800s)....295
Drake, C. M. *Mrs.* (c. 1800s) See ____, C. M. *Mrs. C. L. Drake* (c. 1800s)
Drake, E. S. *Mrs.* (c. 1800s) 296
Draper, Betty Robertson *Mrs.* (c. 1700s)*See* Robertson, Betty *Mrs. J. Draper* (c. 1700s)
Draper, George (c. 1700s)339
Draper, John (1730) 10
Draper, Mary *Mrs. W. Ingles* (1732) 10, 339
Dudley, J. H. (c. 1800s) .. 196
Duerr, Anna Radford *Miss* (1982) 264
Duerr, Finn (c. 1900s) 264
Duerr, Sally Taylor Adams *Mrs.* (1956)*See* Adams, Sally Taylor *Mrs. F. Duerr* (1956)

490

491

492

Figg, James A. (c. 1800s)178, 186, 195, 261, 265, 294, 365, 366

Finch, Mary Phoebe Mrs. L. W. Clark (c. 1800s) ... 280, 301

Finch, May Mrs. L. W. Clark (c. 1800s)See Finch, Mary Phoebe Mrs. L. W. Clark (c. 1800s)

Finch, Mollie Mrs. L. W. Clark (c. 1800s)See Finch, Mary Phoebe Mrs. L. W. Clark (c. 1800s)

Fink, Alva Duval (1905) . 302

Fink, Amanda Mrs. (c. 1800s)See ____, Amanda Mrs. J. Fink (c. 1800s)

Fink, Ambrose Franklin (c. 1899)........................ 301

Fink, Edward Jacob (1870) 203, 281, 300, 301

Fink, Edward Jacob Jr. (1904)...................... 302

Fink, Florence B. Mrs. J. B. R. Cameron (c. 1861).. 300

Fink, Irene Robinson Mrs. (1876)See Robinson, Irene Mrs. E. J. Fink (1876)

Fink, Jacob (c. 1800s).... 300

Fink, Lewis Clark (c. 1900s) 302

Fink, Mary Margaret Mrs. Wilson (1901)............. 302

Fisher, C. W. (c. 1800s).. 424

Fisher, J. M. (c. 1800s) . 226, 227

Fisher, Mary Margaret Mrs. W. H. Howe (c. 1814) . 322

Fitting, Betty J. Mrs. M. Walters (c. 1900s) 265

Fitting, Brad A. (c. 1900s) 265

Fitting, Chris (c. 1900s) . 265

Fitting, Darlene Mrs. (c. 1900s)See ____, Darlene

Mrs. R. K. Fitting (c. 1900s)

Fitting, Jason (c. 1900s).265

Fitting, Maria Mrs. (c. 1900s) See ____, Maria Mrs. R. E. Fitting (c. 1900s)

Fitting, Minnie Harris Adams Mrs. (1912)See Adams, Minnie Harris Mrs. R. D. Fitting (1912)

Fitting, Richard Kent (1948) 164, 265

Fitting, Robert Dancy (1917) 78, 164, 264

Fitting, Robert Eric (1946) 164, 264

Fitting, Stacey Mrs. (c. 1900s)See ____, Stacey, Mrs. C. Fitting (c. 1900s)

Fitzgerald, Mary L. Mrs. (c. 1800s)See ____, Mary L. Mrs. P. Fitzgerald (c. 1800s)

Fitzgerald, Peter (c. 1800s) 302

Fitzgerald, Veda Massie Miss (1888) 302

Floyd, daughter Washington Mrs. (c. 1800s) .... See Washington, daughter Mrs. W. P. Floyd (c. 1800s)

Floyd, John (1783) 54, 62

Floyd, John Buchanan (1806) 53

Floyd, Letitia Preston Mrs. (1779)See Preston, Letitia Mrs. J. Floyd (1779)

Floyd, Sarah Buchanan Preston Mrs. (1802) .... See Preston, Sarah Buchanan Mrs. J. B. Floyd (1802)

Floyd, William P. (c. 1800s) 404

Fraction, Fanny Johnson Mrs. (c. 1802)............. See

494

495

497

499

501

502

504

505

507

509

510

512

513

514

516

517

519

521

522

525

526

527

528

529

531

533

536

537

538

542

Illustration 56: Back Cover, Bust of Dr. John Blair Radford. Courtesy of Bill and Hix Bondurant.

2087788

Made in the USA